WAYWARD LIVES,
BEAUTIFUL
EXPERIMENTS

ALSO BY SAIDIYA HARTMAN

Lose Your Mother

Scenes of Subjection

WAYWARD LIVES, BEAUTIFUL EXPERIMENTS

Intimate Histories of Social Upheaval

SAIDIYA HARTMAN

W. W. NORTON & COMPANY

Independent Publishers Since 1923

New York | London

Copyright © 2019 by Saidiya Hartman

All rights reserved
Printed in the United States of America
First Edition

Photo of two women hugging on p. 296 used by permission of the Charlotte Sheedy
Literary Agency, Inc., on behalf of the Pauli Murray Foundation

For information about permission to reproduce selections from this book, write to
Permissions, W. W. Norton & Company, Inc., 500 Fifth Avenue, New York, NY 10110

For information about special discounts for bulk purchases, please contact
W. W. Norton Special Sales at specialsales@wwnorton.com or 800-233-4830

Manufacturing by LSC Communications, Harrisonburg
Book design by Chris Welch
Production manager: Lauren Abbate

ISBN 978-0-393-28567-3

W. W. Norton & Company, Inc., 500 Fifth Avenue, New York, N.Y. 10110
www.wwnorton.com

W. W. Norton & Company Ltd., 15 Carlisle Street, London W1D 3BS

1 2 3 4 5 6 7 8 9 0

FOR BERYLE AND VIRGILIO HARTMAN,
WHO I MISS EVERY DAY.

FOR HAZEL CARBY,
WHO OPENED THE DOOR.

She was, she knew, in a queer indefinite way, a disturbing factor.

—NELLA LARSEN, *Quicksand*

CONTENTS

Book Three
BEAUTIFUL EXPERIMENTS

A NOTE ON METHOD

At the turn of the twentieth century, young black women were in open rebellion. They struggled to create autonomous and beautiful lives, to escape the new forms of servitude awaiting them, and to live as if they were free. This book recreates the radical imagination and wayward practices of these young women by describing the world through their eyes. It is a narrative written from nowhere, from the nowhere of the ghetto and the nowhere of utopia.

Every historian of the multitude, the dispossessed, the subaltern, and the enslaved is forced to grapple with the power and authority of the archive and the limits it sets on what can be known, whose perspective matters, and who is endowed with the gravity and authority of historical actor. In writing this account of the wayward, I have made use of a vast range of archival materials to represent the everyday experience and restless character of life in the city. I recreate the voices and use the words of these young women when possible and inhabit the intimate dimensions of their lives. The aim is to convey the sensory experience of the city and to capture the rich landscape of black social life. To this end, I employ a mode of close narration, a style which places the voice of narrator and character in inseparable relation, so that the vision, language, and rhythms of the wayward shape and arrange the text. The italicized phrases and lines are utterances from the chorus. This story is told from inside the circle.

All the characters and events found in this book are real; none are invented. What I know about the lives of these young women has been culled from the journals of rent collectors; surveys and monographs of sociologists; trial transcripts; slum photographs; reports of vice investigators, social workers, and parole officers; interviews with psychiatrists and psychologists; and prison case files, all of which represent them as a problem. (Some of the names have been changed to protect confidentiality and as required by the use of state archives.) I have crafted a counter-narrative liberated from the judgment and classification that subjected young black women to surveillance, arrest, punishment, and confinement, and offer an account that attends to beautiful experiments—to make living an art—undertaken by those often described as promiscuous, reckless, wild, and wayward. The endeavor is to recover the insurgent ground of these lives; to exhume open rebellion from the case file, to untether waywardness, refusal, mutual aid, and free love from their identification as deviance, criminality, and pathology; to affirm free motherhood (reproductive choice), intimacy outside the institution of marriage, and queer and outlaw passions; and to illuminate the radical imagination and everyday anarchy of ordinary colored girls, which has not only been overlooked, but is nearly unimaginable.

Wayward Lives elaborates, augments, transposes, and breaks open archival documents so they might yield a richer picture of the social upheaval that transformed black social life in the twentieth century. The goal is to understand and experience the world as these young women did, to learn from what they know. I prefer to think of this book as the fugitive text of the wayward, and it is marked by the errantry that it describes. In this spirit, I have pressed at the limits of the case file and the document, speculated about what might have been, imagined the things whispered in dark bedrooms, and amplified moments of withholding, escape and possibility, moments when the vision and dreams of the wayward seemed possible.

Few, then or now, recognized young black women as sexual modernists, free lovers, radicals, and anarchists, or realized that the flapper was a pale imitation of the ghetto girl. They have been credited with nothing: they remain surplus women of no significance, girls deemed unfit for history and destined to be minor figures. This book is informed by a different set of values and recognizes the revolutionary ideals that animated ordinary lives. It explores the utopian longings and the promise of a future world that resided in waywardness and the refusal to be governed.

The album assembled here is an archive of the exorbitant, a dream book for existing otherwise. By attending to these lives, a very unexpected story of the twentieth century emerges, one that offers an intimate chronicle of black radicalism, an aesthetical and riotous history of colored girls and their experiments with freedom—a revolution before Gatsby. For the most part, the history and the potentiality of their life-world has remained unthought because no one could conceive of young black women as social visionaries and innovators in the world in which these acts took place. The decades between 1890 and 1935 were decisive in determining the course of black futures. A revolution in a minor key unfolded in the city and young black women were the vehicle. This upheaval or transformation of black intimate life was the consequence of economic exclusion, material deprivation, racial enclosure, and social dispossession; yet it, too, was fueled by the vision of a future world and what might be.

The wild idea that animates this book is that young black women were radical thinkers who tirelessly imagined other ways to live and never failed to consider how the world might be otherwise.

CAST OF CHARACTERS

Girl #1   Wanders through the streets of Philadelphia's Seventh Ward and New York's Tenderloin, year 1900. She is young yet so old and raw.

Girl #2   Trapped in an attic studio in Philadelphia, year 1882.

The Window Shoppers   Two young women stroll along South Street, late 1890s.

General House Worker   Appears over the course of the book from 1896–1935. She is always on the lookout for an escape route.

The Rioters   Young women imprisoned at Lowell Cottage, Bedford Hills, New York.

The Chorus   All the unnamed young women of the city trying to find a way to live and in search of beauty.

The Paper Bag Brigade

Women waiting in the Bronx slave market to sell their labor to white housewives for starvation wages.

Sapphire

Authors a radically different text of female empowerment.

Mattie Jackson née Nelson

A fifteen-year-old newly arrived in New York from Hampton, Virginia.

Victoria Earle Matthews

Founder of the White Rose Mission, and member of the National League for the Protection of Colored Women and the National Association of Colored Women.

W. E. B. Du Bois

A young sociologist and newly minted Harvard PhD conducting a social survey in the heart of the Negro slum, 1896–1898.

Katherine Davis

Head of the College Settlement Association and first superintendent of the New York State Reformatory for Women at Bedford Hills.

Ida B. Wells

Radical, feminist, antilynching activist, writer, political speaker, and troublesome woman.

Helen Parrish

A wealthy philanthropist and housing reformer in a companionate marriage with Hannah Fox, also a member of the Philadelphia elite.

Mamie Shepherd, aka Mamie Sharp	A nineteen-year-old beauty who rents a three-room flat in a tenement on Saint Mary Street in Philadelphia.
James Shepherd	Mamie's husband.

Residents of Saint Mary Street

Fanny Fisher	A middle-aged woman who drinks herself to death.
Old Fisher	Fanny's husband.
Mary Riley	A young mother.
Katy Clayton	A pretty young woman fond of men's company.
Old Clayton	Katy's grandmother.
Ike and Bella Denby	A brawling and drinking couple.

May Enoch	A recent arrival to New York.
Arthur Harris	May's husband and defender.
Robert Thorpe	A white man who grabs May Enoch and strikes Arthur Harris.
Gladys Bentley	Entertainer, womanizer, African sculptor, flamboyant and gender-queer stroller, and friend of Mabel Hampton.
Jackie Mabley	Actor, comedian, bull dagger, female impersonator, and friend of Mabel Hampton.

Mary White Ovington	Social reformer, dear friend of W. E. B. Du Bois, and a cofounder of the National Association for the Advancement of Colored People.
Edna Thomas	Stage and screen actor.
Olivia Wyndham	English aristocrat who falls in love with Edna Thomas.
Lloyd Thomas	Edna's husband. A handsome, cultured man fond of quoting Chinese poets and manager of a Harlem nightclub.
Harriet Powell	A seventeen-year-old who loves dance halls.
Eleanor Fagan, aka Billie Holiday	A fourteen-year-old arrested for prostitution in a jump raid in Harlem.
Esther Brown	Chippie and rebel, who insists on being treated the same as white girls.
Rebecca Waters	Esther Brown's friend.
Grace Campbell	Social worker, probation officer, and member of the African Blood Brotherhood and the Socialist Party.
Eva Perkins	A nineteen-year-old factory worker, lover of street life, and wife of Kid Chocolate.

Aaron Perkins, aka Kid Chocolate, aka Kid Happy	Harlem boxer, elevator operator, and dreamer.
Shine	Myth, archetype, and avatar.
Mabel Hampton	Chorine, lesbian, working-class intellectual, and aspiring concert singer.
Ella Baker	Harlem stroller, tenant organizer, and NAACP field investigator.
Marvel Cooke	Communist and journalist.
Hubert Harrison	Socialist, writer, and street-corner lecturer.

Locations

Streets and alleys in the Fifth and Seventh Ward of Philadelphia; streets of the Tenderloin and Harlem; an artist studio on Spruce Street; steerage on the Old Dominion steamer; West Side docks; Jim Crow car on the Atlantic Coast Line Railway; rented rooms and kitchenettes throughout the Black Belt, clubs, saloons, and cabarets; Lafayette Theatre, Alhambra Theater, Garden of Joy, Clam House, Edmond's Cellar; Blackwell's Island workhouse, Bedford Hills Reformatory for Women; Coney Island; and theaters, movie houses, dance halls, casinos, lodges, black-and-tan dives, buffet flats, and chop-suey joints.

Book One

SHE MAKES AN ERRANT

PATH THROUGH THE CITY

The Terrible Beauty of the Slum

You can find her in the group of beautiful thugs and *too fast* girls congregating on the corner and humming the latest rag, or lingering in front of Wanamaker's and gazing lustfully at a pair of fine shoes displayed like jewels behind the plate-glass window. Watch her in the alley passing a pitcher of beer back and forth with her friends, brash and lovely in a cut-rate dress and silk ribbons; look in awe as she hangs halfway out of a tenement window, taking in the drama of the block and defying gravity's downward pull. Step onto any of the paths that cross the sprawling city and you'll encounter her as she roams. Outsiders call the streets and alleys that comprise her world the slum. For her, it is just the place where she stays. You'd never happen onto her block unless you lived there too, or had lost your way, or were out on an evening lark seeking the pleasures yielded by the other half. The voyeurs on their slumming expeditions feed on the lifeblood of the ghetto, long for it and loathe it. The social scientists and the reformers are no better with their cameras and their surveys, staring intently at all the strange specimens.

Her ward of the city is a labyrinth of foul alleys and gloomy courts. It is Africa town, the Negro quarter, the native zone. The Italians and Jews, engulfed by proximity, disappear. It is a world concealed behind the façade of the ordered metropolis. The not-yet-dilapidated buildings and decent homes that face the street hide the alley tenement where she lives. Entering the narrow passageway into the alley, one crosses the threshold into a raucous disorderly world, a place defined by tumult, vulgar collectivism, and anarchy. It is a human sewer populated by the worst elements. It is a realm of excess and fabulousness. It is a wretched environment. It is the plantation extended into the city. It is a social laboratory. The ghetto is a space of encounter. The sons and daughters of the rich come in search of meaning, vitality, and pleasure. The reformers and sociologists come in search of the truly disadvantaged failing to see her and her friends as thinkers or planners, or to notice the beautiful experiments crafted by poor black girls.

The ward, the Bottom, the ghetto—is an urban commons where the poor assemble, improvise the forms of life, experiment with freedom, and refuse the menial existence scripted for them. It is a zone of extreme deprivation and scandalous waste. In the rows of tenements, the decent reside peacefully with the dissolute and the immoral. The Negro quarter is a place bereft of beauty and extravagant in its display of it. Moving in and moving on establish the rhythms of everyday life. Each wave of newcomers changes the place—how the slum looks and sounds and smells. No one ever settles here, only stays, waits for better, and passes through; at least, that is the hope. It is not yet the *dark ghetto*, but soon only the black folks will remain.

In the slum, everything is in short supply except sensation. The experience is *too much*. The terrible beauty is more than one could ever hope to assimilate, order, and explain. The reformers snap their pictures of the buildings, the kitchenettes, the clotheslines, and the outhouses. She escapes notice as she watches them from the third-floor window of the alley house where she stays, laughing at their stupidity. They take a picture of Lombard Street when *hardly no one is there*. She wonders what fascinates them about clotheslines and outhouses. They always take pictures of the same stuff. Are the

undergarments of the rich so much better? Is cotton so different than silk and not as pretty draped like a banner across the streets?

The outsiders and the uplifters fail to capture it, to get it right. All they see is a typical Negro alley, blind to the relay of looks and the pangs of desire that unsettle their captions and hint at the possibility of a life bigger than poverty, at the tumult and upheaval that can't be arrested by the camera. They fail to discern the beauty and they see only the disorder, missing all the ways black folks create life and make bare need into an arena of elaboration. A half-dressed woman, wearing a housecoat over a delicate nightgown, leans against the doorway, hidden by the shadows of the foyer, as she gossips with her girlfriend standing at the threshold. Intimate life unfolds in the streets.

The journalists from *Harper's Weekly* gush in print: "Above the Jews, in the same [tenement] houses, amid scenes of indescribable squalor and tawdry finery, dwell the negroes leading their light-hearted lives of pleasure, confusion, music, noise and fierce fights that make them a terror to white neighbors and landlords alike." Aroused at the sight of elegantly clad domestics, janitors and stevedores, elevator boys in rakish hats preening on the corner, and *aesthetical* Negroes content to waste money on extravagance, ornament, and shine, the sociologist urges them to learn the value of a dollar from their Jewish and Italian neighbors. Negroes must abandon the lax moral habits, sensual indulgence, and careless excess that are the custom of slavery. The present-past of involuntary servitude unfolds in the street, and the home, which was *broken up completely by the slave ship and the promiscuous herding of the . . . plantation*, is now broken again, broken open in its embrace of strangers.

The senses are solicited and overwhelmed. Look over here. Let your eyes take it all in: the handsome thugs lining the courtyard like sentinels; the immoderate display of three lovely flowerpots arranged on the sill of a tenement window, the bed-sheets, monogrammed handkerchiefs, embroidered silk hose, and whore's undergarments suspended on a line across the alley, broadcasting clandestine arrangements, wayward lives, carnal matters. Women, with packages tied in paper and string, flit by like shadows. The harsh light at their backs transforms them into silhouettes; abstracted dark forms take the place of who they really are.

The rag seller's daughters idle on the steps that descend to their cellar flat. The eldest is resplendent, sitting amid the debris in her Sunday hat and soiled frock. The youngest remains mystery and blur.

The sun pours down the stairwell, pressing against the girls and illuminating the entrance to the small dank room, which is filled with the father's wares: rags, papers, cast-offs, piecework, and discarded objects salvaged for future use. He turns his back to the camera and eludes capture.

What you can hear if you listen: The guttural tones of Yiddish making English into a foreign tongue. The round open-mouthed sounds of North Carolina and Virginia bleeding into the hard-edged language of the city and transformed by the rhythm and cadence of northern streets. The eruption of laughter, the volley of curses, the shouts that make tenement walls vibrate and jar the floor. *Yes, oooh, baby that's so good!*—the sweet music of an extended moan that hushes the ones listening, eavesdroppers wanting more, despite knowing they shouldn't. The rush of impressions: the musky scent of tightly pressed bodies dancing in a basement saloon; the inadvertent brush of a stranger's hand against yours as she moves across the courtyard; a glimpse of young lovers huddled in the deep shadows of a tenement hallway; the violent embrace of two men brawling; the acrid odor of bacon and hoe-cake frying on an open fire; the honeysuckle of a domestic's toilet water; the maple smoke rising from an old man's corncob pipe. A whole world is jammed into one short block crowded with black folks shut out from almost every opportunity the city affords, but still *intoxicated with freedom*. The air is alive with the possibilities of assembling, gathering, congregating. At any moment, the promise of insurrection, the miracle of upheaval: small groups, people *by theyselves*, and strangers threaten to become an ensemble, to incite *treason en masse*.

———

There are no visible signs on shop doors barring her entrance, just the brutal rebuff of "we don't serve niggers." If she feels brave, she will shout an insult or curse as she retreats from the shop under the hateful gaze of clerk and customers. She can sit anywhere she wants on streetcars and in theaters, even if people inch away as if she were contagious when she chooses the seat next to them, and she can go to the vaudeville show or the nickelodeon on the same day as the white folks, although it is more fun and she breathes easier when it is just colored and she knows she will not be insulted. Despite the liberties of the city, there is no better life here than in Virginia, no brighter future to grow into, no opportunities for colored girls besides the broom and the mop, or spread-eagle in really hard times. Everything essential—where she goes to school, the kind of job she can get, where she can live—is dictated by the color line, which places her on the bottom and everybody else on top. Being young, she tries to dream another life into existence, one in which her horizon isn't limited to the maid's uniform and a white woman's dirty house. In this other life, she would not be required to take all the shit that no one else would accept and pretend to be grateful.

In this city of brotherly love, she has been confined to a squalid zone that no one else but the Jews would suffer. It isn't the cradle of liberty or the free territory or even a temporary refuge, but a place where an Irish mob nearly beat her uncle to death for some other Negro's alleged crime; where the police dragged her to jail for being riotous and disorderly when she told them *go to hell*, after they had grabbed her from the steps of her building and told her to move on. At Second and Bainbridge, she heard a white man shout, "Lynch him! Lynch him!" after a colored man, accused of stealing a loaf of bread from the corner grocer, ran past.

When she arrives in the Tenderloin, the riot erupts. At Forty-First and Eighth Avenue, the policeman said, "Black bitch, come out now!" Then dragged a woman from the hallway, pummeled her with his club, and arrested her for being riotous and disorderly.

———

Paul Laurence Dunbar caught sight of her on Seventh Avenue, and he feared for American civilization. Looking at the girl amidst the crowd of idle shiftless Negroes who thronged the avenue, he wondered, "What is to be done with them, what is to be done for them, if they are to be prevented from inoculating our civilization with the poison of their lives?" They are not anarchists; and yet in these seemingly careless, guffawing crowds resides a terrible menace to our institutions. Though she had not read *God and the State* or *What Is Property?* or *The Conquest of Bread*, the dangers she and others like her posed was as great as those damned Jews Emma Goldman and Alexander Berkman. Everything in her environment tended to the blotting of the moral sense, every act engendered crime and encouraged open rebellion. Dunbar lamented: If only they could be prevented from flocking to the city, "if the metropolis could vomit them back again to the South, the whole matter would adjust." Better for them and for us, the restrictions of the south, than a "seeming liberty which blossoms noxiously into license." Better the fields and the shotgun houses and the dusty towns and the interminable cycle of credit and debt, better this than black anarchy.

Most days, the assault of the city eclipses its promise: When the water in the building has stopped running, when even in her best dress she cannot help but wonder if she smells like the outhouse or if it is obvious that her bloomers are tattered, when she is so hungry that the aroma of bean soup wafting from the settlement kitchen makes her mouth water, she takes to the streets, as if in search of the real city and not this poor imitation. The old black ladies perched in their windows shouted, "Girl, where you headed?" Each new deprivation raises doubts about when freedom is going to come; if the question pounding inside her head—*Can I live?*—is one to which she could ever give a certain answer, or only repeat in anticipation of something better than this, bear the pain of it and the hope of it, the beauty and the promise.

A Minor Figure

The small naked figure reclines on the arabesque sofa. Looking at the photograph, it is easy to mistake her for some other *Negress*, lump her with all the delinquent girls working Lombard Street and Middle Alley, lose sight of her among the surplus colored women in the city, condemn and pity the child whore. Everyone has a different story to share. Fragments of her life are woven with the stories of girls resembling her and girls nothing like her, stories held together by longing, betrayal, lies, and disappointment. The newspaper article confuses her with another girl, gets her name wrong. Photographs of the tenement where she lives regularly appear in the police briefs and the charity reports, but you can barely see her, peering out of the third-floor window. The caption makes no mention of her, noting only the moral hazard of the one-room kitchenette, the foul condition of the toilets, and the noise of the airshaft. The photograph taken of her in the attic studio is the one that is most familiar; it is how the world still remembers her. Had her name been scribbled on the back of the albumen print, there would be at least one fact I could convey with a measure of certainty, one detail that I would not have to guess, one less obstacle in retracing the girl's path through the streets of the city. Had the photographer or one of the young men assisting him in the studio recorded her name, I might have been able to find her in the 1900 census, or discover if she ever resided at the Shelter for Colored Orphans, or danced on the stage of the Lafayette Theatre, or if she ended up at the Magdalene House when there was nowhere else to go.

Her friends refused to tell the authorities anything; but even they didn't know how she arrived at the house on the outskirts of the Seventh Ward, or what happened in the studio that afternoon. The Irish housekeeper thought she was the black cook, Old Margaret's, niece, and, neglecting her work *as they were wont to do* had wandered from the kitchen to the studio. Old Margaret, no kin to the girl, believed that Mr. Eakins had lured her to the attic with the promise of a few coins, but never said what she feared. The social worker later assigned to the girl's case never saw the photograph. She blamed the girl's mother and the slum for all the terrible things that happened and filled in the blanks on the personal history form, never listening for any other answer. Age of first sexual offense was the only question without certain reply.

From these bits and pieces, it has been difficult to know where to begin or even what to call her. The fiction of a proper name would evade the dilemma, not resolve it. It would only postpone the question: Who is she? I suppose I could call her Mattie or Kit or Ethel or Mabel. Any of these names would do and would be the kind of name common to a young colored woman at the beginning of the twentieth century. There are other names reserved for the dark: Sugar Plum, Peaches, Pretty Baby, and Little Bit—names imposed on girls like her that hint at the pleasures afforded by intimate acts performed in rented rooms and dimly lit hallways. And there are the aliases too, the identities slipped on and discarded—a Mrs. quickly affixed to a lover's name, or one borrowed from a favorite actress to

invent a new life, or the protective cover offered by the surname of
a maternal grandmother's dead cousin—all to elude the law, keep
your name out of the police register, hold the past at a safe distance, forget what grown men did to girls behind closed doors. The
names and the stories rush together. The singular life of this particular girl becomes interwoven with those of other young women
who crossed her path, shared her circumstances, danced with her
in the chorus, stayed in the room next door in a Harlem tenement,
spent sixty days together at the workhouse, and made an errant
path through the city.

Without a name, there is the risk that she might never escape the
oblivion that is the fate of minor lives and be condemned to the pose
for the rest of her existence, remaining a meager figure appended to
the story of a great man and relegated to item number 304, African
American girl, in the survey of his life and work. If I knew her name
I might be able to locate her, discover if she had any siblings, if her
mother was dead, if her grandmother was "living in" with a white
family, if her father was a rag seller or day laborer, or if he had disappeared. A name is a luxury that she isn't afforded—other sitters
are unnamed, but they can be identified; she is the only one who is
anonymous.

In a compelled photograph, a girl's name is of no greater consequence than her desire for a different kind of likeness. (The only
thing I knew for sure was that she did have a name and a life that
exceeded the frame in which she was captured.) When the scandal
erupted and the white girls who lived in large stately homes with
powerful fathers disclosed the things the artist had forced them to
do, no one mentioned her or any other black girl. Years later when
another anatomist, another man of science, was found with a cache
of nude pictures of colored schoolgirls, no one remembered her.
Without a name, it was unlikely that I would ever find this particular girl. What mattered was that she was a placeholder for all the

possibilities and the dangers awaiting young black women in the first decades of the twentieth century. In being denied a name or, perhaps, in refusing to give one, she represents all the other girls who follow in her path. Anonymity enables her to stand in for all the

others. The minor figure yields to the chorus. All the hurt and the
promise of the wayward are hers to bear.

————

It was not the kind of image I was looking for when I set out to tell
the story of the social revolution and transformation of intimate life
that unfolded in the black city-within-the-city. I had been searching
for photographs unequivocal in their representation of what it meant
to live free for the second and third generations born after the official
end of slavery. I was hungry for images that represented the experiments in freedom that unfolded within slavery's shadow, the practice
of everyday life and *escape subsistence* stoked by the liberties of the
city. Beautiful experiments in living free, urban plots against the plantation flourished, yet were unsustainable or thwarted or criminalized
before they could take root. I searched for photographs exemplary of
the beauty and possibility cultivated in the lives of ordinary black girls
and young women and that stoked dreams of what might be possible if
you could escape the house of bondage. This archive of images, found
and imagined, would provide a necessary antidote to the scourged
backs, glassy tear-filled eyes, bodies stripped and branded, or rendered grotesque for white enjoyment. I refused the mug shots and the
family albums of black elites who fashioned their lives in accordance
with Victorian norms, those best described by W. E. B. Du Bois as
strivers, as the talented tenth, as whites of Negro blood.

I looked at Thomas Askew's lovely portraits of the black aristocracy but didn't find the young women whose lives unfolded in streets,
cabarets, and tenement hallways, rather than in grand homes with
parlors furnished with pianos and wingtip chairs adorned with lace
antimacassars. Young women with serial lovers, husbands in the
plural, and women lovers too. Young women who outfitted themselves like Ada Overton Walker and Florence Mills, young women
who preferred to dress like men. I looked at vernacular images, collections of photographs in municipal archives, anthologies of black

photographs, documentary surveys of the slum, black portraits and group pictures displayed in Negro buildings and institutes of social economy at international expositions and world fairs. I browsed thousands of photographs taken by social reformers and charity organizations, hoping to find them, but they failed to appear. They averted their gaze or they rushed past the photographer; they clustered at the edge of the photos, they looked out of windows, peered out of doorways, and turned their back to the camera. They refused the terms of visibility imposed on them. They eluded the frame and remained fugitives—lovely silhouettes and dark shadows impossible to force into the grid of naturalist description or the taxonomy of slum pictures.

The young mothers were the ones pictured most often; they were required to sit with their children in crowded bedrooms and kitchenettes in order to receive the assistance which they had been promised: some milk for the children, or a visit from the nurse because the youngest was ailing, or the loan of a pair of shoes to go out and find work. The mothers had to appear in the reform pictures, and these images were marshaled as evidence in the case made against them by the social workers and the sociologists.

Young women not in desperate need, not saddled with children, and old enough to say *Hell no* and *Get out of my face* evaded capture. The few images of young women between the ages of sixteen and twenty-three are group pictures taken with their families or with their neighbors. They never looked *wild and wayward* or *too fast* in these pictures. Despite their fugitive gestures of refusal—slumped shoulders and side-eyes and radiant anger—they are made into clients and types and examples; they are transformed into social documents and statistical persons, reduced to the human excrescence of social law and slum ecology, pitied as betrayed girl mothers, labeled chance creatures of questionable heredity. The ash barrels lining the street and the ramshackle buildings and the friendly visitors to the poor dominate and infantilize them.

I grew weary of the endless pictures of white sheets draped on the clothesline, leaking faucets, filthy water closets, and crowded bedrooms. I recoiled at the lantern slide show and its oscillating pictures of cause and effect, before and after, the movement of images propelled by moralistic narratives of sexual promiscuity, improper guardianship, and the dangers of the saloon, boarding house, and dance hall. The visual clichés of damnation and salvation: the black-and-tan dive, the sociality of neighbors across the color line, hanging out on the stoop, marrying outside the race, or the model tenement occupied by a monochromatic family of the same race. The outcomes were stark: on one hand, the morgue, prison and the workhouse; on the other, the privatized household and the sovereignty of the husband and father.

The surveys and the sociological pictures left me cold. These photographs never grasped the beautiful struggle to survive, glimpsed the alternative modes of life, or illuminated the mutual aid and communal wealth of the slum. The reform pictures and the sociological surveys documented only ugliness. Everything good and decent stood on the ruins of proscribed modes of affiliation and ways of living: the love unrecognized by the law, households open to strangers, the public intimacy of the streets, and the aesthetic predilections and willful excesses of young black folks. The social worlds represented in these pictures were targeted for destruction and elimination. The reformers used words like "improvement" and "social betterment" and "protection," but no one was fooled. The interracial slum was razed and mapped into homogeneous zones of absolute difference. The black ghetto was born.

The captions transform the photographs into moral pictures, amplify the poverty, arrange and classify disorder. *Negro quarter.* The caption seems to replicate the image, to detail what resides within its frame, but instead the caption produces what appears. It subsumes the image to the text. The words attached to the image— unsightly, broken, typical—seem almost to be part of the picture, like the crumpled bed-sheets or the boards covering the broken windows of the shack. The captions index the life of the poor. The words police and divide: *Negro quarter.* Announce the vertical order of life: *Damaged Goods.* Make domestic space available for scrutiny and punishment: *One-room moral hazard.* Declaim the crime of promiscuous social arrangements: *Eight Persons Occupy One Bedroom.* Manage and segregate the mixed crowd and represent the world in fidelity to the color line: *View of Italian girls, Boys with Cap, and Two Negroes in Doorway of Dilapidated Building.*

Such pictures made it impossible to imagine that segregation was not natural selection based on affinity and that Jim Crow had not always prevailed. Social reformers targeted interracial intimacy or even proximity; the Girl problem and the Negro problem reared their heads at the same time and found a common target in the sexual freedom of young women. The attendant fears of promiscuity, degeneration, and interracial sexual intimacy resulted in their arrest and confinement. Improving the slum and targeting urban vice extended the color line in absence of a legal apparatus or statutory law to mandate and enforce it. Progressive reformers and settlement workers were the architects and planners of racial segregation in northern cities.

The photographs coerced the black poor into visibility as a condition of policing and charity, making those *bound to appear* suffer the burden of representation. In these iconic images of the black urban poor, individual persons were forced to stand in for sweeping historical narratives about the progress or failure of the Negro, serve as representatives of a race or class, embody and inhabit social problems, and evidence failure or improvement. These photographs extended an optic of visibility and surveillance that had its origins in slavery and the administered logic of the plantation. (To be visible was to be targeted for uplift or punishment, confinement or violence.)

Some things didn't appear in the photographs, like the three flowerpots lined up on the windowsill, the crazy quilts covering the tick mattresses, the Bibles wrapped in lace and calico, the illustrations from the mail-order catalogue affixed to the walls. The reformers and the journalists were fixated on the kitchenette. They didn't know that the foyer, the fire escape, and the rooftop were a stretch of urban beach, not until the rich adopted the practice and sleeping on rooftops became fashionable. They didn't know that the hallway and the stairwell were places of assembly, a clearing inside the tenement, or that *you love in doorways*. There is no photograph of the hallway, barely illuminated by a flickering gaslight that hides everything that is unlovely. Even in the daytime, the shadows are too dark and too deep to capture it. The hallway provides the refuge for the first tongue kiss, the place for hanging out with your friends, the conduit for gossip and intrigue. Here you first learn about the world and the role to which you have been consigned, so you scribble *fuck* or *wretched* on the wall in the stairwell. The hallway is where the authorities post the tenement-house laws and the project rules, and the guidelines might as well say, *Negro, don't even try to live*. It is inside but public. The police enter without warrants and arrest whoever has the bad fortune to be found and caught. It is the passageway that leads to the two rooms where you stay with your mother, father, aunt, and your two sisters. Your mother tries to make the drab rooms home by setting out your grandmother's tea set, which is too fancy for the small kitchen table; the set belonged to the white folks she worked for. She said it was a gift, but once let it slip that it was owed to her, she earned it and much more. A Masonic Lodge calendar and lithograph of Frederick Douglass hide the crack on the plaster wall. The sheer curtain hanging in the window filters the weak light of late afternoon. The ivory table mat covering the battered stovetop confirms that even in the worst places one finds beauty. All that effort makes it less terrible. No one forgets that they are here because excluded from everywhere else, so you make do and try to thrive in what's nearly unlivable. It is the Black Belt: You are confined here. You huddle here and make a life together.

In the hallway, you wonder will the world always be as narrow as this, two walls threatening to squeeze and crush you into nothingness. So you imagine other worlds, sometimes not even better, but at least different from this. You and your friends hatch plots of escape and dereliction. This black interior is a space for thought and action, for study and vandalism, for love and trouble. The hallway is the parlor for those who manage to live in cramped dark rooms with not enough air and who see the sunlight only when they step out onto the front stoop.

It is ugly and brutalizing and it is where you stay. It doesn't matter if you don't love the place; you love the people residing there. It is as close to a home as you'll get, it is a transient resting place, an impossible refuge, for those forced out, pushed on, displaced always. They stay but never settle. The hallway is a space uneasy with expectation and tense with the force of unmet desire. It is the liminal zone between the inside and the outside for the one who stays in the ghetto; the reformer documenting the habitat of the poor passes through without noticing it, failing to see what can be created in cramped space, *if not an overture, a desecration*, or to regard our *beautiful flaws and terrible ornaments*. This hallway never appears in the lantern slide show. Only the ones who reside in the tenement know it.

It won't be photographed from the inside until decades later. Not until 1953 will a photograph convey the experience of dwelling within these walls, offer a glimpse of the life worlds made there, capture the breathlessness of a fourth-floor walk-up, know firsthand that how we live and where we stay is not a social problem. It is our relation to the white world that is the problem. Even in the kitchenette one can find the joy of couples dancing under a clothes-line suspended from the ceiling, teenagers playing cards and laughing with their friends, a man sitting at a kitchen table drinking tea, the steaming cup pressed tight against his cheek. He delights in the sensation of the heat against his face, the feel of the porcelain on his skin.

The how-to-live and *the fierce urgency of the now* can be perceived in these other photographs, the images lost and found, imagined and anticipated, like stills edited from an unfinished movie. The tintypes taken at a church picnic. The Kodaks on the beach at Coney Island. Images of *too fast* black girls trying to make a way out of no way, a serial picture of young black women rushing to the city to escape the plantation and intent on creating a free life in the context of a new enclosure. They are as desperate to find an escape route from servitude, as they are hungry for new forms of life. Watching people stroll the avenue or play cards on the step or drink wine on the roof, they are convinced that Negroes are the most beautiful people. The communal luxury of the black metropolis, the wealth of *just us*, the black city-within-the-city, transforms the imagination of what you might want and who you might be, encouraging you to dream. Shit, it don't even matter if you're black and poor, because you are here and you are alive and all these folks surrounding you encourage you and persuade you to believe that you are beautiful too. This collective endeavor to *live free* unfolds in the confines of the carceral landscape. They can see the wall being erected around the dark ghetto, but they still want to be ready for the good life, still want to get ready for freedom.

———

The photograph is small enough to be cradled in the palm of your hand. It is not a lush silver print, but an inexpensive albumen print that measures 1 7/16 × 2 7/16 inches; its tiny size announces its minor status. It is a compelled image, an image taken without the permission of the sitter; it is an image intended to classify, isolate, and differentiate. It is not the kind of photograph that she would have wanted and it was not taken at her request.

The odalisque, an image of a reclining nude, conjoins two distinct categories of the commodity: the slave and the prostitute. The rigidness of the body betrays the salacious reclining posture, and the girl's flat steely-eyed glare is hardly an invitation to look. She retreats as far away from the camera as possible into the corner of the sofa, as if seeking a place in which to hide. Her direct gaze at the camera is not a solicitation of the viewer, an appeal for recognition, or a look predicated on mutuality. The look assumes nothing shared between the one compelled to appear and those looking. The private wish is that the harm inflicted won't be too great and that there will be an exit from this room and others like it.

What knowledge of anatomy did Eakins or his students uncover that afternoon in the studio? They had encountered black bodies before, mostly the corpses at the Jefferson Medical College. The bodies of poor Negroes not claimed by kin, or whose families had no money for a proper burial, or bodies stolen from the colored cemetery. There had been several scandals. She was a living body, not a corpse, but the image of her was not like the other photos of children taken to corroborate or question theories of skeletal development or to determine the movement of the musculature on the frame. I hope he didn't attach electrodes to her to observe the movement of muscle mass. It was unlikely that there was a chaperone attending to this girl. What knowledge of the world did she gain that afternoon? Was Susan Eakins present? Did she take the photograph? Did *she whisper foul things in her ear*? Or encourage her to stay still and not move? Had she done the same with the nieces too? Did she assist him or turn a blind eye to his work? It is hard to look at the photograph and not think about the images that preceded it and the images that would follow in its wake. Afterimages of slavery intended to remind the viewer of the power they exercised over such a body and the threat hanging over the subject captured within its frame of the kinds of terrible things that could be done to a black girl without a crime having occurred.

Was it possible to annotate the image? To make my words into a shield that might protect her, a barricade to deflect the gaze and cloak what had been exposed?

Anticipating the pressure of his hands, did she tremble? Did the painter hover above the sofa and arrange her limbs? Were his hands big and moist? Did they leave a viscous residue on the surface of her skin? Could she smell the odor of sweat, linseed oil, formaldehyde, and clothes worn for too many days? Did she notice the slippers, tattered shirt, and grubby pants, and then become frightened? Had the other models left their imprint in the lumpy surface, the oily patina of the upholstery, and the rank musky odor?

The girl who entered 1729 Mount Vernon Street was not the same one who departed. Rumors about the other girls surfaced: they were white, they were the daughters of the elite, so there was public outrage and the painter disgraced. They had been spared this: the odalisque, the pose of the whore and the slave. They had not been required to look directly at the camera and acknowledge his gaze and pretend to invite it. The other girls might have mentioned her if she hadn't been black and poor.

She left the studio exactly the way she came: down the four flights of stairs into the rectangular garden with the row of elephant ears, past the water hydrant, the four cats, and the setter, exiting through the wooden fence back onto Eighteenth Street, and then made her way back home. Was she able to settle back into her life or did this latest violence leave a mark, a record as indelible as the photograph?

The look says everything about the kind of female property she is—a female not in the class of those deserving protection, and unlike the daughter of the bourgeoisie, whose sexuality is the private property of the father and then the husband, she is one intended for public use. The pleasure yielded by the disavowed assault, by the graphic picture of violated black embodiment provides an inkling, an anticipation, that her body, her labor and her care, will continue to be taken and exploited; the intimate labor of the domestic will define her subjection. It is a stark and brutal image, despite its purported power to arouse. Is the pleasure of looking predicated on the disavowal of violence, the insistence on the girl's agency, the invitation to look signaled by her direct gaze at the camera? Is the precondition of this pleasure indifference, which is the habituated response to black pain? Or is the pleasure achieved through the cultivation of suffering and the infliction of harm?

The odalisque is a forensic image that details the violence to which the black female body can be subjected. It is a durational image of intimate violence. So much time accumulates on her small figure, the girl might well be centuries old, bearing the weight of slavery and empire, embodying the transit of the commodity, suturing the identity of the slave and the prostitute. All of which makes it impossible for her to be a child. The photograph fabricates her consent to be seen. How does she consent to coercion? How does the pleasure taken in the image of sexual assault issue from the girl's invitation? It is a picture redolent with the auction block, the plantation, and the brothel.

It is a picture that confounds our efforts to classify it. Art? Science? Pornography? It is a cold image that makes apparent what can be taken and what can be done under the guise of science and observation. The violence achieved and practiced justifies itself as the study of the Negro, as an anatomy lesson. How does one describe the life that oscillates among the categories of domestic, whore, slave, and corpse? Is it apparent that her life is disposable? Or that she is subject to a regime of brutality so normalized that its violence is barely discernible? How does one make this violence visible when it secures the enjoyment, sovereignty, and bodily integrity of man and master?

Her body is exposed, but she withholds everything. "The body shows itself," complying with the demand, yet "it does not give itself, there is no generosity in it." Is it possible to give what has already been taken?

———

What can a photograph of a girl posed on a horsehair sofa tell us about black life at the turn of the century or about the lives of young black women *rushing to the city* and desperate to enter a new era? How might it anticipate the obstacles awaiting them? How might this photograph illuminate the entanglement of slavery and freedom and offer a glimpse of the futures that will unfold?

Looking at her immobilized on the old horsehair sofa, pinioned like a rare specimen against the scrolling pattern, her small arms tucked tight against her torso like clipped wings, I think about the kinds of touch that cannot be refused. In 1883, the age of con-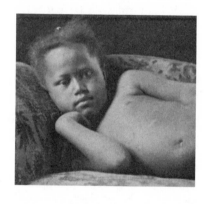sent was ten. There was no statutory rape law to penalize what occurred in the studio, and had such law existed, a poor black girl would have fallen outside its reach. When a rape or assault was reported to the police or the Society for the Prevention of Cruelty to Children, the girl, seduced or raped, might be sentenced to the training school or the reformatory to protect her or punish her for being too fast, too mature, or too knowing. The precocious sexuality of girls *ripened too soon* made them vulnerable to confinement and arrest. Previous immorality negated any claims to protection by the law. Innocence (that is, virginity) was the issue, not what age a girl was old enough for the taking. Previous immorality meant a man could do whatever he wanted. Colored girls were always presumed to be immoral. (One of the arguments against the statutory rape legislation passed in the 1890s, raising the age of consent in most states to sixteen or eighteen, was that lascivious Negro girls would use the law to blackmail white men. Black girls came before the law, but were not protected by it.)

As the photograph makes plain, her body was already marked by a history of sexual defilement, already branded as a commodity. Its availability to be used, to be hurt, was foundational to the prevailing set of social arrangements, in which she was formally free and vulnerable to the triple jeopardy of economic, racial, and sexual violence. This necessary and routine violence defined the afterlife of slavery and documented the reach of the plantation into the ghetto.

———

Looking at the photograph, one wonders if she had ever been a child. By age ten, had she learned everything about sex she would ever need to know? By twelve, had she no interest in it? Did she know the women working the street, the ladies in sporting houses, the sweet men, the badgers and thieves who lived on her block? Had she become prematurely knowing because of what had already been done to her or by observing the world around her? Was the violence experienced in an attic studio or at a neighbor's house irreparable? If so, how did it determine her course? Did it eclipse the possibility of sexual autonomy or stamp it indelibly? Did it make her vow never to love a man or seek his protection? Did it make her yearn for a tender touch capable of assuaging and redressing the long history of violence captured in a pose? Did it make her love fiercely and wildly? Did it make her decide that she didn't want to be a woman, but not a man either?

Looking at the photograph, one can discern the *symphony of anger* residing in the arrested figure. It is an image that I can neither claim nor refuse. Admittedly, it is a hard place to begin, with the avowal that violence is not an exception but rather that it defines the horizon of her existence. It is to acknowledge that *we were never meant to survive*, and yet we are still here. The entanglement of violence and sexuality, care and exploitation continues to define the meaning of being black and female. At the same time, I had to move beyond the photograph and find another path to her. How might this still life yield a latent image capable of articulating another kind of existence, a runaway image that conveys the riot inside? What would a moving picture of a young black woman's life inside the Black Belt encompass? The tenement. The washtub. The dance hall. The house of dreams. Where would it begin? In Farmville, Virginia? In the hold of the ship that conveyed her great-grandmother from Bermuda to Norfolk? In the steamer that delivered her to New York City? And how would it end? With her dancing in Edmond's Cellar or singing at the Clam House or cleaning rooms at the Hollywood Hotel, or waiting for a job in the Bronx slave market or counting the days until her sentence ended and she would receive the gift of her free papers? Would the serial picture of her life be terrible or lovely or heartbreaking?

In the pictures taken with her friends at a church picnic on the Jersey shore or hugging her girlfriend under the boardwalk at Coney Island, we catch a glimpse of this other life, listen for the secondary rhythms, which defy social law and elude the master, the state, and the police, if only for an evening, a few months, her nineteenth year. In the pictures anticipated, but not yet located, we are able to glimpse the terrible beauty of wayward lives. In such pictures, it is easy to imagine the potential history of a black girl that might proceed along other tracks. Discern the glimmer of possibility, feel the ache of what might be. It is this picture I have tried to hold on to.

————

After a year spent looking at a colored girl, posed in the nude, on an old horsehair sofa, I decided to retrace her steps through the city and imagine her many lives. Following in her footsteps and in those of other young black women in the city, I made my way through the

Black Belts of Philadelphia and New York, the neighborhoods and black quarters named after their inhabitants, Little Africa and Nigger Heaven, or their aspirations, the Mecca and the City of Refuge. I traced the errant paths and the lines of flight that in the decades from 1890 to 1935 would enclose the boundaries of the black ghetto. In the end, it became not the story of one girl, but a serial biography of a generation, a portrait of the chorus, a moving picture of the wayward.

For decades I had been obsessed with anonymous figures, and much of my intellectual labor devoted to reconstructing the experience of the unknown and retrieving minor lives from oblivion. It was my way of redressing the violence of history, crafting a love letter to all those who had been harmed, and, without my being fully aware of it, reckoning with the inevitable disappearance that awaited me. The upheaval I experienced looking at her image convinced me that I had to go forward, even if I doubted that I would ever find her. I saw her differently from the others. She was a girl situated on the threshold of a new era, one defined by extremes—the nadir of democracy and the Progressive Era. The age was characterized by imperial wars, an epidemic of rape and lynching, the emergence of the legal and social apparatus of racial segregation, and antiblack racial laws that inspired the Nazis' Nuremberg Laws. Race riots swept across the country. At the same time, legal and social reforms attempted to buffer the vulnerable from the predations of capitalism and free markets, and their necessary outcomes: poverty and unemployment and social violence. Political activists and black radicals battled against the resurgence of racism that engulfed the nation and contested the impaired citizenship and the rightlessness that defined the Negro condition. Club women focused their attention on the plight of black girls and women, determined to protect, defend, and uplift them and eradicate the immoral habits, which were the legacy of slavery.

I envisioned her not as tragic or as ruined, but as an ordinary black girl, and as such her life was shaped by sexual violence or the

threat of it; the challenge was to figure out how to survive it, how to live in the context of enormous brutality, and thrive in deprivation and poverty. The state of emergency was the norm not the exception. The only difference between this girl and all the others who crossed her path and followed in her wake was that there was a photograph that hinted that something had happened, that enabled everyday violence to acquire the status of an event, a forensic picture of an act of sexual violence not deemed a crime at all.

———

I followed her from Philadelphia to New York, the largest black cities in the north, stumbling through the streets of the Seventh Ward and then onto the Tenderloin and after that Harlem. I spotted her everywhere—on the corner, in the cabaret, on the boardwalk at Coney Island, in the chorus; sometimes I failed to notice her. At other times, the headliners and celebrities overshadowed her when she was allowed among their company. She bore faint resemblance to the girl I first encountered, and had I not known about the attic or that she had been forced to sleep in a coal bin or that she was raped by her uncle or assaulted by a neighbor or brutalized by her employer, I would have never guessed from looking at her. It was an age when Negroes were the most beautiful people, and this was no less true of her. Even her detractors reluctantly admitted as much. It's hard to explain what's beautiful about a rather ordinary colored girl of no exceptional talents, a face difficult to discern in the crowd, an average chorine not destined to be a star, or even the heroine of a feminist plot. In some regard, it is to recognize the obvious, but that which is reluctantly ceded: the beauty of black ordinary, the beauty that resides in and animates the determination to live free, the beauty that propels the experiments in living otherwise. It encompasses the extraordinary and the mundane, art and everyday use. Beauty is not a luxury; rather it is a way of creating possibility in the space of enclosure, a radical art of subsistence, an embrace of our terribleness, a transfiguration of the given. It is a will to adorn, a proclivity for the baroque, and the love of *too much*.

In my search for her, I soon encountered all the others hovering about her—the sociologist, housing reformer, probation officer, club woman, social worker, vice investigator, journalist, and psychiatrist—all of them insisting their view of her was the truth. One of them was always there, standing in my way, blocking my path, whenever I encountered her. None of them believed she would blossom. Their notebooks, monographs, case files, and photographs created the trails I followed, but I read these documents against the grain, disturbing and breaking open the stories they told in order to narrate my own. It required me to speculate, listen intently, read between the lines, attend to the disorder and mess of the archive, and to honor silence. The official documents made her into someone else entirely: delinquent, whore, average Negro in a mortuary table, incorrigible child, and disorderly woman. In the statistical chart, the social survey, and the slum photograph, she seemed so small, so insignificant. Everything else loomed large—the condition of the tenements, the perils of the ghetto, the moral dangers of the kitchenette, the risks presented by too many bodies forced into the cramped rooms of the lodging house. It was easier for the professionals to imagine her dead or ruined than to entertain the idea that she might thrive, that chance or accident might permit her to flourish. I had to be mindful not to do damage of my own. Only the chorines, bull daggers, aesthetical Negroes, lady lovers, pansies, and anarchists supported her experiments in living free. She was their avenging angel. Only the wayward appreciated her riotous conduct and wild habits and longing to create a life from nothing; only they could discern the beautiful plot against the plantation she waged each and every day.

―――――

The moving men found the albumen prints among the rubbish of the abandoned house. They might have been aroused by the photograph of a naked colored girl reclining on an arasbesque sofa and not at all concerned about whether she was yet of legal age. A flat-chested, narrow hipped, thick-thighed, prepubescent child arrested in the classic pose of the whore and the concubine was as good an incitement as any other dirty picture. When pleasure yielded to indifference, the photograph was discarded and thrown into a pile with the other debis from the studio.

———

It was not the kind of picture that the girl would have wanted. It didn't even look nothing like her. The eyes are flat and withholding; hard like the eyes of the girls working Middle Alley. They are *eyes in advance of time and experience*. To keep the photographer from coming any closer, she tried to make mean stay away from me eyes, I dare you eyes, eyes of flint, not whore eyes that solicited—*Hey Mister*—and refused—*I don't do that*—in the same glance. When she crossed Du Bois's path over a decade later, the longing in those eyes would betray her.

An Unloved Woman

When the conductor asked her again to give up her seat in the ladies' car, she refused. He didn't say that the other passengers objected to her company, but simply ordered her to surrender her seat and move on to the segregated car. Until he attempted to remove her forcibly, the ladies had assumed she was a servant traveling with her mistress, so were comfortable with the place she occupied in the first-class car. Only after the dispute erupted and the brown-skinned woman insisted that her first-class ticket entitled her to a seat did the white ladies recoil and begin shouting and ordering her to "get away" because they were "not in the habit of sitting on the seat with Negroes." Then their nerves were shocked by her presence and the imposition of such intimate contact. The distress aroused by her proximity was not lessened by the petite stature of the colored schoolteacher—she was a few inches short of five feet—or her discernible refinement. The attractive twenty-one-year-old was attired in a stylish linen duster. The rancor of the women and the threats of the conductor hovering above her did not weaken her determination to continue on her journey from Memphis to Woodstock, Tennessee, or lead her to doubt her right to assume the seat for which she had paid. The conductor's eyes, the harsh tone of his voice, and then the rough hands were not enough to dislodge her. No, she would not budge. The conductor attempted to yank her out of the comfortable upholstered chair, but when he grabbed her arm, she fastened her teeth onto the clenched hand assaulting her and bit down with all the force she could muster.

She took pride in the fact that two additional men were required to assist the conductor in ousting her. She fought like a tiger. They clutched her hands and feet, dragging her through the aisle, tearing her traveling coat. She held on to the seats, scratched and kicked, but there were too many of them and only one of her. The white passengers stood on their seats and clapped when she was ejected. She was not a lady. She was not a woman. She was a Negro. The Jim Crow car had no gender designation. Ida Wells chose to exit the train rather than suffer the humiliation of the segregated coach, which also served as a smoking and drinking car for white men. The conduct prohibited in the first-class car was licensed in the colored coach. White men smoked in the foul car, spat on the floor, drank liquor, cursed, read lewd magazines, ogled and molested colored women. As one young woman recalled, "You were at the mercy of the conductor and any man who entered." Ida was familiar with "all the awful tragedies which had overtaken colored girls who had been obliged to travel alone on these cars." This had been the rationale for the ladies' coach.

Luckily there were no bruises, or black eyes, or battered ribs. For Miss Jane Brown, another colored woman who had earlier been removed from a first-class coach, the action was justified after the fact by the charge that "she was not a respectable person" but "a notorious public courtesan, addicted to the use of profane language and offensive conduct in public places." The damage done to Ida Wells was justified not by a bad reputation, but by her status as "not-quite human." A darky damsel and a black cow were strangely equivalent and indicative of the category crisis she embodied. What kind of woman was she, if a woman at all? The question was no less prescient or urgent than it had ever been. A century later, it would achieve mythic proportions: *Ain't I a woman?* The hold of the uncertainty was so inescapable that it mattered little that Sojourner Truth had never uttered such words. As Ida Wells experienced directly, a colored woman could be labeled a prostitute, cursed as a "slanderous and dirty-minded mulatress," and threatened with castration.

On her way back home, she decided to hire a lawyer and fight the railway company in court. An obedient disposition did not come naturally to her. By her own description, she was tempestuous, hard-headed, and willful which meant she was prepared to confront and stand against white men and the law, and the whole world if need be. She would not stay in her place or kowtow to the ruling race. When she shared the story with her attorney, her voice did not break with the mortification the violent incident sought to produce; rather, it unleashed her innate fearlessness and a quality of courage so fierce and steadfast that it enabled her to do what "reasonable" Negroes declined—to confront, battle, boycott, and oppose white supremacy on all fronts. Only her skin betrayed her as she recounted what had happened; it prickled as she recalled the hands of white men on her arms and legs and tugging at her waist. The bitter taste of the words stuck in her throat might have caused a weaker woman to cry or to retch, but she held it all in check.

The conductor and the baggage handler might have done far worse, and the law would have permitted it. She knew first-hand the terrible things that happened to Negro women. That very day, she had read a story in the *Appeal* about a colored woman who had been lynched in Richmond, Virginia. Terrible things had happened in her family too. She remembered distinctly an exchange between her grandmother Peggy and her father, James Wells, about the old master and his wife. Her father was the offspring of the slave owner, property not son. Her grandmother mentioned that Miss Polly, the old mistress, wanted to see James and his children. The vehemence of her father's response surprised the young Ida: "I never want to see that old woman as long as I live. I will never forget how she had you stripped and whipped the day after the old man died, and I am never going to see her." Her father's hard words raised questions that she dared not ask her grandmother, but which soon found their answer in the sexual violence that engulfed the south. In *The Free Speech*, Ida Wells would write stories about the schoolgirls and domestics and teachers raped and beaten and hanged. *The women of the race have not escaped the fury of the mob.* She would tally the atrocities. She would make a timetable of the deaths. She would denounce mob rule, lynching, sexual violence, and the white man's law until the death threats forced her to flee Memphis and seek exile in the north.

In the parlor of well-appointed homes in Philadelphia and New York, she exchanged stories with other black women about the insults, the obscene propositions, the hateful glances, the lustful eyes, the threats of grievous bodily harm. There was no asylum to be found in the north either. The very words "colored girl" or "Negro woman" were almost a term of reproach. *She was not in vogue. Any homage at the shrine of womanhood drew a line of color, which placed her forever outside its mystic circle.* Together they recounted these stories in a world-weary tone, but without shame—they were treated less kindly than a stray dog, handled less gently than a mule, they were brutalized and abandoned by the law. Then there were the stories that made the room go silent: that woman in New Orleans murdered for living with a white man as her husband; the housekeeper lynched for stealing a Bible; the mother hanged alongside her son for the usual charge; the postmaster's wife, Mrs. Baker, who lost her husband and infant daughter to the mob, enraged that a Negro had taken a white man's job; the thirteen-year-old girl, Mildrey Brown, lynched in Columbia; the eight-year-old Maggie Reese raped in Nashville; Lou Stevens hanged from a railway bridge for the murder of the white paramour who had abused her; and it went on. The Red Record never ceased. More than a thousand Negroes had been murdered in six years. All

the terrible things she and the other survivors would never forget no matter how hard they tried.

As the women drank tea and ate shortbread, they planned ways to prevent such things from ever happening, collectively dreamed of a country in which they might be citizens, weighed the pros and cons of African emigration, lamented the dead. Ida Wells described the virtues of the Winchester and concluded self-defense was the sole protection afforded black women. *One had better die fighting against injustice than to die like a dog or a rat in a trap.* The sentence she penned about the outlaw hero, the attic-philosopher Robert Charles, could well be applied to her. She had already determined *to sell her life as dearly as possible* if attacked.

The delicate clatter of a porcelain teacup placed gently in a saucer, the ring of a silver spoon laid carefully on the Wedgwood pattern seemed to announce—*Still here.* It was the murmur, the music that animated their speech. Still here. They didn't allow their voices to crack or their eyes to glisten at the cold facts, at the brutal calculus of life and death. Only *us* and *we* and *still here* allowed them to utter one atrocity after another without breaking.

An Intimate History
of Slavery and Freedom

Now it was Mattie's chance. Traveling alone on the Old Dominion steamer from Virginia to New York was her first adventure. It seemed as if she had been waiting forever when her mother sent for her, although it had been only a year. Not until the ship was well beyond the James River could she really believe she was on her way. She had taken the smaller auxiliary from Hampton Roads to Norfolk, and, at last, she was heading north. Deep gulps of the salt air calmed the lurching hollow feeling in the pit of her stomach. In nineteen hours, she would arrive at the West Side docks, Pier 26, North River, at the foot of Beach Street. Pier 26 echoed in her head like a refrain, like a rhythm competing with the crest and fall of the Atlantic, with the hiss and spit of the mammoth steam engine. It encouraged the reverie that engulfed Mattie the entire length of the journey and punctuated the list of things she was glad to say goodbye to—the oyster factory and the tobacco fields and the laundry baskets spilling over with soiled linens and dirty clothes. All the places that had once been filled with her father's stories and lies and laughter were bereft, haunted, after Earl Nelson's death. There were the things she would miss, the big porch of their house in Hampton. The smell of rose and crocus. What else? The people, she would miss Nana and her younger brother most. All the rest had been erased by anticipation and desire. She didn't shout from the deck, "Damn you, Virginia," but she was sure glad to be leaving.

Until this very moment, her life had been restricted to a radius of sixty-two miles, which encompassed the homehouse and the farm in Gloucester, the one-room schoolhouse and the small church that her family had attended, and their house in town. She hoped 294 nautical miles was sufficient distance to create a new life. Mattie wanted something else. It was as simple and elusive, as vague and insistent as that. *Something else* was never listed as one of the reasons people left home, only the appalling and the verifiable—the boll weevil, lynching, the white mob, the chain gang, rape, servitude, debt peonage; yet the inchoate, what you wanted but couldn't name, the resolute, stubborn desire for an elsewhere and an otherwise that had yet to emerge clearly, a notion of the possible whose outlines were fuzzy and amorphous, exerted a force no less powerful and tenacious. Why

else pick up and head off to a place where you were a stranger, tolerated at best, but most often unwanted and reviled?

The wide open of the Atlantic made plain the restricted and dwarfed life Mattie was rushing away from, a life where her only possibilities were the same ones that had been imposed on her grandmother and mother. She, too, had been sentenced to servile labor, not trained for it or drawn to it. The house was no better than the fields; domestic work was as merciless and unsparing as shucking oysters and harvesting tobacco—the stench of fish, or hands sticky and yellow from nicotine, the headaches and the nausea; or the unwanted touch, the pressing and grabbing under her dress. Submit or risk a beating. Ass, hands, and capacities owned by mistress and sir. Why pretend there was an opportunity to be found inside the house of white folks or lie about its dangers? Who didn't hate domestic work? No colored woman would ever forget that it carried the taint of slavery. No need to pretend about its dangers. Everyone knew of a girl fired and sent away before she was too big with belly. *The kitchen was the field and the brothel.* No need to sugarcoat the fact: black women were still in the *house of bondage.* Neither Mattie nor her mother or her grandmother had chosen the kitchen or the washtub; they had been conscripted there. Aboard a steamer plowing the waters of the Eastern seaboard, Mattie was steadfast in the belief that *moving on* was the only way to make a better life, and flight the precursor to freedom.

Along with most of the colored passengers, Mattie was consigned to steerage, which they shared with dogs, goats, and chickens. (The few who could afford it occupied the staterooms on the aft side designated for Negroes.) But even the humiliation of the animals and the two dirty bathrooms reserved for them and the rope separating them from the rest of the deck could be suffered because she imagined that New York City promised a release from the color line and believed, willfully and blindly, that everything terrible was behind her now, as did the hundreds of other Negroes crowded around her, eager to disembark. She knew nothing of the riots that erupted in 1900 and 1905, but in 1915, she would experience the threat and the danger first-hand.

Her head was full of dreams. It was 1913 and anything seemed possible. She had done "the one thing which seemed to offer hope," she had left home. She was one of thousands of young black folks rushing to New York from Virginia and elsewhere. Only later would these acts of flight be recognized as a *general strike* against slavery in its new guises, as a fugitive movement from life lived under the heel of white men. When Mattie Nelson landed at Pier 26, she was dreamy with thoughts of what the future would hold. In the crush of folks on the pier, she breathed comfortably inside her own skin, enjoying the self-forgetfulness that she had imagined was possible in a free territory.

———

Had Mattie arrived in New York a decade earlier, Victoria Earle Matthews would have been waiting for her at the pier. I imagine the two of them meeting on that late fall morning when Mattie disembarked. With her gloved hand extended in a half-hearted welcome, Matthews would have introduced herself and then asked Mattie if a friend or relative was coming to meet her. The fate of girls unescorted and left to make their own way was not kind. The *Traffic in Souls*, a silent melodrama, had etched indelibly a tragic picture of unsuspecting girls searching for a room or a job who were lured into prostitution. The girl abducted by the human trafficker bore no resemblance to Mattie, except in Victoria Matthews's eye. (The only black woman in the film is the maid who cleans the rooms at the brothel and appears ignorant or indifferent about what happens behind closed doors.)

Victoria Matthews would have preferred not to welcome Mattie at all; such girls were ill-suited to life in the north and without certain prospects of employment; girls too easily tempted to trick or steal; girls whose movement could not be arrested and who threatened to do even more damage to the reputation of colored women. Had she the power, this upstanding woman and the founder of the White Rose Mission, a home for respectable young colored girls new to the city, would have stopped Mattie from landing on the dock. She would have turned her around, and all the other poor black girls like her, marched them back up the ramp and onto the steamer, and sentenced them forever to the dusty southern towns they had escaped. Matthews's view was not contemptuous, unlike Paul Laurence Dunbar's, who to her mind was too pessimistic about the conditions of the Negro in the north. He let white folks off the hook for the wretched conditions and lack of opportunity Negroes endured; but Matthews also would have preferred it if girls like Mattie never reached the city. It was better for them to starve in the south and "go home to God morally clean, than to helplessly drag out miserable lives of remorse and pain in Northern tenderloins." Better for such girls had they no desire at all; better that they stayed in their place. Unable to deter them or turn them away, she met them at the docks and the railroad stations and offered greetings replete with an account of the hazards and dangers awaiting young women adrift in the city.

Mattie, noticing the reserve and caution of this welcome, might have responded with a shy smile and an eyebrow lifted in doubt. The warning would have been wasted. She had just escaped the shadow of General Armstrong, liberator of the slaves, champion of industrial education, and the iron fist of uplift. At Hampton Institute, bright young women and men were trained for servility. *Every girl in the school received instruction in general housework. The idea of service was inculcated in every possible way.* She had seen the broadsides about the dangers of life in the north, listened distractedly to the stories about frozen, half-starving migrants, and browsed the pamphlets with the before-and-after pictures of Negroes, vital and thriving at work on the farm reduced to shivering impoverished Negroes trapped in tenements, and it had made no difference at all.

Two black women—one barely recognizable as a Negro and the other unmistakable, two women who by outward appearances might

A TYPE OF THE NEGRO GIRLS WHO DO THE LAUNDRY WORK FOR NEARLY 1000 PERSONS, AS WELL AS FOR THE BOARDING DEPARTMENT OF THE SCHOOL. OVER 25,000 PIECES ARE WASHED EVERY WEEK. EACH GIRL IS TAUGHT HOW TO DO ALL PARTS OF THE WORK. AND IS, BESIDES, GIVEN LABORATORY INSTRUCTION IN LAUNDRY CHEMISTRY.

seem like opposites, yet both straddling the fault lines of immorality and decency, violence and desire, an unspeakable past and a blank future. The older woman had been born during the Civil War and marked by a history of sexual shame, the lived experience of intimate violation, and the routine abjection of slavery. Her mother was a slave and her father a master. This history of "monstrous intimacy" and its perverse lines of descent were inscribed on the body, but not visible to the casual observer, who misread the long dark hair without the slightest hint of a wave or curl, and the pale skin for the unmarked category. Sometimes she allowed herself to be mistaken for white, but only when necessary, as when traveling in the south to investigate the savage crimes routinely committed against Negroes. Barring these extreme circumstances, she proudly called herself an Afro-American, rejecting the term *colored* because she believed it stood for nothing. To her mind, *colored* was the negation of her humanity and an injury that had been inflicted by centuries of slavery; now, it was being foisted upon her as an identity to exact even more damage.

In the spring of 1898, the year the race riot in Wilmington, North Carolina, and the Spanish-American War sounded the recurring death knell of Reconstruction and the promise of abolition democracy, two years after *Plessy v. Ferguson* decided that racial segregation was lawful and not a vestige of slavery, and the year Mattie Nelson was born, Victoria Matthews arrived at the pier to meet a girl migrating to the city from Jacksonville, Florida. The letter she received from Miss Morehouse provided the exact time of the ship's arrival and noted that the girl, her student, would be wearing a red ribbon in the buttonhole of her jacket. Matthews arrived on time to meet the steamer, but too late to save the girl from the men lurking there who spotted her first. When Matthews found her several days later, after a diligent search that required the assistance of police detectives, an eager bright-eyed girl had been transformed into "a broken, disgraced young creature, from whom city life [had taken] every vestige of hope, every chance of innocent happiness." This young woman's ruin led Matthews to establish the White Rose Mission. What better symbol of sexual purity and virtue than a white rose? Week after week from spring to late fall Matthews went to the docks to meet girls arriving by the Southern Steamship Line and escorted them to safety.

The sharks and hustlers were waiting too, eager to pick off the fresh arrivals—the near-white quadroons, caramel-colored mulattoes (able to pass for Cuban or Syrian), gorgeous Negresses, and run-of-the-mill colored girls—the young women described as crops ripe for the harvesting. Mattie Nelson would have put Victoria Matthews in mind of this first girl, the one she had lost.

When Victoria Matthews first arrived in New York City, she entered the city empty-handed, and, like every other black woman, with no past to which she could appeal for anything. Slavery, she believed, had destroyed everything decent; the institution had made honor and virtue impossible. All a Negro woman could count on was the future. So she worked hard to define herself and to fend off all that had been put upon her. Like every other southern girl taking her chance in the city, she was treated as if a prostitute (or in her words, a woman of "the depraved class commonly met with on the streets"). She labored as a domestic during the day and studied at night, determined to be *more than nothing*. It mattered little that she eschewed things sensual and disreputable, that she never acted her color, and that she struggled mightily to fortify the degrees of rank and caste that separated the good and decent Negroes from the wayward and the *not uncriminal*. Two-and-a-half centuries of being used, taken, broken, and loved by white folks in whatever manner they decided and by whatever means that suited their fancy, with blows or lashes, with gifts of the mistress's cast-offs or promises of manumission, with curses and sweet talk, with threats and whispers of love in the night—this intimate history of slavery—had indelibly marked black women, and it had marked her too.

While she was determined to turn this shame inside out and to make of it pride; pride and dignity of this sort had at its core something rotten, something spoiled. A life devoted to repairing the damaged reputation of the colored woman did not release Matthews from the sexual stigma of slavery, but merely transformed her from someone tainted by a shameful past into someone who had succeeded in improving and overcoming this past, yet was still bound to it. The taint proved indelible regardless how faint. Stigma isn't an attribute, it's a relationship; one is normal against another person who is not. White women were respectable over and against the degradation of black women. Victoria Matthews and Mattie Nelson were the excluded ones who defined the norms of gender and the meaning of womanhood. The shadow of slavery, wounded kinship, rape, and concubinage had created her and decided the character of her struggle to achieve virtue and decency. But promoting these new ideals, new if only because impossible to achieve or maintain in the context of chattel slavery, produced its own kind of shame and deviance. Her decency also required someone to be respectable against.

———

It was still too early for the whores, sissies, and toughs who plied their trade at the docks. Families gathered awaiting daughters and brothers and cousins; thugs and gangsters lurked at the outskirts of the crowd on the lookout for naive young women in search of direction or in need of help with a heavy piece of luggage. When Mattie Nelson arrived in New York City, she was barely a woman at fifteen. She was a tall, thin, dark-skinned girl, the kind only a father would have ever described as lovely, and the kind white people labeled a *Negress* to make apparent their contempt and scorn. It would be a decade before the thick hair tamed in braids and pinned in a bun on the top of her head, prominent cheekbones, almond-shaped eyes, and wide full lips would be compared to the beauty of an African mask. Even when dressed in her Sunday best, Mattie was decidedly unsophisticated. Yet despite the not-quite-polished picture the black, but comely, small-town girl presented, Mattie was determined to be more than nothing.

It was hard for Mattie to make a distinction between the city and freedom itself. Like those provincials and fools whom Paul Laurence Dunbar derided in *The Sport of the Gods* as intoxicated by "the subtle and insidious wine" of the streets, who translated the Bowery into romance, made Broadway into lyric, and Central Park into a pasto-

ral, and thereby failed to read the city as it really was, or apprehend it in a mode commensurate with its dangers, or properly adjust to its rhythms and demands, Mattie, looking past the cold facts and the risks, mistook the city for a place where she might thrive. "The real fever of love" would take hold of her, and the streets and the dance halls did become her best friends. All the sentimental causes for this rush and flight—the freedom to move, the want of liberty, the hunger for more and better, and the need of breathing room—explained her presence in New York. She too would fall prey to the pleasures and dangers of the city while trying to make a feast of its meager opportunities.

————

None of the factories, shops, or offices would hire colored girls, especially girls as dark as Mattie. Housework and laundry were her only options. It is hard to say whether it was the disappointment at the lack of opportunity or the assault of the coldest winter she had ever experienced that landed her in bed, sick for more than a month, only a few weeks after she had arrived. When Mattie recovered her strength, she found a position as a domestic at a boarding house with twenty-three rooms where she was the sole maid. Washing, cleaning rooms, making beds, and trudging up and down the five flights of stairs in the boarding house wore her out. She hated the drudgery and boredom. But her mother said if she wasn't going to school, she had to work. Most nights, she fell into bed exhausted, too tired to think about going to the moving pictures or the dance hall. When she wasn't tired, she was lonely. The evenings were long and dull and not at all as she had imagined New York. After five weeks she quit the boarding house and found a new job at a Chinese laundry in Bayonne, New Jersey, which was different, but no better.

The days were still long and exhausting, but now spent doubled over, pressing clothes. Few white girls were willing to work for the Chinese. The sexual panic about the dangers of Chinese men reached a new height after the body of a young white woman was found in the trunk of a Chinatown bachelor. The daily papers fed the hysteria and fueled the idea of the yellow peril by regularly reporting stories of unsuspecting girls lured into opium dens and turned into drug-addled mistresses, or seduced by lonely bachelors at taxidance halls, or murdered by their lovers. The queer arrangements of Chinatown, the all-male households, were the result of immigration statutes that restricted the entry of Chinese women, and, as a consequence, the brothel or another man's embrace were the most likely opportunities for intimacy, unless one looked for love across the color line. For Mattie, the Chinese laundry was just another job. Unlike black washerwomen who resented the *washee washee* men because they competed for the same clients, Mattie didn't care. The job was just a way station until something better became available.

———

Herman Hawkins was her first friend in New York. He worked as a waiter in a boarding house not far from where she lived with her mother. At twenty-five years old, he appeared worldly to the not yet sixteen-year-old Mattie, who, by her own admission, knew nothing at all, but was eager to learn. Herman boasted that he would show her everything—the Tenderloin, Harlem, Coney Island. He was a recent migrant from Georgia, so no doubt he enjoyed showing Mattie *his* city.

Mattie looked forward to the evenings spent with her gentleman friend. They would go to dance halls and parties where couples did the Slow Drag, Funky Butt, and Fish Tail to rags played on player pianos and the ditties and love-and-trouble songs the white world derisively called "coon songs." One night after such a party, they were walking home through Allen Park, when Herman started talking about the things he wanted to do to her. Mattie did not know if he started talking this way because of how they had been dancing when the lights were dimmed (wrapped up so tight in each other, that the boundary between her body and his gave way to flesh), or if the seclusion of the park in the early hours after midnight encouraged him to speak to her like she was a woman, like she was *his* woman, like she was the kind of woman who enjoyed listening to *that* kind of talk. In hot pursuit of the virginal-but-curious Mattie, Herman described in explicit detail what a body could do and how it would make her feel. Mattie had never done any of those things before and she tried to picture the intimate acts he described and the sensations aroused by such acts, and wondered if she would be embarrassed with her bloomers down around her ankles, and what his body would feel like on top of hers, and if the bed-sheets would be clean, or if the cot would squeak when they made love (like her mother's bed when she and Mr. Smith were going at it). It wasn't right for Herman Hawkins to say such things. He had never spoken to her like this before, no one had. Mattie told him to stop, and yet, he continued to talk and she continued to listen. She knew what he was saying was bad, but it also sounded thrilling. He kept on talking as if she had not asked him to stop, and, instead of getting angry or upset, she just listened. Mattie was not aware that she was giving him an answer to his question and that she had said yes.

———

Shortly after that walk in Allen Park, he convinced Mattie to remove her camisole and bloomers. It is not difficult to imagine the things Herman Hawkins taught Mattie inside the rented room of a lodging house. There were so many lessons to teach a girl who knew nothing, so much for her to discover. What to do? How to hold him? How to not be embarrassed by her naked body or ashamed of her smells and the things she wanted to do? First she had to breathe deeply and let go of the body armored in anticipation of insult and attack, surrender in consequence of pleasure, allow the body to yield to another, to be entered, joined, and bridged, to risk all defense, yet not be made into the mule of the world.

If a tender lover, he might have lingered kissing her mouth, traced the length of her back with his tongue, discovered the ways she liked to be held and the best ways to make her come. Had he been a selfish and demanding one, he would have trained her for his pleasure, instructing her how to move, what to say, when to keep her mouth shut. Did he force her to repeat words that humiliated and excited her, or plead with her to admit what she wanted most, but feared? Or perhaps they spoke no words at all, just hands fondling genitals, tongues thrust into ears, fingers exploring every orifice? Were they loud? Did they even care if the lodgers next door or the spying neighbors downstairs heard them? Would they have minded if a lonely bachelor caught a glimpse of flesh or an abandoned wife savored the moans escaping through the open window and made them her own? Or were they quiet and intent on denying others their sound? Did the men hanging out on the corner wink at Mattie as she made her way home or the women exchange knowing and hungry glances?

Mattie had no other person to compare him with, no scale to weigh his respective merits and weaknesses, talents and areas in need of improvement. Perhaps his skills were little more than the accumulated lessons he had acquired from the women he had been with, women his age and older, women capable of training and directing him, women unafraid to tell him to hush and get to it? Women who expected little else of him, because they also worked hard for meager wages and realized that although twenty-five, like most colored men in New York, he couldn't afford to marry or support a family, even if he had wanted one. Had the boasts of other men prodded him to lie, as they did, about what he could do or had done and to be as adamant about what he would never do, that is, the kinds of habits one indulged occasionally, but never disclosed?

Perhaps, what mattered most to Mattie was that she had found the way to her own pleasure, had learned to enjoy the smell of herself on her hands and in his hair, found a way to lessen the boredom, and diminished the hours spent waiting and trying to find a way out. Whether her lover valued her as a prize or took advantage of a gullible young woman matters less than what Mattie discovered in that room—what she wanted might actually matter. *Or that "I want that" becomes a way to cleanse the stench of "ain't (got)," "can't (get)," "don't."*

———

It is possible that Mattie experienced this opening of her desire as a refusal of all that kept her fixed in place, stuck at the laundry, chained to an ironing board, suffocating and without any possibility of change. An unremarkable act of coitus, a deed of no import, except to those involved, a routine practice not in any way to be confused with matters of significance, just an everyday act of fucking, a quasi-event, would not have been noticed had it not been part of a greater social upheaval. Intimate acts shared in rented rooms in boarding houses and tenements throughout the city fueled the social panic about wandering, dissolute young women and the great numbers of young black people rushing to New York. Mattie's restiveness and longing and the free love practiced in a private bedroom rented by the week were part of a larger ensemble of intimate acts that were transforming social life and inaugurating the modern, which was characterized by the entrenchment and transformation of racism, emergent forms of dispossession, and the design of new enclosures, and by a fierce and expanded sense of what might be possible. Girls on the cusp of womanhood, young colored women like Mattie, were at the center of this revolution in a minor key. Despite the efforts of the state to contain it as pathology and as crime, it proved impossible to stave the tide of desires not bound by law, coupling and procreation outside the embrace of marriage, and the ardent longing to live as one wanted.

A small rented room was a laboratory for trying to live free in a world where freedom was thwarted, elusive, deferred, anticipated rather than actualized. Mattie was a hunger artist wasting away before the eyes of the world for lack of opportunity while everyone gawked and watched. *And like any artist with no art form, she became dangerous.* Mattie was desperate not to be a servant or drudge, but there was no ready blueprint for another life that she could follow besides the one she crafted, an inchoate plan and radical thought in deed were her resources. *If she could feel deeply, she could be free.* She knew that beauty was not a luxury, but like food and water, a requirement for living. She loved cashmere sweaters, not because they were expensive, but because the fabric felt so exquisite against her skin, like a thousand fingers caressing her arms, and the cool slip of silk undergarments against her flesh, smooth and releasing all that heat and fire, and the way a gold bracelet glinted and flashed in the sunlight and made the tone of her blue-black flesh so lush, as if right below the skin there were layers of indigo and ochre, a vortex of deep black in which you could lose yourself. Beauty and longing provided the essential architecture of her existence. Her genius was exhausted in trying to live.

What took place behind the closed doors of a rented room in a lodging house was a moment, *an iteration of the revolution of black intimate life* that was taking place in New York, Philadelphia, and Chicago in the first decades of the twentieth century. It was part of the general unrest that came to define the age and the New Negro. Experiment was everywhere. It was a ubiquitous term employed to describe a range of social projects—from the settlement house to a laboratory of sociology to a model tenement, from aesthetic and scientific innovations to radical designs for living. It was a term bandied about. There was nothing precious or unusual about seeking, venturing, testing, trying, speculating, discovering, exploring new avenues, breaking with traditions, defying law, and making it, except that hardly anyone imagined that young black women might be involved in this project too. Few guessed that Mattie was trying to make something of herself, however uncertain she was about *what might be* and however desperate to shake loose the expectations and demands of others, which always boiled down to drudge and whore. Better an errant path than the known world. Better loose than stuck.

If it is possible to imagine Mattie and other young black women as innovators and radical thinkers, then the transformations of sexuality, intimacy, affiliation, and kinship taking place in the black quarter of northern cities might be labeled *the revolution before Gatsby*. Before the queer men and lady lovers and pansies congregated at the Ubangi Club, or the Garden of Joy or the Clam House, before the Harlem Renaissance, before white folks journeyed uptown to get a taste of the other, before F. Scott Fitzgerald, and Radclyffe Hall and Henry Miller, before black communists and socialists preaching on Harlem street corners noticed girls like Mattie, eager as any to hear news of a future world—this *reconstruction of intimate life commenced*. After the slave ship and the plantation, the third revolution of black intimate life unfolded in the city. The hallway, bedroom, stoop, rooftop, airshaft, and kitchenette provided the space of experiment. The tenement and the rooming house furnished the social laboratory of the black working class and the poor. The bedroom was a domain of thought in deed and a site for enacting, exceeding, undoing, and remaking relations of power. Unfortunately, the police and the sociologists were there also, ready and waiting, for Mattie Nelson on the threshold of want.

———

Inside Herman Hawkins's bedroom, a young laundress, an exhausted drudge, a clothesline muse, and reckless dreamer tried to unmake the colored girl scripted by the world. Two lovers huddled in a rented room engaged in chance acts of intimacy that might well be blamed on the promiscuity afforded by crowded city streets and by young women navigating the world on their own. The things experienced and explored surpassed the status crimes—the disorderly conduct, moral depravity, vagrancy, and prostitution—for which black girls and young women were regularly convicted. The modern existence wrought by girls like her was apprehended as crime and ascribed to the backwardness of "plantation holdovers." Mattie has been credited with nothing, deemed unfit for every role except servility, condemned in advance of wrongdoing, and destined to be a *minor figure* even in her own *verified history*. To esteem her acts, to regard rather than vilify Mattie's restive longing, is to embrace the anarchy—*the complete program of disorder*, the abiding desire to change the world, the tumult, upheaval, open rebellion—attributed to wayward girls. It is to attend to other forms of social life, which cannot be reduced to transgression or to nothing at all, and which emerge in the world marked by negation, but exceed it.

———

To yield, to be undone and dispossessed by the force of her desire, and for no other reason than that she *wanted to*, made Mattie feel vital, untethered. And this freedom was sensual and palpable—like the taste of Herman Hawkins in her mouth, a force so arresting it could stop her in her tracks, make her ache in anticipation of what could happen. When he was inside her, when she was inside him, when he kissed her so hard that his teeth were bruising her lips, she left that other Mattie behind, the plain dark-skinned girl whom no one had ever described as pretty. The sweetness of bodies was stoked by self-forgetting. In that room she tried to slip away, elude the hold of the plantation and the police, and pry open time into an endless stretch of possibility.

At other moments, it was harder to discern the difference between something painful and something beautiful. *Take all of me. Don't lie to me. Use me. Hit it. Don't hurt me.* There was a thin line between loss and expenditure, between yielding and breakdown. The violence of it when he forced her to do things she didn't want to do. How he might punish her. How he misused her. *How he loved her.* Trained her to want what she didn't, as if every black woman's life was destined to a blues, an autobiographical chronicle of love and disaster, or a secret history of pain and joy. *How he loved her.* A rough hand caught in Mattie's hair, which unfurled and then drew up in tight curls in sweaty palms, and the light playing on dark bodies at dusk said what the world withheld—beauty. It was a practice of care and an offering of the self for the use of the other in the confines of enormous brutality. The beauty of things taken and things given by those living in defeat. Mattie wanted so much from the world and had been allowed so little—the force of all that *want* drove her to the small rented room. She was moved by lust, which was not an exercise of her will, but *the mere force of existing*, a kind of submission that was insistent, an act that confused the doer and the deed. In the enfolding of flesh, in this most base and exalted act of entries and exits, Mattie threatened to disappear, the force of it exceeding her and erasing the boundaries of the discrete body, making her something less than she was and something more. To be undone, against her will and with her consent. A state that was neither autonomy nor capture. It broke her down, it made her nothing at all, it laid her low, it transformed her into anything else she longed to be: like a bird flying high or a thing vast and boundless, oceanic—not a person at all. In the reek and warmth of a rented room she was all flesh and sensation; she was hovering at the end of the world. And she welcomed it.

————

When her mother, Caroline, asked, "Who been messing with you?" she struggled hard to explain. The dislocation of desire and the pangs of lust were impossible for her to describe, except in the language provided by others. *I went wrong with Herman Hawkins. I liked doing it. He forced me. I knew better. I wanted it.* How could she communicate the exquisiteness of the unexalted or the lovely repose of bodies spent after the act? Or the courage entailed in refusing shame or risking it? Decency demanded omission; otherwise she would be forced to lie. She didn't care about decency, or about respectability. Better words were needed to convey all that transpired in that room—the things taken and given. So Mattie offered only his name: Herman Hawkins. He's the one been messing with me.

———

The baby girl was born dead. He never saw his daughter. He wanted nothing to do with the child or the mother. The dead baby girl should have been the end of the business with Herman Hawkins, but because Mattie was only fifteen years old when they became lovers, the Society for the Prevention of Cruelty to Children became involved and the social worker pressured Mattie to charge him with statutory rape. Mrs. Burns told Mattie that according to the law, a girl her age, even *a Negress*, was too young to consent to sexual relations, too young to know what she wanted. Mattie's story defied the logic of right and wrong, wanting and being taken. Did she want something that she didn't consent to or desire something bad for her? Was yielding to a lover the moment when everything went wrong? So Mrs. Burns imposed a language. Clarity required blame or guilt, and wrongdoing, his or hers, lurked in every phrase and admission. For the social worker, consent was the way to shift the burden of criminality from her shoulders to his. It was the factor that determined the distribution of punishment and that underscored the danger of intimacy and all the ways it could put a young woman at risk.

After hearing the evidence in regard to statutory rape, the grand jury dismissed the charges against Herman Hawkins, and he walked out of the courthouse free and clear. (Mattie figured that because she was colored the court didn't care. They believed she asked for it. After he abandoned her, it was hard to sort out the truth of what happened. It was difficult to believe that she had ever wanted him.) His only obligation was to pay for his daughter's funeral.

———

For another kind of girl, the disappointment with Herman Hawkins might have crushed her, or induced her to make vows about never traveling down that road again, or convinced her that there was a moral lesson to be found in this experience or lead her to renounce her sexual adventure. For Mattie, the experience unleashed her. If she set out to make a new life after Herman Hawkins, then clearly she intended on one that was wild and wayward. At sixteen, she was still anticipating something better than the life she had. Like other young black women, she exercised her talents and ambitions in the streets and cabarets. Each day she struggled to acquire a bit more breathing room in a world becoming more and more restricted by the color line, more and more defined by the routine brutalities of racism. Mattie never stopped *clutching at a way of life* better than what she had. Everyone had an idea of who she should be and what she should do. It was clear that her own desires mattered to no one but herself. If she didn't decide how she wanted to live, then the world would dictate, and it would always consign her to the bottom. Refusing this, Mattie carried on *as if she were free*, and in the eyes of the world that was no different from acting wild.

———

By the time Mattie met Carter Jackson, she had lost the veneer of a small-town girl. Everything else was different too. For one thing, the first time they had sex, Carter promised to do right by her, unlike Herman Hawkins, who had preferred to risk prison rather than be tied to a wife, or, at least, bound to her. Carter seemed like the kind of man she might build some kind of life with. What kind of life was not certain? When Carter spoke, he made everything seem possible. He was hungry to exist on his own terms and establish the measure of his acts. It was hard to tell whether he was earnest or just better at talking shit than Herman Hawkins and the men she had known after him. For the time being, she was content to give Carter the benefit of the doubt. It didn't matter that the outlines of what might be were vague, and if she was pressed about how and when, it all threatened to disappear.

Carter Jackson hadn't seen much more of the world than Mattie had and knew less because he had not grown up with a father with a splendid education who filled his head with stories of the Philippines, Cuba, and Haiti. Her mother had traveled too, but in Caroline's stories she always sounded like the same woman, and the world appeared little different from the one Mattie knew, a world familiar in its limits, a world that made her weary. Caroline recounted her journeys, as if traveling across the world hadn't changed her at all, as if Cuba and Jerusalem were the same as New York, because housework was housework. If she remembered fondly the nights dancing in open-air bars, or the feeling of freedom or possibility that attended leaving everything you knew behind and moving as if nothing tethered you to a time or place, if she in any way enjoyed this sense of the big sea, she didn't share it with Mattie, perhaps not wanting to encourage her daughter's dreamy recklessness.

Her father had scrubbed and cooked and hauled his way around the globe, but Earl Nelson made it sound as if he were navigating the oceans for the first time. He had wanted his children to know how big the world was, as if knowing this would be enough to battle everyone and everything trying to confine colored folks to a six-by-nine-foot existence. Mattie had believed every word of her father's. The way she told it, when he was alive, she had not wanted for anything. They lived in their own house in Hampton with a large back yard and garden. Her father had a successful business in town in addition to the farm in Gloucester, so when he died he left her and her brothers several hundred dollars each. Had she done anything bad when Earl Nelson was alive, he would have beaten the daylights out of her.

———

A daughter knows one man and a wife another. After Earl Nelson's death, Caroline had vowed never to get married again. Nearly a decade later, she had remained faithful to that pledge. Her husband had saddled her with five children and then decided to spend most of his days at sea, shipping out for stretches that sometimes lasted more than a year. Despite earning good money, he sent home very little, ten or fifteen dollars folded inside a perfunctory note. Some men hurt a woman by the cruel things they do or say; Earl hurt Caroline by all things he withheld. He had deceived her. Midway through their marriage, she was convinced he no longer loved her. *It seemed evident he cared little for his family.* Why else had he decided to spend most of his days at sea? Caroline couldn't even say whether he loved his children. He had hardly sent home enough to support them, forcing her to wash and clean for white folks.

The last letter was from the freight company. His vessel had been shipwrecked. He should have been dead in her heart by the time she read the words *presumed dead. Lost at sea.* Since that first crossing, the water had never stopped punishing Caroline's family, inflicting new losses on each generation. When her grandmother was a girl in Bermuda, Virginia "traders" had kidnapped her and four brothers while they played on the shore. The white men lured them aboard, promising them safety from an approaching storm and then bound them below decks until the hold was packed and "a full complement of cargo" secured. The five stolen children were sold as slaves in Virginia. They never saw their mother again. Mother-dispossessed defined what it meant to be a slave. The stillborn baby girl died the same year as Mattie's great-great-grandmother. Of this, Caroline was certain. She felt it in her bones.

————

Carter Jackson did not have a prosperous business or a large house that he had built with his own hands. No doubt, he knew better than anyone the distance between where he was and where he wanted to be, the gulf between what he had and what Earl Nelson had created for his family, according to Mattie's elaborate stories. At twenty-six, Carter had not realized any of the grand things of which he dreamed, but when Mattie met him, he was not resigned to this.

He was young, so he did not yet know the wonderful things or the awful things of which he was capable. He did not yet know whether he was a good man or a bad one because he hadn't been tested.

Mattie believed Carter was a good man, but she would not be spared from witnessing what the world could do to a good man and the damage he would inflict as his sole line of defense. With this lover, she did not give permission without realizing it; she wanted Carter as much as he wanted her. She took him at his word. He would not bring a child into the world and then turn away from it. During her seventh month, Mattie started calling herself *Mrs. Jackson* and introducing Carter as her husband. *Mrs. Carter Jackson*—it rolled off her tongue as sweetly as if the words were honey. Caroline didn't believe it for a minute. Mattie hoped like every would-be bride that the *Mrs.* would provide a sufficient foundation to secure the future, to keep her man and child together. Was this pretend marriage an attempt to make her child legitimate, or a rehearsal for the normal conjugal life that they failed to achieve but which they desired? Was *Mrs. Jackson* an exaggerated performance of what was expected or imposed? Was there another Mrs. Jackson somewhere with a legal right to the name? Who needed the law to decide what went on between them or to endow *husband* and *wife* with meaning?

Mattie might have suspected that the four weeks they shared in a rented room in a New Jersey lodging house in the eighth month of her pregnancy was as much of a marriage as they would ever have. She returned to her mother's house in the last weeks before the baby was due. Carter stayed in New Jersey, although he visited regularly. When the baby was born, Carter was so tender with her that she never suspected that anything could go wrong, or that there was any reason to worry. In truth, he was drowning, but he filled her head with promises about all he would do and all they would have. Even if he never uttered the words, "You can count on me," every gesture of love seemed to prove it. Even if he never said, "Girl, no need to worry," she relied on him.

The baby, Scott, was just a month old when Carter disappeared. Caroline called the boarding house in Bayonne, but there was no trace of him to be found. He had moved out without leaving a forwarding address or telling any of his friends where he was headed. He quit his job and vanished.

Mattie grieved for her missing husband, not knowing whether he was dead or alive. No matter, he's dead to you and your child, Caroline might have counseled. But she held her tongue. She knew that the same man dead to Mattie might now be another woman's prize, another Negro resurrected through flight and the gift of an alias.

Probably drowned was the exact phrase used in the cargo company's letter to Mrs. Earl Nelson. He was "presumed dead." It was a cruel term that announced loss, but left open the door for unreasonable hopes, foolish expectations. Just last year, Caroline had received a letter from one of Earl's friends informing her that he had seen her dead husband walking through the streets of New York. She might have hired a detective to find him had she believed that Earl Nelson ever loved her or if anything rested on the distinction between dead and dead to her. What would be the point of catching him in this last and biggest lie? Caroline preferred to think of him as dead and continued to take comfort in being his widow. It was best for everyone that way and she never planned to tell Mattie any different.

———

Aurelia Bush recognized her undergarments. The new silk combination camisole-and-bloomers that had disappeared after the second washing were hanging on the hussy's clothesline as if they rightfully belonged to her. She fumed at the thought of that lowdown whore in her intimate apparel. She had never liked Mattie Jackson and would never be fooled about the kind of women she and her mother were because she knew the whole story. She knew about the dead baby girl and the bastard son and Herman Hawkins and the two husbands, and the white men who regularly came to the house. Aurelia wasn't a fool. Mattie was living out of wedlock with *Chester* Jackson, a boarder inside her mother's house, and still calling herself *Mrs. Jackson*, the name she had started using when she was pregnant with *Carter* Jackson's baby. She was no better than her mother, Caroline Nelson, who was living with the boarder Smith and calling herself Mrs. Smith. There was no truth to none of it. Of this Aurelia Bush was dead certain. What most offended her were the Italian men who called at the house looking for Mattie. She watched them as they climbed the stairs and entered the back door. What decent colored woman entertained the company of white men? It explained why Mattie and her mother could afford to live better than everyone else.

The clothesline belonged to Mattie, but she allowed Aurelia, who lived downstairs, to hang her clothes there too. The missing undergarments could have been an innocent mistake, but it was also true that Mattie had little regard for private property. *Mine, I own it, belongs to me*—were terms that didn't carry much weight with her. She treated possession as if it were conditional, rather than absolute, as if beautiful objects were intended to be shared, as if the loveliest things were rightly a communal luxury. Once she came home wearing a gold bracelet, which belonged to a woman whose clothes she laundered. When her mother asked about it, she said she found it. Another time, she came home from work draped in a cashmere sweater that was the favorite sweater of her employer's daughter. The next day she returned to work wearing it. As with Aurelia's undergarments, Mattie made no attempt to hide these items. Her employer believed that Mattie was as honest as the average colored girl, but had not failed to note that she was somewhat careless with the property of others. She didn't accuse Mattie of stealing because she didn't hide the items but wore them openly. As far as she was concerned, Mattie did not deliberately take anything. It was the kind of *cheap socialism* commonplace among Negroes. When Mattie found a locket and chain belonging to one of the children and placed it around her neck, she wore it in plain view, as if indifferent to rightful ownership and innocent of the notion of theft. Beautiful objects solicited her and she yielded to them, not caring about who owned them, not believing that she had stolen anything.

When Aurelia confronted her, Mattie apologized and offered her the $3.97 that she had paid for the underwear, but Aurelia Bush wanted more than an apology. She was the one who told the police detective about Carter and Chester, the two Mrs. Jacksons. Mattie Jackson was a low-down prostitute. Aurelia had repeated this accusation so often she was certain it was true. The field investigator never found any evidence to confirm this, but the accusation exacted its damage.

———

The sociological note appended to the case file stated: *The maternal home was a poor environment. The mother did not appear to feel very keenly disgraced by daughter's behavior. She is lax in supervising her daughter. Her immoral conduct has been repeated by her daughter. Probation officer did not believe her home would be a good place to send patient. She considered probation quite seriously because this is the girl's first offense, but felt that the institution would be better than probation in this case. The staff agrees.*

Had her mother been Mrs. Smith by law, had Mattie really been Mrs. Jackson, had she not given birth to two children out of wedlock, had the police detective been willing to drop the charges when Aurelia Bush had a change of heart, had the probation officer not disappeared halfway through Mattie's trial, had the House of Mercy or the Magdalene Home been willing to accept colored girls, had the superintendent of the reformatory not believed the prison a better and more nurturing environment than the average Negro home, had the officers of the court not concluded that the lives of the two Mrs. Jacksons constituted moral depravity, had Mattie Jackson been white, it is unlikely that she would have been confined to the New

York State Reformatory for Women at Bedford Hills for nearly three years.

The case against Mattie was the case against her mother. This maternal inheritance placed her at risk for arrest and confinement, marked her as pathological and immoral, if not criminal. Given her poor upbringing and broken home, it was not a surprise that the girl had gone wrong. It was another example of maternal neglect. In the deliberations about Mattie's future, this maternal inheritance was far more important than Aurelia Bush's missing undergarments. Caroline's lack of shame regarding Mattie's sexual behavior and bastard children proved that the young woman was in need of better supervision than what could be offered by a lax Negro mother. Despite attending church regularly, clearly Mrs. Caroline Nelson, also known as Mrs. Smith, had very poor moral standards and transmitted her own lawless conduct to her daughter. Without batting an eye, Caroline told the investigator that she vowed never to marry again, but clearly this didn't exclude extramarital relations.

As damaging were Mattie's own words. In "The Statement of the Girl," she said: *I liked doing it. I went wrong. He forced me. I knew better. I wanted it.* Her remarks yielded no clear sense of guilt or regret. Nor did they convince anyone that she had learned her lesson after Herman or Carter. The Italian men raised the matter of prostitution, although there was no evidence of this. Her lack of remorse and her refusal to acknowledge any wrongdoing turned the tide against her. Nothing she had done justified her arrest, let alone being incarcerated. By insisting that she had not done anything wrong, Mattie served to confirm her guilt in the eyes of the social worker and the psychologist.

———

Even if Caroline Nelson hadn't heard Mattie screaming on the second Sunday in November of the second year of her imprisonment, in all likelihood, she had read in her daughter's eyes that things were

not well. When she visited with Mattie a guard was always present, so her daughter couldn't say much. She was waiting for Mattie
in the visitors' room when the matron, Mrs. Engle, informed her
that Mattie wouldn't be allowed visitors. Caroline could hear Mattie
screaming and so she kept asking, *Mrs. Engle, what is wrong? What is
wrong? I hear my daughter.* Then she started shouting Mattie's name,
hoping her child might hear her. The matron demanded that Caroline stop shouting and insisted that everything was fine. The whole
time Mattie was screaming in the background. Mrs. Engle escorted
Caroline out of the visiting area and through the front gates. On the
train back to New York City, Caroline, distraught and afraid, questioned: What are they doing to my child? Mattie's screams echoed
in her head the entire ride.

Mattie wrote her mother twice a month, but the matrons read all
the letters, so she would not have been able to say, Mama, they are
hurting me. Please get me out of here. They have handcuffed me
to the bars of my cell. They have locked me in the dungeon of the
Disciplinary Building. They have denied me food and water. They
have tied my wrists with a rope and suspended me from the ceiling

of my cell. They have choked and beaten me. They have slapped my face. They have called me nigger and ugly black bitch. Mother, please get me out of here.

Had Mattie written any of this in one of the two letters she was allowed to send each month, the letters would have been seized and she would have been subjected to even greater punishment. (Soon the torture and abuse would be made public. But it would be decades before anyone questioned whether young women should be incarcerated for having children out of wedlock or staying out overnight or having serial lovers or intimate relations across the color line.)

———

Caroline got off the train in Harlem. She was determined to track down two girls who had been friends with Mattie at Bedford. What they reported broke her and made her want to hurt somebody. Awful things had been done to her daughter, her flesh and blood. Caroline might have felt as her great-grandmother had when her children were kidnapped from Bermuda. What could she do? Not a damn thing. It might have reminded her of her grandmother, stolen and mother-dispossessed, or made her worry about her grandson, mother-dispossessed too. Wounded kinship repeated across generations. That evening, Caroline, determined to do something, wrote a letter to the superintendent of the prison:

November 26, 1919

Dear Miss Cobb
Just a line or two to ask you what was the trouble with Mattie that she was screaming? Was you whipping her? I saw a woman and she say you all treat my daughter as if she was a dog. Why you do [so?] She was not in when I got there.

I was told twice after I leave there before the train came I heard Mattie crying my self that [was] why I was standing up when you came in.

I heard her and I want to know was you whipping her [?] I was told by a girl that was in there that the two of you get on Mattie and beat her choke her.

If I had heard that before I came up on Sunday I would have told you about it, but on my way home I stop uptown and these girls was telling me about it. I am sorry to write to you but I have to because I want you to know it, for it made me sick to know such cruel people was up there. I can't believe it. Will [you] give Mattie this note. You read it [to see] if I put anything in there [that] is not right, cross it out.

Please I will tell you more of the girls' news to me Miss Cobb, if you allow me to. This is [all I] ask of you: when can I see [Mattie] or when can I see you? I will (sign) yours respectful

Mrs. Earl Nelson

Pleas answer.

———

Mattie's letters are missing from the case file, although she corresponded with her mother and wrote notes to her friends. On at least one occasion, she was punished for passing notes to a girl in another cottage. In the spring of 1918, she was sent to the Disciplinary Building for hiding stationery and stamps in her room. But there are no copies of the letters she drafted and hoped to smuggle out of the prison or of the notes that she passed to a girlfriend. What stories were shared in all the letters lost and disappeared, the things whispered, and never disclosed? Is it possible to conjure the sentences and paragraphs and poems contained in that lost archive? Or find a way to Mattie's language of self-expression? Her desire to write was so great that she was willing to risk punishment. A note slipped under a door or a crumpled message passed from cell to cell, hand to hand is called a kite—words travel even when we can't.

Did Mattie keep a journal or write love poems? Did she record her dreams? Did she write stories about stillborn babies or stolen children or ships lost at sea or missing fathers? In her letters home, did she remind her mother to sing Scotty a lullaby so he could fall asleep real easy? Did she think about her great-great-grandmother exiled in Bermuda and separated from her children? Did she regret what had happened with Herman Hawkins? Or accept how hard it was to divorce the things she wanted and the things that hurt her, or separate the beauty of what she had experienced from the violence of it? In her letters to Caroline, did she ask about her girlfriends in Harlem or if her mother had seen Chester lately? Mattie would not have dared ask about the Red Summer of riots. She would not have been able to tell her mother whether she loved a girl in a neighboring cottage or had joined her friends in the riot at the reformatory, turning over beds, setting curtains on fire, and destroying everything in reach; or explain that *if they destroyed much it was because they had suffered much.* If her mother read between the lines, would she have been able to discern what Mattie's letter implied: she was struggling to get free.

Manual for General Housework

anual: of or pertaining to the hand or hands, done or
performed with the hands. Now especially of (physical)
labor, an occupation, etc., as opposed to mental, theoretical. Manual as distinguished from the mind and the intellectual.
Manual: as of a weapon, tool, implement, etc.; that is used or worked
with the hand or hands. Actually in one's hands, not merely prospec-
tive. (Manual: short for manual exercises, i.e., physical labor, and not
the exercise of reason or imagination.) A tool or an object, within
one's grasp, not speculative, not a proposal for black female genius.
The use of the body as tool or instrument. Of occupation or possession. Able to have in one's own hands, as in possession is three-fifths
of the law, as in possession makes you three-fifths of a human, as in
property handled by another. Also to be possessed. To be handled
as if owned, annexed, branded, invaded, ingested, not autonomous.
Manual: to be wielded by another, to be wielded on a whim; to be
wielded as an exercise of another's will, to be severed from one's own
will or motives or desires. Manual: as opposed to mental, as in not an
exercise of rational faculties. As opposed to the formation of critical
reflections; as opposed to contemplation of the self or the world. A

method of operating or working. A function. Short for manual exercise. Short for manual tool.

Manual: as opposed to automatic, as opposed to starting or functioning by itself and for itself, as opposed to deliberation and judgment, as in the need for direction, as in the imposition of a mistress or master.

Manual: As of pertaining to the hand or hands. The hands to be outmoded or made obsolete by the machine. Of or pertaining to the mule more than the machine. Worked with the hands, finished with the hands. No more than a pair of hands. Hands cracked and swollen from harsh soap and ammonia. Hands burnt taking the pies out of the oven. Hands stiff and disfigured from wringing cold sheets and towels outside in the winter before hanging to dry on the line. Hands, no longer yours, contracted, owned, and directed by another, like a tool or object. The hands that handle you. The hands up the dress, the hands on your ass, the hands that pull down your undergarments, the hands that pin you to the floor. The hands that pay you two dollars for the day or thirteen dollars for the week. Manual: as of subject to use, made a tool, handled, grasped, palmed, slapped, fondled, hugged, harassed, caressed; as of pertaining to the hand.

Manual: as opposed to contemplation, or theory. As opposed to the use of the intellect. As opposed to looking, viewing, contemplating. As opposed to thinking, reflecting, scheming, plotting, planning, weighing, brooding. The use of the hands as opposed to a conception or mental scheme or paradigm. Manual: the concrete, the physical, the embodied as opposed to abstract knowledge and the formulation of it. As opposed to reason. Manual: as pertaining to ignorance, obtuseness, stupidity, and as opposed to erudition.

As related to handle, as to be handled, as to be handled with no regard, as to be handled as a tool or instrument; as to be handled like a slave, like a wench, like a bitch, like a whore, like a nigger. Handled as pertaining to that part of the thing which is to be grasped by the hand in using it or moving it. To be grasped by the hand or sometimes by the neck, the ass, the throat. Colloquial: to fly off the handle; to go into a rage; to fuck shit up. Figurative: that by which something is or may be taken hold of; one of two or more ways in which a thing may be taken or apprehended. To manipulate, manage; to subject to the action of hands, to touch or feel with hands. As opposed to: Don't touch me. As pertaining to: Hands up, don't shoot. To manage, conduct, direct, control. To be handled by men, to be manhandled, to be seized by men, to be used by men, to be used up by men. Handled, as related to use of the thing, to do something with the tool, as opposed to directed by will and desire; as opposed to consent, as opposed to leave me the fuck alone. To deal with, to treat as you wish, to serve, to use, to accumulate, to expend, to deplete.

Manual: as related to a book, etc.—of the nature of a manual intended to be kept at hand for reference. A concise treatise, an abridgment, a handbook.

An Atlas of the Wayward

On South Street, two young women walking hand in hand along the sidewalk attracted the attention of the sociologist. His eyes settled on them, but they paid him no mind. One girl nudged the other with her elbow, and they stopped in front of one of the shops and peered into the window filled with rows of shoes. The large plate glass window allowed them entry into the world of radiant objects, and they too became part of the beautiful display. Their reflections floated on the surface of the glass, the brown faces resplendent as they hovered above the sea of items, lulled by the surfeit of goods. The shop window fascinated them and for a few moments interrupted their stroll while they gazed at the display window as if it were a moving picture. The glass window offered confirmation: Girl you look fine; chided: A threadbare coat can't fool anyone; instructed: Tilt that hat over the right eye, create the mystery you want to be.

Her eyes filled with longing, one of the women extended her arm, pointing toward a pair of men's shoes.

Do you see those shoes?

Which ones?

An assortment of men's shoes: conservative black wingtips, ankle-

high boots with silver eyelets, highly polished boots with compli-
cated hooks, plain humble shoes, and heavy work boots. The shoes
that caught her eyes were for the man who dared to exceed under-
statement, cared nothing about being respectable, and delighted in
turning every head as he strode down the block. Who could resist
a man in a pair of two-toned oxblood and ivory boots with buttons
on the side?

With a pointed finger, she directed her companion's gaze.

Those?

That's the kind of shoes I'd buy my fellow.

The pair burst into laughter. Each one imagined the kind of man
who would wear those shoes and the kind of woman she would have
to be or become to stroll beside him. It wouldn't be a shy girl or a
homely one, but a woman just as sharp and dangerous as he was.
The kind of man who could get you to do the things you'd never do,
even if you wanted to do them, without him being the excuse or setting down the law or acting the master, or the kind willing to get on
his knees begging you to relinquish your boundaries to your desire:
Can I kiss you there? Your brothers would hate him, rightly convinced
that he would be the ruin of you, but the kind of man your girlfriends
would desire and envy you for having. *She's not that pretty.* Loving
that kind of man would make *your mother call you reckless and your
father call you wild.*

He was the man the crowd opened up for, permitting the woman
hanging on his arm to pass through, following alongside him or trailing behind him without having to push the jealous ones out of her
path. The girl on his arm was no longer just a face in the crowd, but
the face that the other women searched for, scorched with their evil
looks and disfigured with their jealousy.

The shoes incited the fantasy of the man. For the shoes fit only
the kind of man who raised your temperature with a gesture: the
flick of his tongue over a dark, plum-colored bottom lip, or the way
he perched his leg on the stoop and tugged at his trousers so that

his splendid shoes were on full display, or the way he tilted his head and set his mouth when he cast you a sideways glance. One of those roguish *Don't ask* types who arrogantly assumed they knew what you wanted, and if you had picked the right one, they did. He was the kind of beautiful, dangerous man who risked everything to keep his head raised, who would love you and leave you, the kind of man who talked *sweet*, trampled your heart, and left a trail of distraught lovers in his wake. The kind of man capable of far worse than he had done to you, so when he walked away, he felt decent and you considered yourself lucky for having survived love with only a few bruises to show for it and a handful of nasty words that still delighted you. The very idea of this wild break-you-down love thrilled the young women because they imagined it as *something akin to freedom*, the submission enjoyed by *the one who chose it*, a reckless act of self-expenditure.

Two colored girls, not yet futureless, desired a beautiful pair of shoes that lured them into a world so much better, so much bigger than ugly tenements and the press of poverty. They looked long and hard at all the objects on display in the shop window, expectant and dreaming of a way out.

———

The sociologist lingered at the corner of Seventh and Lombard, an onlooker determined not to let a single detail of the teeming life of the streets escape him. The intersection was the hub of Philadelphia's Black Belt, and from the corner he had a view of the worst slum in the city. Outfitted in a well-cut three-piece gray suit, with a gold timepiece nestled in the vest pocket and an elegant cane resting beneath his manicured hands, he looked every inch the dandy. Beneath the fashionable appearance beat the heart of a Victorian and a libertine. The cane and the gloves, a habit acquired as a student in Germany, were a shield and a second skin, which the twenty-eight-year-old Dr. W. E. B. Du Bois hoped might better protect the first. He was desperate to believe that the refinement of style might make plain what escaped the gaze of the white world—every Negro was not the same. All noticed him on the corner, but no one stared or threw a stone at him.

Day and night, the streets bustled. The corner offered refuge to loafers, gamblers, thieves, and prostitutes, as well as stevedores, porters, day laborers, and laundresses. The raucous laughter and shouting that passed for conversation, and the loud irregular rhythms of ordinary life, were discordant to the ears of the investigator, and his head pounded from the assault. If not vigilant, he would be swallowed whole by the raw angry need, by the insistent hunger of the slum. Even beauty was an affront in these circumstances—the elegantly dressed boys and brash lovely girls, reckless enough to have staked every penny on an outfit.

He feared being engulfed by the crowd and cultivated detachment as his defense. The distaste was sharp and visceral. If there was hope to be found in the tumult and upheaval of the slum, in the waves of raw Negroes from the south, in the countrified excess, in the lust for more and better than this, in the ward's outlaw sounds, he searched for it. Who are these people? he wondered. *Just because I am a Negro doesn't mean I understand what these Negroes think or feel or want.*

The August heat was oppressive, suffocating. The stench of water closets and garbage-strewn streets forced him to take only shallow gulps of air. The summer weather, like the Seventh Ward, was intemperate and volatile, bright and clear one hour and stormy the next. In a moment, a wandering eye, an unwelcome joke, or a sharp retort could turn laughter into threats and curses. A loud and angry exchange erupted in the block, attracting his attention and that of the crowd. Two young men were embraced in battle. The pugilists locked arms around each other to ward off the damage of reciprocating blows. A young woman screamed as they rocked and lunged. Onlookers begged them to stop; others goaded them to destroy each other. A hat was knocked to the ground and a collar torn. With the flash of a blade, the crowd scattered. The Italian and Jewish peddlers swung into motion, retreating from the danger and speedily navigating their rickety fruit and dry-goods carts away from the brawling Negroes. The white ladies from the College Settlement dared not enter the fray and diligently attended those waiting for lunch. The clamor of the street drowned out their welcome and defeated the platitudes, but soup was soup and the promise of a free meal beckoned even the recalcitrant. By the time the police arrived, the victim lay bleeding on the sidewalk and alone. No one had seen a thing.

Block after block of the ugly and unsightly was as sweet as freedom got. Three decades after Emancipation and black folks had nothing. No matter. The flood of migrants did not cease, and the scramble to live did not squelch dreams of the north, the city, and the good life. All they heard back home, in dusty southern towns, were the lies and the assurances—things were easier up there and the white folks ain't as evil. It took only a week to discover that neither was true. Still, it was better than Virginia or North Carolina. To the newcomers entering the city, the only lasting evidence of what the Civil War had won for them was their ability to catch a steamer north and roam the streets in search of opportunities that eluded them.

The Seventh Ward was marvel and blight, the heart of a rag-tag black metropolis, the seed of the emergent ghetto. Philadelphia housed the largest black population in the northeast, until 1900, when New York's Black Belt surpassed it and Chicago replaced it as the second-largest city in the nation. But in 1896 it was still impressive. Since 1780, Philadelphia had been a laboratory for the nation's experiment in racial democracy and the premier stage on which *the future after slavery* was enacted. The city boasted a gilded history of triumph and accomplishment. The first act for the Gradual Emancipation of Slavery was passed in 1780. The Free African Society was established in 1787, and the doors of Bethel African Methodist Episcopal Church opened in 1794. The American Anti-Slavery Society was founded in 1833. Before the Civil War, the city was home to the largest free black community in the country, and it boasted a small prosperous black elite. Then there was the underside: An outbreak of yellow fever in 1793 divided the city along racial lines. The black residents were blamed for the spread of the epidemic, conscripted to nurse the sick and cart the dead, and then excoriated for acts of theft and extortion rumored to have happened during the crisis. The Eastern State Penitentiary opened in 1829 and inaugurated the practice of solitary confinement. The first prisoner was Charles Williams, a Negro. In 1838, Negroes were disenfranchised after the state legislature decided that black and white citizens were not equal in the eyes of the law and changed the qualifications for suffrage in the state constitution from every freeman to every *white* freeman twenty-one and over who had paid taxes. Race riots in 1839, 1842, 1849, and 1871 rocked the city and tested the meaning of slavery and freedom, citizen and alien, on northern soil. Black men did not regain the right to vote until 1870, after the Fourteenth and Fifteenth Amendments were ratified. Octavius Catto, a young teacher and civil rights activist, had played a central role in the campaign to ratify the Fifteenth Amendment in Pennsylvania. In the election of 1871, he and other black men exercised this hard-won right in a vote for the Republican Party. After casting his ballot in Philadelphia, he was murdered by an Irish mob deputized by the police. After the 1876 compromise that ended Reconstruction and returned slavery to the south in the guise of debt peonage, sharecropping, domestic servitude, and the convict leasing system, waves of black migrants began arriving in the city. They rushed from the plantation and assembled in the streets.

Slick, fresh-mouthed boys, comely, buxom girls, policy runners, ne'er-do-wells, petty gangsters, domestics, longshoremen, and whores—the young and the striving, the old and the dissipated— gathered on the corner of Seventh and Lombard. The air was thick with laughter, boasts of conquest, lies bigger than the men who told them. Idlers loud-talked one another in an orchestrated battle of words. Pimps crooned, "Hey girl, send it on" to each and every woman under thirty who strolled by. Bull daggers undressed the pretty ones with a glance. Passersby could overhear wishful stories shared about the good things yet to come. Hardworking folks and jaded pleasure seekers joked and despaired—this is the future we was waiting for?

The beautiful anarchy of the corner refused no one. It was the one place where they could quit searching and rest for a while, and still believe they were moving and on the way to some place better than this. Free association was the only rule and promiscuous social life its defining character. All were permitted to stay briefly, catch their breath, resist the pull of roaming, hustling, and searching. Every hour someone remarked, I got to go, and then lingered. Newcomers refreshed the crowd; strangers became intimates. The flow of those arriving and departing kept it alive. The same folks were always there and yet it always looked different.

Every rank and shade of black life could be seen in the Seventh Ward. A quarter of the Negroes in the city resided there. The aristocrats and the poor brushed elbows, not intimate (in fact, rarely on speaking terms), but forced by the color line to share the streets as well as the bottom rung of social life. The slum had spread from the Fifth Ward into the Seventh, expanding westward. Colored folks occupied the streets from Seventh to Eighteenth and from South Street to Spruce. They had remapped the ward, messing with the organization of the city by the ways they inhabited and used public space. Their political clubs, churches, rooming houses, barber shops, make-do establishments serving fried fish and biscuits, and saloons renowned for piano-playing, dance parties, easy women, dangerous men, sissies, and tribades had created the Black Belt in a northern city. Now the white folks wanted it back.

Falling-down tenements and alley dwellings sprouted in the shadows of Philadelphia's best homes. Ignorant Negroes and drunken

Irish willing to exchange a vote for a few dollars or a chicken dinner had decided the last mayoral election and defeated the reform candidate. The elites complained that political clubs merely provided cover for gambling and prostitution. Barbarians from the south had changed the face of the city and threatened to do more harm if the tide wasn't turned. The daily papers belittled the newly arrived migrants: they were unlettered country folk unsuited for modern life and intoxicated with dreams of freedom.

Concerned citizens, alarmed by the political corruption and crime in their city, held the growing population of black migrants responsible, so they hired him—a Harvard PhD and a Negro—to conduct a survey of the Seventh Ward, where they believed the cancer resided. Susan Wharton, the head of the College Settlement Association, and Dr. Charles Harrison, Provost of the University of Pennsylvania, invited the young social scientist to Philadelphia to write a comprehensive study of the Negro problem. The motives behind the invitation did not escape him. *There was a widespread feeling that something was wrong with a race responsible for so much crime.* It was clear that they wanted him to confirm what they already knew: The city was going to the dogs and the Negroes were to blame.

———

For a year, he and his new bride, Nina, were required to call a sparsely furnished one-room flat in the worst section of the Seventh Ward home. They were still shy lovers practicing the roles of husband and wife. He acted paternal, like a genial tyrant, as he imagined what a husband and head of the household should be. Nina, a beautiful dark-eyed slip of a girl, heeded his instructions, following his lead as if she were still his student. When he was a lecturer at Wilberforce, she had been a student enrolled in his classics course. At the beginning of the semester, he took notice of the delicate beauty. Utterly smitten by her lustrous black hair, hourglass figure, large trusting eyes, and cinnamon complexion, Du

Bois proposed, and by the end of the school year they were married. Her refinement and solid family background secured the match. Nina's father was a respected chef, and her Alsatian mother, an attentive and loving housewife who had cultivated her daughter's graceful and excellent manners. Du Bois doted on his bride, indulging her with small gifts and surprises. Eager to please, Nina was a fastidious housekeeper and devoted wife. She learned quickly to cede first place to his work and life out in the world.

700 Lombard Street—the College Settlement House—sat in the ugly heart of the slum. Here they lived alongside those he had come to study, residing in *an atmosphere of dirt, drunkenness, poverty, and crime.* The settlement house was built on the ruins of the notorious Saint Mary Street, another defeated project of slum clearance and urban renewal. "Model tenements" had once lined the street, offering the decent poor an example of how they should live, with charitable ladies, nurses, and friendly visitors, and the police providing the requisite instruction in uplift and betterment. (This time Susan Wharton intended to do a better job and not *labor blindly.*) When the old tenements were razed, the residents were scattered elsewhere, but little else had changed. The surrounding streets were packed with shiftless Negroes, a sprinkling of Russian and German Jews, and a handful of Italians. The College Settlement House replicated this earlier thwarted effort to improve the slum and uplift the Negro. But slum clearance only exacerbated the color line, displacing poor black folks who had occupied the worst blocks into the areas where the better class had fled, hoping to escape the conditions of less fortunate Negroes. *It was best not to clean a cesspool until one knew where the refuse could be disposed.* One slum disappeared and another emerged. The settlement workers and the housing reformers failed to realize that the slum was not a simple fact; it was a symptom of greater social and historical problems. Over the next two decades, the Negro quarter would become *the ghetto*—a racial enclosure, an open-air prison.

After one week's residence in the ward, Du Bois learned that murder was commonplace and the police were the only government. By the end of August, he knew not to get up and look out the window when he heard pistols firing. Two blocks away, the police had once rounded up forty-eight prostitutes in a morning's work. The *Inquirer* had reported that the raid in "Little Africa netted a courtroom full of women of all shades, from inky black to gold, all young, all tough, and all much given to swagger and vile oaths."

Poverty, crime, unemployment, overcrowding, lack of decent affordable housing, and broken families plagued the Seventh Ward. It exemplified the problems of the emergent black ghetto. Du Bois blamed the lax morals, promiscuity, children born out of wedlock, and the disregard of marriage for the social crisis or revolution of black intimate life that was taking place in the slum. The home, which had been destroyed by slavery, struggled to emerge after Emancipation, but it was at risk again. He blamed the plantation and the city for the sorry state of domestic life. The casual liaisons, transient marriages, and households that failed to conform to the pattern daddy-mommy-child disturbed him: unwed mothers raising children; same-sex households; female breadwinners; families composed of siblings, aunts and children; households blending kin and strangers; serial marriages; "widows" without legal standing; young women living out of wedlock with their lovers; lodgers and boarders acting as transient husbands; a man missing from one home resurfaced in another, raising a stranger's children as his own. *Cohabitation was a direct offshoot of plantation life and was practiced considerably.* Ten percent to twenty-five percent of the unions in the slum were common-law marriages, temporary cohabitation, and liaisons that lasted for two to ten years. Such kinship was labeled broken and immoral, and the home environment deemed unhealthy and a danger to society. Women assumed the duties of men, and men were dependent on the wages of their sisters, mothers, and wives to support families. Men searching for work left partners and children behind, started new families elsewhere, and acted as substitutes for other men gone missing. Perhaps an aunt or lover or lodger did the same for him, taking on dependents and assuming obligations that others had abandoned or were unable to meet, yet such practices enabled survival. Flexible and elastic kinship were not a "plantation holdover," but a resource of black survival, a practice that documented the generosity and mutuality of the poor.

To the young sociologist, the tone of black social life was promiscuous. He blamed this condition on the disproportionate number of young folks and the surplus of young women who had migrated to the city—all of which encouraged free love and sexual excess. In this surplus, he envisioned *as deep and dark a tragedy as any in the history of human striving.* The rush to the city and the wandering from place to place in search of a better life had produced a social upheaval. Sixty percent of the black population was under thirty years of age. The tendency to marry later, economic distress, the high death rate of black men, and changing sexual mores were revolutionizing black intimate life. Women outnumbered the men. Charlotte Perkins Gilman, the writer and feminist, had first identified the danger of "cheap women" in the city. These surplus women were unable to secure marriage or produce proper families because the number of single women exceeded the available men. They troubled the marriage plot and produced nameless children.

The drama hiding behind the statistics and skewed gender ratios went something like this: Two young people not in a financial position to wed or support a family entered a thoughtless marriage. The husband, being unable to support the wife and now a child on his wages, needed her to work too; it was a state the sociologists described as being half a man. The couple struggled to survive and experienced marital strife, and then the wife turned laundress, or the husband deserted, or the couple chose to separate. Other scenarios included sexual promiscuity and men being supported by women. Du Bois feared that "armies of black prostitutes" and "undetected prostitutes" passing for regular women were overtaking the race, such women figured prominently in his anxieties about the future.

The great numbers of unmarried women lowered the standards of life and fostered casual relations, cohabitation, the taking up and casting off of lovers at will. The lax moral habits of the slave regime were apparent in relationships broken by whim and desire. Casual sex was commonplace. Desertion, voluntary separation, and death explained the large number of homes without husbands and fathers. More than half the women in the ward were single, widowed, or separated, and this imperiled the newly fledged black family. Such were the fruits of sudden social revolution.

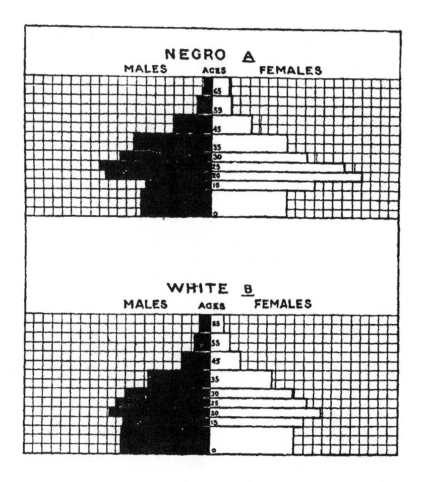

Men, unable to support families on low wages, ruined girls, abandoned mothers, and deserted wives. *So sudden a change in marriage customs posed grave dangers. Sexual looseness arose as a secondary consequence, bringing adultery and prostitution in its train.* Sexual immorality was a blot on the character of black folks. Slavery and the *utter disregard of a black woman's virtue and self-respect, both in law court and custom* were responsible for this shame, this wretchedness.

His views wavered, as the *heart-quality of fairness*, the heartbreak of shared sentiment, overtook the cold statistician. A betrayed girl-mother abandoned by her lover might embody all the ruin and shame of slavery and also represent all that was good and natural about womanhood. Du Bois equivocated regarding sexual freedom and decades later he came close to endorsing free love when it coincided with maternal desire. For him, motherhood would always be noble and virtuous because it was defined fundamentally by devotion, sacrifice, heroism, and the wealth of natural affection, which was distinct from selfish and carnal pleasures. He would come to embrace *betrayed girl mothers* and perceive *the up-working of new revolutionary ideals* in the choices they made and the way they lived. Circumstance forced his hand, leading him to recognize that black women's lives were not dictated by married motherhood and to accept that frank sexual longing was a sign of health in a culture that worshipped virgins and reviled whores. In a novel, he possessed the ability to transform a ruined girl who grew up in a brothel into a heroine, but achieving the same in a sociological study proved nearly impossible. Literature was better able to grapple with the role of chance in human action and to illuminate the possibility and the promise of the errant path.

———

No wall surrounded the Negro slum separating it from the rest of the world. The Jewish and Italian neighbors in the adjoining tenements weren't yet white. Their comfort and identity didn't yet

depend on restrictive covenants that prevented black folks from living on the block; they didn't yet relish the word *nigger*, or utter it with
a pride and patriotism akin to waving the flag and with the certainty
that the epithet as much as the stars and stripes established their
position and security in the republic. The Negro quarter wasn't yet
the dark ghetto, but each day a new stone was set in place. It was
not yet a zone of racial enclosure characterized by extreme deprivation and regular violence. It was not yet a reserve for the dispossessed and those relegated as fungible, disposable, surplus, and not
quite human. The ghetto was not yet a foregone conclusion. In two
decades, this would no longer be true.

Every year more and more Negroes flooded the ward, concentrat-
ing the death and poverty of the city in the black quarter, making it
harder to see beyond the slum or to dream of ever escaping it. The
dirty streets and the poor housing conditions weren't the heart of
the matter. The slum was the symptom of a problem 250 years in
its evolution, but no one welcomed explanations that began with the
arrival of twenty-odd Africans in Jamestown, Virginia, and went
on to enumerate crimes that could never be forgiven. Three decades
after Emancipation, freedom was an open experiment. For most
white folks, it was still unthinkable and, at worse, it was a crime.

From his window one floor above the street, Du Bois watched his
neighbors. The good elements mixed with bad and lived side by side
in apparent harmony. To the indifferent eyes of the white world, they
were all just Negroes, and nothing more. The poorest of them lined
up for soup and bread at the settlement kitchen. From his perch, he
could smell their poverty as keenly as he did the day's meal. Before
him was a sea of black faces. Some were pinched by poverty, others, still open, were questing and bright. Day laborers, sullen and
exhausted, trudged home, brushing past rawboned migrants awe-
struck by the sport and squalor of the ward. His eyes roamed from
the group of idlers gathered on the corner to the reckless young
women, and embittered old ones. On Lombard, on Kater, in Middle

Alley, folks gathered on the front steps of tenements enjoying the reprieve from the kitchen, the boss, the Missus, and the drudgery, if only for a few hours.

Not seen from his window were the women gathered in the court-yard, drinking cups of beer and playing cards. In one another's eyes, they were smart, crazy, wild, not to be messed with. They gossiped about the ones who had moved to New York, hoping to find a life better than Philadelphia had to offer, join the stage, or leave their troubles behind. The women swapped tales about the sharpers on the corner, cursed the no-good men not worth fighting over, they bragged about grinding all night, they lied that they were married, and never let on that their sister was really their girlfriend. *All pimps look alike to me*, one exclaimed, humming the popular tune. Yet the strident assertions—*I don't want him; you can have him*—and the full-bellied laughter that erupted after each anecdote shared about a beautiful, awful *no-count* man did not mask the tender silence that followed when the one talking the wildest confessed, *All I ever wanted was a nigger who would be true.* Yet the confidences shared in the courtyard and the collective knowledge of a woman's sorry condition would not prevent friends from coming to blows over a good-for-nothing Negro or taking up with another's husband. They delighted in rumor and created scandal by embellishing *he said* and *she said* until the truth was no longer possible to discern, but they sobered sharing the news of the day: the three colored policemen hired by the mayor, and the story in the paper about the colored milkman lynched in Ohio.

Had Du Bois seen the women from his window, they might have appeared spent and misshapen from the long day's work of clean-ing up after white folks, lumbering home to squalid tenements and alley dwellings. The sight of a laundress, burdened with a basket of dirty clothes, slogging her way through the filth of the alley, might have encouraged his despair. The clop of her scuffed black boots was accompanied by oaths and curses muttered about this damn city.

A few men sat in open doorways, forced outside to escape stifling, airless rooms. Young women roamed the streets, adrift and headed for trouble. Where were their fathers and uncles and brothers? he wondered. Not the idle men lounging on the street in straw-backed chairs, or the thugs gathered on the corner. Where were the decent hardworking men? In this great industrial center, black men were locked out of the steel mill and the railroad yard, they were barred from the factories and the skilled trades. *They were loiterers on the ragged edge of industry.* The women outnumbered the men. This produced an unhealthy condition, encouraged women to couple casually, and men to take up and exchange women as it suited them. Statistics and ratios were not bloodless and abstract, but antagonists in the tragic tale of black womanhood.

In the graphs documenting the conjugal unions of black folks, the bars of the horizontal chart appeared like a banner; all that was missing in the black and gold bar graph of the "Mortality of American Negroes" was the red indexing the death and suffering that had produced this state of things. A hand-colored diagram provided a stark picture of the crisis, a visual document of an imperiled future. Nothing in the statistical tables asserted *me too* or risked being mistaken for an autobiographical example or required the sociologist to yield to the heartbreak of cold facts, although charts and graphs could prick as readily as any photograph. A whole world could be made and undone by a row of figures and the future eclipsed by ratios or the lines of a flowchart. The table of unions created, severed, and thwarted was a historical epic of love and trouble, a long chronicle of violation and unwanted touch. The lives crushed and destroyed appeared bloodless in the diagrams; the moral tableaus were cool, objective, no matter how devastating the social pictures they painted.

The women lured into prostitution and forced to sell themselves for ready cash disappeared into the column labeled *disorderly and bawdy houses.* Sex work was a crime masked by other categories, like

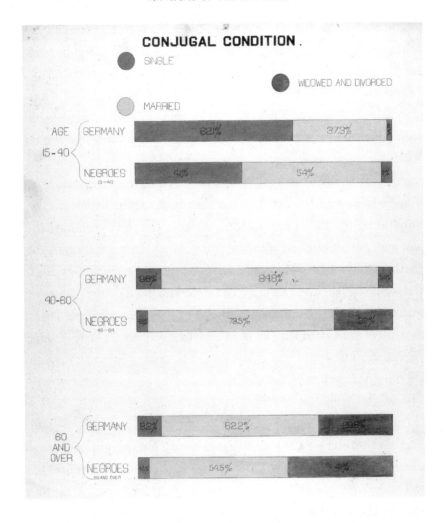

CONJUGAL CONDITION.

SINGLE

WIDOWED AND DIVORCED

MARRIED

AGE 15-40
GERMANY — 62.1% / 37.3%
NEGROES 15-40 — 41% / 54% / 9%

40-60
GERMANY — 9.6% / 84.8% / 5.6%
NEGROES 45-64 — 4.5% / 73.5% / 22%

60 AND OVER
GERMANY — 8.2% / 62.2% / 29.6%
NEGROES 65 AND OVER — 4.5% / 54.5% / 41%

larceny and assault and battery. Under slavery, the law of property dictated that black women submit to any white man who wanted them; now poverty dictated their course. Black women, once sold, now were coerced to sell their bodies for ready cash. This new traffic in women bore the imprint of the older trade in human commodities. In the throes of the moral panic that ushered in the first decades of the twentieth century, reformers and the journalists decried prostitution as "white slavery" and so would the legislators and the prosecutors, yet there was nothing white about it, at least not as it concerned the black women of the ward, whose violated bodies and exploited capacities were the norm, not the exception. Every one-dollar woman and fifty-cent whore working Ratcliffe Street or Middle Alley was another name entered in the ledger book.

The crushing weight of slavery had fallen on black women. Out of this, what sort of women could be born into the world of today? Adultery and degradation were their heritage and their condition today. What good could come from such women? It would take decades until Du Bois could find his way to an answer that didn't condemn them or forever consign them to a terrible fate. For the present, he concentrated on elaborating the social and historical forces that had produced the problem. A straight line could be traced from the plantation to the ghetto. Unlike his fellow sociologists content to *count the bastards and the prostitutes* and call it a day, he recognized the long history of sexual defilement that stamped the face of the present. Looking at the trail of exhausted women plodding their way home, he feared for the future. The world had relegated these women to an awful fate. He trembled at the sight of them.

———

The house-to-house canvass required him to put in eight- and nine-hour days surveying the ward and interviewing his neighbors. He had little experience with this type of poor urban Negro. Most had been in the city for only a few years, but already they had been scarred by the cold, hostile welcome of northern antipathy and hardened by the deprivations and brutality of the slum. They were nothing like the faithful, open peasants of the Tennessee hills whom he had taught during his summer breaks from Fisk University, where he first experienced an all-Negro world. The Dowells and the other families were united in the common hardship of poverty, but still they welcomed him, a stranger, and shared their scrupulously neat tiny homes and forced him to eat second helpings of their meals of fried chicken, wheat biscuits, corn pone, string beans, and berries. In the ward, such welcome was rare. When he knocked on doors in the Seventh Ward, he often encountered flat withholding faces and eyes that were suspicious and doubtful. Long hard stares met his gaze. Most residents of the ward knew to be wary of the ones studying them.

How could he explain the purpose of his study: to educate the world about how the Negro lives and the reasons why we are forced to live as we do? Who was he? Nobody. He was just a stranger prying into their lives and asking intrusive questions. The white world, he wanted to tell them, is ignorant of our circumstances. If we educate them, we can change our condition.

In the 835 hours of conversation with five thousand people in the ward, they asked, *Why are you studying us?* Wouldn't it be better to study white folks, since they are the ones who need changing? They wondered what Negro was earnest or naive enough to believe that truth alone would change white people? As if they were blind to the world they had created? Or didn't know no better than to treat Negroes like dogs?

We ain't specimens!

———

The sight of an impeccably dressed colored man entering cellar dwellings, tenements, and alley houses did not go unnoticed. No doubt, the appearance of the effete gentleman making his way through the stinking back alleys of the ward amused some. Others distrusted his hincty manner and the standoffish way he held himself in their company. A few closed the door in his face; those less hostile participated reluctantly, giving terse answers to his questions, so the interviews lasted no more than fifteen minutes. The brothels and the gambling dens refused him entrance, as did the impeccable homes of the black elite, albeit for different reasons. This small upper echelon avoided the worst blocks, riding in their elegant hansoms; they preferred to maintain their distance from the lower ranks, to the extent that this was possible. They kept their distance from him, holding the young sociologist at arm's length. Strangers rarely secured entrance to their circle. Many in this tier hardly even looked like Negroes and might best be described as whites with a small percentage of black blood.

Any race pride aroused by their success was mixed with disappointment. Their obsession with self-advancement, and their single-minded pursuit of wealth and comfort, blinded them to the condition of the lowest classes, except when inconvenienced or embarrassed by some new crisis or scandal created by the criminal element, but for which they too would be forced to pay.

"Are we animals to be dissected and by an unknown Negro at that?"

"Thank you for your time ma'am." He scribbled *unwilling to respond* on the schedule of questions.

———

"What's the object of this investigation?" the woman asked, eyeing him suspiciously.

"Simply to get at the truth," he answered.

"Do you propose to do anything after you get the facts?" she inquired.

"We simply collect the facts," he replied. "Others may use them as they will."

"Then you are trying only to get the facts and not to better things," she said.

"Yes," he answered.

"Humph," she replied and then refused to tell him anything.

———

"Why Negroes are doing badly—that's the mystery you trying to solve?"

When the laughter subsided, Du Bois proceeded with the next question.

He learned far more about the Negro problem from them than he had imagined possible. Being born of a race didn't endow him with a storehouse of knowledge. He had come late to the experience of being a Negro. He started the survey with no research methods, just visiting and talking with people. In interview after interview, black folks made it clear they wanted more and deserved better than they had received. While most doubted the survey would make any difference, they shared the details of their lives with him. No one had ever asked them how they managed to scrape together a living, or what they wanted for their children, or what were their experiences with the white world or the difficulties they faced in trying to find a place to live or why so many lived in so few rooms. He listened to their stories about low wages, about being shut out of the professions that used to be theirs—butlers, chauffeurs, barbers, and headwaiters—and being barred from the new jobs at the steel plant. Despite the absence of signs clearly stating, "Colored need not apply," no one wanted to hire them. The men couldn't find work and the women were trapped in domestic service. Unskilled labor and low wages were the only opportunities awaiting them in the city. A third of the Negroes in the city were servants. Nine out of ten women were domestics. Many, almost 20 percent, lived in the homes of white folks, where they were lonely and isolated. *No, they never felt like one of the family.* Those who didn't live-in spent virtually all of their wages on rent. Some weeks their children ate only what they could take home from white women's kitchens. The white folks thought of it as stealing. But how was it wrong to take home leftovers from meals they had prepared? Were their labor and care to be denied their own family? Were the hours that went into making biscuits and pot roasts not to benefit their own homes? How could it be a crime to feed their children?

Every day was a test of the assertion, *I am not a slave.* Things seemed like they were getting worse. *Kind of employment?* He didn't really need to ask.

Many of the questions were matters of public knowledge—Name and address? Sex? Age? Place of birth? Length of time at residence? Other questions were more intrusive: Able to read? Able to write? Conjugal condition? Relation to the head of household? Family members residing in the apartment?

Du Bois had been foolish enough to expect unequivocal answers to questions like: Are you married or widowed? But such questions about their intimate and private affairs were at the very heart of the deviance he assumed and sought to document. Their experiments with conjugality exceeded the law and defied it. The blank looks, evasions, tortured explanations, and lies surprised him. Either you were married or you weren't. Or so it first appeared. Was the head of the household the father of your children or the lover helping you to support them? Was she the head of the family if she was the one who worked steady? Or what about the child whose father had disappeared before the mother ever became *Mrs.*? Wasn't calling herself a widow the right thing to do for her child? How was Lady Washington to admit she was a prostitute or explain that she had once been a stevedore with a different name? Was it best not to explain? *Where no information is given, put "unknown" or "unanswered."*

A woman in questionable circumstances might answer his question with a question of her own. Perhaps, she discerned his thoughts: *Degraded homes like this [are] a plain survival from the past. The family group is struggling to recover from the debauchery of slavery.* Were the distaste and the judgment apparent in the gaze of the sociologist or in the tone of his voice? Elaborate stories were concocted to hide the truth of embarrassing circumstances or disguise the complexities of intimate arrangements. Withholding and stony silence often circumvented the relay of questions. Had the interviews been recorded, we might expect to hear such evasions:

"Husband? Which one?"

"Why does it matter what the law say, isn't it how you live that counts?"

"He was my husband though we didn't have any paper. We have morals just like everybody else."

"He took care of me and my children, so I have every right to use his name."

"A widow. I don't know when, but I'm sure that he's dead."

"No, I didn't know my father. It was my mother who put the food in my mouth."

———

His father was a shadowy memory. The only details he remembered were those he had salvaged from the stories told by his mother. Alfred Du Bois abandoned his family a year after his son William was born. Like many of those he interviewed, Du Bois had grown up not knowing if his father was dead or alive. Half of the mothers in the ward claimed to be widows. He took comfort in the fact that at least his parents had been married. He had been spared the shame of being a nameless son, which would have made greater the wound of being deserted and never knowing his father. His older brother, Adelbert, had been born a bastard (of a different father). The web of lies fabricated by his uncles and aunts about a thwarted romance, or was it a broken engagement, between his mother and the cousin to whom she was betrothed did little to cloak the hard truth or make it less painful.

The spare truth of wounded kinship sounded like a blues: *It's an old story, every time it's a doggone man. Baby, come back home. If he don't care about me no more it don't matter? Poppa, what you got now that you didn't have before? That man treats me so mean. You never get nothing by being an angel child. You better change your way and get wild. You don't want no one woman, you don't do nothing but run around. I followed my daddy to the burying ground.* Other stories, sober and plaintive, like a minister's sermon, warned about the dangers waiting right outside the door, being rebuked and scorned, or dared to question God as to how much a Negro was expected to bear.

———

Whether they lived in one room or five, black folks shared the same hopes. They wished and prayed that the terrible things that had happened to them and to their mothers and fathers would not happen to their children. They cursed white men and the world. Wasn't forty years in the desert enough? What else were they expected to endure?

"I want something better for my daughter than cleaning house."

"I know I am not what I ought to be, but I don't want her to be like me."

Their eyes looked straight into his, as if imploring Du Bois for a solution. Was there some answer or remedy that might have escaped them? The sociologist was silent.

The conversations humbled him. By outward appearances he remained a dispassionate observer. His gentlemanly comportment and reserved New England manner—even his friends called him *dear Du Bois*—was off-putting, and it exaggerated the gulf between him and ordinary black folks. The distance was a requirement of the research and a studied performance. He was torn apart by the stories he collected each day in his interviews. Eight hundred thirty-five hours of hope and despair—and he was the Atlas bound to shoulder it. He was the repository for all that striving and disappointment, the collector of anecdotes and stories, the one cleaving to all those bruised lives. What could he set down in orderly sequence on schedules, when so much exceeded this? This other information he stored in his memory. He mourned the ability and intelligence gone to waste because the world failed to recognize the gifts and noted only the problems, as if the poverty and the ugliness weren't the outcome of an ongoing relation between masters and slaves, except now it was conducted by their sons and daughters, and it conscripted each and every person to a world divided by the color line. This was the meaning of progress. Yet innocence and indifference prevented the wider world from being accountable, from acknowledging its debt, from owning their crimes.

Black talent and ambition had no outlet but the street. Under other conditions, what might they accomplish? In the face of every bootblack lurked a physician, an engineer, and an artist; and in the too fast girls, easy prey to the affliction of desire, he saw teachers and social workers and upstanding matrons, if only things had been different. It hurt him—the sight of all these young people prevented from stepping any higher than their mothers and fathers and forced to earn their bread and butter by menial service. They were bitter, discontented, and refusing to work because barred from their chosen vocations. Who could blame them for rejecting servitude, for their unwillingness to pretend that being conscripted to manual labor was opportunity? Who could blame them for declining to be trained for servility?

To witness such intellect thwarted and ambition derailed affected him deeply. It changed the way he looked at black folks and in time it would transform radically his understanding of the problems they faced. When he first arrived, he thought of them as *raw recruits* and *barbarians* and blamed them for the crime and squalor of the ward. The *inconsiderate rush of backward Negroes* to the city had stoked the antipathy of whites and precipitated the decline of the best Negro neighborhoods. Dense pockets of poverty and vice were concentrated in the ward. He understood that the newcomers were propelled by the universal desire to *rise in the world* and escape the choking narrowness of the plantation and the lawless repression of the south. Yet, unless their movement into the city was checked or real opportunities created, how would they avoid becoming paupers, loafers, whores, and criminals? The lowest ranks struggled for sheer physical existence. How would they not impair and threaten the tenuous foothold of the better class of Negroes?

Always he had imagined people like these poor uneducated folks as waiting for someone like him to come along and improve their condition. While he remained attached to the idea that the best-equipped *men* of the race were the ones who would lead the rest and direct *the mass away from the contamination and death of the worst,* he discovered that the lower orders weren't waiting for him or anyone else to rescue them. The knowledge they imparted far exceeded the scope of his survey. The schedule of questions addressed their circumstances and material conditions, but their existence could not be reduced to the jobs held, years of education, the family members residing in an apartment. Much of what they wanted to say had little to do with his questions. Yearning and rage suffused the interviews, and despite the armor of the sociologist, these feelings touched him too. He understood why they felt the way they did, and he felt it too.

—Each and every day another door is closed. Used to be you could find work as a butler or waiter, now white folks don't even want to see you. They would rather hire Irish or German than a Negro. They are foreign, but they are white.

—They don't see a human being.

—My daughter makes good grades in school and her teacher told her that one day she would make an excellent maid. A teacher is supposed to model what you can be, not tell a child that there is nothing waiting for her.

—I've never been insulted in the streets, but my daughter has. White boys called her and her friends all kinds of low-down names. She came home in tears. My mother can remember when a Negro could not ride in a streetcar or walk on a public road in peace.

—Everyone knows that in a city like Philadelphia a Negro does not have the same chance as a white man.

—How do you explain to your children that the white man stands between them and the future?

Was it better to withhold the stories and say nothing about what the world could do to you? How it would try to cut you down to size to fit the cramped space allotted Negroes? A box no bigger than a coffin or a cell or a kitchenette? No, it was not good to explain too much to the children; they discovered the world soon enough, experienced the dead end of opportunity, were enclosed by the blunt corners of the small, small world to which they had been confined. So mothers and aunts withheld the worst stories and whispered the atrocities, but the children already knew. It wasn't hard to figure. They knew how they lived, and they knew how white folks lived. Even before they had the language, they sensed the world was against them. They knew they had been condemned. Out of love, they spared their parents this knowledge, shielding them from the fact of their powerlessness.

The young were angry, disappointed and in *open rebellion*. Sixty percent of the population was under thirty. The avid desire for something better confronted the utter lack of opportunity; such circumstances created rage and despair, encouraged tumult and upheaval. Young folks were apt to be dangerous. This unsatisfied ambition, unrewarded merit, and the dismal prospects positioned them at war with the given. They were reckless. What did they have to lose? What was crime, but *the open rebellion of an individual against his social environment? There was a widespread feeling that something was wrong with a race that was responsible for so much crime and that strong remedies were called for.* Yet, how could they not rebel against circumstances that made it impossible to live?

How long could a city teach its black children that success required a white face? How long could it exclude Negroes from every opportunity the city afforded and expect them to accept it, to remain patiently at the bottom and be grateful? In 1896, one out of ten arrested in the nation were black. This was seven times greater than their portion of the total population. Given these circumstances, the rising incidence of crime was no surprise. It was to be expected when criminality was anticipated. Crime, he believed, was the result of misdirected intelligence under severe economic and moral strain, failing to see that crime was the necessary outcome of racial policing and essential to the remaking of a white-over-black social order.

————

The long steady movement of Negroes into northern cities made plain the political implications of flight, although the idea that this refusal of the plantation was a general strike had not yet occurred to him. He watched thousands from Virginia and Maryland as they *rushed to the city* and *swarmed in the vile slum.* Unable to fashion the world in their own terms, they could, at the very least, resist the world imposed. The collective movement against servitude and debt, the choreographed flight from rape, terror, and lynching was a reiteration, a second wave of an earlier exodus of slaves from the plantation during the Civil War. Decades later he described the general strike in quite similar terms as *the swarming of the slaves* for the purposes of seeking freedom behind the lines of the Union army. He likened this movement to *a great unbroken swell of the ocean.* The slaves who escaped the plantation did not merely desire to stop work. *It was a strike on a wide basis against the conditions of work. It was a general strike that involved directly in the end perhaps a half million people. They wanted to stop the economy of the plantation system, and to do that they left the plantations.*

At the dawn of the twentieth century, the general strike was again a way of saying "no" to the known world and the vestiges of slavery. *The Negro was on strike.* By 1920, it was undeniable. The small movement of black folks from the south, which began as early as the 1880s, had become a mass movement. It was nothing short of a refusal of the plantation regime. The general strike was *a great human experiment.* Black folks were "seeking political asylum within the borders of their own country." Year after year, decade after decade, black folks fled the south, entering Philadelphia and New

York (as well as Chicago and Detroit). After he left Philadelphia for Atlanta, after Sam Hose had been mutilated and lynched and his knuckles put on *exhibition at a grocery store on Mitchell Street*, after Du Bois's firstborn had died, after an epidemic of rape and lynching, after sitting on the front steps of his home in Atlanta with a Winchester cradled in his arms in anticipation of the white mob, after the Red Summer of race riots, Du Bois would be able to recognize this tumult and upheaval, this rush to the city, as a way of contesting *slavery in all but name*. He would appreciate this flight as a refusal of the conditions of work and as a desperate attempt to make another kind of life.

In 1897, what he felt surpassed his vast knowledge. He discerned the hunger and the want. The verbs tell the story: riot, rush, tremble, flight, and strike. In the Seventh Ward, "all is good and human and beautiful and ugly and evil, even as Life is elsewhere."

———

In the evenings he returned exhausted to the settlement house. The newlyweds usually dined alone. He and Nina rarely invited anyone to their modest flat. Katherine Davis, the head of the settlement, and Isabel Eaton, who assisted him with the survey, had come by for tea on a few occasions, an invitation most white women would have declined for fear of the damage done to their reputation by keeping company with Negroes. Both were of good New England abolitionist stock and also opponents of segregation, unlike other settlement workers. Those lonely years at Harvard had taught him how avidly the liberal north policed the race lines. His fellow students sped across Harvard Yard and averted their gaze on Brattle Street rather than utter hello or good day to a Negro. Harriet Beecher Stowe captured it in Miss Ophelia's benevolent antipathy and sentimental aversion to Topsy. Lofty ideals and racist aversion went hand in hand. His classmates were enlightened enough to be seated in the same lecture hall with him, but that defined the extent of their hospitality and engagement. When circumstance or proximity made conversation unavoidable, it followed a predictable course. He wanted to say, no to shout: *One is not compelled to discuss the Negro question with every Negro one meets or tell him of a father who was connected with the Underground Railroad; one is not compelled to stare at the solitary black face in the audience as though it were not human; it is not necessary to sneer, or be unkind or boorish, if the Negroes in the room or on the street are not all the best behaved or have not the most elegant manners; it is hardly necessary to strike from the dwindling list of one's boyhood and girlhood acquaintances or school-day friends all those who happen to have Negro blood, simply because one has not the courage to greet them on the street.*

After dinner, he returned to work. His books and notes covered the dining table. He pored over histories of Philadelphia, reviewed three centuries of state law, consulted surveys of London and New York and Chicago, and compiled statistics about birth rates, age of marriage, births out-of-wedlock, crime, divorce, and death. He charted graphs and plotted statistical tables, consulting Charles Booth's nine-volume study, *Life and Labour of the People in London.* The hand-colored maps reflected the expansion and density of the black quarter, made visible the different classes that constituted the race, and documented the segregation of the Negro from the rest of the city. He translated the stories of the ward into statistics and graphs, muting the voices and aggregating the lives of those he interviewed into a grand sociological pattern, rendering the dire conditions of everyday existence into numerical tables. Society was *the regularities of human action.* The figures, charts, and graphs aspired to be a moving picture of black life that documented the Negro's modernity and made clear that the race had a future. A moving picture was a living image, a story in motion. The Negro was not fixed, but a changing and variable entity. The diagrams tried to render the great vicissitudes of black life and represent historical development over the course of a century.

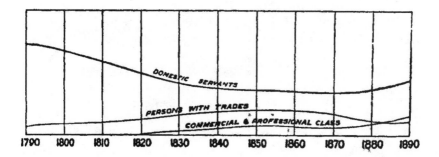

While the best minds at the University of Chicago and Columbia might want to believe that black folks were dying out and would one day be extinct, he intended to prove otherwise. The graphic pictures contested Hoffman's statistics about the increasing rates of mortality among urban Negroes and projections regarding their eventual disappearance.

Contrary to photographs, which arrested motion and fixed time, making the contingent and unfolding present into the eternal, his charts and graphs represented change over time; they detailed the advances and regresses, the stops and starts of history, offering a visual account of black movement—rush, strike, and swarm. Diagrams captured the primary and secondary rhythms of black life; the visual lexicon anticipated the cinema, formed its prehistory, recording the movement of the Negro from small towns to the city and the steady movement forward over the course of time. The vertical graphs established the scale of measure and enabled the Negro to be seen in relation to whites and the world at large. Horizontal bar graphs revealed the fluctuation of crime rates and the similarity between black and white patterns of conjugal union. History wrote itself in figures and graphs, and statistics transposed lives into bars and curves, densities of ink and color. Tables contrasted the rates of black and white poverty, detailed the frequency of separation and widowhood, showed the incidences of disease, and differentiated the race into distinct classes. The colored maps charted the diffusion of residence, morality, aspiration, and need.

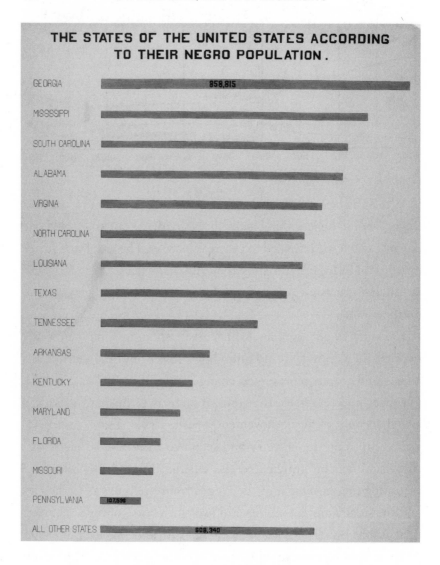

THE STATES OF THE UNITED STATES ACCORDING TO THEIR NEGRO POPULATION.

GEORGIA	858,815
MISSISSIPPI	
SOUTH CAROLINA	
ALABAMA	
VIRGINIA	
NORTH CAROLINA	
LOUISIANA	
TEXAS	
TENNESSEE	
ARKANSAS	
KENTUCKY	
MARYLAND	
FLORIDA	
MISSOURI	
PENNSYLVANIA	107,596
ALL OTHER STATES	608,340

The 40,000 Negroes of Philadelphia, including the 9,675 living in the Seventh Ward, could be divided into ranks or grades, ascending from the bottom rung to the aristocracy. Grade One: families of undoubted respectability earning sufficient income to live well; Grade Two: the respectable work class living in decent homes and steadily employed; Grade Three: the poor, not always energetic or thrifty, but with no touch of gross immorality; and Grade Four: the lowest class of criminals, prostitutes, and loafers, the submerged tenth. By his admission, these were moral categories rather than class designations. Poverty and crime were not the natural condition of the Negro, contrary to popular belief. The sociologists fixed their gaze on the worst elements, *gleefully counting the prostitutes and the bastards.* The dregs and the refuse fascinated them, but Du Bois knew that the best elements determined the future of the race. His visual graphics offered a true portrait of the Negro as changing and variable, not an outcast of evolution.

There was no average Negro, no composite *darky*, but distinct classes and modes of life that merited precise and accurate representation. There was no surer way of misunderstanding the Negro problem than by ignoring manifest and glaring differences of character and condition among the black people of Philadelphia. *It was only the color line that cordoned them together.*

By the time he retired for bed, the streets were still bustling with activity. Revelers stumbled their way home after an evening of dancing. Rags, banged out on an old piano at a neighboring saloon, sounded past midnight. In the early hours of the morning, gamblers reentered the world exhilarated and depleted after days hidden away in dim smoke-filled dens. Shouts and laughter pierced the night air as if daring the ward to sleep.

———

"That's the kind of shoes I'd buy my fellow." It was the only part of their conversation that the sociologist heard, but the look in the girl's eyes betrayed her. The sharp edge of lust cut him like a knife. He looked at the gaudy shoes in disgust and turned back toward the two young women, searching their profiles for the telltale characteristics of the prostitute evident by the indecency of their words. *The remark fixed their life history; they were from among the prostitutes of Middle Alley, or Ratcliffe Street, or some similar resort, where each woman supports some man from the results of her gains.* They were no longer *undetected* prostitutes.

He could already see their faces in the police file, and try as he might he was unable to discern any beauty or virtue in their dark faces. A distinct picture of their lives unfolded. At an early age, they had been ruined; whether by particular circumstance or the general environment mattered less than the indecency of the brazen display. The newspapers offered a daily chronicle of colored women arrested for stealing and brawling and rioting. Young women were stabbed and beaten in tenement hallways because of old grudges and petty jealousies; impressionable girls were led astray by their lovers. In the *Ledger*, Du Bois read a story about a young woman, Etta Jones, who had been a responsible servant until she met a smooth-faced, cross-eyed mulatto, who was a crap-fiend who took every cent of her earnings and pawned all of her clothes. Then she began to steal from her employers. She was arrested for petty larceny after stealing a silk dress from her mistress and attempting to sell it at the pawnshop for seven dollars. A few weeks earlier, a young woman from Baltimore was arrested after stealing a ten-dollar bill from a white man in a badger scheme. One need not work hard to imagine what the white man had in mind when he approached a Negress on the streets and accompanied her home. There were the tragic stories of seduction and suicide: the naive young woman from Virginia lured into a house of prostitution or the broken-hearted domestic found lying unconscious in an alleyway after attempting to end her life with a bottle of benzine. Grown women bore the signs of ruined girlhood—the cold, hard eyes of having *been ripened too soon.*

————

Illicit sex had introduced Du Bois to lovemaking and nearly undone him. He never lived down the guilt, which had accompanied the pleasure of losing his virginity in an act of adultery with an unhappy wife. When he arrived in the hills of Tennessee as a lonely young teacher, he was so ignorant about sex that he lacked even the basic knowledge of the anatomical difference between men and women.

None of his peers believed that anyone could be so innocent and stupid, until they realized he was telling the truth. The country boys taunted the seventeen-year-old mercilessly, introduced him to lewd women, and gossiped about the women in town who were willing and skilled. He had never even held hands with a girl. The only woman he had ever embraced was his mother. He adored her, and his virginity was proof of this devotion.

When he arrived in Wilson County, Tennessee, Josie Dowell helped him find his schoolhouse. *She was a thin, homely girl of twenty, with a dark brown face and thick hard hair, a common sort of girl, with a good heart, and she talked fast and loud.* He called her a girl-woman, but at twenty, Josie was older than him. "We need a teacher at the school over the hill," she told him. "You can stay with my family." The Dowells' home was a simple, dull frame cottage with four rooms, perched just below the brow of the hill, amid peach trees. Josie was the eldest daughter and the center of family life. Mr. Dowell, her father, was an unlettered, faithful man, *with no touch of vulgarity or immorality.* Mrs. Dowell was quite the opposite. She was attractive and vibrant, with a quick, relentless tongue, and *an ambition to live like folks.*

Unlike her daughter Josie, Mrs. Dowell was not decent or humble; she was dreamy and reckless. She was flawed and vulgar and attracted to the young teacher. He stoked her desire for a life very different from the one she shared with her husband. She might have confided "the things she had done and had not done and the things she had wished for." That summer she taught the schoolmaster how to hold a woman, where to put his hands, what to do with his mouth. He could hardly believe what had happened and that it was his body thrashing and entangled with hers, his wetness and shame.

He would write about those two summers in the rolling hills of Tennessee over the course of his life. Never did he describe it as a sexual watershed. Each time, he narrated a slightly different version. He never committed her name to print, perhaps fearing that if he identified her, the rest would be obvious, and the guilt as palpable on the page as if he were uttering her name, again and again, a name repressed rather than cried out in the passion and exuberance of a novice lover. He blamed her for what had happened: *I was literally raped by the unhappy wife who was my landlady.* He held her responsible for the appetite that was unleashed and the *desperately recurring fight to keep the sex instinct in control.* To control his lust and to check the lowest impulses meant everything to him, not only because of his own moral standards, but also because of his ambition to lead his people and model what they should strive to achieve. After all, he was *the living example of the possibilities of the Negro race.* Nothing was as critical for the race as a whole than to chasten its appetites, to better manage carnal life.

In his essay "A Negro Schoolmaster in the New South," Du Bois immortalized Josie in her place, making the daughter's tragic moral heroism into a feminine ideal. Unlike her mother, who hungered for better than she had, who was not satisfied with her husband, and lusted after young men, Josie sacrificed to keep her family afloat. Weary and faithful, she toiled until defeated by a lover's infidelity and marriage to another. Du Bois grieved Josie's death. It made him question, if not doubt, the meaning of progress in a world that held dark-faced girls so cheaply. Her fate might have reminded him of his exhausted mother. She had been a young woman broken by hard work and poverty and fatally weakened by betrayal and abandonment. Josie was tragic, but she didn't make him fear for the future the way her mother did. The needs and wants of Mrs. Dowell were immoral, excessive. The thought of their intimacy still made him shudder. Glancing at the pair of gaudy shoes, a wave of shame washed over him.

———

That's the kind of shoes I'd buy my fellow! In the girls' longing for beauty lurked something criminal and promiscuous. Too great a love of beauty was often the sign of ungovernable wants and errant ways.

Crime and ornament were bedfellows. His mentor, the Reverend Alexander Crummell, had said as much, condemning the *aesthetical character* of young Negroes, suspecting something prodigal, sensual, and godless in the *will to adorn.* "Dandies" and "Clothes-bags" were "full of vanity and pretense, poisoned with lust and whiskey, and too proud and lazy to work." False notions about style and elegance were ruining colored girls "crazy for delight, swept away by animal desires, alien from domestic duties, and devoted to pleasure." The minister's stern lessons were unequivocal: "No people can live off of flowers, nor gain strength and robustness by devotion to beauty. No people can get their living and build themselves up by refined style and glittering fashion, or addiction to harmonies, colors and delights that please the senses."

Du Bois also bemoaned this tendency to excess, the too much, the love of the baroque; the double descriptive: down-low, Negro-brown, more great and more better; the frenzy and passion; the shine and fabulousness of ghetto girls. Ignorant Negroes and reckless women, trying to subsist on beauty. The vulgar pleasures, the glitter and shine afforded on city streets had degraded the human desire for beauty, so claimed Jane Addams. The "newly awakened senses" of *urban youth* were attracted to "all that is gaudy and sensual, by flippant street music, the highly colored theater posters, the trashy love stories, the feathered hats, the cheap heroics of the revolvers displayed in the pawn-shop windows." The untutored longing for beauty was dangerous because it was "without a corresponding stir of the higher imagination." The arousal of the senses unrestrained by the faculty of judgment created an "aesthetic insensibility" which yielded a destructive sensuality and encouraged the appetite for greater and more intense sensory experiences, guided only by "dumb and powerful instinct" and "without awakening the imagination or the heart."

The want of beauty expressed in "preposterous clothing," or "the huge hat, with its wildness of bedraggled feathers" was the way the poor girl announced to the world: *I am here.* She "demanded attention to the fact of her existence; she was ready to live, to take her place in the world." Two young colored women longing after a pair of men's shoes were guilty of the same—the ardent desire to live, the hunger to find a place in the world in which they were not relegated to the bottom.

While Du Bois knew the girls were not to blame, he blamed them anyway. *Contempt* was too strong a word for his feelings—*chagrin* better captured the swirl of emotion that overtook him. Under his gaze, they were no longer two girls promenading on South Street and transported into amorous fantasies by all the wonderful commodities soliciting them; rather they were composite figures, representatives of the worst tendencies of the race, the products of many generations of immoral habits and unhealthy bodies.

All his arguments about advancing the cause of science and demonstrating the progress of the race stood or collapsed before them. What plan of reform could change their lives? What future world awaited a race of disappointed men and degraded women? What kind of mothers would these two ever be? In his eyes, two young black women enraptured by a pair of shoes embodied the threat of decline and made it palpable. The naked expression of desire offended him deeply. Girls like these occupied the public gaze and pushed upstanding and decent colored women into the shadows.

This feeling of something distinctly sexual and the shame that followed like a powerful blow nearly toppled him. To his dismay, he thought of Nina, his steadfastly virginal wife and reluctant lover, and cringed at the comparison. Just in time, he had married her; otherwise he might have grown comfortable with other men's wives or worse. He had rushed into marriage in a desperate attempt to leave all of that—the risks and dangers of adulterous affairs and mistresses and lovers not bound by law—behind him. Nina was a good wife and had been preparing for the role since she was a child. Her lifelong training as a virgin, the dedicated protection of her chastity as the property of her father which was then to be transferred to her husband, was the ironclad law of the respectable Negro home and the first line of defense against the enduring sexual taint of slavery. All of which made it almost impossible for her ever to regard sexual intercourse as not fundamentally indecent. She wanted to please him, so tried to oblige less grudgingly his sexual appetites. It was the great difficulty of their married life. Lovemaking required much coaxing on his part and produced great shame on hers, no matter how passive and minimally encouraging she had been. No rush to strip away undergarments, enter stealthily and extract as much pleasure as possible in the short window before her husband and children returned home as he had with Mrs. Dowell. No hips active and thrusting to meet his like the whores of Paris, no encouraging words whispered in his ears as had his lover in Berlin, or fervent instructive embraces as had the genteel wife of his colleague at Wilberforce College. The act of coitus required careful restraint on his part so as not to make his *dear wife* unhappy. *No easy task for a normal and lusty young man.*

Who else but the prostitutes of Middle Alley or Ratcliffe Street dared utter such words? Their history was apparent in the open expression of desire. He knew exactly what kind of man they imagined in those shoes. Idlers and libertines accustomed to living on the wages of prostitutes. Of this he was certain, if only because he was unable to imagine what else could account for such desire in a woman. Looking at the girls' reflections in the glass, he questioned, *Who are they?* He couldn't really see their faces, only everything that he feared. They returned his gaze with a penetrating look that asked, "What are you staring at?" Before he could venture a reply, the young women locked arms, turned away and continued their stroll.

———

On his walk home, he steered clear of the shrewd merciless men who lined the curbs and exited from seedy lodging houses, quickening his pace to bypass any danger. The day's number reverberated along the block as it was relayed from house to house, like a code unlocking the secret of the ghetto: wild hope and the gift of chance. Every shady girl who crossed his path brought to mind the indecent laughter of brash young whores. The guilty Victorian, he could regard wayward colored girls as nothing more than the victims of a long history of violation and destined for the trade. Sold on the auction block, defiled, coupled with masters, locked away in cellar rooms, molested in attic studios, and selling ass in Middle Alley—this was not the only story. Colored girls, too, were hungry for the carnal world, driven by the fierce and insistent presence of their own desire, wild and reckless. Most were determined not to sell anything, but content with giving it away.

A Chronicle of Need and Want

The whole house was in an uproar. Curses and complaints escaped from the windows of 635 Saint Mary Street. Two women were in a state of open war. Fanny Fisher was taking down Helen Parrish, the rent collector, in a manner so scandalous that everyone on the street had paused to listen to the torrent of abuse. "Go to hell!" Fanny shrieked. Mary Riley closed her door so the children wouldn't hear Fanny's swearing. Katy Clayton didn't enter the fray but delighted in Helen's humiliation and encouraged Fanny with her laughter. "To hell with you!" The entire neighborhood heard Fanny's tirade about the rent: "I don't care what the book say. We don't owe nothing!" Fanny was belligerent and drunk. The rent collector was not sure how much Fanny owed because the books were in a hopeless muddle. She had shown Mr. Fisher the garbled book of receipts. He could not read and so for an hour she patiently tried to figure out the sums and explain to him what was involved, and yet not daring to let him see how much everything was in a mess. Helen Parrish would not allow Fanny Fisher or her husband to doubt her authority or correctness in any way. "Mrs. Fisher, you will pay what is owed or you'll find yourself in the streets!" "Damn you and the rent!" Fanny responded. A small flat wasn't the world.

Raising her voice above the thundering expletives, Helen ordered Fanny Fisher to be quiet. "Don't ever dare speak to me in that manner again! Mrs. Fisher, take hold of yourself." The command only invited another round of cussing and abuse. Damn bitch! Katy Clayton doubled over with laughter. Once again they had succeeded in defeating Lady Bountiful and bringing her down to their level.

Luckily, the police had not been summoned. Lieutenant Mitchell liked nothing better than dragging a colored woman off to jail. Twenty-four hours locked down for rioting and disorder, a few days more if he could call her by name, and he knew everyone on Saint Mary Street.

———

Fanny, spent and exhausted, returned to her room. Her neighbors heard the curses; but Fanny as easily might have said, I'm so tired. I'm just broke down. No doubt, her dreams were bigger than two small rooms on a block reeking with the stench of human waste and garbage. The ugliness was so brutal it could bring you to tears. She never forgot for a moment the violence required to make life so ugly, or the hate necessary to keep Negroes trapped in the awfulest quarters of the city. The injustice of having nothing and owing everything made her shout at Miss Parrish, as well as the shame of having been reduced to this. Fanny objected to the rent and the book that transformed their lives into columns of credit and debt. What you owed was just a way of saying that you were in their debt, still a slave. It was no different in the north. White folks loved to talk about what Negroes owed them personally, what they owed the country, what they owed themselves. It was a debt that could never be paid. Rent was just another burden intended to break you; and jail or the workhouse the threat intended to keep your black ass in line. A feeble act of charity could not repair all this damage, and the good intentions of Miss Parrish and Miss Fox did not make a damn bit of difference.

Fanny would never beg and plead like Old Clayton, brought so low she was willing to sell the clothes off her back to make the rent, so that Miss Parrish, someone so clearly not in need at all, could write some numbers and notes in a book, scribbling furiously all the time like she was studying them, like their lives were just raw material for an experiment.

Fanny was past wondering what kind of life was possible on Saint Mary Street. Nothing was promised except hustling and scraping to get by. There was no way to win, just rage or submit, just get from one day to the next. So far this had taken Fanny from one bad place to another, but that was the case for most Negroes. When she first arrived in Philadelphia, she was just coming into the young woman she wanted to be, but she never got there, there was so little for her, only the meanness of the city. What could she do? Saint Mary Street was not so bad as the other places, but it was still the bottom.

———

It was a block infamous for gambling, brawling, and whoring. Saint Mary Street was in the ward of the city with the highest death rate and the poorest residents of Philadelphia. The street was only two blocks long and crowded with small wooden houses about to collapse and dark courts with houses even uglier leading from the main street. *Dark Hebrew women, patient Negroes, and stout Germans live out their story day after day before the eyes of the street.* Outliers, lawbreakers, and bad characters called it home. Decent folks suffered the bad. Black migrants, wide-eyed and unschooled, affected a pose of sophistication not rightly theirs; others idled on the front steps, deciding on the day's lucky number and sharing the names of the few enterprises willing to hire Negroes. Men, by all appearances unattached because their wives were still waiting in Virginia or working as live-in maids in Chester or Camden, consorted with wild girls and deadbeat foreign women, making love in public view. Mom Hewitt,

a low-life Irish as dissolute as her tenants and married to a colored man, had managed the tenements at 635 and 637 before Hannah Fox purchased them. Hannah Fox and Helen Parrish intended to set a very different tone.

They were the daughters of Philadelphia's elite. Helen's grandfather had been a surgeon at the Pennsylvania Alms Hospital, an opponent of capital punishment, a member of the Friends Yearly Meeting Committee on Indian Affairs, and the president of the Pennsylvania Society for Promoting the Abolition of Slavery. She and her first cousin Susan Wharton had grown up playing hide-and-seek in their grandfather's cellar, which had been a station of the Underground Railroad. Susan was the grandniece of the steel magnate Joseph Wharton and a founding member of the College Settlement Association, the Saint Mary Street Library, and the Starr Center settlement house. Hannah Fox's newly acquired wealth had not yet been cleansed by a family history of philanthropy and social reform. Her father had made a fortune speculating in oil ventures in western Pennsylvania, but she

made good this inheritance by purchasing two tenements on the most infamous block in the slum. Here she and Helen began in earnest their career as housing reformers and their lifelong companionship.

Subjective need—their desire to live a purposeful and meaningful life—explained the presence of two wealthy white women in the heart of the Negro quarter. For Helen and Hannah, slum reform provided a remedy for the idleness of the privileged, a channel for the intelligence and ambition of college-educated women, and an exit from the marriage plot and the father's house. No longer girls at thirty, they had eluded the conscription of wife. Without a Mr. to shield them from the dangers of life or prohibit them from associating with bad elements, they charted a path through streets peopled by Negroes, Russian Jews, Italians, thieves, prostitutes, sodomites, thugs, and anarchists. In the slum, they avoided the indictment: spinster, surplus woman, invert, and listened for the sounds of their name—Miss Parrish and Miss Fox—linked in good deeds rather than malicious gossip.

In the fortress of her office, Helen recorded all the details of her awful fight with the Fishers. The doubt and despair filled two pages of a schoolgirl's composition book. Only a month earlier, she had been foolish enough to believe that surly Negro women might come to trust her and even call her a friend. It had been a gorgeous summer day. All the tenants from Saint Mary Street were invited to the colored lending library for cookies and lemonade. A handful of the women came, but none of the men. She wished the men had been there. It was easier with them than with the women. Most would bite their tongues rather than speak out of turn to a white woman. She thought she could trust the men, but not the women. The women were a different matter. *It was mindful to be as wise as a serpent surely in dealing with the women.* She must remember never to speak a word of one to any other. Even the most casual was sure to breed trouble. They were too much together, too much at home, and they loved to talk and gossip. She found knots of women in the yard, and whatever she did was sure to bring about some discussion—alone they were amenable, but en masse far from it.

That brilliant July afternoon, Helen offered no advice and issued no demands, but simply enjoyed the party. She finally heeded her aunt's advice about the harm done by those who strive to regulate things too much, so she didn't scold Poor Mary Riley for the chamber pot, which she kept under the bed for the children and which made her rooms foul-smelling and unbearable in the summer heat, or complain about Mary's do-nothing husband, Charles, who had been out of work for weeks and gambling away the few pennies for milk and bread. More than once, Helen had berated Mary's husband for failing to meet his duties. Charles Riley was a man easily defeated, so Helen conquered nicely, lecturing him about what he should be doing, never giving him a chance to speak. Did he not have enough spunk or did he have too much courtesy to fend off the attack? Poor Mary, a plain listless wisp of a girl, just sat perfectly meek and cowed.

At the tea party, even Poor Mary managed a smile. Too fast Katy Clayton was quite charming, when not steadfastly opposed to every good deed simply to prove she was not to be governed by anyone. *They feel, poor things! Their ignorance and powerlessness,* and yet such sick half-crazy ones like Fanny Fisher rage against it, taking hold of any little mistake to skirt her duties. What was to be done with a girl like Katy, who had been sleeping in the foyer to escape the summer heat, and sitting on the front steps, half-dressed, flirting with men in public view? Helen held her tongue. She didn't caution Katy about the damage done to a girl's reputation when she had too many gentlemen friends, or lecture Rebecca Clark about drinking beer in the yard. She didn't stop Old Clayton, Katy's grandmother, from making a meal of shortbread and consuming more than her share of lemonade. Bella Denby said if she could have lemonade like this every day, she would stop drinking whiskey. "Oh, if you would only have a saloon where I could get a drink like that, I never tasted anything so good in all my life." With her hair pinned neatly to the top of her head, Bella could almost pass for a decent woman. Even with her bruised eye and dirty rags, she was still pretty. *She seemed penitent & rebellious and gentle & rough all together.* Her husband, Ike, had combed and plaited her hair in two braids as if she were still a country girl. An act of devotion by the same hands that had blackened her eye and cut her lip.

At the library, Helen and the women spoke freely, as if they were equals. They chatted about small things—the weather, the rising price of milk and bread, the new display in John Wanamaker's window, a church outing in Cape May. Katy Clayton had gone to Chester for a camp meeting and the ladies' evening was beautiful. She had her tintype taken, but it did not begin to be as pretty as she was. For a few hours, Miss Parrish did not threaten anyone with eviction or lecture Negro women about how to live. On a lovely July afternoon with the sun pouring through the windows, Helen felt satisfied that they were friends.

Every Monday Helen made the rounds, knocking at every door at 635 and 637, intent on the impossible—collecting the rent. She addressed the tenants by their surnames, almost always preceded by a Miss, Mrs. or Mr. It was the one sign of formal equality that they could count on. For her, it was an act of détente. Bella and Ike Denby didn't even open their door, pretending not to be home week after week, and fooling no one. She had a talk with Joe Robinson and told him that if he married his white girl, he could not stay in the building. Too bad, she trusted him *even though he was a darkey.* Fanny Fisher, in lieu of the rent, offered to sweep the stairs. Old Clayton begged for a little more time and schemed to get what she didn't have. She promised to pawn her shoes to meet some of what she owed if Miss Parrish would allow her another week. Her sons had not been able to help her and Katy was out of work, but looking. Soon as Katy finds something, we'll catch up. Katy's a good worker, she just need a chance. Mary Riley apologized as she had for the last five weeks. Poor Mary seemed content to stay home and sit on the edge of the bed all day minding her children. It was hard to think of her as a homemaker, and not an idle Negro woman. Helen scolded her about the need to meet her obligation as the tears brimmed in Mary's eyes. *Rent was a just debt.* Mary had no right to expect any more of her and Miss Fox than clean rooms. As she left, Helen gave Poor Mary fifty cents for soup meat to feed the children and promised to bring her a pair of shoes the next week.

Old Clayton and Mary Riley were never able to meet the rent; they were always in debt. They swept the hallways and scrubbed the water closets and cleaned vacant rooms and passively received Helen's abuse. They pawned their clothes and household items and they found piecemeal work—shucking oysters, washing clothes and linens, and repairing garments. On occasion, Helen extended loans, despite her belief that it would encourage laziness and a sense of entitlement. These calculated acts of kindness were not enough to bridge the gulf between poverty and the minimal requirements necessary to live. None of these stopgap measures afforded a way around the truth: more than sixty percent of the Negroes in the city lived in a state of poverty.

———

On Monday afternoons, Gallen, the porter, came to Helen's office to report the events of the weekend. Her own efforts at spying had proven fruitless, turning up little besides a pack of playing cards and three pots of flowers in Ida Haines's room and a half-emptied bottle of gin in Bella Denby's cupboard, so she depended on the porter. Gallen seemed disappointed when nothing sensational happened, and relished the ugly details: Bella Denby was rioting on Saturday night. Ida Haines was arrested on Hirst Street in a disorderly house and locked up twenty-fours for getting in a rage. Fanny Fisher had been drinking all weekend since the doctor told her there was no hope. Now she said she could drink as much as she wanted. Gallen saved the worst for last, displaying the Negro trait for drama. On Saturday night, he had caught Katy Clayton making love with one of the Gallagher boys in the foyer. By the time he unlocked the door, he found Jim Gallagher, but no Katy. They must have heard his keys in the front lock. Gallen ordered him out and found Katy at the faucet in the backyard, she tried to pretend like nothing had happened, but he was no fool. He heard them going at it. He knew what the girl had been doing with Gallagher. All that commotion wasn't holding hands. He had not believed the gossip about Katy; now he knew the rumors were true.

After the conversation with Gallen, Helen headed straight to the police precinct. She sought Lieutenant Mitchell's help whenever the problems of Saint Mary Street were too big for her. Hannah was in London, and without her companion, Helen faltered. In the evenings, she would regale Hannah with the details of street life: "The other day a very good-looking darkey stopped me and asked for a room for himself and one other. You are married then? Oh yes, he replied. Then it is for you and your wife? No, for me and a young lady friend!"

Helen blanched at the word *prostitute*, but there was no getting around it. Lieutenant Mitchell promised that Katy would be arrested if caught in the act. She could be sent away for as long as three years for what she had done. Walking home from the station, Helen wondered if she had pursued the right course. The comfort she felt when the lieutenant assured her that he would handle the problem had disappeared. It was too late to stop what she had set in motion. Now Katy Clayton was at risk. If the lieutenant had his way, she would soon be off to the Magdalene House or the Eastern State Penitentiary. Helen hoped that no one had seen her at the police station. Whatever she did was sure to bring about some discussion. It was hard to blunder on as she did. She waited 'till circumstances impelled some action, then did what she knew was right, and yet felt no safety in being right. She didn't know what was best.

Things sometimes turned out right after she did them, but she wanted a clear conscience before. Aunt Sue said that their *feelings of rebellion* against her dictating about their rooms or trying to legislate for them ought to be respected. Helen should never look into their closets or sneak into private homes, her aunt counseled, but Helen failed to heed this advice. Whenever she tried to dictate, they insisted that they had paid for the room and she had no right to interfere.

Helen failed to reach the women. Each sharp word and cut of the eye was the reminder. The women were as likely to send her to hell as to utter good day. Watching them gather in the courtyard, she looked on jealously, believing their intimacy to be a rejection of her. They were backlit by the late afternoon sun, the flat black shapes like silhouettes against the flank of sheets hanging behind them. Every indifferent glance and back turned toward her was a barricade keeping her outside the circle. When they withheld their recognition and made plain that they had no clear need of her, when she was unable to find her better self reflected in their eyes, when their hostility was so piercing it threatened to crush and destroy her, then the cluster of women assembled in the yard on a late August afternoon involved in the mundane tasks of hanging clothes, cracking pecans, and tying off buttons collapsed into a faceless *them*, a threatening crowd, a race without distinct features or characteristics. At such moments, Helen could see only *treason en masse*, the lines of battle were drawn; she thought, *All are against me.* She doubted if she would ever be able to reach them. Who would have guessed that the battle to be waged was against them as well as the slum?

Face to face with Katy or Fanny or Bella, she forced herself to remember that they were not the enemy. If it had been possible, she would have slipped into their skin just to know what they knew and to feel what they felt; and the women, as if sensing this desire to occupy their inner lives and stake claim, rebuffed her, refused her the right to enter their heads and hearts; they confided nothing.

———

Two colored women in well-cut dresses, tasteful hats, and impeccable gloves entered the office. Helen was not surprised to see them because few landlords would rent to Negroes, and the ones willing charged the highest rents for the shabbiest tenements in the ward. An interview with the two ladies would not be necessary. She turned the better sort away. Clearly they needed no help and were not suited for the neighborhood. Before Mamie Shepherd and her mother, Mrs. Eunice Berry, had a chance to say hello or give their names, Helen had dismissed them. There was no need of improvement that her eye could detect. The daughter, her resemblance to the older woman being unmistakable, was quite striking. She was lovely and disarmed Helen with her respectable manners and receptive doe-eyes. The sort easily led astray, Helen thought, making the case against her. A girl so gentle and yielding wouldn't last a week before Katy Clayton lured her into trouble or a handsome thug seduced her.

Ladies, you would do best to steer clear of the neighborhood, she advised. Mamie's mother agreed that it would be best for her daughter to look elsewhere. Eunice Berry had not failed to notice the garbage scattered in front of the other buildings and the brash, insistent stares of the men idling on the corner. Mamie would be safer with her until she found suitable rooms. Helen could see that the young woman was too refined for Saint Mary Street and had been accustomed to better. But Mamie insisted that she couldn't stay in her mother's house forever; a married woman needed her own place. It was only Mamie and her husband and she promised to be steady. It was impossible to find a room elsewhere. She was willing to try Saint Mary Street, if only temporarily. The appeal of the girl's lovely upturned face and penetrating dark brown eyes turned Helen around. *What a pretty, attractive little thing.* Mamie Shepherd took possession of apartment number 5.

On Thursday evening, James Shepherd arrived. Nothing about Mr. Shepherd gave Helen reason to doubt his ability to guide Mamie in the right direction. Their rooms were already fixed nicely. At the first opportunity, she planned to speak privately with him about Katy Clayton and the others; they were young women Mamie would do better to avoid. On Saturday Helen visited again. It was Mamie's birthday. She was nineteen years old and looking very bright and attractive. With the necessary support, the young couple might be able to create a decent life. For now, Helen intended to do what was within her power to shield Mamie from the others. She would not lose her as she had Ida Haines and Katy Clayton. She would try hard to influence her and keep her out of danger's way, and she vowed to protect Mamie from her surroundings, especially with her husband away from home most of the week. He had been unable to find employment in Philadelphia, so like most colored men, he worked outside the city. With this girl, Helen would redouble her efforts.

Seated at the window, Mamie listened to the clamor of Saint Mary Street. The block pulsed with a hunger so sharp it made her ache just hearing it. All the violence and beauty and misery reverberated through the slum, winding through the streets and alleys and echoing in tenement flats. On any given night, Mamie might hear the piano rags drifting through the alley from the saloon on Seventh Street; the steady pound of fists as Irish hoodlums beat a black boy for sport; Old Clayton, absentmindedly humming *My Way's Cloudy*, perched in the window one floor below; Lady Washington haggling over the price of what had already been done with a deadbeat patron still attached to her hips; the Gallagher brothers planted on the front steps swelling Katy Clayton's head with sweet talk and coaxing her with promises; a white man from Pat O'Brien's place in the courtyard flirting with Rebecca Clark and her friends, trying his hardest and getting nowhere, but with each round of beer the women becoming more forgiving and he more attractive. Mamie got to know her neighbors living with their sounds. People, in every other way strangers, became intimates. She recognized Bella's sobs and knew to listen for the soft murmur of regret and the volley of pleas that followed Ike's violence. Even with cheeks hurt purple and blue, Bella was still pretty, but everything else was destroyed. Charles Riley shouted at Mary and the children, believing they would be better off without him. He knew what a man was supposed to do and Mary begging him to stop talking like that. The peals of William Sutton's laughter, sharp and shrill, piercing the air as he charmed his company, men and women alike, into surrender. Fisher's baritone warning, "Enough Fanny. You trying to run to the grave?"

When she grew tired of listening to the lives of her neighbors, Mamie would get dressed and wander the streets, peering in store windows and making up stories about what she would do in that black velvet dress or what her life would be like if she lived in a stately limestone row house on Spruce Street as Miss Parrish did. On these aimless journeys through the city, Mamie moved as freely as she wanted. Her mother had warned her often that it wasn't safe for her to drift and stray or to keep company with strangers. People would form the worst impression of a colored woman cruising through the

streets on her own, especially at night. Anything might happen to her. So far, she had been lucky. No white man had ever insulted her, so she still felt comfortable going about alone. Strolling across the grid of streets that ordered the city, she slipped in and out of dozens of conversations. Roaming about unloosened a wild something that made her feel alive, a sharp pang of want that caused her to tremble. The black city at night was alive with possibility.

Some nights she would make her way to Gil Ball's saloon on Seventh to have a beer and listen to a favorite rag. Or she would go to the Academy of Music if there was a vaudeville act or a minstrel show playing. She liked to go to the theater and dime amusements, and no one ever insulted her there. Sitting in the darkened auditorium, she experienced the transport that allowed poor girls to dream. It was why she loved the stage. She sat in the audience enchanted, gazing at the "airily dressed women" who "seemed to her like creatures from fairy-land." A hundred other girls had experienced it: the feeling of being "lost" and "transfixed" and her soul "floating on a sea of sense." It was grand. Looking at the actors on stage, she wondered what it would be like to be an actress and be up there. The glare of the footlights could convince anyone that a wonderful life awaited her somewhere. Absorbed in the brilliant musical acts, lost in the silks and laces, she preferred not to think about her life at all, instead claiming the glamour and pleasure of the stage as her own. It was the antidote to the stereopticon views of the poor in dilapidated homes and the miserable melodramas narrated by Miss Parrish.

The world was so vast and she had seen so little of it: leopards in snow-covered mountains, views of the North Pole and Japan, panoramic views of Paris, picture plays, an illustrated sequence of *The Raven*. With ten cents she could buy an excursion to the beautiful places she would never visit, experience lives she would never inhabit except in a darkened auditorium, yet it all seemed more real to her than the three-room flat in which she lived. As one image dissolved and another appeared, her heart raced. The images flickering across

Dilapidated home.
Man, wife and
two children.

the screen transported her from a decent tenement on an awful
block, ushered her into grand palaces, and conjured up the promise of a different life. It was the opposite of staying in place, locked
inside the cramped rooms of Saint Mary Street, pretending to be
content, and expected to be grateful. She became another person in
another place, as in a dream, where the self you are is nothing like
you at all, but at the same time so clearly you. The slides moving
across the screen transformed the world in the blink of an eye; each
image was ripe with the promise that the distance between now and
what the future might hold could be easily bridged; it was as if that
glorious you blanketed in the darkness of the theater was the only
self who had ever existed.

Desire enchanted the city and made it beautiful to her. Otherwise, it appeared unsightly and hostile, the way it felt when she
was trapped in her dismal apartment, bored and with no prospects
besides what James or some other man could offer. When the city
was no more than the harsh face of poverty—buildings tightly
packed on too-narrow streets, ash barrels and trash containers clut-
tering the sidewalk, the stench of scavengers hauling their wagons of
excrement through the streets after midnight, the dreary washed-out

garments of domestics and haulers draped across the alley, and the sickly sweet smell of cheap bread from a tenement bakery—then she was less than she imagined, not her own woman at all, but just a colored girl adrift, a sad lonesome thing.

Like every other person on the block, Mamie wanted better than she had, better than the deprivation and unsightliness of the Negro quarter. Her waking hours were devoted to imagining what this might look like. At the end of the nineteenth century, it was still possible to believe that she would not be trapped in a tenement, even a decent one, forever. It was still possible to suppose that a plain, whitewashed room filled with cast-off furniture on an ugly block was a way station to someplace better. The Negro quarter was not yet "encircled by disaster," so it didn't seem foolish to believe that another kind of life was within reach.

———

Mamie Sharp was the name she had given at her previous address. Miss Parrish, you said you rented only to decent people. If you rent to Mamie Sharp, it's clear you'll take anyone. Soon this place will be as bad as it was when Mom Hewitt was in charge. The prying Mrs. Joyce rambled on, but Helen had stopped listening.

She had not expected good news when her neighbor appeared unexpectedly at the office. She listened but couldn't square the story with the lovely nineteen-year-old residing in apartment number 5. Many thoughts rushed about in her head; but to affect an appearance of being in charge of the situation, she replied curtly: Mamie was there on trial—if she did not behave rightly, she would have to go. Helen refrained from asking anything that might give Mrs. Joyce the impression that she knew more about the tenants than Helen did. Rising from her chair, Helen thanked her for the information and forced the interview to close sooner than Mrs. Joyce had expected and to her clear dissatisfaction, but Helen was too agitated to remain seated. She dashed out, leaving Mrs. Joyce at her desk.

Had she been terribly wrong in her estimation of Mamie? As wrong as she had been about Ida, although even at the first meeting she suspected that Ida might drink. She had been wrong about Mrs. Henderson, thinking her respectable and well-to-do with her fine set of false teeth until the woman threatened to strike her. But Mamie was different. Helen had not had the chance to work with a girl of her quality, and so much might be accomplished with such fine material. But supposing the awful things Mrs. Joyce said were true?

When Helen knocked at the door, Mamie welcomed her inside. It was a bright hello, not the sullen "What?" that often met the rent collector's arrival, with the door opened slightly, just enough for the protruding head to say, "I don't have it" or "It ain't right coming here on Sunday to conduct business," and then banged shut after the last word uttered, without even the slightest courtesy of "Good afternoon" or "Pleasant evening."

There was no easy way to lead into the matter of adultery, so Helen broached the issue directly. "Mamie, have you been going around town with other men? Have you?" The question was as much an accusation as inquiry. Mamie's reply was no less direct: "Yes, I like to go about as I please." Mamie didn't apologize or offer any excuses for not being able to hold steady; she did not try to temper Helen's judgment by admitting that she had been lonely. Loneliness could prompt reckless acts that one later regretted. Helen understood this well, laboring blindly, as she did in Hannah's absence.

Mamie offered no excuse. She refused to apologize or explain.

"Mamie, have you no sense of right and wrong?" asked Helen.

Right and wrong didn't have anything to do with it. "I am not the kind of woman to stay on my own. I like to go out with my friends."

"Mamie, you can't go around with a man who is not your husband. Surely you realize this?"

"I am no worse than anybody else," replied Mamie. "I am not anymore bad than the majority of them. Yes I have been bad. But for the last week or two, James has been working by day and coming home at night, and I have not been going up around the theatres or anything like that."

Mamie didn't accuse Miss Parrish of interfering or call her a nosy bitch, as Bella Denby or Fanny Fisher would have. "Ever since James talked with you, he told me I must not go with Maizie Gibbs," said Mamie. When Ida Haines came to visit he refused to let her in. Mamie didn't feel the need to explain what she had done. James was the only one she had to answer to. Without guilt or remorse, she said, "Maybe I have been bad, but you can't understand what I need."

———

On the Saturday night of their third week on Saint Mary Street, James Shepherd kicked in the door of their apartment. He had been away for the week, and the man who had been keeping company with Mamie ran out with his shirt and shoes in his hands. It isn't hard to imagine James consumed by rage and breaking the door in; the rest is uncertain and the details are sketchy, although the scene of love and betrayal unfolds along a familiar track, repeated endlessly and as often as the promise to be true:

James had not intended to bust up the rooms that had taken two weeks of arranging to make less inhospitable, but destroying one of the dining room chairs prevented him from putting his hands on Mamie. He could have demanded why, but didn't because there was no point to it. There was nothing she could say to soften the blow or make it hurt less. He shoved her into the little room off the entrance that was his sanctuary. More of a closet than a room and outfitted only with a small card table, one chair, a box of cigars, and a Bible with the names of his parents and grandparents, the names and dates of birth of his brothers, and the few names of other kin they could still recall inscribed on the first page. James punched the wall above Mamie's head to avoid looking into her eyes and to erase that

I don't have anything to be ashamed of look from her face. Her eyes were without a glimmer of conscience to which he might appeal. The empty stare nearly destroyed him. It made plain that he would never be enough and that there would never be enough in the world for her. Desperate to erase that look, he destroyed the room but the vacancy remained. He pushed her against the wall, pressed his body against hers, devoured her mouth and found his way through the obstacle of her underskirts. Mamie, Mamie, he called until the emptiness in those eyes drained away.

The picture is as painful as it is moving, a handsome young man, betrayed and reckoning with what he cannot possess, a woman who loves him, but who does not belong to him. It isn't a scene anywhere described in Helen's notebook. Mamie mentioned it briefly to Gallen. Perhaps she confided more to Maizie Gibbs or Katy Clayton. So one can only speculate about the fighting and pleading incited by her infidelity or the reservoir of love that enabled Mamie and James to weather it. The vulnerable and fragile relation of a couple as tender as newlyweds trying to make a life together without anything to support them or keep them from drowning is not likely to end well. Seen from her eyes or his it is no less heartbreaking.

James Shepherd was a thoughtful man, perhaps even a bit brooding or melancholy. He had lost too many he loved to be careless with relations. Loss threatened to diminish him; it was as if the people gone took away that particular part of him they had made special. Too many pieces had gone missing on the journey from his home in Florida to Philadelphia. He had lost two brothers he would have given his life for, still no word from them. He and Mamie were the only society that he required. He was content with that. They had so little time together with him working outside of the city, it was a relief to have a place all their own, not her mother's house and secluded from the world.

He had traveled enough to know that you kept meeting the same folks wherever you arrived. The Negro quarter, Little Africa, the Tenderloin, the Bottom—looked and smelled the same no matter where you were, Richmond or Philadelphia, New York or Washington, Chicago or Pittsburgh. There was never enough air to breathe, no room to grow, no corner of earth hospitable enough to allow you to put down roots. Negroes were drifters, nomads, fugitives, not settlers. They had not been allowed "me" and "mine." Even when you had the hubris to believe that you had staked a lasting claim, built a homehouse with enough space for your children and your brother's children, where great-grandchildren sitting on the front porch might one day ask, "Poppa how did we get here?" and you would say something like: I made this house with my own hands, and this is yours, and within our gates no white man rules and other things that massaged them into feeling safe, yet put enough steel in their spine so that when they found out there was no protection against white folks, they would be able to hold the knowledge and stand down a hostile world. Even with all this, one day a white man could ride up to your front porch with a piece of paper in his hand that said none of this belonged to you; it was not yours and never had been, and what a fraudulent deed failed to accomplish, a torch and a rifle surely would. When that day came you had no choice but to fight and die or pick up and move on. And as long as this was so, Negroes had to be ready to take flight in a heartbeat, as he and his brothers had.

The first generation after slavery had been so in love with being free that few noticed or minded that they had been released to nothing at all. They didn't yet know that the price of the war was to be exacted from their flesh. People were too busy dreaming of who they wanted to be and how they wanted to live and the acres they would farm, and searching for the mother they would never find, wondering what happened to their uncle, was their sister dead, and was it true that someone had seen two of their brothers as far north as Philadelphia? Freedom was the promise of a life that most would never have and that few had ever lived. But who could bear this? So colored folks were still looking, picking up and moving on, again and again.

With his two brothers gone, James had no one but Mamie. Too long had passed with no word for him not to imagine them in the grave, in chains, on the run. He was exhausted, waiting for a reply that would never come. All he had was Mamie. There were women prettier, women willing to buy him shoes and pocket watches and silk vests, women who would kiss the ground he walked on. A few left him before he had the chance to say goodbye first, but it hadn't mattered much. There was no more to it than mixing it up and the fast life. Then his brothers went missing and he knew he had nothing. Mamie found him when there was so little of him left. He held onto her, fearing he might otherwise disappear. Don't let me go. She held on as he learned to stop waiting for the sound of his name, as it was uttered by his brothers with the roar of the Gulf Coast in it.

———

Everything calm at 635 with the exception of Mamie. Helen questioned Gallen about Mamie and James. The gossip had spread, so others also had started to complain about Mamie. Contrary to what Helen wanted to believe, it appeared Mamie was very unprincipled. She didn't even know if Mamie had ever been faithful to James. Gallen repeated what Mamie told him: when Shepherd was away, she had another man staying with her, and when her husband came home, he broke the door down. Gallen hadn't seen or heard anything. If she didn't tell him, the others might have.

Intimate arrangements on Saint Mary Street, as Helen learned, were never what they appeared. Was a husband a husband or a wife a wife after all? The terms of intimacy were so elastic for Negroes it was uncertain exactly what they meant—the wife of his youth or the woman he was living with now? Was the head of the household the father of the children or the man who supported them? One could never be sure if a young couple had been separated by work as they claimed, or if theirs was a free union not bound by the law. It was hard to decide whether the Negro family was really a family at all. A child arrived with one mother, only to be claimed months later as someone else's child. Men were fathers, but separated from their children; or a husband might have two families. Women on the loose were unable or unwilling to make a home for anyone, or they lived in with white families while their own children were untended. Helen knew all of this, yet she was not prepared for Mamie. Not even her name was right. Mamie Sharp. She had been married when she was fifteen years old, and her husband abused and ill-treated her. Mamie left him about two years ago. Since then he had "married" again and she had "married" James Shepherd.

To make matters worse, now Mamie and James were behind on the rent. Helen went to see Eunice Berry on the pretext of collecting the past-due rent, but it was information that she wanted. Mamie's mother confided that she had not been able to keep her daughter at home because she enjoyed the company of men. She feared for her.

———

The room was stifling. Mamie had spoken with James about the plan for them to separate, but he was unwilling to hear any of it. Helen Parrish sat trembling in the chair, waiting for James to emerge from the little room adjoining the front room. He was calm and polite, not raging, as she had feared. Helen waited for James Shepherd to speak. Mamie remained silent and distant, as if a bystander to the scene that was taking place in the front room. Helen knew everything now, and she would ask them to vacate the apartment, giving them a week's notice, as was her usual practice. If he knew the law allowed three months, he might insist on taking it. Helen counted on his not knowing this or surmising the limits of her authority. James Shepherd didn't say anything, so she began the conversation.

"Mr. Shepherd, this situation cannot bring Mamie any good," Helen's voice wavered. "When you applied for the room you pretended you were married. Had I known the truth, I never would have rented you the room. You cannot stay here."

"Miss Parrish, we plan to leave as soon as we can find another place."

Helen, surprised to hear this, looked at Mamie for confirmation, but Mamie ignored her. "In this unlawful relation, you cannot do her any good or protect her. She is in constant danger and temptation. Can't you see that Mamie would be better off without you?"

James looked surprised. "Miss Parrish, I care for her. Don't you suppose I would marry her if I could?"

"Whose fault is that?" Helen asked sharply. "Mamie rushed into a hasty marriage and must now pay for that." The young couple had paid and they were paying now, but Helen carried on about the law and morality, blind to this essential fact.

"You can't leave a husband on a whim and take up with another man. You are bound by those vows. You can't just walk away and start over with someone else." Helen looked at James as she spoke, but the words were directed at Mamie. "There is a civil and a religious law to condemn how you are living."

"I love her," said James. "This is no sudden thing."

"But can you protect her?"

He had protected her. He had put a roof over her head and clothes on her back.

"You are no protection with her running the streets and in constant danger. Mr. Shepherd, you have given her nothing."

James was silent.

"What have you done besides drag Mamie so low she can't tell right from wrong? There is no protection in this arrangement."

James allowed Helen to lecture on with few interruptions. He listened with a bowed head, waiting to speak. When Helen paused, he lifted his head and asked, "Miss Parrish, have you ever loved someone? Have you ever been married?"

Helen trembled. The arrogance of his question filled her with rage. At that moment, she decided not to spare James Shepherd, this man pleading about love and trying to save himself with words so pretty they might have been taken from a sonnet.

Helen did not reply.

"Then you do not know what you ask. I love that woman as I love myself."

This was the trouble with Negroes—the law did not determine what was right and wrong in their eyes, as if they could live outside or oppose it. She had heard others besides the Fishers insist that no paper can decide if a thing is right or wrong, no paper can settle the matter of truth. Owning nothing and subsisting on so little, they let the heart decide everything. Love was their only anchor. It was clear to Helen that the sole thing that mattered to James Shepherd was: Do I want Mamie? Does she want me? Damn the law and Miss Parrish.

"Don't you suppose I would marry her if I could?" he repeated.

Helen appraised the tall, striking young fellow and decided to break him.

"Mamie wants you to leave. She told me she is willing to give up her room and her 'friend' and find a new place. She wants you to leave. She is willing to do as I wished."

James didn't call Miss Parrish a liar, but he was unwilling to believe what she said was true. "Mamie?" James waited for her to reply, waited for her to deny it, but she didn't answer. "Mamie, did you tell Miss Parrish you were willing to give me up?"

"I told Miss Parrish I would get another place."

"Mr. Shepherd, Mamie told me she would not mind leaving anyone much."

"Yes," Mamie said, "only to get another place."

"You are evading my question," James said.

"I said I would leave and find another place," admitted Mamie.

The air was thick with all the things they refused to say in front of

Helen Parrish. I have forgiven you everything, James might have said. You know what kind of woman I am, Mamie might have ventured in reply. None of this was uttered, but it hung in the air between them.

"You know what I asked," James implored.

"Yes," Mamie said. "I told her that I'd leave you, as far as getting the place. I never intended to."

"That is not what I understood. She told me that she would leave you," Helen repeated. "Mamie, you said, 'Oh no, I would not care.'"

James looked at Mamie, wishing it were just the two of them in the room.

"If you love Mamie, you can do more for her by letting her go. You can bring her no good."

"Mamie, do you want me to go?" James asked in disbelief. His eyes made the appeal.

"Yes," Helen insisted. "There is nothing you can do for her."

"I have nowhere to go," James said quietly. "I have no home. I have no people. I have brothers, but I don't know where they are. I have a friend in New York."

"You can find work and a home," Helen replied curtly.

"A job and a room? Peace of mind is the only thing I will be looking for," he responded.

"You will need to leave," Helen insisted.

"Give me a little time," James pleaded.

"I will be back tomorrow," said Helen.

"I tried going away before, leaving her, but I could never stay away, but two or three days. Give me a little time. Please."

———

That evening at home Helen tried to recount the exchange in her journal, but it proved difficult to write down. *It was hard to know what to think—how deeply to take the meaning of it all.* Helen transcribed the conversation, trying to recollect each word spoken, so she could better understand the strange experience of this triangle. The relay

him all I thought – that I had not
known they were unmarried. When they
came – that it was unlawful, that it
was Mamie's punishment for her hasty
marriage before, that they could not
live together – That it could bring
her, and does bring her no good – She
is in constant danger, and temptation and living with him is no protection for her, but there is both a
civil & religious law to condemn such
unions – etc. etc – He let me talk
most but he said several things –
Early in the time he said he cared
for her, then later he looked up
and said "Have you ever been
married? – "then you do not know
what you ask – I love that woman
as I love myself – Again he
said to me "don't you suppose I
would marry her if I could –
again that it was no sudden thing,
that they have been together for
nearly four years – (it is only
four since Mamie told me she
married her husband! She is 19 now)

of "he said" and "she said" yielded a queer parlor drama. Despite her dutiful transcript, the truth of what had happened eluded her. In other circumstances, she might have written: *I conquered nicely.* To do so would have required her to own this need to hurt and possess. To acknowledge that James, this tall, handsome Negro, her foil, was the one sacrificed to jealousy.

In clashes with the other tenants, the lines of battle had been unmistakable. All were aware of the state of *open war* in which they were embroiled. With the Fishers and the Denbys, the boundaries were clear-cut and the antagonism open and unavoidable. When she gave Mrs. Henderson notice, the woman threatened to strike her. When she first arrived at number 5, Helen had been afraid that James Shepherd might threaten and curse, as had the others. The week before when she had called the police on Ike and Bella Denby, the officer remarked that Helen had a great deal of nerve to go among such people and that once a man had been thrown out of a window in this house. What would make one man throw another from a window? Was it a fight over a woman? she wondered. What kind of person was capable of such an act? So determined to finish off a man? Was it an act decided upon with a cool head and a brutal hand or a crime of passion?

Helen understood the cruelty unleashed by want. She and James had sparred for Mamie. She intended to rescue the girl, to train and manage her, to mold Mamie's life in accordance with her designs. The best thing would be to send her to the country. The city promised only trouble for her. Helen wasn't ashamed to admit that she cared deeply for the girl. The success of the work depended upon this mutual affection. When James Shepherd stepped into his front room, he had not been prepared to fight for his life; he never suspected that Mamie would be the weapon used against him. It was a rout—Helen had broken him as his beloved Mamie watched passively from the sidelines. He would leave the city in a matter of days. She would find a safe place for Mamie in the country where the girl would be far from temptation and in her hands.

If James truly loved Mamie, he could do more for her by leaving. Helen would make sure that Mamie was shielded and protected, something her consort could not do. Never before had Helen been so confident about what love required or how a woman should be loved. *Miss Parrish, have you ever been married?* Helen had skirted his question. Her heart was not the issue at hand. She wondered what Hannah would make of this—a black man trying to teach her about love and devotion.

———

The headline in the *Philadelphia Inquirer* identified him as Joseph Spanks, but Helen knew it was James Shepherd. Her first thoughts were about Mamie and how she might have been involved. She retrieved a pair of scissors from her desk drawer and carefully cut the article from the newspaper and pasted it into her journal:

SHOT IN THE NECK

The Mysterious Affray That Startled

Lisbon Street

SEVERAL CONFLICTING STORIES

George Grant, for Some Unknown Reason,

Pulls Out a Pistol and Deliberately Shoots

Joseph Spanks.

Joseph Spanks, colored, aged 23, of No. 635 Saint Mary Street, lies in Philadelphia Hospital in a dying condition from the effects of a pistol wound inflicted by George Grant, also colored, of No. 610 Barclay Street. So many conflicting stories are told that it is difficult to determine the cause of the affair. The police are inclined to believe that the shooting was the result of a drunken quarrel.

A few minutes after 5 o'clock yesterday afternoon passersby in the vicinity of Fifth and Hirst Streets were attracted by a commotion in Lisbon Street, a thoroughfare running off Hirst, between Fifth and Sixth streets. The noise proceeded from a shanty on the East Side, near Sixth Street. When the door was open Grant had fled and Spanks was standing in the centre of the room, bleeding profusely from a bullet wound in the neck.

A bystander who was in the apartment at the time said that Spanks was wrestling with another colored man when Grant said that if Spanks would move to one side he would shoot him. Spanks did so, and according to the bystander, he was shot on the spot. Another person, who claimed to be a witness, but who could not be found afterwards, said that it was an accident.

Spanks at the time had no idea he was seriously injured. Stopping the flow of blood with a handkerchief, he staggered out of the house. He got along all right until he reached Sixth and Lombard Street, when he sank down exhausted from the loss of blood.

James Shepherd was on his deathbed. Mamie had been at the hospital every day for the past two weeks. The couple was still together and with Mamie living in number five—to Helen's dismay. Mamie continued to pose as James's wife, except now she was running to the hospital and back, fearful of becoming a widow. There had been no quarrel between the two men, and, according to Mamie, they were friends. It was now clear that Mamie had deceived *her* as well as James. She never had any intention of leaving him or going to the country as she had agreed. Even Eunice Berry seemed to be singing a different tune now, saying that it was only right and appropriate for Mamie to attend her dying *husband*.

It was hard to believe that it had been only a month since Mamie had moved in. Helen browsed the pages of her journal. September 5th Mamie applied for the room. September 6th James Shepherd arrived, although it had seemed like weeks before he had appeared. The next week Mrs. Joyce showed up at Helen's office with her rumors. By the second week, Mamie was late with the rent like everyone else. By the third week, Helen knew enough to write The Secret History of Mamie Sharp. Then lies, lies, lies.

After his release from the hospital, James and Mamie disappeared. Gallen heard a rumor they had gone to New York. Mrs. Joyce said they were living in a very disreputable house in the Seventh Ward. Helen had planned to ask Lieutenant Mitchell if they were still in Philadelphia and when George Grant was scheduled for trial, but decided against it.

Mamie had disappointed Helen far more than the others. It was her fault for trying to rescue a girl who didn't want to be saved. Had Helen taken notice of the fierce desire in that wide-open face or really looked into those suppliant eyes, she would have known that Mamie Sharp wasn't meant for a sheltered life in the country or the cut-down-to-size respectable poverty that was all Helen had to offer. In the end, Mamie turned out to be no different from Katy and the others. She, too, refused to be governed.

In a Moment of Tenderness
the Future Seems Possible

The right couple exists in a state of peril. The future promised by the marriage plot will be derailed when the mother asks, "What that niggah got to marry on?" It is the question on which black marriage founders. The numbers doom love. The death table, the rate of unemployment, the skewed gender ratios, the murderous abstractions. The numbers secure the law and determine the dire outcome. What kind of anchor is love against all that? The happily-ever-after will elude them. The beautiful life that might have been is captured in a moment of tenderness that in no way betrays what is to come—the mother cloaking her daughter in a burial garment. All the maternal toil and sacrifice fail to assure any better prospects for her daughter or provide an escape from the unspeakable. For this too the black mother will shoulder the blame. She has given all she has, all that matters, but to no avail. A vague disquieting feeling hangs in the air. It will cost her and the daughter everything.

The narrative is disjunctive. The story is in fragments. The chain of cause and effect goes awry. It is impossible to be confident about what happens and what is imagined. The whole story is unbelievable, so it is hard to reconstruct the chain of events. Dream and flashback thwart the attempt to order time into tidy categories of past, present, and future. The story advances and stumbles in uncertainty. So the account of the romance is necessarily speculative.

The threat of ruin hangs over the head of the right couple. Is it all just a waking nightmare? Is there an alternative scenario, a parallel

track where they live happily ever after? Where invention is capable of sustaining love?

A storm descends. It is not from paradise, but the kind of storm that reminds them hellhounds are on their trail. The weather causes them to lose their way. It threatens to devour them. Engulfed in the storm, they can't find a path of escape, a route to safety; they keep going in circles. Will they make it? They search for shelter and find an old house, but the domestic offers no refuge. The closed doors hide the hurt, make the brutality a secret history. In another telling, the rape never happens and a perfect life awaits them. In another telling, the nightmare ends and love triumphs.

Book Two

THE SEXUAL GEOGRAPHY
OF THE BLACK BELT

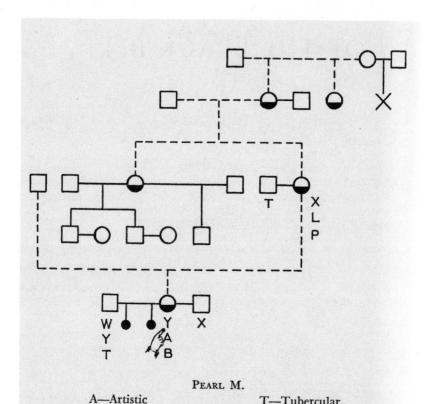

PEARL M.

A—Artistic	T—Tubercular
B—Bisexual	W—Alcoholic
L—Syphilitic	X—Promiscuous
P—Psychotic	Y—Separated

1900. The Tenderloin.
241 West 41st Street

I t was two a.m. The August heat was brutal and no one could sleep. Heads peered from the windows of rented rooms, drowsy and irritable; the desperate lay on makeshift beds; tick mattresses and folded sheets were spread on fire escapes and rooftops. Bodies scantily clad in undershirts and nightgowns rested in public view. The temperature hovered near one hundred degrees, driving decent and hardworking folks into the company of whores, thugs, policy runners, and gamblers: the folks who owned the street after midnight. Mothers with their children camped out on front stoops, small groups of men clustered at the corners, those with an extra nickel or dime to spare elbowed their way into crowded saloons for a pitcher of cold beer. On a night like this, all conspired to escape the suffocation of tenement flats, airless back bedrooms and sweltering buildings, to flee the assault of rank bodies, crying babies, embattled couples, and to shake off the general misery.

May Enoch couldn't sleep either. The rented room on the top floor of Annie Jones's house was unbearable. With each flight of stairs the temperature inched toward boiling, so the upper rooms were like hell. The heat ascended from the apartments below, and the sun beating the tar roof nearly baked them alive. It was too hot to prepare a meal, so she and Kid decided to go out for a bite to eat. They were on their way to Dobbins's restaurant, but first he needed a cigar. He probably expected her to pay for that too. "Get the money from my woman" was a phrase that passed from his lips more frequently now that they were in New York. He didn't ask her for any money but disappeared into McBride's saloon to buy a cigar.

At the bar with his friends and a cold drink in his hands, Kid lost track of time, while May waited outside on the corner, trying not to sweat up her dress. He smoked a cigar, drank a glass of ginger ale with his friends Kid Black, Sam Palmetto, and George Bartell, and lounged at the bar. The man loved to kill time. May didn't go inside McBride's, but, impatient, hollered from the door, "Kid, come on up home," and then waited. She had been waiting for nearly an hour, not just for him, but for something she couldn't name that made her heart race whenever she turned phrases like *I want* and *if only*. What must she have looked like waiting for a man on the corner in all this heat? Like a fool? Like a beached whale? Like a woman on no one's clock but her own? The folks walking across Forty-First Street or moving up Eighth Avenue trudged slowly, as if their legs were too heavy to lift. They moved indifferently, weighing whether to surrender to the lethargy, or anticipating something or someone to urge them on. It was too hot to move. Damn Kid. She was tired.

To wait idly on the corner for her man, to stroll the wide avenues of the city, to straddle Kid in a rented room on the top floor of a Tenderloin boarding house, to love and to hurt, as the black eye evidenced—defined the choreography of her life as much as scrubbing and cleaning and serving. The coital embrace of a young couple in a tenement bedroom, which was their own by the week and costing twice what white city dwellers were required to pay, was as sweet as freedom would get. She was from Philadelphia and he was from Virginia; they met in New Jersey, and expected the world from New York. What they found was a small perch in the Negro quarter. She lingered on the corner of Forty-First Street, unaware that by tomorrow she would long desperately for this, the liberty to waste time lost in her thoughts. She would remember this night vividly.

It was only their second week in New York, so she didn't yet know what the city would hold. Did it have anything to offer her, something better than Philly, or Newark, or D.C., or just the same but at a price more dear? En route, she had left behind one man, a proper husband, after four years of marriage. She wondered what John Enoch was up to these days. Was he dead? Had he remarried too? Luckily there had not been a child. Had there been a child, she might not have left home or met Kid or ever moved to New York. Had there been a child, would she have dared to leave anyway? It was hard to pull up stakes and run with a baby. A child might have sealed her fate.

Next month, the fourth of September, would be their first anniversary. Things with Kid had been good enough for them to try their luck in New York. If there was luck to be found anywhere for a Negro, it was here. New York was the largest black city in the north. It was more alive, more dangerous than Philadelphia. This was an auspicious year and she, like every other Negro, hoped 1900 was a portent of change. Yes indeed, New York was the city for a new life and a new century. Black folks yearned desperately for a break with the past, a rupture with the dark days, so they fashioned themselves New Negroes and spoke tirelessly of regeneration and awakening in the hope that the world might follow their lead and yield a better set of arrangements.

The hand was tight on her left arm, before she turned and saw his face. He was pulling her up the street before she could utter a word. What the hell was this white man doing? People were watching but no one did anything, said anything. A colored woman could be grabbed in the street and no one said a damn word or uttered a peep. No matter where you went there was always some white man you had to tell to get his hands off you. When you least expected it, when you were lost in reverie about the good life in the city, these hands suddenly appeared, as if always waiting to snatch you; the moment you let your guard down, they did exactly that. What are you doing? He kept on pulling her. Being new to the neighborhood, May didn't recognize him, she didn't know that he made it a regular practice to stand on the corner and "abuse black men and women at will." He was a terror and he took pride in being every Negro's nightmare. Colored folks hated him, but he didn't care. It stoked his appetite for violence; the fear and the hate inspired him. So when he dragged May up the block, Thorpe didn't say a word. Often the threat was enough to force them to their knees, others times they had to be rough-handled to yield. No matter how they pleaded, no matter what they had been forced to do, he booked them without fail. (The corruption and harassment in the Tenderloin was legend. Graft, bribery, and extortion transformed the police into wealthy men. The great yield—the most succulent part of the loin—had bestowed the area with its name.)

When Kid exited from the side door of McBride's, he saw a white man with his hands on May, pushing and pulling at her. He ran up the block after them. "Hey, let go of my woman." In court, when he recounted everything that had happened, he spoke in the standard, the way white folks did, proving he wasn't some ignorant nigger. On the stand, he would say, "What is the trouble? Why are you abusing her?"

"It is none of your damn business. Don't you like it?" said Thorpe.

"Hell no."

Kid ordered May to get the hell out of there and she did. Then the white man grabbed his collar. The first blows landed on Kid's face and head, toppling him onto the sidewalk. He was sprawled in the street, and the white man pummeled him with a club, taunting him, daring him to rise. "Get up, you black son of a bitch." Kid reached for the penknife in his pocket. He jabbed two or three times, and then the white man fell into the gutter. Blood covered the front of his shirt, slick and glistening. Kid stood there, frozen, glaring at the white man moaning and cursing in the street. Then he fled.

A white man smoking in the alley next to the theater saw a light-skinned colored woman with a black eye rush up the street. He was the one who told the police where they could find May. She didn't know where to go, so she ran back to the house.

When the police appeared at her door, May told them that the white man never said he was the police. He had been in plainclothes. He never said he was the police. How was she supposed to know? Was she to treat every white man like he was the law? Nothing she said made a difference. She tried to explain. Kid, her husband—his real name was Arthur Harris—was just trying to defend her. They asked her who did the cutting. She hadn't seen the fight, but she knew it was Kid. He was the only one interested in her; the only one who cared if a white man tried to drag her off the street or send her to jail because every black woman was a prostitute in the eyes of the law. Didn't she have no rights? "When you lose control of your body, you have just about lost all you have in this world."

She didn't know where Arthur Harris was hiding. When Officer Thorpe was stabbed, why did you watch and do nothing? The cops dragged her back to the corner. Thorpe was bleeding in the street. The other flatfoot called his name. Thorpe, is this the one? He looked up at May and said, That's the one. They arrested her for prostitution and then took her to the Tombs. When the following day the newspapers reported that a Negro, Arthur Harris, had murdered a police officer in the Tenderloin, they identified her by name, followed by indictments and qualifiers like "would-be wife," "girl-friend," "common-law-wife," "negress," and "wench." Her guilt was established with the words "loitering" and "soliciting." Description condemned her: dissolute, criminal, and promiscuous.

May Enoch *passes as a wife*, but they didn't say what she was, like she was nothing at all. It was in the *New-York Tribune* for everyone to see. Passing for a wife or acting like one was not the same as being one. Love not bound by the law and sanctioned by the city clerk's seal had no standing. The district attorney never failed to describe her as a prostitute and Arthur Harris as a rapist. It didn't matter that there was no evidence for either charge. The white world had made the rules about how to be a man, how to be a woman, how to live intimately, and May and Kid lived outside those rules. Everyone kept asking the same questions: Why was she out after midnight by herself? Why had she waited on the corner after she had spoken with her husband? What exactly did the officer say to her and what was her reply? Why didn't she do anything to stop her *consort*, to stop Arthur Harris, once Thorpe was sprawled in the street?

It became apparent that she was guilty too. Her crime was moving through the city and taking up public space; his was the belief that he had a right to defend them from a white man's violence. Other black folks agreed. If their refusal to submit and battle with the law were celebrated or memorialized in *The Ballad of Arthur Harris* or *May Enoch's Rag*, such tunes have been forgotten.

> You saw he had my woman.
> I fixed that son of a bitch didn't I?
> That fellow who hit me.
> He tried to lock up my woman.
> I fixed that son of a bitch.

———

"He didn't say nothing to me, he took hold of me—this officer did. Arthur stepped up before he had a chance. I had just got done talking with Arthur as soon as the officer placed his hands on me. Arthur said, 'What are you doing that for? She ain't done anything.' The officer let go of me and grabs him. Then a man by the name of George told me to go up to the house. . . . Twenty minutes after that two officers came for me."

Sam Palmetto said, "There is a man got your woman."

Kid said, "What are you doing to her?"

Kid pushed Thorpe's hands away; then Thorpe grabbed him.

"I'll take you," Thorpe said, seizing Kid by the coat collar.

———

Then Thorpe hit Kid with his club.

Then the blows fell on Kid's face.

Then there was a scuffle.

Then Thorpe hit him for the third time with the club.

Then Kid reached for a knife.

Then the white man fell into the gutter.

———

You saw he had my woman. I fixed that son of a bitch didn't I?

———

On the steps of the house where Thorpe's body lay for viewing, one of the mourners, a white woman overcome with grief, cried out, "Get all the black bastards." The crowd of police officers, and the friends and relatives of Thorpe, seized the first Negro they saw—a seventeen-year-old on his way home from work. Other white folks who didn't give a damn about Thorpe and had little regard for the police joined the mob intent on beating, maiming, and killing. White women shouted and cursed, inciting vengeance and stoking the fury of their men. "These coons have run the avenue long enough." "Lynch the niggers!" "Kill the black sons of bitches!" "Give us a coon and we'll lynch him!" The *New York Herald* reported: "At every street corner white men had gathered, and the general theme of conversation was that the blacks had had too many privileges in the city, that they had abused them, and that the time had come to teach them a lesson. . . . It was asserted on every side that [Negroes] had been entirely too bold, and had assumed improper sway in Sixth, Seventh and Eighth Avenues and that the white must assert themselves." White men beat Negroes in the street, pulled them from streetcars, and broke into their homes, determined to quash and extinguish this improper sway, this black swagger betraying the sense that they were at least as good as any white man. Maybe Kid did want to be "the coolest monster on the corner."

Three days of white violence engulfed the city. After the rout abated, the Reverend William Brooks condemned the police who had goaded the white mob, orchestrating and directing the violence and encouraging brutality as civic duty. Brooks asserted that the Negroes would not suffer such injustice passively or quietly. In his remarks to the press, he didn't mention May Enoch's name, but spoke of decent and upstanding folks. They were citizens and would not stand for this blatant disregard of the law; they would not succumb to the white mob and the force of lynch law. Negroes would tell their story so the whole world would know; and even if the police didn't bother to take their testimony they would record it. When the Reverend Brooks and the Citizens' Protective League assembled the pamphlet *Story of the Riot*, May Enoch's story was nowhere to be found. She was mentioned in passing as the wife of Arthur Harris and otherwise merited little attention. Kid was the only one who cared about her. The League feared dissolute types like May and Kid. Too loud women loitering on street corners and black men with too much swagger would confuse the matter, defuse the righteous anger about what had been done to decent black folks, innocent, law-abiding, and respectable people. She and Kid were on the other side of that line.

It was as if what had happened to May was in a different class than the terrible things the police had done to all those other Negroes, as if good and decent folks had suffered because of *them*, because of her. Was it Arthur Harris who incited the mob? Was she responsible in the end because he tried to protect her? Was the blood of every

Negro battered and brutalized by the police and the white mob to be blamed on her? She was as bad as Kid, and everyone concurred what he had done was terrible. He had tried to defend his wife; he had refused to be beaten like a dog. May had been standing on the corner waiting for him to have a drink and finish a cigar. Was that a crime? Was the knife in her hand, too? He had done it to protect her. Was she glad he had fixed that son of a bitch? Glad that he refused to stand by idly while a white man grabbed her? Proud that he resisted and "resolved to sell his life as dearly as possible," like Robert Charles battling the police and the white mob in New Orleans a few weeks earlier? If courage made him an outlaw, so be it.

The city rocked with violence as May Enoch waited in a small cell in the Tombs. Every blow the police delivered to black mothers in the company of their children, every colored woman and girl cursed as a black bitch or wench, every daughter and sister and grandmother manhandled and paraded through the streets in their nightclothes and undergarments, every indignity hurled at them—was intended to make them pay for what Kid had done and for the dangerous thought incited by a black man who had raised his hand and dared strike back. All of them, the newcomers and natives, the disorderly Negroes and the established ones, would pay for what Arthur Harris had done.

———

For four days, all colored people in the city were to answer for May Enoch and Kid. He was still a fugitive. Until he was captured, all Negroes would suffer the violence intended for him. When Annie Hamer exited the Seventh Avenue streetcar, the mob surrounded her. She was instantly struck in the mouth with a brick. As police officers surrounded her, she was separated from her husband, and did not know what became of him until three the next morning, when he came home all covered with blood. On the same night two police officers in plainclothes broke into the home of Elizabeth

Mitchell at half past eleven. When Kate Jackson heard the pounding on the front door, she feared that the white mob would harm her and her children, maybe murder them. "She caught up her youngest child (three years old) in her arms, and in her frenzy and fright jumped out of the window onto a shed . . . the child still in her arms." She was bruised, unable to walk, but at least they were alive. Rosa Lewis was sitting on the front stoop of her building with her husband and neighbors when a police officer walked by and ordered them inside and threatened to beat anyone who didn't move. She obeyed, preferring not to risk a broken jaw or bashed skull. "I had reached the foot of the stairs leading up to my rooms when the officer, who had rushed into the hallway, struck me over the back with his club."

Irene Wells was sitting on the front stoop with her three children, as were her white neighbors. On any warm night, folks relaxed on the front steps and waited for a breeze. At eleven thirty p.m., police moved through the block. One stepped toward her and said, "Get in there, you black son of a bitch" and struck her across the right hip. When she ran into the building with her children, the cop followed her in, "striking at her until she reached the top step." He threatened to strike her again if she left home. At 2:55 a.m., police officers passed through the block again, clubbing colored people. It didn't make a damn bit of difference if you were a woman or a man.

Those naive enough to appeal to the police for protection were clubbed and beaten by officers, then arrested. Once inside the precinct, they were beaten again before being locked away in jail cells. The mob and the police were united in their effort to "treat niggers the same as down South." It was impossible to distinguish the mob from the law. The threats and curses were shared: "We're going to make it hot for you niggers!" "Kill every damned one of the niggers!" "Set the House afire!" When the police forced their way into Lucy Jones's apartment at 341 West 36th Street, they shouted, "You God damned black son of a bitch, you know a lot about this damned shooting, and if you don't tell me I'll blow the brains out of you." She had watched as the police had beaten and dragged away her neighbor, William Seymour, who lived in the flat next door to hers. He had been wearing only his undershirt when they pulled him outside. The added humiliation of his nakedness produced a collective state of shame. One of her white neighbors caught sight of Lucy peering from the window. He shouted, "Look at the damned nigger wench looking out of the window. Shoot her! Shoot her!" The scene of the mob dragging Lavinie Johnson from the Eighth Avenue streetcar was illustrated in the *New York World*, but her face was a black mask, featureless and indistinct; the folds and creases in the trousers of the man kicking her back were rendered more precisely than her expression. The excess of dark pigment blotted her out, making her a shadow.

When they seized Nettie Threewitts from her house, she protested, "You are not going to take me without any clothes on?" "You don't need any clothes," the police replied, shoving her down the

The mob dragging Lavinia Johnson, a colored woman, from an Eighth Avenue car at Forty-third street. The rioters pelted her with stones and clubs until passengers on the car and the police rescued her.

stairs and onto the stoop, where she was in full public display. When the patrol wagon came, the officers cursed her for sport. They called her a black bitch, laughing and enjoying her humiliation. "One of them struck me in the head with his fist, another one deliberately spit in my face, and another took his helmet and jabbed it into my eye." One suggested they "burn up all the nigger wenches." Another shouted, "Shut up, you're a whore, the same as the rest of them." The black women of the Tenderloin came before the law as May had, as future criminals, prostitutes, nobodies.

People were crying, "O Lord! O Lord! don't hit me! don't hit me!" *Lord Help Me! If he made a way. If he brought them out.* Women pleaded for their fathers and husbands and friends only to be beaten and cursed and clubbed alongside them. The police did more harm than the mob. *Look, a Nigger! Lynch the Nigger! Kill the Nigger!* Such were the rallying cries of neighbors and citizens. Less than three weeks after the brutality in New Orleans and a year after Sam Hose was lynched in Georgia, burned and mutilated before a crowd of over two thousand, white men gathered in the streets of New York, determined to instruct Negroes about the limits of liberty and intent on quashing the arrogance and swagger that evidenced a misguided belief in equality. Mob rule in the Tenderloin was as vicious and indiscriminate. North and south were just directions on a map, not placeholders that ensured freedom or safety from the police and the white mob.

————

Reverend Brooks defended Arthur Harris, but he would not call him a hero, as Ida Wells had in her defense of Robert Charles after he killed seven white men, including four police officers in New Orleans in self-defense. Nor did he assert his right to self-defense. Reverend Brooks and the self-appointed leaders of the race hoped that the banner of innocence might protect them from orchestrated and random brutality. The Citizens' Protective League repeated to no avail, "We are citizens, even though we are black, and there should be some redress in the courts for all we have suffered. The city should be responsible for the brutality that has been practiced upon innocent people. . . . If we cannot get [redress] now, when can we get it?" When can we get it? This question would be repeated endlessly over the course of the century.

The terror unleashed in the heart of the city's blackest and most populated ward brought to mind the Draft Riots of 1863, so open was the hatred, so voracious the violence and the fury. Between 1890 and 1900, New York City's black population doubled, and the white folks living in closest proximity greatly resented their presence. The more than forty thousand Negroes made up less than 2 percent of the population, but the threat represented by their presence was magnified a thousandfold. The effects of the riot in the Tenderloin were far-reaching and accelerated the racial segregation that more and more defined the city. The violence was a major catalyst in the making of Harlem. After being attacked by their white neighbors, black New Yorkers sought protection by huddling with their own. The daily racial assaults and clashes in downtown, coupled with the availability of housing in Harlem, spurred this migration within the city. By 1915 at least eighty percent of black New Yorkers lived in Harlem. The numbers steadily increased despite the attempt of "The Save Harlem Committee" organized by Anglo Saxon Realty to stanch the flood of black folks. What the riot made clear was that the color line was hardening and that segregation and antiblack racism were not only augmented by way of state and federal policy, but also stoked by the antipathy and the psychic investment of even the poorest whites in black subordination and servility. Their ancestors had never owned slaves, yet they regarded Negroes as "slaves of society." What stake had survivors of famine and immiseration in recreating the plantation in the city, in gratuitous violence directed at any and every black face, in defending the color line as if their very lives depended on it, as if their sense of self was anchored in this capacity to injure others? What stake had the survivors of pogrom in excluding Negroes from the factory floor and refusing to hire them? As four days in August made plain, the enclosure of the Black Belt was to be as sharply defined in northern cities as it had been in the south; poverty, state violence, extralegal terror, and antiblack racism were essential to maintaining the new racial order.

As if anticipating what the future held, as if the Red Summer of 1919 and the riots in Harlem in 1915, 1935, and 1943, and Watts in 1965 or Detroit in 1967, were already within his sights, Paul Laurence Dunbar advised the Negroes of the Tenderloin not to do anything to stir up trouble and invite the wrath of white folks. On a tour of the homes of Negroes in the riot district, he counseled them "to stay at home and refrain from doing anything that might incite the rioting element to break out again," as if white rage were a storm that had landed in the Tenderloin, or a spate of bad weather that they could wait out if only they were patient. Worn out after his encounter with their bruised and battered lives and mouthing what he was expected to say but was hard-pressed to believe, he refreshed himself at a saloon at Thirty-Second Street and Sixth Avenue. The Negro bard passed out—a condition with which he was not unfamiliar—except in this instance he claimed the blackout was the consequence not of excessive drinking, but of being drugged in the saloon. When he awoke the next day, his watch was missing, as well as a $150 diamond ring and forty dollars in cash. His personal history of debauchery and wastefulness failed to temper the stern lessons he offered the lower ranks of the race, whose lives he had made into lyric securing his fame. His song for the riot was belated, and penned when even a fool was capable of reading the handwriting on the wall, listening for *the deep impassioned cry.*

1909. 601 West 61st Street.
A New Colony of Colored People,
or Malindy in Little Africa

Half a man—it sounded less harsh than the third sex or queer or invert and had the advantage of endorsing the aspiration to be a full and true man. As critical was the related question shadowing this as-yet unrealized ambition: When would the colored female achieve her full status as a woman? In her official role as friend of the race, Mary White Ovington sought to improve the lot of the Negro, not be another cold statistician tallying the crimes and calculating rates of illegitimate birth. While it could not be denied that what it meant to be a man or a woman in the Negro world diverged wildly from what was to be expected in the world at large, it was still possible for the Negro to fall into line. In spite of the things she witnessed daily—men who lived on their wives and paramours and ample evidence of lusty life and infidelity—she was optimistic about the future of the race. Such indelicate matters were hard to escape as the night wore on; although she tried not to pry, such issues were not beyond her concern. Intimate lives were on view on the streets and in the corridors. The airshaft made public the things that happened behind closed doors.

For nearly a year she had observed first-hand this anomalous, yet beautiful, world by dwelling within the thick precincts of black life.

Idle men and female breadwinners blurred the lines between man and woman, husband and housekeeper, spouse and lover. "Dandified looking men without work preached their doctrine of an easy life with a hard-working girl to make life happy." Colored men commanded their mark and there were plenty of girls to "keep them in polished boots, fashionable coats, and well-creased trousers."

For nine months she lived in a third-floor flat of a model tenement in San Juan Hill, the only white woman among her Negro neighbors. In the black ghetto, no one ever bothered or molested her, a fact she often repeated to white friends and colleagues "since the Negro had acquired a reputation for brutality." She was "never freer from insult or harm than in this spot in New York." No strange men ever spoke to or approached the conspicuously blond, blue-eyed woman; she came and went unmolested from morning until midnight. The sense that she would be all right wherever she landed was born of wealth and comfort, education and opportunity, a fundamental sense of belonging in the world, wherever that might be. Her comfort among Negroes was backed by her political convictions. She found it easy to relate to the poor black women who were her neighbors, easier than to those more properly described as peers, whom she found difficult and troublesome. A white woman living among Negroes, even one in her forties—well, the imagination ran wild. Her secrets and indiscretions did not involve them, despite the horrible things written about her in the newspaper, painting her as a high priestess of social equality, who encouraged interracial marriage, dined and socialized with Negroes, and hosted an "equality love fest" and "miscegenation banquet." It was bad enough that a cultured woman of wealth submitted to "a fraternity of perverts," but to lure young white women into the company of black men was unspeakable. Of course, she was a race traitor.

With a quick glance, her neighbors could tell she was not one of the two-dollar Irish women on Tenth and Eleventh Avenues, she wasn't a Jewish or Italian woman passing for black so she could live in peace with her husband and children or her lover without attracting contempt and violence, nor was she one of those white Negroes discernible only to members of the group. The exaggerated kindness

of her eyes and the noblesse oblige that colored the simplest acts of care and decency settled the matter. When she entered their small homes, she appeared too large and assessed too nakedly their lives. She did not disclose that she was conducting a social survey or living among them to collect "Negro material," yet it was obvious. No less apparent were the pleasures taken in the company of Negroes.

Mary White Ovington delighted in being lost in the sea of blackness. The crush and pressure of the densely packed blocks of San Juan Hill, the flesh-to-flesh intimacy that would make most white folks recoil, provided a sense of joy and vitality, which she perversely likened to "a mass of humanity approximating that of the slaver's ship." The apartments were "human beehives, honeycombed with little rooms thick with human beings."

San Juan Hill was "a poor neighborhood running from West Sixtieth Street to Sixty-Fourth Street, between Tenth and Eleventh Avenue. Whites dwelt on the avenues, colored on the streets, and fights between the two gave the hill its name; black men were required to battle as fiercely here as they had on San Juan Hill during the Spanish American War." Fifteen thousand inhabitants were squeezed in an area of five blocks. Sixty-First, Sixty-Second, and Sixty-Third Streets were entirely Negro blocks. San Juan Hill was as "a bit of Africa as Negroid in aspect as any district you are likely to visit in the South." Every time she turned from Eleventh Avenue onto Sixty-First Street, she was glad to enter the black world again.

The influx of black migrants was changing San Juan Hill, and the Upper West Side as far north as Ninety-Ninth Street bordering Central Park. As the *New York Times* observed: "A constant stream of furniture trucks loaded with the household effects of a new colony of colored people who are invading the choice locality is pouring into the street. Some of them are grotesquely picaresque. . . . The buildings are *swarmed* as soon as they are thrown open. Another equally long procession moving in the other direction is carrying away the household goods of the whites from their homes of years." The Black Belt had extended its reach. A walk through Manhattan made it clear that segregation had taken hold in the city. Negroes were cordoned into exclusively black streets and neighborhoods, and the good and bad elements were intermixed. As a social worker noted, "It was a surprise to find addresses of the delinquent girls leading into the very houses where respectable people of my acquaintance lived and very near their apartments." Segregation leveled the distinctions of rank by forcing all black folks to huddle together.

All the vice and untoward desires of the white world were channeled into the Negro quarter of the city. It was an interzone where disparate worlds met and anything could happen, where opium-addled girls turned tricks in dark hallways and suicidal poets leapt to their death and lady lovers and female impersonators sought refuge. The telltale signs of Negrophiles seeking adventure in Little Africa were apparent in the wide, hungry glances, the radiant carnality, the palpable sense that base pleasures might be countenanced here.

In 1910, John Rockefeller Jr. commissioned a door-to-door survey of prostitutes in the worst dens of the city. Irish, French, German, and Italian women selling hand jobs and French style lived in close proximity to black working girls. Had they uttered good day, had they been willing to cross the color line, had they imagined Negroes as neighbors, they might have sounded a whore's *Internationale*. This was the very thing that Rockefeller and other Progressive reformers feared—the promiscuity sociality of the lower ranks, love and friendship across the color line. Law and order depended on the color line to segregate vice and quarantine it within the black ghetto. The white working class fell into line and shored up the project.

More striking to Ovington than the crime and the blight was the beauty of black folks. Whether in San Juan Hill or in the hills of Jamaica, she found the dark bronze faces, the plum and purple lips, the brilliant eyes, the handsome figures, and the regal carriages of the Negroes so lovely. Her brother-in-law, sharing this admiration for the beauty of the darker race, teased her: "She was attacking Negro equality the wrong way. Just get a law passed that everyone must go nude. Then you'd get not equality but Negro superiority." In her eyes, the Negro quarter was Little Africa. It was characterized by the torpor and pleasure of the libertine colony, by the license that made dark bodies available for sale and use. Within this distinctive geography, gender norms and sexual mores were "inverted, mocked or completely ignored"; keenly apparent was the gulf between her life and the lives of her black neighbors.

The color line in the city was as deep and wide as the ocean. She traversed it, preferring the Negro world and breathing easily again when engulfed in the sea of black faces, when lingering in a "cool tenement hallway" in the company of "stout, good-natured colored women," reluctant to enter their private flats and "slow to turn the latches of their door." The "ceaseless sounds of humanity filled the air." The bedrooms opened up to airshafts, which were conduits for sounds, passageways for the collective life of the tenement. This noise, if not a kind of music, at the very least, inspired it. Ethel Waters made music of it, all the sounds of life, the loving and fighting and laughter and suffering, and described the deprivation and vitality of cramped living from the inside: "I would hear a couple in another flat arguing, for instance. Their voices would come up the airshaft and I'd listen, making up stories about their spats and their love life. I could hear such an argument in the afternoon and that night sing a whole song about it. I'd sing out their woes to the tune of my blues music." Ellington also prized the airshaft and the sounds of life it conveyed: "You hear fights, you smell dinner, you hear people making love. You hear intimate gossip floating down. . . . An airshaft is one great loudspeaker. You see your neighbors' laundry. You hear the janitor's dogs. . . . An airshaft has got every contrast. . . . You hear people praying, fighting, snoring." You might hear a woman in a rear tenement "calling her husband out of the front house and threatening death to the degraded creature who had lured him in."

The beauty of the Black Belt, whether in the Lowndes County, Alabama, or Jamaica or the tenement districts of New York, was unmistakable, and at night, despite the assault of electric lights that dimmed the stars, there was "the laughter of men and women returning from the theatre, or some dance that last[ed] until dawn. Light and intermittent noises, the heat of the long day climbing up from the pavement, this [was] the night at San Juan Hill. The plantation songs sound[ed] in the night, melodious, quavering: 'All the people talking about heaven ain't going there.' Only the old people sang these noble songs filled as they were with thought of a future bliss. Today brings *no acquiescence in slavery's status* but a long, heavy battle for more of heaven on earth."

The Beauty of the Husband

"It's strange but I sometimes think the more trifling the man, the more he is sheltered and cared for, and you will see the same love given to a selfish woman," a neighbor confided. Mary's close friend, *dear Du Bois*, explained the intimate arrangements and strange couplings—the kind of man who lived at the expense of a woman and the woman willing to support him—as a holdover of the plantation and as a kind of prostitution. While she felt it a poor expression of love and an act of self-expenditure unfathomable to her, she did discern the shades of difference between giving everything and prostitution. This excessive generosity was a race trait. Even when used and cast away, black women too easily pardoned those who had wronged or disappointed them; even the roughest were openhanded. This capacity to share all they had and expect nothing transformed private homes into places of refuge that welcomed all, indifferent to judgments regarding who was worthy and who was no-good. "To shelter the undeserving quite as much as the deserving," one woman lamented, "to slave for some trifling colored man as though you were back in the cotton field, there is a great deal of this among the women inside these doors." In tenement hallways, black women confessed their heartbreak and voiced their defeat and took pride in what they could give one another, as if giving satisfied want and transformed all you didn't have into plenty.

It was obvious that gender as category was not elastic enough to encompass the radical differences in the lived experience of black and white women. In slavery, stolen labor, violated flesh, and negated maternity (black women were legally denied a mother's access to her child or choice about reproduction) had defined this difference. In the twentieth century, wage labor, servitude, improper guardianship, failed maternity, chance coupling, serial marriages, and widowhood marked the difference. *Half a woman* announced the black female's failure to realize the aspirations of womanhood or meet the benchmark of humanity. Great dangers awaited those who lived in the lexical gap between black female and woman. This category crisis defined the afterlife of slavery. "The Negro comes north and finds himself half a man. Does the woman, too, come to be but half a

woman? What is her status in the city to which she turns for opportunity and larger freedom?"

The black woman was a breadwinner—this was the most glaring problem. In short, she threatened to assume and eclipse the role of

the husband. As early as 1643, black women's labor had been classified as the same as men's. The Virginia General Assembly placed a
tax on African women's labor. Tithes or taxes were usually imposed
on men in agricultural labor and the heads of household. No tax
was imposed on the labor of white wives and daughters laboring in
the household of their husbands and fathers. Unlike white women's
labor, black women's labor was treated as if they were men, inaugurating a centuries-long crisis about the status of black women's
work and their deviation from gender norms. The tax introduced this
gender variance, which would be made absolute two decades later
when their reproductive capacity and maternity was also targeted
and deemed the property of slave-owners; the womb was made into
a factory and children transformed into commodities for the market.
The failure to comply with or achieve gender norms would define
black life; and this "ungendering" inevitably marked black women
(and men) as less than human.

   This state of affairs—black women as providers, heads of households, and wage laborers—transgressed what was deemed normal
and proper: "With her, self-sustaining work usually begins at fifteen, and by no means ceases with her entrance upon marriage,
which only entails new financial burdens. The wage of the husband . . . is usually insufficient to support a family, save in extreme
penury, and the wife accepts the necessity of supplementing the
husband's income. This she accomplishes by taking in washing
or entering a private family to do housework. . . . She has but few
hours to give her children. She is ready to be friend and helpmate
to her husband, but should he turn out to be a bad bargain, she has
no fear of leaving him, since her marital relations are not welded
by economic dependence." A woman who didn't need a man or
depend on one raised concerns and instigated doubts about her own
status—was she a woman at all? This nagging, insistent question
placed black females on the threshold between the dangerous and
the unknown.

Despite the pleasantries exchanged in the hallway, the visits to the ailing and needy, and the books and cookies offered to their children, Mary Ovington considered her neighbors sexually immoral. In part, it was a matter of history and habit. In part, it was a matter of numbers. There were too many colored women in the city. What did it mean to be a surplus human? Were they unnecessary, expendable, or without value? When weighing the danger they presented against the value of their lives, was it a matter of who they loved multiplied by how many times they had loved divided by the losses of death and separation? Did the surplus woman produce a social deficit or create a drain on public resources? Was the relation between surplus and debt and danger particular to the Negro quarter? What measure was used to calculate the cost of love and survival, and why were black women always found wanting? "In their hours of leisure, the surplus women are known to play havoc with their neighbors' sons, even with their neighbors' husbands, for since lack of men makes marriage impossible for about a fifth of New York's colored girls, social disorder results. Surplus Negro women, able to secure work, support idle, able-bodied Negro men. The lounger at the street corner, the dandy in the parlor thrumming on his banjo, means a *Malindy of the hour* at the kitchen washboard."

————

Mary Ovington was not unfamiliar with playing havoc with another woman's husband, with loving someone else's man. While her affairs were confined to more luxurious surroundings than a model tenement and in a wealthier neighborhood of the city, she too was subject to *degrading temptation,* and guilty of the extramarital relations frowned upon by common decency, except in this case intimacy outside the law couldn't be blamed on an upbringing in a poor environment or the history of slavery. Hardly anyone knew about her affair with John Milholland, the wealthy industrialist. Perhaps dear Du Bois, her friend and colleague, might have suspected. He was experienced in this arena, having had several extramarital affairs, although it was all very discreet and without scandal. His formality and aloofness provided the perfect mask for the adulterer. While her social intercourse with Negroes was the cause of public uproar and fueled outrageous rumors, and the lunches and dinners with Du Bois at the Marshall Hotel tracked by private investigators, her secrets remained safe elsewhere. The only traces of the affair were to be found in her lover's diary, in a married man's prayers to "subdue the flesh" and "purify his filthy imagination."

When she described her black female neighbors as immoral, if she felt the pang of hypocrisy or the sting of such judgment as it redounded on her own life, she never let on. It was easy enough to pretend to be what the world recognized: a respectable woman of means. Never did her own passion and indiscretion temper her judgments about the Negro girl in New York. Without hesitation, she searched for a long history of degradation and maternal "weakness in the contour and color of her face" and expressed grave doubts about her future. Had a "vicious environment . . . strengthened her passions and degraded her from the earliest girlhood?" Did the fact that colored women met with more severe race prejudice than men make her less likely to succeed or break free of the past? "We don't allow niggers" blocked her entrance to the office and the retail shop. The colored girl in New York "gets the job that the white girl does not want." What the white girl "desires for herself, she refuses to her colored neighbor." For black women, there was no path through the city where they might avoid insult or obscene proposition. After being insulted at a public park, one young woman declaimed, "I wish the ocean might rise up and drown every white person on the face of the earth."

What might bring about "a diminution in sexual immorality?" Was it a gesture as simple as "the raising of the hat to colored women?" Or offering help with too heavy a load? Often "the white man most blatant against the 'nigger'" was "the one most ready to enter into illicit relationship with the woman whom he claims to despise." Had history and social custom dictated an irrevocable course? Would the colored woman ever achieve her *full status as a woman*? "Slavery deprived her of family life, set her to daily toil in the field, or appropriated her mother's instincts for the white child. She has today the difficult task of maintaining the integrity and purity of the home. Many times she has succeeded, often she has failed, sometimes she has not even tried."

————

She climbed the four flights of stairs to the top floor of the dark tenement to visit Annabel's mother, a delicate woman broken by the physical strain of laundry work and housekeeping. Inevitably, it seemed that whomever she needed to visit lived on the highest floor of the tenement. The girl's mother was sick with tuberculosis and had sold off all the family furniture to pay the ten-dollar rent and then lost the bill on her way back home. They had sold everything, but now they would still be evicted. "It's the end," the mother said quietly, "there's nothing left for us." "There's not a penny but what goes for the rent . . . Annabel don't have enough to eat, and look at her shoes." Her handsome towering son was unemployed and could do nothing for his mother. He skulked away quietly. "There was the look of embarrassment on his mother's face, although she said nothing, but only picked up the plate he had left on the chair and called to him a good-night."

Annabel swept the floor and washed the dishes. She was the perfect little helpmate to her mother. What future awaited Annabel? she wondered.

"What are you going to do when you grow up?" Mary asked the child.

Annabel replied immediately, "I shall play at the theatre. I can make lots of money that way. I mean to dance and sing. I can dance now," she added.

Indeed she could. The fifteen or eighteen dollars a week earned

by a Negro chorus girl could be earned a dozen other ways by white girls. She had seen Annabel coquetting at the playground. "Couldn't you do something nicer than that?"

Annabel knew the material side of a Negro's life better than Miss Mary ever would. "I want a home," she said with some emotion. "I want mamma to be where she can keep her things." Annabel glanced at the bare, dismantled room.

Yes, she would dance on the stage, maybe at the Lincoln Theater or on Broadway. Even if it was just a saloon with a small sand-covered floor and just enough room for her to dance, no matter, because everyone would come just to see her, not to drink gin and beer. The audience packed into the small tables clustered around the floor would never take their eyes off her, they would adore her, and she would never have to scrub until her knees were raw or her hands swollen. She would never have to be a servant like her mother, who worked so hard, but had nothing. Yes, she would shake her hips and wear rouge and powder and smile brightly and kick her legs in the air higher than any other dancer ever had. She would be ravishing and Negroes would lie and say that they knew her back in the day; they would pretend they expected great things from her and she had been a close friend. They would tell the story of how she escaped a dark tenement on Sixty-Second Street, how she never tricked or threw herself down three flights of stairs because she was so unhappy she couldn't bear to live or took opium because that was the only road out she could see. They would say that since she was a little girl she wanted to dance and the story of "when I knew her" and "what happened was" ended on a pleasing note. Annabel would never have to walk down Sixty-Second Street crying, bawling in the street because she had lost her last ten-dollar bill and would be evicted from two rented rooms, tears streaming down her face while folks watched or shook their heads in pity or whispered "dumb bitch." No, she would have a handful of ten-dollar bills, so many that if she lost one, she wouldn't even notice. So many that she would give them to the children playing in the street and then she would put her arms around their shoulder and her eyes would say, "One day things will be better," and they would all try very hard to believe this was true.

Mistah Beauty, the Autobiography of an Ex-Colored Woman, Select Scenes from a Film Never Cast by Oscar Micheaux, Harlem, 1920s

f Gladys Bentley's life were an Oscar Micheaux film, it might open with a shot of the three-story tenement house in Philadelphia in which the entertainer grew up. Four boys play in the alley behind the house. The camera settles on the eldest, distinguishing him from the others as the film's protagonist, but not exaggerating any difference between him and the other boys. Nothing about the way he jumps from the top of the stairs to the bottom of the landing or shoves his young brother aside, which causes him to fall and to cry Mama, establishes or fixes the categories "boy" or "girl," "brother" or "sister." Or the story might start earlier, with a pair of empty hands filling the frame, but cut off from the body and suspended in the air, expectant. Then a shot of the young mother staring indifferently at an infant she cannot love and refuses to embrace, the rejection would be punctuated or underscored with dramatic music that would announce that this failed embrace is an event, a significant moment, a nodal point in the story to unfold. A melodramatic gesture like the mother's downcast eyes, averted gaze, or forehead cradled in her palms as she sobs would telegraph her anguish. Or a long take of the mother as she retreats from the baby nestled in her husband's extended arms. The self-loathing would be apparent on her face as she turns her back to the infant, her firstborn, but the child she would never be able to love. The one who would remind her always that she was not a good-enough mother. It would hurt too much to say the words *bad mother*, even when the fact couldn't be avoided. The next scene might be shot in deep shadow, and we would struggle to make out the dark figure in the even darker room, until the door was thrown open and the harsh light from the hall-way flooded the windowless room, and the fourteen-year-old andro-gyne resting on the narrow cot wearing his brother's Sunday suit and lost in a daydream about the third-grade teacher whom he still loves madly. Before he could open his eyes and pull himself from the fantasy of her arms, her kisses, and return to the dark stuffy room, he would be exposed and berated. Next scene, extreme close-up of the letter written by the distraught sixteen-year-old in the early hours of the morning, addressed to his mother and father, explaining that he was heading to New York, that he could not live at home anymore; he could not pretend to be the daughter his mother could never love, she could love only a son and he became one. Yet she failed to love him. The long objective stare of the camera as he walks down the hallway and creeps out of the house with everything he owns, which isn't much, packed in a satchel, and pulls the door closed very quietly behind him. Or the story might open in a cabaret, with a close-up of Bentley as the Bad Nigger, as the flashy gentleman (the physiog-nomy or a gesture would signal to the audience his tragic flaw, his moral defect).

In the film, the telltale gestures, tics, and queer traits would give Bentley away: his tendency to swagger; the too-big body, the too-loud voice, the mountain of flesh, the vocal intonation, the distribu-tion of hair, the masculine distribution of weight, his brazen flouting of law and custom and civilization, the preening defiance and naked display of pleasure. Seated at the best table in the club, he would be surrounded by a bevy of beauties. The camera lingers on the five bot-

tles of champagne accumulated at the table, so the audience doesn't miss the clue and the condemnation: he has been plying the young chorines with alcohol and all of them are intoxicated, and the many bottles make plain that the rogue has money to burn. The eyes brim with lust. The sideways smile and the inviting mouth are certain to be the cause of a young chorine's downfall.

Cut to the dance number on the club floor, which is pivotal, obligatory, and never inessential in a Micheaux film. Everything terrible about the club—the alcohol, the debauchery, the infidelity encouraged by the environment, the loose, jaded women—would be balanced by this scene, which would condemn the cabaret and at the same time exalt it. In the cabaret scene, black virtuosity is on display. Then comes the chorus, and the dancing bodies are arranged in beautiful lines that shift and change as the flourish and excess of the dancers unfold into riotous possibility and translate the tumult and upheaval of the Black Belt into art. The extended musical numbers might first seem like digressions, except that they establish the horizon in which everything else transpires and foreground the lovely actuality of blackness. The dance scene is crucial, the movement of bodies, the chorus as well as the ordinary folks crowding the floor, reveal the other lineages of black cinema, understood broadly as a rendering of black life in motion in contrast to the arrested and fixed images that produce and document black life as a problem. The cabaret scene illuminates the indebtedness of the moving picture to the limbo dance (which, practiced on the slave ship, was "the gateway to or threshold of a new world and the dislocation of a chain of miles") and to the ring shout danced in the clearing. The long legs of the high-brown chorus girls propel through the air, and their collective movement creates a series of beautiful lines that they arrange and break. The café-au-lait beauty shimmies as she sings a popular ditty with her hips swiveling and arms cutting the air, and the flow of this segment cuts and deranges the regimented units of the melodrama's plot, and before all this beauty we forget for a few minutes that things will end badly for the sheik at the table. The chorus conjures the promise that this night might never end, that there is no world but this one, that everything is possible, that the reservoir of life is limitless. The hyperextended bottom, the contracted figure, the rotating pelvis, the arms akimbo and then raised to the sky and bringing down the house, the motion of bodies—they collapse the distance between the plantation and the city, the quarters and the tenements, producing the "annihilation of time and space" characteristic of modernity and definitive of the cinema. The Shimmy, the Turkey Trot, the Funky Butt, the Black Bottom, the synchronized rhythm of the chorus all attest to the flow and frequency of black locomotion, to the propulsion and arrest of history. Bentley's life refracted through Micheaux's cinema is the wild, deregulated movement that refuses the color line and flees the enclosure of the ghetto. The bodies in motion, bodies intimate and proximate, recklessly assert what might be, how black folks *might could* live. The slave ship is as central as the railroad in the collapse of time and space that produce modernity and black cinema. The scene pivots around the breach and the wound and endeavors the impossible—to redress it. The beauty resides as much in the attempt as in its failure. What it envisions: life reconstructed along radically different lines. The chorus elaborates and reconstructs the passage, conjures the death in the fields and the death on city pavements, and reanimates life; it enables the felled bodies to rise, plays out in multiple times, and invites all to enter the circle, to join the line, to rejoice, and to *celebrate with great solemnity.*

Such scenes could be witnessed each night in the dozens of nightclubs and cabarets where Bentley performed. La Bentley was a star in Harlem's Jungle Alley, one of its high priests. Bentley was abundant flesh, art in motion.

Huge, voluptuous, and chocolate-colored, Bentley always worked in a tuxedo and top hat or flashy men's attire. The hair was cut short, tamed and waved by a handful of pomade that plastered it to the scalp. Any day of the week, Bentley could be seen marching down Seventh Avenue attired in the threads of a Harlem sheik and usually with a pretty chorus girl hanging on his arms. He thrived on the fact that his "odd habits" were "the subject of much tongue wagging" because he lived and loved as a man. He wasn't a radical, but a brilliant performer, one smart enough to make the corporeal malediction of black and mannish into a kind of costume that delighted, aroused, and solicited others. Risk or reward attended the offer of

the thick dark body as an object of veneration and ridicule, condemnation and pleasure. The appreciation and the laughter of the onlookers crowded in the cabaret domesticated the danger of La Bentley, but he conceded no ground. There was nothing feminine about him; it was more than glamour drag, more than a woman outfitted as a man, as several of his wives, both white and colored, could attest. Black and white audiences loved the risqué lyrics, the sonorous deep voice, the open flirtation with the most attractive women in the audience, the jokes about sissies and bull daggers. They cried, laughing so hard; they were doubled over from the ache of it, they blushed, and they fed on the anomalous beauty of Bentley. "The large dark masculine figure," according to Langston Hughes, was "a piece of African sculpture animated by rhythm." A modern surface. An exemplary architecture of black possibility.

In a Micheaux film, all this virtuosity would seem to be an aside, a break in the narrative, a digression in the plot of seduction or betrayal, but in fact everything else that happened in the film was merely a supplement to this. When the camera eventually returned to Bentley or to the shady antagonist and his struggle with the good man, the hardworking one devoted to the improvement of the race, laboring ceaselessly to raise funds for a Negro school, willing to marry a girl to save her from the gutter or an abusive father, or too honorable to abandon a woman of questionable morals and remaining true even when a better woman waited in the wings—it didn't really matter; it was hard to recall the story line or keep track of which was the good woman and which was the bad, separate the actualities from the dream sequence. The viewer watches and waits with bated breath for the next interruption of the cabaret scene and betrayal of the plot. The duel or competition between the two men that would decide the fate of our heroine and the future of the race would be dull, uninteresting, and anticlimactic. In a Micheaux film, the lustful, prodigal Bentley, sharp and rough as any Harlem sweet man and able *to lay down their jive just like a natural man*, could only be cast as villain. The player flitted from woman to woman; never capable of being sated, at best, he could love them and leave them. There were not enough women in the world to make him feel loved. So he ran through the chorus girls, ruined women, spoiled them, used and abused them. *They got a head like a sweet angel and they walk just like a natural man.*

A heartbreaker like Bentley, a womanizer, a carouser, and a libertine, would meet a bad end. The story punished those deviating from the marriage plot, from the script of racial uplift, from the ought and should of what a woman was expected to be. As if repenting for the lavish club scenes, the half-dressed bodies, the promiscuous life and intimate trespass afforded by the nighttime, the denouement of the film would restore the trampled ideals and imperiled norms of temperance, monogamy, and heterosexuality. Bentley's queer masculinity ran roughshod over the righteous propagation that resided at the heart of every racial melodrama. Bentley trashed the gendered norms and family ideals central to the project of racial uplift—self-regulation, monogamy, fidelity, wedlock, and reproduction—and scoffed at the moralism of the latter-day Victorians, the aristocrats of uplift. Alas, the villain cannot escape the end that awaits him. By the time *The End* rolls onto the screen, virtue's antagonist is long gone. A car crash, a bullet to the head or the heart, or the penitentiary has resolved the drama. (For our protagonist, the political climate would propel the story toward a tragic end. In the 1930s, state law would require female performers to apply for a license to wear men's clothing in their acts. Cross-dressing was now labeled as subversive. Queers were placed in the sightlines of Senator McCarthy and the House Un-American Activities Committee [HUAC]. Bentley's much discussed marriage to a white woman in a civil ceremony made the entertainer vulnerable.)

A car crash or bullet would not kill this celebrated sharper and lady lover, this husband to many beautiful women, black and white. A brutal twist in the plot of the film Micheaux never directed leads

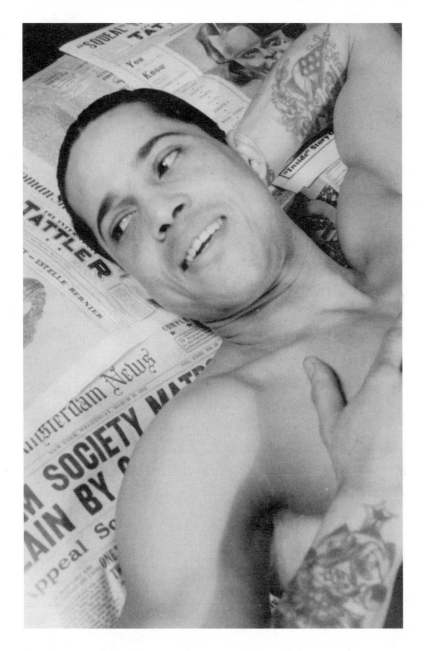

to the demise of our protagonist. An act of self-immolation moti-
vated by state repression and declared in a coerced confession forces
the beautiful husband to assume the role of wife, signaling his defeat.
It is a crushing last act of self-renunciation. The lines from the death-

bed: *I inhabited that half-shadow no man's land which exists between the boundaries of the two sexes. Throughout the world there are thousands of us furtive humans who have created for ourselves a fantasy as old as civilization itself; a fantasy which enables us, if only temporarily, to turn our back on the hard realm of life. Our number is legion and our heartbreak inconceivable.*

The hard-hearted no-count man, sharper, sheik, sweet man, queer fellow, seducer must be handled or dispatched so that the right couple can emerge—the true husband and wife. So that the girl ruined by the promise of a part in the show, the girl willing to meet the gambler, pimp, or shady producer later at the after-hours spot, the girl willing to do anything to get the part can be rescued, so that no one else will savor the words or hum the tune: *Women ain't gonna need no men. They got a head like a sweet angel and walk just like a natural man.*

Family Albums, Aborted Futures:
A Disillusioned Wife Becomes an
Artist, 1890 Seventh Avenue

There were few memories of her childhood she could recollect with any pleasure. It would not be wrong to say that she had never been a child, or at least, she had never been a happy child. Are precocious children ever happy? To learn about the world or to blossom too early was dangerous. It wasn't clear if her *father*, the man who raped her twelve-year-old mother, was the son of the family that had owned her grandmother's people; all she knew was that *he was the sort of southern gentleman who had no scruples against making concubines of their servant girls.* Although a term like *concubine* inadequately described the violence experienced by her mother, grandmother, and great-grandmother, three generations of women who, in her words, became very practiced at submission. Her great-grandmother had been a slave; her grandmother and mother were nominally free. The *monstrous intimacy* of chattel slavery, the violent coupling and compulsory reproduction, marked each generation of her family. The child follows the condition of the mother—*partus sequitur ventrem*—so that the daughters labor even now under the outcome. What happened to Edna's mother, grandmother, and great-grandmother was neither unique nor exceptional. It was to be expected if you were a servant in the house. House service, wrote Du Bois, preserved "the last vestiges of slavery and medievalism." The "personal degradation of the work" was so great that "any white man of decency would rather cut his daughter's throat than let her grow up to such a destiny." Throughout the world, there was "no greater source of prostitution than this grade of menial service." Du Bois echoed Frederick Douglass, who a century earlier described the kitchen as brothel. The kitchen contained a "whole social history," not only of racism and servility, but sexual use and violation.

Her grandmother joined "the wild rush from house service, on the part of all who could scramble or run," and moved the family to Boston so that Edna might avoid this fate. The awful things they escaped were described only through euphemisms like *loyal servants* and *concubines* and *fathers*, but her grandmother was too honest to disguise the brutality part and parcel of intimate labor as love or consent. Dissemblance was the way they managed and lived with this violence. What Edna knew was: *All the women in the family were beautiful* and *They probably often submitted to the white men.* She also knew never to speak the name of her father or her mother's father or her grandmother's father. The secrets and lies and the perverse lines of descent encompassed slavery and its afterlife. Only when she was an adult did her mother share the graphic account of her rape. A white family had hired her mother as a nursemaid. Her family was so poor they permitted it. When she was in bed sleeping beside her three-year-old charge, her employer, a fine Virginia gentleman, entered the bed and raped her. At twelve, she didn't even realize that she was pregnant, she was too young to know anything about sex or babies, and so believed the old people when they said *there were snakes in her belly.*

———

My sister, my mother. Until she was about six years old, Edna believed her grandmother was her mother. She and her mother lived with her grandmother and the Negro man she had married after giving birth to her second child by a white man. They were poor but lived on the outskirts of a very nice colored neighborhood and strived to assume their place among decent and respectable Negroes. Being nearly white endowed them with status; being nearly white also raised questions about the circumstances that afforded Edna's ivory complexion, golden wavy hair, and blue eyes. The missing father exposed the lie of any presumed respectability. Once it became apparent that Edna had no father and was nameless, the other children on the block mocked her and called her terrible names, making cruel sport of the things their parents whispered behind closed doors. They adored and reviled her, envied her near-white beauty and held her in contempt as the child of a white man's whore. *Half-white bastard.* Her fate was sealed. Even her aunt Nancy believed Edna would never amount to anything and would be a *bad woman* like her mother.

When in a fit of jealousy, her grandfather murdered the fiancé of his then-sixteen-year-old stepdaughter and was sentenced to life in prison, Edna was condemned as the granddaughter of a murderer too. All hopes of blending invisibly with the upper ranks were dashed. The scandal of the murder and the stepfather's envy of his daughter's lover cast an additional layer of shame on their house.

Her mother was *too free.* She did what she wanted. Her sexual relations were social. She was never kept by anyone. This excess—being reckless enough to have sex with a number of men, both colored and white, could not and would not be forgiven. Her mother was beautiful, loose, and unrepentant in her sexuality. She was attracted to men who were gentle and to men who abused her. Burdened by the weight of her mother's history, Edna felt guilty and condemned. It wasn't hers to carry, but the world punished her anyway. The knot of shame that blossomed inside her had as much to do with the names their neighbors called them as with what she now believed. It was hard to look at her mother and not judge her a bad woman.

As they lived in three small rooms, Edna found it impossible to avoid the sight of her mother in bed with colored and white men.

White man's whore, the neighbors spat. The words *promiscuous* or *dissolute* weren't in the six-year-old Edna's vocabulary. *Lax in sexual matters, loose-living, abandoned, unrestrained in behavior, unruly, lavish, wistful.* When she was old enough to understand the meaning of such words, she preferred to describe her mother as *too free.* A flood of tears accompanied the conviction that what the neighbors said about her mother was true. It was not the picture of her mother's body entwined in the arms of a casual friend or stranger that made her sob inconsolably; rather, it was the vision of her mother applying rouge to her cheeks. The blood-red color was the same as that of the artificial rose she had soaked in water, loosening the pigment, and then painted onto her face. Her mother was beautiful, cut-rate, and deep scarlet. *Only bad women did that.*

Guessing at the World

Masked behind the quiet demeanor, the cultivated manners, the very fair and very pretty appearance, was a quiet turbulence. Edna was slow to realize it was not simply that her circumstances were unsettled; rather, there was something decidedly unsettled about her. A *riot inside* was palpable, but its source she couldn't discern. Perhaps it was simply unhappiness, the brutal loneliness that characterized a failed and unhappy marriage. Perhaps it was the three generations of hurt transmitted along the maternal line. There was the creeping fear and the risk that her resolute passivity might yield to something dangerous and unexpected. Maybe it was the blind groping for something she could not name.

Lloyd Thomas did not try to seduce her as so many others had. The lovely twenty-nine-year-old Edna traveled in the best circles. As the social secretary of Madame C. J. Walker, the first black woman millionaire, she quickly gained entry to the worlds of the wealthy and the fashionable. The aspiring actress was courted by admirers, both white and black, and moved easily between the worlds of

Greenwich Village and Harlem, taking pleasure in the opportunities and the glamour afforded by the city, at least for the beautiful and talented, and she was both. Edna was fascinated by Lloyd's indifference. This dour, taciturn man, who managed aspiring singers and actors as well as several Harlem nightspots, did not appear to want or desire her, and that made her desire him fiercely. She initiated the courtship, and they married in a very short time. He was attractive, debonair, cosmopolitan; most importantly, he was a master of withholding. Even when surrounded by a roomful of beautiful chorus girls, his eyes never wandered. He remained aloof, cold, unreachable. This amazed and aroused her, encouraging her determination to make him want her fiercely. He loved her from a distance, if he loved her at all. He had never said that he did, and refused to utter those three words—I love you—despite her badgering, as if it were an outrageous or unreasonable thing to expect of a man. It surprised her although he had never expressed ardor or tenderness before they married, she wrongly assumed he would relent and soften. Certainly, he wasn't a conventional man; he enjoyed the company of artists, writers, and entertainers whose desires were not fixed by the coordinates of identity, who outrageously defied expectations regarding who they were supposed to be and who they were required to love. (As with Edna, he might have enjoyed the experience of being wanted by those he did not want; more likely, he was attracted to the queer men regularly in his company, the poets, singers, and club owners who made Harlem beautiful; or maybe he wanted them with an intensity that Edna never could have guessed. Rumors circulated that it was a marriage of convenience.)

Despite his indifference, Lloyd proved to be a passionate lover; he satisfied her physically, and he was faithful insofar as he seemed completely unaffected by other women, yet his heart belonged to him alone. The very qualities that initially made him so attractive—his sexy reticence, Olympian reserve, and striking impassivity—caused a great deal of grief.

What was at stake in trying to transform indifference into love and adoration? Should she be satisfied with his cold constancy and a fidelity ensured by boredom with other women? Was the impossible effort to transform aloofness into devotion yet another attempt to break loose from her mother's life? Or make up for what her mother failed to give? She had escaped her mother's fate, and had been lucky when compared with the women in her family. No rapists, murderers, or mercurial violent men. No savage love and fierce carnality. At sixteen, she had rushed into marriage still a virgin, determined to escape poverty and scandal. All she and her mother noticed was the veneer of respectability and the gilded family name. Her husband, the son of a wealthy self-made man, enjoyed a secure place in "brown society." What could be more attractive to a bastard child than social standing, than the protection of fathers and husbands? Only after she became a Mrs. did she discover that he was spoiled and irresponsible; he never worked; he drank and gambled away their money. It was a colossal mistake. She quietly planned and plotted a way out and vowed never to become a mother. The first abortion was difficult, but she was as resolute the second time.

With the first marriage, she miscalculated, confusing appearance with substance, seeking safety from the turbulence of her childhood in the priggish straight-laced milieu of the Negro upper classes, but she had been wrong to believe that by preferring constancy to passion, and a well-scripted life to uncertainty, she could avoid being damaged by the world. Only the wealth of her father-in-law had protected her and her husband from the streets. The second time, there was no one to whom she could turn. And to protect her from what? A tepid marriage, a lukewarm coital embrace, waning affection, boredom? All the secrets harbored inside a marriage: the remoteness of the husband, the abrading routine of daily life, the monotony of domesticity, the thousand missed opportunities for an act of tenderness or a small proof of love. The loneliness of the marital bed threatened to break her.

On stage, she had purpose. She was no longer a disappointed wife;

she was alive, resplendent. It didn't matter that this feeling was transient and ephemeral. The freedom of being less like Edna and more like others was exhilarating. To be lost to the world of marriage and duty and disappointment and tedium as she entered the space of the ensemble and the intensity of creating and inhabiting a world with others, a domain of collective bodies, kinesthetic experience and gestural language. All other roles had to be relinquished. The stage enabled her to escape her paltry individual life and slip into someone else's existence—prostitute, queen, toiling laborer, flawed heroine— and to shed every petty concern. When she stepped into a character and lent her body to the gesture, she was nobody and everyone at the same time, no longer bound to her personal history and yet able to express deeply all the pain and failure and want, sharing it with the world but not shamed by it.

She disappeared into other lives; she became other selves. This was exquisite. It was the most sustained joy she had ever experienced. In the world of actors, directors, singers, playwrights and stagehands, she found a vehicle, an outlet for her tamped-down passion; she let go the impulse to seek safety within the confines of restraint and to settle for a dispassionate existence.

As her career soared, Lloyd became jealous and resentful. Her name appeared regularly in the theatre reviews, first in amateur productions, next as a member of the Lafayette Players, and then as a leading lady. Each success she enjoyed made him feel smaller and smaller, like there wasn't enough air in the room for the two of them; like she was trying to become the dominant one, like they were in a competition, and he wouldn't be anyone's second. He had opposed adamantly her career as an actress and now she intended to go on tour. After six months on the road with *Lulu Belle*, she returned home to find him dating younger women, frequenting cabarets and theatre clubs without her, spending the night at other Harlem apartments. Things unraveled but it was all very civil: no cussing and fighting and cutting up clothes and throwing his belongings into the streets. They were moderns. They were bohemians. Again, she was alone and dis-illusioned in marriage; she had become practiced at being let down, accustomed to heartbreak.

Whether it was Evelyn Preer or Fredi Washington or Rose McClendon—she never confided. All she disclosed was that a roman-tic encounter with a colored leading lady turned her life around. One dance sent her hurtling down a radically different path. Embraced in the arms of this lovely lady, Edna felt something electric, and it made her feel alive; it let her know that she was someone other than who she imagined herself to be. It was her first experience with a woman. They danced together and something very terrific happened, a very exhilarating thing. *It made her know.* Rumors circulated. It was the theatre so no one was shocked. Then there was the gossip about her relation with A'lelia Walker. Edna was among the circle of beauti-ful women who surrounded the Harlem heiress. They were intimate friends. She left it at that.

She met Olivia at a party at A'lelia's house. For six months Lady Olivia Wyndham pursued Edna relentlessly, claiming to be madly in love after their first meeting and not giving a damn about Lloyd. The English aristocrat was mannish, elegant, addicted to opium, and reckless. She had once cut herself on the head with a knife and thrown herself down a flight of stairs so that she might be hospi-talized and attended by a nurse she loved. The intensity and force of her desire made Edna recoil. It frightened her. It was the oppo-site of everything she sought in a husband. For six months, Olivia, undeterred, regularly appeared at Edna and Lloyd's Seventh Ave-nue apartment stylishly outfitted like a gentleman of wealth. Folks in Harlem accepted it as the English way after Radclyffe Hall, Sackville-West, and Nancy Cunard. She was after all a distant cousin of Oscar Wilde. Wyndham was the tempest threatening to destroy what remained of Edna's staid and loveless marriage. After months of relentless pursuit, Olivia conceded defeat and decided to return to England. On the night she was scheduled to depart, she made a last visit to Edna, presumably to say goodbye, but not without hope. Edna had done everything possible to quash Olivia's expectations, never reciprocating her affection or encouraging her desire. Yet, somehow after months in this sustained war of position, rejecting Olivia at every chance and determined not to feel anything at all for Lady Wyndham, she had succumbed to her charms. Had her resolve simply been worn away? Or was it more like rain after a long dry season? Unexpected, startling and necessary. If forced to do so, she would have no choice but to admit that she did harbor feelings for Olivia. Now that her departure was imminent, it was easier to admit. When Olivia arrived that evening, Edna invited her inside the apartment and then refused to let her go. They lived together for decades.

The romance of the English aristocrat and the Negro leading lady captivated the press. The articles stepped gingerly around the obvious—never mentioning the words lady lovers or homosexuals or lesbians—and cast no aspersions. People wrongly assumed *ménage a trois*; Edna and Olivia were the couple, but expansive enough to include Lloyd as a housemate. Lloyd didn't seem to mind releasing her and enjoyed the attention they received in the press: *Rich British Woman Forsook Own People to Reside in Harlem* or *She Renounced British Tradition for Her Negro Friends*. He and Edna had drifted into the arms of other lovers, creating parallel lives, but the three of them lived together in their Seventh Avenue flat, hosted dinner parties for their mutual friends, and regularly appeared in the society columns as the Lloyd Thomases and friend, whether attending A'lelia Walker's soirees, charity benefits, theatre openings, or the Hamilton Lodge Ball. Wallace Thurman, Dorothy West, and Jimmy Daniels rented a room in their place and Lloyd's beautiful young lover, Harlem's *It girl* Blanche Dunn, made a second home there until she jilted him for an English oil magnate. Olivia's fortune allowed them to live comfortably. After his Harlem nightclub closed, Lloyd never worked again. Marriage provided the cloak that allowed them to live as they wanted and without public censure.

From The Brilliance Of Mayfair To--

SHE RENOUNCED BRITISH TRADITION FOR HER NEGRO FRIENDS

OLIVIA WYNDHAM
"There's nothing unusual about me."

EDNA THOMAS
They met at a party—and a firm friendship started.

It was all so unexpected—late love and a successful career, a farmhouse in Connecticut and European holidays in English castles and French chateaus. For a poor girl who had been raised in a three-room apartment on the outskirts of respectability, it was astonishing and unbelievable—unless you were a leading lady or a brilliant entertainer or member of the beautiful set. She was one of the lucky ones: "the remnants of that ability and genius . . . whom the accidents of education and opportunity have raised on the tidal waves of chance," a rare bird, a Negro artist.

The world kept Edna guessing about what she might do and who she might become. She had *done all of the shocking things imaginable* and the only reason she could summon was the urge for expression, an urge that no one experienced more fiercely than black women and that none paid as dearly when this need was unmet, when one remained *an artist without an art form*. Everywhere you looked you could find it. *No modern intelligent person was content merely existing. Sometimes it was good to take a chance.*

Book Three

BEAUTIFUL EXPERIMENTS

Revolution in a Minor Key

It was past midnight and Harriet Powell was still on the dance floor. At first, she couldn't make sense of what the police officer said. She was under arrest? For what? The music blaring in the background and the couples dancing around her offered no hint that she would spend the next few years in and out of prison and that a decade would pass before she received the gift of her free papers. Who would have expected that involuntary servitude was the price for two nights of love in a rented room in a Harlem tenement? Or that unregulated black movement was still a risk, a threat, and a crime? Or that the "rebellious flame" of her "nocturnal wanderings" and sexual variance made her a potential prostitute and vagrant? How had the state come to set its sights on a seventeen-year-old black girl and make her the target of its violence? Even after the police officer uttered the words: *You are under arrest*, she protested, insisting that she had done nothing wrong. How had living become a crime?

Everyone was talking about freedom and democracy. One year, six months and twelve days of war hadn't produced any agreement about what the war meant and what it would bring. The police didn't give a damn if a Negro was wearing a uniform. *Move on nigger.* But even the dissenters, the radical Negroes who opposed transforming young men into cannon fodder for capitalism and who condemned the war as a crime and an extension of the color line on a global scale, expected something decisive at the outcome. Would the colored people of the world be united in the fight against imperialism? The hopes of revolutionary change ignited by 1917 reached deep into the heart of the Black Belt. *The New Negro has no fear*—was the declaration that echoed through the crowd. The spirit of Bolshevism was palpable in the streets of Harlem. Would a better world unfold in its wake? In editorials in the *New York Age*, the *Amsterdam News*, the *Chicago Defender*, and the *Afro-American*, everyone was asking when, if ever, the Negro would be free. But no one had Harriet Powell in mind or the war waged against her. Walking with the "conscious sway of invitation," gathering and assembling at the cabaret, and engaging in the very ordinary everyday practice of defiance were incommensurate with the political idiom of adjustment, betterment, and reward, the holy grail of self-appointed race leaders and friends of the Negro, and, as well, beneath the scrutiny of black socialists and street-corner radicals. Harriet's beautiful lack of restraint, her spectacular refusal to aspire to a better job or a decent life, and her radiant lust solicited only the attention of the police and the sociologist.

Charlie Hudson wasn't a soldier, unlike many of the young men Harriet knew who were lingering and tormented in the south and desperate to get to France. Theirs was not a romance stoked by the passions of war or the imminent threat of separation. If they became involved too quickly and made their way from the dance floor to the bedroom in a week, their only excuse was pleasure. On the Tuesday evening when Harriet left home to meet him, she told her parents she would return home shortly. Her father didn't believe it for a minute. He complained that *the girl made no pretense of listening.* She was always running the street. After work, she came home only long enough to change her clothes before rushing off to a dance or a movie and did not return until well after midnight. *Why shouldn't I go out sometimes if I work?* she challenged. He said he wouldn't stand for it in his house. It wasn't fair, she countered; she worked like an adult, so why shouldn't she be treated like one?

The rented room was just a few blocks from the Palace Casino, where she first met Charlie. It was in the fast part of Harlem, filled with lodging houses, cabarets, clubs, and saloons, and it was where the police focused their raids. Harriet had been intimate with others, mostly boys her own age, kissing and groping in dark hallways and on rooftops. The first time she did it was with an Italian she met at the park. He took her home and raped her. Few were the girls who consented the first time. It was different with Charlie Hudson. He was not brutal. He didn't force her, nor did he want her to hustle. For two days and nights, they lay idling in bed in a furnished room indistinguishable from hundreds of others, which had been carved out of lovely row houses now amputated and transformed into the tenements and rooming houses that lined 134th Street. In the tiny but glorious world of the rented room, she did whatever she wanted to do, not what others expected her to do, and it made her feel grown. When she and Charlie finally ventured outside, they made their way back to the dance hall.

On the floor of the Palace Casino, Harriet savored the joy of losing herself in the crowd. She absorbed the waves of heat emanating from all the bodies shimmying and shaking and grinding and it made all the pleasure of the past forty-eight hours even sweeter. Only when Officer Johnson grabbed her arm as she moved across the dance floor did it come to an end.

Causes Sister's Arrest in Dance Hall as Incorrigible

Helen Peters, 17, a waitress, of 229 E. 75th St., was arrested early Thursday morning in the Palace Casino, 135th St. and Madison Ave., on complaint of her sister, Mrs. Mildred Wellington, of the same address, who charged her with being incorrigible.

The girl disappeared from her home on Oct. 18th. On Thursday night Mrs. Wellington traced her sister to the Palace Casino, where nightly dances are held.

Policeman Johnson, of the E. 126th St. station, arrested Helen in the dance hall. The girl told the policeman that she had been living in a furnished room house on W. 42d St.

When arraigned before Magistrate Healy, in the Washington Heights Court, the matter was referred to the Yorkville Court.

The growing black presence in New York exaggerated the menace of colored women and the sexual dangers posed by young black folks rushing to the city. Each decade the population had doubled. It was impossible to walk through the streets of the Tenderloin or San Juan Hill or Harlem without encountering rambunctious girls, street waifs, baby-faced whores. They were the daughters of day laborers, Southern migrants, and West Indian immigrants flooding the city. The bohemians called them chippies, anarchists, lady lovers, sporting girls, bull daggers, and wild women.

Social reformers and yellow journalists sounded the alarm: The seduction of "unprotected" girls had reached epidemic proportions, so extreme measures were required. White slavery incited the moral panic and the national movement to protect young women from sexual predators. Rumors circulated about white slavery conspiracies, Jewish slave trafficking networks, Negro predators, and Chinatown opium dens, and the utter lack of evidence did little to dampen the fear and hysteria. Common sense held that black girls were the most vulnerable because of the corrupt employment agencies recruiting them from the south, the lack of decent job opportunities, and, most important, the centuries-long habit of consorting with white men, which had been their *training* in slavery. "Black women yielded more easily to the temptations of the city than any other girls," explained Jane Addams, because Negroes as a group, as "a colony of colored people," had not been brought under social control. Policy makers and reformers insisted they were "several generations behind the Anglo-Saxon race in civilizing agencies and processes." For this reason, they were in need of greater regulation. Slavery was the source of black women's immorality, observed the criminologist Frances Kellor, because "Negro women [were] expected to be immoral and [had] few inducements to be otherwise." Even W. E. B. Du Bois lamented, "Without a doubt the point where the Negro American is furthest behind modern civilization is in his [or her] sexual mores."

Moving about the city as they pleased and associating freely with strangers, young women risked harassment, arrest, and confinement. Wayward minor laws made them vulnerable to arrest and transformed sexual acts, even consensual ones with no cash exchanging hands, into criminal offenses. Phrases like "potential prostitute," "failed adjustment," and "danger of becoming morally depraved" licensed the dragnet. Casual sexual encounters and serial relationships were branded as "moral depravity," an offense punishable with a prison sentence. All colored women were vulnerable to being seized at random by the police; those who worked late hours, or returned home after the saloon closed or the lights were extinguished at the dance hall, might be arrested and charged with soliciting. If she had a sexually transmitted disease or children outside of wedlock or mixed-race children, her conviction was nearly guaranteed. Young women between fourteen and twenty-one, but sometimes girls as young as twelve, were sentenced to reformatories for visiting or residing in a house with a bad reputation or suspected of prostitution, or associating with lowlifes and criminals, or being promiscuous, or not working. Those who dared refuse the gender norms and social conventions of sexual propriety—monogamy, heterosexuality, and marriage—or failed to abide the script of female respectability were targeted as potential prostitutes, vagrants, deviants, and incorrigible children. Immorality and disorder and promiscuity and inversion and pathology were the terms imposed to target and eradicate these practices of intimacy and affiliation.

It was one's status that determined whether an intimate act, an evening spent with a stranger, or a proclivity to run the streets was a punishable offense. A status offense was a form of behavior deemed illegal only for a particular group of persons. These offenses fell within the jurisdiction of magistrate courts, and judges had great latitude in deciding a young woman's fate. Subjective evaluations of "behavior and conduct" produced dire outcomes. The Women's Court was created to address matters of sexual delinquency and it had the highest rate of conviction of all New York City courts. Not surprisingly, black women made up a significant percentage of those convicted.

Sex wasn't a crime, yet some forms of intimacy were unlawful and immoral—premarital sex, sex with a girl or boy under the age of consent, sodomy, sex in exchange for gifts or money rather than a marriage proposal. A wayward minor, as defined by the Code of Criminal Procedure, was: "Any person between the ages of sixteen and twenty-one who (1) 'habitually associates with dissolute persons,' or (2) 'is found of his or her own free will and knowledge in a house of prostitution, assignation, or ill-fame, or habitually associates with thieves, prostitutes, pimps or procurers, or disorderly persons,' or (3) 'is willfully disobedient to the reasonable and lawful commands of parent, guardian or other custodian and is morally depraved or is in danger of becoming morally depraved,' or (4) '. . . without just cause and without the consent of parents, guardians, or other custodians, deserts his or her home or place of abode, and is morally depraved or is in danger of becoming morally depraved,' or (5) '. . . so deports himself or herself as to willfully injure or endanger the morals of herself and others.'"

Only young women were adjudged wayward under these statutes (between the years 1882–1925). The intent of the legislation was to police and regulate sexual offenses without the "stigma of the conviction of crime." Young women's sexual activity, it was believed, led "directly to the entrance of the minor upon a career of prostitution." Yet such "protective measures" served only to criminalize young black women and make them even more vulnerable to state violence.

Serial lovers, a style of comportment, a lapse in judgement, a failure of restraint, an excess of desire—these were not crimes in and of themselves, but indications of impaired will and *future crime*. Those charged were not technically guilty of breaking the law or having commited a crime, so as a result, they were not protected by regular forms of due process, but subject to the discretion of the magistrate as to whether to suspend sentence, offer probation or commit the accused to the reformatory or other appropriate institutions. As a result of this discretion, many young black women who were first-time offenders, or to be more exact, young black women who had their first encounter with the police were likely to be sentenced to the reformatory for three years.

The wayward were guilty of a manner of living and existing deemed dangerous, and were a risk to the public good. Formally, they were not juvenile deliquents because "delinquency includes the commission of an act which if committed by an adult would be adjudged a crime and punished as such." In contrast, the provisions of the Wayward Minors Act held that "the definition of a wayward minor includes only *non-criminal acts but which indicate the immi-nence of future criminality.*"

The paradox was that minor infractions and statutory offenses were subject to more severe forms of punishment than actual crimes. A girl convicted as a wayward minor might receive an indeterminate sentence of three years, while a woman convicted of prostitution might receive sixty days at the workhouse. When the young Billie Holiday apppeared before the Women's Court after being arrested in a disorderly house, the fourteen-year-old Elinora Harris gave her name as Eleanor Fagan, which was her grandmother's surname, and pretended she was twenty-one in order to avoid a custodial sentence of three years at the reformatory in favor of a short stint at the work-house. As she had hoped, the judge (Jean Norris) sentenced her to four months in the workhouse at Blackwell's Island. This sentence was a month longer than the sentence received by the neighbor who raped her when she was eleven.

Wayward minor laws brought conduct such as drinking, danc-ing, dating (especially interracial liasions), having sex, going to parties and cabarets, inviting men to your room, and roaming the street under the control of the police and the courts. These counter-conducts (different ways of conducting the self directed at challeng-ing the hierarchy of life produced by the color line and enforced by the state) or errant ways of living were seized by the state in its cal-

culation of social risks and dangers. Risk was the metric for tabulating future crimes and this foreshadowing determined the outcomes of young black women already targeted and vulnerable to myriad forms of state violence. The actuarial logic at work predicted the kind of persons and the kind of acts that were likely to lead to crime and social disorder. State racism exacerbated the reach of wayward minor laws, marking blackness as disorderly and criminal.

———

Harriet Powell has been credited with nothing: she remains a surplus woman of no significance, a nobody deemed unfit for history and destined to be a minor figure. What errant thoughts and wild ideas encouraged her to flout social norms and live outside and athwart the law in pursuit of pleasure and the quest for beauty? Or to never settle and keep running the streets? Was it to experience something akin to freedom or to enjoy the short-lived transport of autonomy? Was it the sweetness of phrases like *I want you*, *I go where I please*, *Nobody owns me* rolling around in her mouth?

Wayward: A Short
Entry on the Possible

Wayward, related to the family of words: errant, fugitive, recalcitrant, anarchic, willful, reckless, troublesome, riotous, tumultuous, rebellious and wild. To inhabit the world in ways inimical to those deemed proper and respectable, to be deeply aware of the gulf between where you stayed and how you might live. Waywardness: the avid longing for a world not ruled by master, man or the police. The errant path taken by the leaderless swarm in search of a place better than here. The social poesis that sustains the dispossessed. Wayward: the unregulated movement of drifting and wandering; sojourns without a fixed destination, ambulatory possibility, interminable migrations, rush and flight, black locomotion; the everyday struggle to live free. The attempt to elude capture by never settling. Not the master's tools, but the ex-slave's fugitive gestures, her traveling shoes. Waywardness articulates the paradox of cramped creation, the entanglement of escape and confinement, flight and captivity. Wayward: to wander, to be unmoored, adrift, rambling, roving, cruising, strolling, and seeking. To claim the right to opacity. To strike, to riot, to refuse. To love what is not loved. To be lost to the world. It is the practice of the social otherwise, the insurgent ground that enables new possibilities and new vocabularies; it is the lived experience of enclosure and segregation, assembling and huddling together. It is the directionless search for a free territory; it is a practice of making and relation that enfolds within the policed boundaries of the dark ghetto; it is the mutual aid offered in the open-air prison. It is a queer resource of black survival. It is a *beautiful experiment* in how-to-live.

Waywardness is a practice of possibility at a time when all roads, except the ones created by *smashing out*, are foreclosed. It obeys no rules and abides no authorities. It is unrepentant. It traffics in occult visions of other worlds and dreams of a different kind of life. Waywardness is an ongoing exploration of *what might be*; it is an improvisation with the terms of social existence, when the terms have already been dictated, when there is little room to breathe, when you have been sentenced to a life of servitude, when the house of bondage looms in whatever direction you move. It is the untiring practice of trying to live when you were never meant to survive.

The Anarchy of Colored Girls
Assembled in a Riotous Manner

sther Brown did not write a political tract on the refusal to be
governed, or draft a plan for mutual aid or outline a memoir
of her sexual adventures. A manifesto of the wayward—*Own
Nothing. Refuse the Given. Live on What You Need and No More. Get
Ready to Be Free*—was not found among the items in her case file.
She didn't pen any song lines: *My mama says I'm reckless, My daddy
says I'm wild, I ain't good looking, but I'm somebody's angel child*. She
didn't commit to paper her ruminations on freedom: *With human
nature caged in a narrow space, whipped daily into submission, how
can we speak of potentialities?* The cardboard placards for the tumult
and upheaval she incited might have said: "Don't mess with me. I
am not afraid to smash things up." But hers was a struggle without
formal declarations of policy, slogan, or credo. It required no party
platform or ten-point program. Walking through the streets of New
York, she and Emma Goldman crossed paths but failed to recognize
each other. When Hubert Harrison encountered her in the lobby
of the Renaissance Casino after he delivered his lecture on "Marriage Versus Free Love" for the Socialist Club, he noticed only that
she had a pretty face and a big ass. Esther never pulled a soapbox
onto the corner of 135th Street and Lenox Avenue to make a speech

about autonomy, the global reach of the color line, involuntary servitude, free motherhood, or the promise of a future world, but she well understood that the desire to move as she wanted was nothing short of treason. She knew first-hand that the offense most punished by the state was trying to live free. To wander through the streets of Harlem, to want better than what she had, and to be propelled by her whims and desires was to be ungovernable. Her way of living was nothing short of anarchy.

Had anyone ever found the rough notes for reconstruction jotted in the marginalia of her grocery list or correlated the numbers circled most often in her dog-eared dream book with routes of escape not to be found in McNally's atlas or seen the love letters written to her girlfriend about how they would live at the end of the world, the master philosophers and cardholding radicals, in all likelihood, would have said that her analysis was insufficient, dismissed her for failing to understand those key passages in the *Grundrisse* about the ex-slave's refusal to work and emphasized the limits of black feminist politics. *They have ceased to be slaves, but not in order to become wage labourers*, she had amen-ed in enthusiastic agreement at all the wrong places, *content with producing only what is strictly necessary for their own consumption* and embraced wholeheartedly *indulgence and idleness as the real luxury good.*

What did untested militants and smug ideologues know of Truth and Tubman? Unlike unruly colored women, they failed to recognize that *experience was capable of opening up new ways, yielding a thousand new forms and improvisations.* Could they ever understand the dreams of another world that didn't trouble the distinction between state, law, settler, and master? Or recount the struggle against servitude, captivity, property, and enclosure that began in the barracoon and continued on the ship, where some fought, some jumped, some refused to eat. Others set the plantation and the fields on fire, poisoned the master. They had never listened to Lucy Parsons; they had never read Ida B. Wells. Or envisioned the riot as a rally cry

and refusal of fungible life. Only a misreading of the key texts of anarchism could ever imagine a place for wayward colored girls. No, Kropotkin never described black women's mutual aid societies or the chorus in *Mutual Aid*, although he imagined animal sociality in its rich varieties and the forms of cooperation and mutuality found among ants, monkeys, and ruminants. Impossible, recalcitrant domestics weren't yet in his view or anyone else's. So Esther Brown's minor history of insurrection went unnoted until she was apprehended by the police. (It would be a decade and a half before Ella Baker and Marvel Cooke wrote their essay, "The Bronx Slave Market," and over two decades before Claudia Jones's "An End to the Neglect of the Problems of the Negro Woman.") The revolt of black women against "the personal degradation of their work" and "unjust labor conditions," expressed itself in militant refusals: "'soldiering,' sullenness, petty pilfering, unreliability, and fast and fruitless changes of masters." Yet it had no chronicler. None responded to the call to write the great servant-girl novel.

It is not surprising that a *Negress* would be guilty of conflating idleness with resistance or exalting the struggle for mere survival or confusing petty acts for insurrection or imagining that a minor figure might be capable of some significant shit or mistaking laziness and inefficiency for a general strike or recasting theft as a kind of *cheap socialism* for too-fast girls and questionable women or esteeming wild ideas as radical thought. At best, the case of Esther Brown provides another example of the tendency to exaggeration and excess that is common to the race (and further proof of the fanciful thinking that mistakes loafing and shirking for embodied protest and a flock of black girls at rest for radical assembly). Nobody remembers the evening she and her friends raised hell on 132nd Street or turned out Edmond's Cellar or made such a beautiful noise during the riot that their screams and shouts were improvised music, so that even the tone-deaf journalists from the *New York Times* described the black noise of disorderly women as a jazz chorus.

———

Esther Brown hated to work, the conditions of work as much as the very idea of work. Her reasons for quitting said as much. Housework: Wages too small. Laundry work: Too hard, ran away. General housework: Tired of work. Sewing buttons on shirts: Tired of work. Dishwasher: Tired of work. Housework: Man too cross. Live-in service: I might as well be a slave.

At age fifteen, when Esther left school, she experienced the violence endemic to domestic work and tired quickly of the demand to care for others who didn't care for you. She ran the streets because nowhere else in the world was there anything for her. She stayed in the streets to escape the suffocation of her mother's small apartment, which was packed with lodgers, men who took up too much space and who were too easy with their hands, men who might molest a girl, then propose to marry her. She had been going around and mixing it up for a few years, but only because she liked doing it. She never went with men only for money. She was no prostitute. After the disappointment of a short-lived marriage to a man who wasn't her baby's father (he had offered to marry her, but she rejected his proposal), she went to live with her sister and grandmother, and they helped raise her son. She had several lovers to whom she was bound by need and want, not by the law.

Esther's only luxury was idleness, and she was fond of saying to her friends, "If you get up in the morning and feel tired, go back to sleep and then go to the theatre at night." With the support of her sister and grandmother and help from friends, lovers, dates, and consorts, she didn't need to work on a regular basis. She picked up day work when she was in a pinch and endured a six-week stretch of "Yes, Missus, I'll get to it" when coerced by need. So really, she was doing fine and had nearly perfected the art of surviving without having to scrape and bow. She hated being a servant, as did every general house worker. Service carried the stigma of slavery; white girls sought to avoid it for the same reason—it was nigger work, the kind of hard, unskilled work no one else wanted, the kind of work that possessed the entire person, not just her labor-time but her lifetime. The servant in the house—the ubiquitous figure of the captive maternal—was conscripted to be friend, nurse, confidante, nanny, and bed-warmer. The insult was that she was expected to be grateful, as if cooking and scrubbing were the colored woman's piano day, as if her sole talents were the ability to "wash and iron until her fingers bled and burned" and sacrificial devotion. Had her employers suspected that the better the servant, the more severe the hatred of the mistress, Esther would not have been "entrusted to care for their precious darlings."

Why should she toil in a kitchen or laundry in order to survive? Why should she work herself to the bone? She preferred strolling along Harlem's wide avenues to staying home and staring at four walls, and enjoyed losing herself in cabarets and movie houses. The streets offered a display of talents and ambitions. *An everyday choreography of the possible* unfolded in the collective movement, which was headless and spilling out in all directions, strollers drifted en masse, like a swarm or the swell of an ocean; it was a long poem of black hunger and striving. It was *the wild rush from house service on the part of all who [could] scramble or run.* It was a manner of walking that threatened to undo the city, steal back the body, break all the windows. The people ambling through the block and passing time on corners and hanging out on front steps were an assembly of the wretched and the visionary, the indolent and the dangerous. *All the modalities sing a part in this chorus*, and the refrains were of infinite variety. The rhythm and stride announced the possibilities, even if most were fleeting and too often unrealized. The map of what might be was not restricted to the literal trail of Esther's footsteps or anyone else's, and this unregulated movement encouraged the belief that something great could happen despite everything you knew, despite the ruin and the obstacles. What might be was unforeseen, and improvisation was the art of reckoning with chance and accident. Hers was an errant path cut through the heart of Harlem in search of the open city, *l'ouverture*, inside the ghetto. Wandering and drifting was how she engaged the world and how she understood it; this repertoire of practices composed her knowledge. Her thoughts were indistinguishable from the transient rush and flight of black folks in this city-within-the-city. The flow of it carried everyone along, propelled and encouraged all to keep on moving.

As she drifted through the streets, a thousand ideas about who she might be and what she might do rushed into her head, but she was uncertain what to make of them. Her thoughts were inchoate, fragmentary, wild. How they might become a blueprint for something better was unclear. Esther was fiercely intelligent. She had a bright, alert face and piercing eyes that announced her interest in the world. This combined with a noticeable pride made the seventeen-year-old appear substantial, a force in her own right. Even the white teachers at the training school, who disliked her and were reluctant to give a colored girl any undue praise, conceded that she was very smart, although quick to anger because of too much pride. She insisted on being treated no differently from the white girls, so they said she had a bad attitude. The problem was not her capacity; it was her attitude. The brutality she experienced at the Hudson Training School for Girls taught her to fight back, to strike out. The teachers told the authorities that she had enjoyed too much freedom. It had ruined her and made her into the kind of young woman who would not hesitate to *smash things up*. Freedom in her hands, if not a crime, was an offense, and a threat to public order and moral decency. Excessive liberty had ruined her. The social worker concurred, "With no social considerations to constrain her, she was ungovernable."

————

Esther Brown longed for another world. She was hungry for more, for otherwise, for better. She was hungry for beauty. In her case, the aesthetic wasn't a realm separate and distinct from the daily challenges of survival; rather, the aim was to make an art of subsistence. She did not try to create a poem or song or painting. What she created was Esther Brown. *That was the offering, the bit of art, that could not come from any other. She would polish and hone that.* She

would *celebrate that every day something had tried to kill her and failed.*
She would make a beautiful life. What is beauty, if not "the intense
sensation of being pulled toward the animating force of life?" Or the
yearning "to bring things into relation . . . with a kind of urgency as
though one's life depended upon it." Or the love of the black ordinary? Or the capacity to make *what we do* and *how we do it* into sus-
tenance and shield? What Negro doesn't know that a few verses of
song might be capable of stoking the hunger to live, might be the
knowledge of freedom that leads you out of the enclosure? Brings
you back from the dead or kills you a second time? Who could fail to
understand seeking a way out, inhabiting a loophole of retreat, and
escaping the imposed life as anything else, anything *but beautiful?*

To the eyes of the world, Esther's wild thoughts, her dreams of
an otherwise, an elsewhere, her longing to escape from drudgery
were likely to lead to tumult and upheaval, to open rebellion. She
didn't need a husband or a daddy or a boss telling her what to do.
But a young woman who flitted from job to job and lover to lover
was considered immoral and likely to become a threat to the social
order, a menace to society. The police detective said as much when
he arrested Esther and her friends.

––––––

What the law designated as crime were the forms of life created by
young black women in the city. The modes of intimacy and affiliation being fashioned, the refusal to labor, the ordinary forms of
gathering and assembly, the practices of subsistence and making do
were under surveillance and targeted not only by the police but also
by the sociologists and the reformers who gathered the information
and made the case against them, forging their lives into tragic biog-
raphies of crime and pathology. Subsistence—the art of scraping by
and getting over—entailed an ongoing struggle to live in a context in
which deprivation was taken for granted and domestic work or general housework defined the only opportunity available to black girls

and women. The acts of the wayward—the wild thoughts, reckless dreams, interminable protests, spontaneous strikes, riotous behavior, nonparticipation, willfulness, and bold-faced refusal—redistributed the balance of need and want and sought a line of escape from debt and duty in the attempt to create a path elsewhere.

Mere survival was an achievement in a context so brutal. How could one enhance life or speak of its potentialities when confined in the ghetto, when subjected daily to racist assault and insult, and conscripted to servitude? *How can I live?*—It was a question Esther reckoned with every day. Survival required acts of collaboration and genius, guessing at the unforeseen. Esther's imagination was geared toward the clarification of life—"what would sustain material life and enhance it, something that entailed more than the reproduction of physical existence." The mutuality and creativity necessary to sustain living in the context of intermittent wages, controlled depletion, economic exclusion, coercion, and antiblack violence often bordered on the extralegal and the criminal. Esther's beautiful, wayward experiments entailed an "open rebellion" against the world.

———

She had been working for two days as a live-in domestic on Long Island when she decided to return to Harlem to see her baby and have some fun. It was the summer and Harlem was alive. She visited her son and grandmother, but stayed at her friend Josephine's place because she always had a houseful drinking and carousing. Esther had planned to return to her job the next day, but one day stretched into several. People tended to lose track of time at Josephine's place. 5 West 134th Street had a reputation as a building for lovers' secret assignations, house parties, and gambling. The apartment was in the thick of it, right off Fifth Avenue in the blocks of Harlem subject to frequent police raids and tightly packed with crowded tenements, which offered refuge to runaway domestics and recalcitrant black girls; with as many as eight to ten persons crowded in two rooms, they flocked together forming transient communes, pooling their meager resources and sharing dreams. She was playing cards when Rebecca arrived with Krause, who said he had a friend he wanted Esther to meet. She didn't feel like going out, but they kept pestering her, and Josephine encouraged her to give it a try. Why not have some fun?

Do you want to have a good time? Brady asked. Rebecca gave him the once-over. Esther didn't care one way or the other. A smile and the promise of some fun was all the encouragement Rebecca needed. Krause would go anywhere as long as he could get a drink. Rebecca took Brady's arm and the others followed, aimless but determined to have a good time. If a man half-looked at her she would light up. Rebecca's free-floating lust was not directed at any one person. She liked company as much as Esther, maybe even more. When she was in school, the teachers often discovered her hiding out in a closet or hallway, locked in a tight embrace and kissing some boy. She had been "going around" since she was fourteen or fifteen. Others might have called her a "charity girl," because she accepted presents from her friends. All the girls did. She hardly ever asked for money, although there was no clear line between desire and necessity. Sex wasn't cordoned off from the need to live, eat, have a roof over your head and clothes for you and your baby; it explained why the names of lovers and husbands and baby's fathers were not the same. More than anything else, Rebecca loved going to moving picture shows and the theater, and her friends supported such pleasures. Rebecca had moved in with Josephine after her man Dink caught her at the picture show with another man. He cut her, but still pleaded his love, saying if she would do right, then he'd marry her. But she wasn't one of those *He beats me too, what can I do? Oh my man I love him so* kind of women. Nobody owned her. As quick as she could pack up her things, she moved out of the rented room where they had been living for the past six months and walked a few blocks up Madison Avenue to Josephine's place.

Brady didn't want to go to Josephine's place and said anywhere else would do. A tenement hallway was as good as any lounge. In the dark passage, Brady snuggled up with Rebecca, while his friend tried to pair up with Esther. Krause asked Brady for fifty cents to go buy some liquor. That was when Brady said he was a detective. Krause took off quick, as if he knew what was coming as soon as the man opened his mouth. He would have gotten away if Brady hadn't shot him in the foot.

At the precinct, Detective Brady charged Krause with white slavery (the trafficking of women or girls for the purposes of prostitution or debauchery) and Esther and Rebecca with violation of the Tenement House Law. They were taken from the precinct to the Women's Court at the Jefferson Market Courthouse for arraignment. Because they were seventeen years old and had no previous offenses, they were sent to the Empire Friendly Shelter while they awaited trial, rather than being confined in the prison cells adjoining the Jefferson courthouse. At the shelter, they cut up, dancing lewdly, cursing at the other girls, shouting at the windows to the people passing by, clowning folks, noting the virtues and defects of strangers, berating someone if he or she dared to look offended.

—Who you trying to be all dressed up like Mrs. Astor's horse?

—Hey you, yeah you, this ain't Virginia looking like a field hand in those clodhoppers.

—Off-brand nigger.

—You could buy that one for a quarter.

—Hey baby, you can haul my ashes.

—That dicty bitch thinks she cute.

—What the hell you looking at?

—Hey sweet poppa, I could put a hurtin' on you.

Esther was considered the worse of the two. As an unwed mother, she was deemed an outlaw, a pariah for procreating outside marriage and bringing a nameless bastard into the world. Her parents had set a better example than this. They had been married, but after her father died, her mother and grandmother were forced to work as live-in domestics, so she and her sister were sent to the Colored Orphan's Asylum for four years. There were rules and codes regulating the conditions under which children should be conceived and she had violated those codes. She had "thrown herself away" and given birth to a chance creature. Pregnancy could be made a status offense. Maternal neglect and improper guardianship were the easiest ways to "catch a case" at the Society for the Prevention of Cruelty to Children, and protection was the fast route to the reformatory and the prison.

A week of observing Esther and Rebecca's wild conduct was enough to convince the social worker, an avowed socialist, that the two young women should be sent away to be rescued from a life in the streets. They were waiting to appear before the judge when Krause sent word he was free. The detective failed to appear in court, so the charges against him were dismissed. Esther and Rebecca wouldn't be so lucky. It was hard to call the cursory proceedings and routine indifference at the Women's Court a hearing, because the court had no jury, produced no written record of the events, required no evidence but the police officer's word, and failed to consider the intentions of the accused, or even to require committing a criminal act. *The likelihood of future criminality*, rather than any violation of the law, determined their sentence. The magistrate judge barely looked at the two colored girls before sentencing them to three years at the reformatory.

———

Until the night of July 17, 1917, Esther Brown had been lucky and eluded the police, although all the while she had been under their gaze. Harlem was swarming with vice investigators and undercover detectives and do-gooders who were all intent on keeping young black women off the streets, even if it meant arresting every last one of them. Being too loud or loitering in the hallway of your building or on the front stoop was a violation of the law; making a date with someone you met at the club, or arranging a casual hook up, or running the streets was prostitution. The mere willingness to have a good time with a stranger was sufficient evidence of wrongdoing. The court, like the police, discerned in this exercise of will "a struggle to transform one's existence," to stand against or defy the norms of social order, and anticipated that this non-compliance and disobedience easily yielded to crime. "The history of disobedience," enacted in every gesture and claimed in the way Esther moved through the world, announced her willingness "to be ruined by standing against what is instituted as right by law."

The only way to counter the presumption of criminality and establish innocence was to give a good account of oneself. Esther failed to do this, as did many young women who passed through the court. They failed to realize that the readiness or inclination to have a good time was evidence enough to find them guilty of prostitution. It didn't matter that Esther had not solicited Krause or asked for or accepted any money. She assumed she was innocent, but the Women's Court found otherwise. Esther's inability to give an account that would justify and explain how she lived, or atone for her failures and deviations, was among the offenses levied against her. She readily admitted that she hated to work, not bothering to distinguish between the conditions of work available to her and some ideal of work that she and none she knew had ever experienced. She was convicted because she was unemployed and "leading the life of a prostitute." One could lead the life of a prostitute without actually being one.

With no proof of employment, Esther was indicted for vagrancy under the Tenement House Law. Vagrancy was an expansive and virtually all-encompassing category; like *the manner of walking* in Ferguson, it was a ubiquitous charge that made it easy for the police to arrest and prosecute young women with no evidence of crime or act of lawbreaking. In the 1910s and 1920s, vagrancy statutes were used primarily to target young women for prostitution. To be charged was to be sentenced because nearly 80 percent of those who appeared before the magistrate judge were sentenced to serve time; some years the rate of conviction was as high as 89 percent. It didn't matter if it was your first encounter with the law. Vagrancy statutes and the Tenement House Law made young black women vulnerable to arrest. What mattered was not what you had done, but the prophetic power of the police to predict the future, and anticipate the mug shot in the bright eyes and intelligent face of Esther Brown.

———

The first vagrancy statute was passed in England in 1394. The shortage of labor in the aftermath of the Black Death inspired the law. Its aim was clear: to conscript those who refused to work. The vagrancy laws of England were adopted in the North American colonies and invigorated with a new force and scope after Emancipation and the demise of Reconstruction. They replaced the Black Codes, which had been deemed unconstitutional. Vagrancy laws resurrected involuntary servitude in guises amenable to the principles of liberty and equality.

In the south, vagrancy laws became a surrogate for slavery, forcing ex-slaves to remain on the plantation and radically restricting their movement. In the north, vagrancy statutes were intended to compel the labor of the idle, and, more importantly, to control the propertyless, by denying them the right to subsist and elude the contract. Those without proof of employment were considered likely to commit or be involved in vice and crime. Vagrancy statutes provided the legal means to master the newly masterless. The origins of the workhouse and the house of correction can be traced to these efforts to force the recalcitrant to labor, to manage and regulate the ex-serf and ex-slave when lordship and bondage assumed a more indirect form.

Vagrancy was a status, not a crime. It was *not* doing, withholding, nonparticipation, the refusal to be settled or bound by contract to employer (or husband). Common law defined the vagrant as "someone who wandered about without visible means of support." William Blackstone in his 1765 *Commentaries on the Law of England* defined vagrants as those who "wake on the night and sleep in the day and haunt taverns and ale-houses and roust about; and no man knows from where they came or whither they go." The statutes targeted those who maintained excessive notions of freedom and imagined that liberty included the right *not* to work. In short, vagrants were the deracinated—migrants, wanderers, fugitives, displaced persons, and strangers.

Status offenses were critical to the remaking of a racist order in the aftermath of Emancipation and they accelerated the growing disparity between black and white rates of incarceration in northern cities at the beginning of the twentieth century. While the legal transformation from slavery to freedom is most often narrated as the shift from status to race, from property to subject, from slave to Negro, vagrancy statutes make apparent the continuities and entanglements between a diverse range of unfree states—from slave to servant, from servant to vagrant, from domestic to prisoner, from idler to convict and felon. Involuntary servitude wasn't one condition— chattel slavery—nor was it fixed in time and place; rather, it was an ever-changing mode of exploitation, domination, accumulation (the severing of will, the theft of capacity, the appropriation of life), and confinement. Antiblack racism fundamentally shaped the development of "status criminality." In turn, status criminality was tethered ineradicably to blackness.

———

Esther Brown was confronted with a choice that was no choice at all: Volunteer for servitude or be commanded by the law. Vagrancy statutes were implemented and expanded to conscript young colored women to domestic work and regulate them in proper households—most often white homes, or male-headed households, with a proper *he*, not merely someone pretending to be a husband or merely outfitted like a man, not lovers passing for sisters or a pretend Mrs. shacking up with a boarder, not households comprised of three women and a child. For state authorities, black homes were disorderly houses because they were marked by the taint of promiscuity and illegality. The domestic was the locus of prostitution and criminality. Is this man your husband? Where is the father of your child? Why is your child unattended? Such questions, if not answered properly, might land you in the workhouse or reformatory. The discretionary power granted the police in discerning *future crime* would have an enormous impact on black social life and the making of a new racial order.

———

The letter her ex-husband sent didn't say if the article appeared in the metro column of the *Amsterdam News* or the "New York City Brief" in the *Chicago Defender* or the City News section of the *New York Herald*, in which event only a few lines dedicated to the when, where, and how would have appeared, just the cold, hard facts. It would not have been a showy or sensationalist headline like "Silks and Lights Blamed for Harlem Girls' Delinquency" or "Lure for Finery Lands Girl in Jail" or a lead story of moral crisis and sexual panic manufactured by vice commissions and urban reformers. If the details were especially sordid, a column or two might be devoted to the particulars of a young woman's fall.

All her ex-husband said was that "a rush of sadness and disbelief" had washed over him as he tried to figure out how his Esther, his baby, had come to be involved in such trouble. He encouraged her to be a good girl and he promised to take care of her when she was released, something he had failed to do in the few months they lived together as husband and wife in her mother's home. Now that it was too late, he was trying to be steady. The letter was posted on

U.S. Army stationery and it was filled with assurances about his love, promises about trying to be a better man, and pleading that she try to do better. *You will not live happy,* he cautioned, *until [your] wild world end.* He hoped she had learned a *long lost lesson in the wild world of fun and pleasure.*

Esther's grandmother and sisters didn't know she had been arrested until they saw her name in the daily paper. They were in disbelief. It wasn't true. It couldn't be. Anyone in Harlem could tell you that stool pigeons were paid to lie. Everyone knew Krause was working for the cops. He would sell his own mama for a dollar. Stories appeared in the newspapers about stool pigeons framing innocent young women and matrons, sometimes to extort money from them or to be paid directly by the police for their service. Besides, if anyone was to blame for Esther's trouble, her grandmother thought, it was her mother, Rose. She was jealous of the girl, mostly because of the attention paid to Esther by the men boarding in the rented rooms of her flat. Rose was living with one of them as her husband, although the relation, properly speaking, was outside the bounds of the law.

When Rose heard the news of her daughter's arrest, it confirmed what she believed: The girl was headed for trouble. Some time in the country and not running the streets might steady her, she confided to the social worker, tipping the hand that would decide her daughter's fate. What passed for maternal concern was a long list of complaints about Esther's manner of living. Rose told the colored probation officer, Miss Grace Campbell, that her daughter had "never worked more than six weeks at a time and usually stayed in a place only a couple of weeks." She just wouldn't stay put or keep a job. She had a good husband and she left him. She was young and flighty and did not want to be tied down to one husband, one man, any man. What more was there to say? Esther just wanted to have her own way.

The neighbors told a different story. The mother is the one who needed to be sent away. Everyone knew Rose Saunders consorted with one of the men who lodged in her apartment. "What kind of example is that for a girl? That's no straight road."

The letter from Esther's girlfriend was nothing like her husband's. It didn't plead for her to be a good girl or beg her to leave the wild world behind or caution her to take the straight road, but reminded her instead of all the pleasures awaiting her when she received her free papers, not the least of these being Alice's love:

Dear Little Girl, Just a few lines to let you know that everything is o.k. I suppose you think I was foolish to leave Peekskill but I could not stand the work. I have not been used to working so hard when I leave Bedford and why should I do so when I don't have to, you stay where you are as you expect to live in New York when you are free. . . . It will surprise you, I am going to be married next month, not that I care much [for him] but for protection. I went to New York Sunday and seen quite a number of old friends and heard all the scandal and then some. . . . New York is wide open, plenty of white stuff & everything you want so cheer up there are plenty of good times in store for you. So I must close with the same old love wishing you well.

Within a few weeks of Esther's release, she and Alice reconnected with their friend Harriet Powell. They crashed at her place until they could find a place of their own. Harriet's mother welcomed both girls, not caring that one of them was white. They enjoyed a wild time in the city, making up for the twenty-five months stolen, dancing until nearly dawn, going to the theatre and the movies, eating at chop-suey joints, and keeping company with whoever they wanted, at least until the parole officer found them. "Both were free and neither good," Miss Murphy told their employer at the midtown hotel, making sure that the head housekeeper knew exactly what kind of girls they were. She began with the word *dangerous*.

———

Not quite two centuries after the conspiracy to burn down New York was hatched at a black-and-tan dive called Hughson's Tavern, the city's ruling elite still lived in fear of black assembly and the threat of revolt. The state was no less intent on preventing the dangers and consequences posed by *Negroes assembled in a riotous manner.* In the eighteenth century, slaves and free blacks who gathered in illegal assemblies were whipped. A 1731 "Law for Regulating Negroes & Slaves in Night Time" prohibited Negro, Mulatto, or

Indian slaves older than fourteen years old to be about at night without a lantern or lighted candle so that they could be plainly seen.
No more than three slaves could meet together on penalty of being
whipped not more than forty lashes. For "playing or making any
hooting or disorderly noise" the penalty was twenty lashes. Every
social gathering provided an opportunity for potential conspiracy.

In the twentieth century, the unregulated movement and assembly of black folks remained a matter of public safety. Gatherings
that were too loud or too unruly or too queer—or venues like hotels
and cabarets that welcomed black and white patrons; black-and-tan
dives frequented by Chinese men and white girls or black women
with Italian paramours or women who preferred dancing with each
other—were deemed disorderly, promiscuous, and morally depraved.
These forms of free association and open assembly threatened the
public good by trangressing the color line and eschewing the dominant mores. The governing elite, targeting this promiscuous sociality, manufactured a moral panic to justify the extravagant use of
police power.

Wealthy private citizens endowed with the authority of the state
and directing the police, ruled the Committee of Fourteen (the vice
commission comprised of rich New Yorkers and reformers) and ran
the State Board of Charities and State Prison Commission. One
of their central goals, beyond dominating the propertyless, was
to impose racial segregation in the absence of legislative decree at
the state or city level. Segregation was seen as a way to maintain
the health and morality of the social body and police power was
critical to achieving this goal. In the most general terms, police
power endows the state with the capacity to regulate behavior and
enforce order in the service of the public good. Policing blackness
was deemed essential to ensuring the health of the social body and
minimizing danger. In the eyes of the city's ruling elite, racial segregation was synonymous with the public good, and the imposition
of the color line a means of controlling crime by funneling prostitu-

tion, gambling, drugs, and other vice into black neighborhoods and containing it there.

In 1912, the Committee of Fourteen refused to grant the Marshall Hotel a liquor license. It was a gathering spot for progressive intellectuals, artists, and musicians. Paul Laurence Dunbar resided there. W. E. B. Du Bois and Mary White Ovington and other members of the NAACP gathered there for conversation, for drinks, for planning to undo the color line. A letter from Du Bois stating that it was a respectable meeting place and assuring the committee that there was nothing illegal or unseemly about the interracial encounters and meetings hosted there failed to sway the committee. The Marshall Hotel was one of the few decent establishments in the city that welcomed or tolerated a mixed crowd. Du Bois was not able to convince the committee that the Marshall Hotel was not a haunt for the degenerate. Interracial intimacy and friendship across the color line, not prostitution, were the issues with which the committee was most concerned. As the executive secretary, Frederick Whitten, explained in his reply: The Marshall Hotel encouraged "the unfortunate mixing of the races which when individuals are of the ordinary class, always means danger." When Du Bois objected to this moral defense of the color line, especially as it violated the civil rights laws of New York state, the secretary only affirmed the committee's position: "If we find that the association of the two races under certain conditions results in disorderly conditions and their separation results in discrimination based on race or color, we must choose between the horns of the dilemma. . . . *Disorderly is worse than discrimination.*"

———

The Tenement House Law was the chief legal instrument for the surveillance and arrest of young black women as vagrants and prostitutes. The black interior fell squarely within the scope of the police. Plainclothes officers and private investigators monitored private life and domestic space, giving legal force to the notion that the black household was the locus of crime, pathology, and sexual deviance. The Tenement House Act (1901) was crafted by Progressive reformers, official friends of the Negro, and the sons and daughters of abolitionists intent on protecting the poor and lessening the brutal effects of capitalism with clean water closets, hot water, steam heat, and fire escapes. From its inception, the effort to protect tenement dwellers from decrepit and uninhabitable conditions was linked inextricably with eradicating crime and social vice. The Act took for granted the criminality of the poor and identified the diseased home as the incubator of crime. Progressive intellectuals and reformers believed that social evils emanated from the slum rather than the structural conditions of poverty, unemployment, racism, and capitalism. While the Act was designed to prevent the overcrowding that was the prolific source of sexual immorality and to improve the housing conditions of the poor—insufficiency of light and air due to narrow courts or air shafts, dark hallways with no light or windows, overcrowding of buildings on lots, fire hazards in design and use, lack of separate water-closet and washing facilities, overcrowding, and foul cellars and courts—the benefits and protection provided by the law were overshadowed by the abuse and harassment that accompanied the police presence inside private homes.

While the Act did little to improve the housing of the black poor (with irregular enforcement of building codes or legal prosecution of landlords), it did consolidate the meaning of prostitution, and suture blackness and criminality, by placing black domestic life under surveillance. The specter of prostitution earlier attributed to the influx of Jewish immigrants now became a Negro problem. In 1909, the Tenement House Act was amended and revised into a series of laws with a particular eye toward eradicating prostitution and with an understanding of "the vagrant as the chrysalis of every criminal." The new law defined the vagrant as:

A woman who knowingly resides in a house of prostitution or assignation of any description in a tenement house or who commits prostitution or indecently exposes her person for the purpose of prostitution or who solicits any man or boy to enter a house of prostitution or a room in a tenement house for the purpose of prostitution, shall be deemed a *vagrant*, and upon conviction thereof shall be committed to the county jail for a term not exceeding six months from the date of commitment.

Any young woman residing in a tenement who invited a man into her home risked being charged with prostitution. The Tenement House Law expanded the provisions of the Criminal Code, making vagrancy an elastic, indiscriminate, all-encompasing category.

By 1914, "the majority of prostitution charges were executed through the vagrancy clause of the Tenement House Law." Thirty-six percent of these convictions were of black women. They were the largest single group prosecuted under this rubric. In the guise of housing reform, the police were given great latitude in the surveillance and arrest of black women and tenement residents. The bulk of the arrests were justified less for what had been done than on the suspicion of who these young women might become.

In 1915, the criminal code was amended again to "simplify" or streamline the evidentiary requirements, making it easier to arrest and prosecute young women on *suspicion* of prostitution. To secure conviction, all that was required was the officer's testimony. In the earlier statute, an overt act of prostitution was required—solicitation and the exchange of cash. Now only the *willingness* to have sex or engage in "lewdness" or appearing likely to do so was sufficient for prosecution. Most of the women convicted of prostitution were deemed vagrants.

Jump raids were commonplace. In a "jump raid," plainclothes officers, having identified a suspicious person and place, knocked at the door of a private residence, and when it opened, they forced their way across the threshold or they followed behind a woman as she entered her apartment. It was common to see the doors of rented rooms and apartments scarred, broken, and hanging off the hinges after the police officers entered homes by force and without warrants.

In its annual report, the Committee of Fourteen endorsed the jump raid as a reasonable response to the black presence in the city. While ordinarily a police raid without a warrant would be a "dangerous procedure" because it violated basic civil liberties, and the "unrestricted use of this custom would probably lead to police oppression," the Committee found these measures were warranted. By their assessment, the police exercised good judgment in conducting raids in such manner because "the conditions found to exist in the resorts so raided have fully justified the action taken." For those under the surveillance of the police, there was no difference between "good judgment" and police oppression.

Black tenants were policed more intensely and violently than their white neighbors, so it is not surprising that as a result of these regular encounters with the law, the buildings in which they lived contained more "disorderly houses" and "disorderly persons." The coordinated efforts of social reformers and the police had a precipitous effect on the formation of the black ghetto, since landlords who rented to black tenants were more likely to be prosecuted for violation of the Tenement House Law and fined as much as a thousand dollars. This contributed to the unwillingness of white landlords to rent to black folks, and then only the worst and the most wretched housing at the most exorbitant prices.

A police card illustrates the typical sweep of Harlem tenements, and the routine arrests. Once police entered a flat, everybody they encountered was subject to arrest. Billie Holliday was arrested in one such sweep, where more than a dozen women were arrested in a five-block radius. The irony was that Holiday's mother had boarded her in Florence Johnson's home to keep her daughter out of harm's way and to shield her from the danger of the streets.

4/20/29 Viola Taylor ar. conv.
        69 W. 135 St. Bedford

4/5/29 - Margaret Cornish
        40 W 132 . 180 days.

4/27/29 - Doris Hunter
        121 W 129 - 100 days

4/9/29 - Ampola Rogas
        75 W 118 St. Disch.

4/9/29 - Rita Giminez
        75 W 118 St.   100 days

5/2/29 - Alice Murphy - 329 Lenox Av. 100 days
5/7/29 - 146 W 129 - Patronta Dade - Disch
5/26/29 262 W 129 - Irene Cobb - Disch
5/17/29 40 W 132 - Estelle Stevenson 30 days
5/26/29 6 W 135 St Mary Williams 180 "
   "   "   Edith Thompson 100 "
   "   "   Marion Streets 100 "
5/3/29 122 W 137 Florence Jones Disch
   "   "   Mackie Thompson "
5/3/29 151 W 140 Gladys Johnson 100 do.
   "   "   Florence Williams 5 ds.
   "   "   Eleanor Fagen Hosp.
   "   "   Iney Allen Disch
   "   "   Julia Harris "
5/2/29 305 W 143 Florence Walker 100 ds.
5/10/29 125 W 144 Florence Jackson Disch
   "   "   Lorenza Payne "
   "   "   Lois Huntley Prob
   "   "   Alice Hogan Prob
6/4/29 at 100 W 141 - 7 fl. Lillian Willis 10 ds
6/2/29 at 42 W 138 Rebecca O'Bee Prob
        Frances Thompson
        Margaret Vyson Disch.
        Ellen Walker
        Louise Price

Mother and daughter were both arrested, but they did not disclose their relation to the police out of fear that it would invite harsher punishment.

Women were arrested on the threshold of their homes and inside their apartments, while exiting taxicabs, flirting at dance halls, waiting for their husbands, walking home from the cabaret with friends, enjoying an intimate act with a lover, being in the wrong place at the wrong time. In short, anywhere and at any time a young black woman encountered the police, she was at risk. Billie Holiday described the 1920s as an awful decade for this reason: "Those were rotten days. Women like Mom who worked as maids, cleaned office buildings, were picked up on the street on their way home from work and charged with prostitution. If they could pay, they got off. If they couldn't they went to court, where it was the word of some dirty grafting cop against theirs."

––––––––

In 1922, Trixie Smith recorded her first song, "My Man Rocks Me with One Steady Roll," for Black Swan Records. Its lyrics celebrated the sexual freedom of the age in explicit detail:

> My man rocks me, with one steady roll
> There's no slippin' when he wants take hold
> I looked at the clock, and the clock struck one
> I said now, Daddy, ain't we got fun
> Oh, he was rockin' me, with one steady roll

Smith had accompanied Fletcher Henderson at several notable Harlem venues and recorded with him on Paramount Records, had performed on Broadway, and was well on her way to becoming one of the famous classic blues singers, when a police detective entered her apartment and arrested her, along with her friend Nettie Berry, a stage performer and film actor. The detective had been watching

Smith for several weeks. He had first encountered her in a Harlem cabaret and then entered her home, accompanied by an acquaintance, a paid informant, who assisted him in "meeting women" and had introduced the two. The undercover agent returned a week later. On this visit, he asked for a glass of gin and then arrested Trixie Smith and Nettie Berry. Smith was charged with renting a room for prostitution and Berry with being a prostitute. Trixie Smith's two small children were home at the time when the alleged act was said to have been committed; in this case it entailed the willingness to entertain the plainclothes detective and offer him a drink. The two artists were arraigned in Jefferson Market Court in the early hours of the morning.

The headline of the story, which appeared in the *Afro-American* a few weeks later, read: "Race Actresses Said Framed by Cop." Only

the contracts displayed by their booking agent and community outrage that two distinguished artists could be treated with such blatant
injustice resulted in the dismissal of the charges against them. They
had been able to produce "witnesses to prove that they were both
working at their professions and bore reputations as being respectable members of the community."

Prostitution was a charge levied to extract information, extort
money, harass and abuse, and establish the boundaries of what a
black woman could and could not do. The *New York Age* and the
Amsterdam News warned women about the dangers of corrupt police
officers and stool pigeons, and advised them to avoid encounters with
strangers. Chatting with men on the street or inviting them into your
homes posed great risks, as did accepting dates with strangers. The
threat of punishment wasn't enough to deter young women from
associating with "bad company" or divert them from the errant
path, even when the costs were great.

————

The afterlife of slavery unfolded in a tenement hallway and held
Esther Brown in its grasp. She and her friends did not forget for a
moment that the law was designed to keep them in place, but they
refused *to live in its clauses and parentheses.* The problem of crime
was the threat posed by the black presence in the northern city, the
problem of crime was the wild experiment in black freedom, and
the efforts to manage and regulate this crisis provided a means of
reproducing the white-over-black order that defined urban space and
everyday life. With incredible ferocity, state surveillance and police
power acted to shape and regulate intimate life. State violence, involuntary servitude, poverty and confinement defined the world that
Esther Brown wanted to destroy. It made her the sort of girl who
would not hesitate to smash things up.

The Arrested Life of Eva Perkins

t was the first night of August and the third night in a row with a temperature near 100 degrees. It was too hot to sleep. At 11:30 p.m. Eva Perkins walked over to 135th and Lenox Avenue and picked up Aaron's supper at the café, three sandwiches and two slices of pie. Her routine had been the same for nearly a year, except for the two days she was in the hospital when she lost the baby. Usually, she arrived at the building where Aaron worked as an elevator operator by midnight. In the daytime, all the elevator runners were women, but the law wouldn't allow them to work at night. Sometimes, the runner from the neighboring building joined them for dinner and conversation. After an hour or two, Eva headed back to their apartment. By the time Aaron finished work and arrived home in the morning, she was at the factory, so they relished the midnight supper.

It was nearly 1:30 a.m. when Eva reached the front door of the apartment. She had a leftover sandwich in one hand and her keys in the other. In the hallway, she noticed a man she hadn't seen in the building before. "You want to have a good time?" he asked her. "I'll give you two dollars." "I am not interested," she said and left it at that. When she pushed open the apartment door, three detectives forced their way in behind her. They winked at the colored man and told him to disappear before they charged him too.

"Tell us where Shine is?" She didn't know anything about Shine, except that he lived one flight up. The rumor was that he was in France, but she didn't say that. "I don't know anything," she replied, trying to explain she had just come back from taking dinner to her husband. "Husband? You're not married," one of them said, laughing in her face. "You are just another woman of Kid Happy." Did he say woman or something worse?

The detectives called Aaron by his fighting name, like they were friends of his rather than the law who had busted their way into his house to harass and threaten his woman. Everyone knew Aaron because he had been boxing at many of the clubs in Harlem and at benefits for the soldiers and the Red Cross. The detective said he knew Kid; then barked, "Go ahead, tell us something." "I don't know nothing about Shine," Eva repeated. That's when one of them said, "You better come with us." The other one snickered and said, "Charge her with the Tenement House Law." Before they dragged her out, Eva asked to leave a note for Aaron. When he came home in the morning, he found it on the table. All it said was: I am locked up.

In Harlem, the police snatched you first and found an excuse later. After the 1905 riot in San Juan Hill, the police commissioner gave the officers a stern warning: They couldn't beat Negroes up without charging them with a crime; it didn't look good. Now if they decided to drag you to the station or beat your ass, they charged you with disorderly conduct, public nuisance, rioting, Tenement House Law. Eva didn't know anything about Shine. Half of the Negroes in Harlem were Kid somebody. Kid Happy. Kid Chocolate. Kid Midnight. If they weren't Kid, they were Sheik or Shine. It was hard to know if the "bad nigger" the police were after even existed; if he was one man or a composite, a monster to them and a hero to us; or if he was a figure colored folks made up, just a bundle of capacities endowed with a name, a badass hero of extraordinary talents, a Stagger Lee, a street-corner philosopher, a miracle worker able to find a way out from under the thumb of white folks and elude the everyday disasters of the color line. To defy a world unable to see Negroes as anything other than shines—shine my shoes, wash my clothes, and adore me. Shine was a beautiful myth about a Negro who could survive anything and everything a white man could send his way, and yet weather the catastrophe that was life under Jim Crow.

Shine was the hero of a thousand folk ballads; the alter ego of ex-colored men; the leader of a black Republic never to be; he was every Harlem Big Shot or striver with a dream; he was every man who wanted more and had failed. You could find him in nearly any tenement in Harlem. The stories eclipsed and overreached any one person or mere mortal, so it was hard to distinguish the lies from the truth, the fantasy from the facts. Had he been the only passenger to survive on the Titanic? Was he still a soldier in France or just a fugitive on the run? Was he a Harlem maroon or a ghetto rebel endowed with the gift of nine lives?

And what of Shine's woman—his mate, his friend, his sister, his comrade? Shine, not unlike Caliban, was cast into the fight without a female companion. The most significant absence of all in the dramaturgy of struggle, in the cosmic shattered history of black life, in the unfolding plot of the wretched, was that of his woman. Was the native son ever to be accompanied by a native daughter? Or was there no one at his side as he faced the world? As it faced him? Am I not an ally and a sister? Am I not here? Am I an absent presence? If the text of the human was written over and against him, she fell out of the order of representation all together. Neither subject nor object, but a mute, silenced thing, like an impossible metaphor or a beached whale or a form yet to be named. Her coming of age has been endlessly deferred. What place was there for Eva in the stuff of myth and imagination? Could the *Coming of Eva Perkins* or its tragic eclipse ever stand as allegory of the race, as the representative tale of blackness? In the drama between the world and him, she disappears, she falls into the black hole; she is the black hole, a person of no account. Unnamed, she waits in the wings, but without her own part to play, the catalyst of nothing. What has she to do with matters of life and death writ large? What about her desire and defiance? Or was she "reduced to having no will or desire except that prescribed" by master and mistress or coaxed by a lover?

What was the text of her insurgency? Did she also possess knowledge of freedom—the miraculous, unfathomable ways of escaping from under the heels of white folks? How did she strike back and lash out? She too had survived a thousand deaths, so why were there

no folk ballads about her or exaggerated accounts of her endurance? Stories about how she made a way out of no way? Was her fate to remain trapped within the impoverished realm of realism, or worse, confined in the sociological imagination that could only ever recognize her as a problem? And even in the absence of any evidence of wrongdoing always found her guilty? Yes, she was always to blame.

Had she no say in how the world made use of her? No way of talking back to power? How much rage could the body house before it exploded? What were the harsh words she was forced to swallow or the curses she uttered or the prayers she mumbled under her breath? Were refusal and nonparticipation and dissemblance her only ways to fight? Was acquiescence the mask of retribution and destruction? *Overcome 'em with yeses and grins . . . agree 'em to death and destruction.* "Yes sir" to hell and back.

Eva hated the police detectives who had forced their way into her home and arrested her simply because they could, because Shine eluded them and she could be seized as his surrogate. Next time, she would give them a reason. Silently, she harbored the protest and the complaint. No talking back, no expletives—not even a whisper. She vowed to tell them nothing.

Riot and Refrain

The reporters were most interested in what happened to the white girls. Ruth Carter and Stella Kramer and Maizie Rice were the names that appeared in the newspapers. Ruth was the first one to tell the State Prison Commission about the terrible things done to them at Bedford Hills: They were handcuffed in the cells of Rebecca Hall, they were beaten with rubber hoses and handcuffed to their cots, they were hung from the doors of their cells with their feet barely reaching the ground, they were given the "cold water treatment" and their faces immersed until they could hardly breathe, they were isolated for weeks and months, confined in the cells in the Disciplinary Building. The thick wooden double doors blocked all light, and the lack of air made the dank smell of the dark chamber and their waste and rank unwashed bodies unbearable. The stench, the sensory deprivation, and the isolation were intended to break them, to make order out of disorder, to wrench obedience from anarchy.

There were two hundred and sixty-five inmates and twenty-one babies. The young women ranged in age from fourteen to thirty, the majority were city girls exiled to the country for moral reform. They came from crowded tenements on the Lower East Side, from Chinatown, from the Tenderloin, from Harlem, and from all that these districts imply. Eighty percent of the young women at Bedford had been subject to some form of punishment—confined in their rooms for a week, confined in the cells of Rebecca Hall, confined in the Disciplinary Building. Even the State Prison Commission was forced to concede that it was cruel and unusual punishment. It was a reformatory in name only, and there was nothing modern or therapeutic about the disciplinary measures.

The aim was civil death: the mortification of the self, everything a young woman had been and might be ended at the gates. The numbers assigned replaced her name, possessed the body and indexed the state's dominion. In the identification photograph found in the case file, the numbers are attached to a plain gingham jumper, trans-

forming a singular life into a statistical profile, arresting her a second time. The numbers impose an identity and produce an account of her, severed from family and friends, sequestered from the world, held in the body of the state, and vulnerable to gratuitous violence. Her likes and dislikes, her capacities and talents no longer matter: she is now a statistical aggregate, a member of an abstract social category; she is an inmate, a prisoner. There are no props in the photograph, just an austere white wall behind her. She stares ahead blankly, steely-eyed, withholding everything, owning nothing. Her life and labor now belonged to the reformatory. The "before" shattered when Mrs. Engle drove her through the front entrance and escorted her inside the Reception Hall. Even a century later, reading through the materials assembled in the case file and poring over her letters, I am prohibited from calling her name, less to protect her than to guarantee her disappearance. The state never releases her, but claims forever this part of her past as its property. The photograph, which was intended to classify, measure, identify, and differentiate, offers no clue about the riot or her role in it, but I am unable to look at her face without anticipating it, without straining to hear its music.

When asked if hanging girls up, handcuffing them, tying them to their cots, and beating them with hoses was abusive, one matron replied: "If you don't quell them or rule them with an iron hand you cannot live with these people." When questioned why she neglected to mention such punishments, the prison superintendent, Miss Helen Cobb, responded that she hadn't discussed such practices because she considered them "treatment, not punishment."

The smallest infractions invited brutality: a complaint about dinner, a box of stationery found tucked under a mattress, or a note passed to a friend in another cottage might be punished with a week locked in your room or confined in Rebecca Hall or stripped and tied to a cell door in the Disciplinary Building. Black girls were more likely to be punished and to be punished more harshly. Esther and her friends were disciplined for talking too loudly and doing the Black Bottom and the Shimmy, which the white matrons considered dancing in a lewd manner; they were punished if they grumbled about being assigned to the kitchen and the laundry or questioned why they had to do the hardest chores at the reformatory; they were punished if they protested that it wasn't fair that they were not allowed to take the few secretarial or academic classes; they were punished if they were too friendly with the white girls. They were punished if, on visiting day, their sisters or mothers or husbands talked back to the matrons listening to their conversations, who interrupted whenever they wished, censored topics they deemed inappropriate, and never allowed them a moment of privacy. At Bedford, a colored girl was expected to work like a drudge and be treated like an inferior.

Most of the black women had been labeled "feeble-minded." It did not matter if they were intelligent, avid readers, songwriters. Ryan Lane, an opium-addicted poet, wrote a one-act play in verse, *In the*

Woods, and composed thoughtful, melancholy letters. None of this mattered, only the results of the battery of intelligence tests to which she had been subjected. She was labeled a borderline case of mental deficiency with a mental age of eleven. The Binet-Simon test provided "scientific proof" of inferiority and placed them beyond the possibility of civilization; as well, the feeble-minded were at risk of being confined to the custodial care of state hospitals for the rest of their natural lives and never returning home.

Rarely were black women paroled home, even when their husbands were working or their children were waiting for them, or if they had an aunt or mother with a decent place in which they could live. No Negro home was really a proper home by the measure of the state. All a "Bedford girl" was good for was general housework, and the demand for such labor was great. Katherine Davis, the first superintendent of the reformatory, admitted as much: "In placing a woman [in a reformatory] there is just one avenue open to her and that is domestic service. The present economic conditions are such that there is a larger demand for domestic help than we can supply. I usually have waiting lists for cooks, general housework girls and domestic servants of every kind. So great is the demand, particularly for general housework, that one lady said to me, 'I don't care if she has committed all the crimes in the Decalogue if she can only wash dishes.'" It was not the case in any other trade or employment. Serving time at Bedford made the "reformatory girl" a social outcast and trained her for nothing.

After two or three years confined in segregated housing, the black women were sent to white homes in upstate New York and forced to labor as live-in domestics. Parole meant being barred from the city, separated from family and friends, and forced into the grueling work that made the Mr. and Mrs. of the private home into wardens of the state, bureaucrats and overseers of domestic space. General housework was the sentence that awaited you after the first sentence had been completed. To the eyes of the conscripted domestic, the white household was an extension of the prison.

After twenty-two months and three weeks at the Reformatory, Eva had been paroled but not allowed to return home. Aaron was renting a room in someone else's house, and this wasn't a proper home in the opinion of Miss Cobb, the superintendent, although nearly half of the folks in Harlem lived this way. So Eva had been prevented from joining her husband; the marriage certificate with the official seal and the clerk's signature had not made any difference at all. The conditions of parole forced her to live-in as a general house worker for a white family in upstate New York.

Mr. and Mrs. Outhouse—literally, their names provided a cruel allegory of Eva's condition. The couple owned a boarding house, and in addition to taking care of them and their two children, Eva also had to cook and clean for eight boarders. Mrs. Outhouse worked her to exhaustion; she worked from the moment she awoke until she fell into bed—the duties didn't end until her body hit the sheets. Then there were the boarders and their demands, the propositions— a fifty-cent fuck or doing French for seventy-five. There were the hands she had to fight off. "Men who would not accost a respectable servant girl," acknowledged Katherine Davis, "think [Bedford] girls are fair game because they have been in an institution and presumably have been criminals." It wasn't surprising that many Bedford girls doubted the rewards to be gained by the straight road. "What is the use?" they complained. "Do you think I am such a fool as to be willing to go out to domestic service and do hard work for four or five dollars a week when I have been accustomed to spend more money in a week than you can earn in a month?"

Eva had written Miss Cobb and begged to be placed somewhere else, but after months with no reply, she decided to leave the Outhouses. She packed her street suit, two working dresses, and two sets of underwear, put on her sole pair of shoes and walked away. It was a violation of her parole. Now she was on the run—a fugitive from justice and an outlaw domestic. The investigator found her a few months later.

To be confined again at Bedford compounded the wrong of her initial arrest and extended the time stolen. How the hell had this happened to her? Like every other woman incarcerated, she had vowed that once she left Bedford she would never return. It was difficult to elude the state when servility and confinement was the script into which you had been cast. Staying free proved nearly impossible. Eva had never adjusted to the reformatory, which was what you were supposed to call it, but she was a prisoner. Two hundred acres of farmland and a lake could not disguise the fact. The beauty of the Hudson Valley didn't diminish the violence of confinement. The cottage system had been designed to provide the "good home environment" that poor girls—"economic and human wastage"—lacked. The cottages didn't have bars, but no one forgot they were cells. A matron locked you in at night and released you in the morning, yet you were supposed to see her as a mother figure guiding you to the straight road. The poorly paid white women employed to lead and instruct ranged from incompetent to cruel. No one in Lowell Cottage mistook it for a home. Technically the only prison buildings were Rebecca Hall, which had traditional six by nine cells, steel bars, mattress on the floor, and a bread-and-water diet, and the Disciplinary Building, with its ten isolation cells "having no furniture whatever, no window, the light coming from a glass in the roof" and double doors— the solid wooden outer door made it as dark as a coffin, except in a grave you had more air. The Disciplinary Building was a medieval dungeon, a tomb for the living, a laboratory for self-mortification.

Even if Eva resigned herself to the cruelty and deprivation and risked becoming complacent, an irate letter from Aaron reanimated her rage. Her captivity arrested them both, put their lives on hold, and wrecked the vision of all they had believed was possible. The glamour and hard-edged angular beauty of Harlem turned their head, made their hearts race, and catapulted them into the rush of street life. They were fast together and living the sporting life. It didn't matter that they were on the outer ring; they were close enough to brush shoulders with the beautiful people—the celebrities, the politicians, the club owners, and the gangsters. The sense of the possible was stoked by the visions of all the other strivers, running the streets, dancing in the cabarets, listening to street-corner lectures about the revolution and the new day, watching the parades and the fancy cars glide along Seventh Avenue: all of this made Harlem a Mecca, not a ghetto, and they were among the fortunate as residents of the black capital. It made romance all the sweeter and convinced them to hire a minister and go down to City Hall to get a proper license.

Love was their anchor—not a deed to a house, not property inherited from their parents, not a mortgage or a car note or five scrappy acres in Virginia or North Carolina. But love had no standing in the

eyes of the law. It didn't matter to the prison superintendent or the parole board. It didn't matter that they were happy, although living no better than average folks in Harlem and struggling to get by. Aaron's letters were dream books of some other life, an elsewhere they would soon experience; the letters were jeremiads animated by complaints three centuries old, tracts for abolition, promises for a grand life. He enclosed business cards from his latest endeavors as well as those from failed enterprises of which he continued to be proud—notary public, employment agent, producer, real estate broker, and boxer. In his letters, he shared his plans for the future; he was not afraid to dream, still confident that they could make a good life. As soon as Eva was free, he intended to move her to a nice house in Washington, D.C., where she would live a respectable life among some of the finest colored people in the world. Eva laughed at the thought of it—her in the company of the finest colored people in the world. In another letter, he railed at the superintendent for the contempt she displayed toward his wife and warned Miss Cobb to tread carefully because he wasn't a prisoner, but a free man with recourse to attorneys and state officials and the important people of Harlem.

Aaron and Eva wanted nice things like everyone else, but like most black folks they didn't adore property, believe in it as a principle like freedom or love or Jesus, or idolize and worship it like white folks did. What Aaron and Eva esteemed was autonomy, what they sought was an escape from servility. Owning things, land, and people had never secured their place in the world. They didn't need others beneath their feet to establish their value. For white folks—settlers and masters and owners and bosses—property and possession were the tenets of their faith. *To be white was to own the earth forever and ever.* It defined who they were and what they valued; it shaped their vision of the future. But black folks had been owned, and *being an object of property*, they were radically disenchanted with the idea of property. If their past taught them anything, it was that the attempt to own life destroyed it, brutalized the earth, and ran roughshod over everything on God's creation for a dollar. As items of cargo, they had experienced first-hand the ugliness and violence of the world as seen through the ledger and double-entry bookkeeping. They had endured the life of the commodity. They had been propagated and harvested

Miss Cobb I am a man and what is more I am man who is capable of making a dollar every and some time 20 and some times more. I can live comon life that is marriege life. I have more chartcher about me than that. Women with sympathetic immoral chartcher and unclean chartcher the reformatory is where

like any other crop, treated no differently from the tools and the animals owned by massa. They knew a corporation was not a person, not flesh and blood, and that a piece of paper secured nothing that a white man was bound to respect; they knew starvation wages weren't freedom, but another kind of slavery. The things they valued most had no price on them.

In the steady stream of letters Aaron wrote to the head of the prison, he maintained the injustice of Eva's confinement, debated points of law, challenged the devaluation of their life by social workers and parole officers, voiced her repentance, threatened to take the superintendent to court for suppression of his letters, denounced prison officials for keeping them apart, questioned Miss Cobb's decency and authority after she taunted Eva and told her that even if her mother was on her dying bed, she would never be released to see her. As long as he lived, Aaron vowed, this would never happen. In one letter, he questioned whether Eva was being used for immoral purposes. He had just read a book about such things happening in prison and needed assurance that his wife wasn't a victim of such abuses. Every letter insisted that he was nothing but a man, every inch of him, and as such he should be allowed to provide for his wife, and despite what her jailers believed, she was not a tramp or a whore. What right had the state to interfere in their lives? What authority had social workers and bureaucrats to decree that the life he and Eva had created was not good enough for Eva to be released and returned home, as if she were alone in the world, with no home, with no mother, no husband, as if their lives were trash? It destroyed them.

In his letters to Eva, Aaron promised that he would find them a place of their own instead of renting rooms in somebody else's house. Yet, this was nearly impossible on thirty dollars a month. Average rents in Harlem were twenty or twenty-five dollars a month for two or three small rooms with a bathroom in the hallway. If he could make more, fifty or sixty dollars a month, then he could swing it. When he boxed, he did, but he couldn't count on that.

The truth was that he could only take care of Eva if she was on the outside and working too. His letters boasted confidence in the future, but each strident assertion of what might or could be masked the doubt lurking in every line: How would they live? Would they ever be able to do better than struggle to survive? Or live the beautiful life they never stopped imagining for themselves? Reading his letters, Eva didn't know whether to laugh or cry: "I am going to get the house and I do not need any help. It will be my home in my name, my furniture, all new stuff: one brass bed, a rug, a parlor suite, four kitchen chairs, a kitchen table, one dresser, four large pictures for the parlor. It will be a home for you. I will do this because it is my duty as a man."

What kind of man couldn't provide a home for the woman he loved? What kind of woman could be treated as a mule or drudge, reduced to hands and ass, worked like a man and treated like a slave? There was no doubt or question about him and his place in the world that didn't redound upon her and cost her dearly as well. Maybe if they could find their way beyond this language of being a man and being a woman, this grammar of the human that regarded them both as monsters and deviants, and break free of a scheme never fashioned for them but imposed indifferently and cruelly, they might find their way to another kind of love and support, one capable of withstanding the daily assault of a world dead set against them. Why should they be tethered to white folks' notion of what or who they should be? Notions responsible for Eva's imprisonment and every nagging doubt they had about whether this love would last. Would he amount to anything? Could she trust him? Could she support him and respect him too? Could he trust her? Could they not hurt one another as their sole line of defense? Was it possible to refuse the roles that the world imposed? Was this required not to wound each other and to hold on to something as fragile as love in the white man's world? The barracoon, the hold, and the plantation had changed everything irrevocably, and the ghetto would exacerbate the difference between their intimate lives and those of white folks, make apparent that vows and contracts couldn't protect them or their children.

Eva and Aaron were bold in daring to risk love at all. Why even try to hold on to each other when the law could seize you on a whim? Why heed any of it? Was the failure to live like white folks only injurious? Or was there a gift too that resided in the "detour around the proper"? Certainly, *the Negress* occupied a different rung of existence than the mistress and the lady of the house, the very term signaled a

break or caesura in species life, a variant in the human, an antagonism or dimorphism more fundamental than man and woman. Yet,
was there an opportunity that resided in the infidelity to supposed
to be? In the refusal to emulate and mimic the standards of who and
what you were directed and commanded to be (but never would be)?
It was difficult to put this visceral and abiding sense of existing otherwise, at odds with the given, into words. Hadn't they spent the last
centuries asking: *Am I human flesh? Am I not a man and a brother?
Ain't I a woman?* Such queries and appeals had been imposed, desperate assertions that circumstance and necessity forced them to mouth
and inhabit. The humiliation of having to prove and assert over and
over again, *they were human flesh.* To what end? What opportunity
might be found in never uttering such questions again? What possibility for living a radically different scheme of being? Such wild
notions proved nearly impossible to articulate or to embrace con-
sciously and unreservedly, even as they suffered the truth of it, even
as they paid the cost.

Eva and Aaron had been married less than a year when she was
imprisoned. When he moved from their apartment in search of a
smaller, cheaper place, he put her wardrobe in storage because he
never intended for another woman to wear her clothes. He packed
each item carefully, including her best outfits: three ball dresses, an
evening coat, and two parasols, placing them in a cedar trunk for
safekeeping until his wife would be free. He pledged to be true, so
he swore to Eva and Miss Cobb.

Eva loved Aaron, but she also blamed him: "If my husband would
only use his head and get a little home together I would not have all
this trouble." She would be free and in her own house. Other times
she felt lucky that he loved her at all. He was dapper, handsome, and
a resolute dreamer, an unflappable idealist. For three years, he never
stopped trying to get her out, and most of the time he succeeded
in convincing her that he would find a way. He wrote all the time.
His letters were honest and passionate; they described the thousand

other lives they might create if they so desired. The handwriting was labored and nearly perfect, as if every letter was intended to be a public document. The tone of the letters was defiant, and for these reasons the prison authorities suppressed them, pretended they were lost, withheld them, and destroyed them. Eva wrote him, lovesick and feeling guilty, acknowledging that when he said, "I do," he hadn't bargained on all this. She joked that the blues had become his constant companion: "I bet that husband of mine is singing 'Sometime you get a good one and sometimes you don't.' And I laugh. Kiss for you indeed my baby."

> *Attitude about situation: Is quite upset about her commitment to Bedford. Says that her arrest is a frame-up and that it was an outrage to send an innocent girl to a jailhouse.*

> *Sociological note: My feeling is that she has probably been prostituting though we have no actual verification of it.*

———

Loretta Michie was the only colored girl quoted in the newspaper article. The prison authorities resented that the inmates had been named at all. It fueled the public hysteria about the abuses and endowed the atrocities with a face and a story. Loretta and several other black women testified before the State Prison Commission about how Miss Cobb and Miss Minogue treated them. Perhaps it was the sixteen-year-old's curly hair, dark brown eyes, and pretty face that caught the attention of the reporters and prompted them to record her name. Perhaps it was the graphic account of brutality that made her words more noteworthy than the others. Did she describe more vividly the utter aloneness of the dungeon—how it felt to be cut off from the world and cast out again, trapped in the darkness, how shouting out to the others and hearing their voices was your lifeline; or how your heart raced in fear that you might drown, even when you knew it was just a pail of water, but hell it might as well have been the Atlantic. The fight to breathe was waged again. How long could one live under water? The world went black and when your eyes opened you were beached on the dark floor of an isolation cell. Was the body suspended from the door of a neighboring cell yours too? Or the sense that the pain radiating from lifted arms down into the shoulder blades and cutting through your insides as your flesh was transformed into an instrument of the jailer could be felt by everyone else confined in the ten cells of the Disciplinary Building, and that these cells were connected to all the other cells that had ever existed and the awareness of being locked down and cast away could make a fourteen-year-old believe she was ancient.

The newspaper offered a pared-down description: Loretta testified that she had been "handcuffed to the bars of her cell, with the tips of her toes touching the floor, for so long that she fell when she was released." The colored girls, she noted, were treated worse and assigned to the heaviest and nastiest jobs in the kitchen, the laundry, and the psychiatric unit. Other women reported being stripped and tied naked to their cots; they were fed bread and water for a week; they were strung up and suspended in their cells, denied even the small relief of toes touching the ground. Their mouths were gagged with dirty rags or washed out with harsh soap and water.

Eva could have told the reporters about Rebecca Hall and about Peter Quinn slapping and kicking the girls had she been asked to appear, had she not been a fugitive (wanted for violating parole). But Peter Quinn didn't need anybody to testify against him. He was one of the few guards who owned up to some of the terrible things he had done, mostly to make Miss Cobb look bad. By his own admission, he helped string up girls about one hundred times. He was the one who "showed Miss Minogue how to first handcuff a girl to the cell partition with her hands back of her," and he knew that "at that time the feet were always wholly on the floor." Under the direction of Miss Minogue the practice "just grew" to lift them a little higher.

In December 1919, the women in Lowell Cottage made their voices heard even if no one wanted to listen. Lowell, Gibbons, Sanford, Flower, and Harriman were the cottages reserved for colored girls. After the scandal about interracial sex and lesbian love erupted in 1914, segregation had been imposed and cottages sorted by race as well as age, status, addiction, and capacity. A special provision of the Charities Law permitted the state to practice racial segregation while safeguarding it from legal claims that such practices were unconstitutional and a violation of New York's civil rights laws. State authorities justified segregation on the basis of natural racial antipathy, when in fact interracial intimacy—love and friendship—were what they hoped to eliminate.

The *New York Times* described the upheaval and resistance of Lowell Cottage as a sonic revolt, a "noise strike," the "din of an infernal chorus." Collectively the inmates had grown weary of gratuitous violence and being punished for trifles, so they sought retribution in noise and destruction. They tossed their mattresses, they broke windows, they set fires. Nearly everyone in the cottage was shouting and screaming and crying out to whomever would listen. They pounded the walls with their fists, finding a shared and steady rhythm that they hoped might topple the cottage, make the walls crumble, smash the cots, destroy the reformatory so that it would never be capable of holding another "innocent girl in the jailhouse." The "wailing, shrieking chorus" protested the conditions of the prison and insisted they had done nothing to justify confinement; they refused to be treated as if they were not human. The *New York Tribune* reported: "The noise was deafening . . . Almost every window of the cottage was crowded with Negro women who were shouting, angry and laughing hysterically." "The uproarious din emanating from the cottage smote the ears of the investigators before they got within sight of the building." Songs and shouts were the instruments of struggle. Terms like "noise strike" and "vocal outbreak" described the soundscape of rebellion and refusal.

The chorus spoke with one voice. All of them screamed and cried about the unfairness of being sentenced to Bedford, being arrested in frame-ups, the three years of their lives stolen. Were they nothing or nobody? Could they be seized and cast away and no one in the world even give a damn? Eva worried about her little sister Viola, who had been sentenced to Bedford the year after her. Was she safe? Was her cottage in open rebellion? Were Harriman and Gibbons and Sanford and Flower also up in arms?

A month after Miss Minogue put her in a chokehold, beat her head with a set of keys, and pummeled her with a rubber hose, Mattie Jackson joined the chorus. Thinking about her son and how he

was growing up without her made her wail and shout louder. It is
not that she or any of the others imagined that their pleas and complaints would gain a hearing outside the cottage or that the find-
ings of the State Commission on Prisons would make any difference
for them. This riot, like the ones that preceded it and the ones that
would follow, was not unusual. What was unusual was that the riot
had been reported at all. The state investigation of abuse and torture
at the reformatory made rioting colored women a newsworthy topic.

Loretta, or Mickey as some of her friends called her, beat the walls,
bellowed, cursed, and screamed. At fourteen years old, before she
had had her first period, before she had a lover, before she had penned
lines like "sweetheart in my dreams I'm calling you," before she had
received the first love letter from her sweetheart outlining in graphic
detail how she would take and be taken, she had been confined to
Bedford Hills on an indeterminate sentence. Mickey waged a small
battle against the prison and the damned police and the matrons
and the parole officers and the social workers. She was unwilling to
pretend that her keepers were anything else. The cottages were not
homes. Miss Cobb didn't give a damn about her and Miss Minogue
was a thug in a skirt. The matrons were brutes and there not to guide
or provide counsel or assist the girls in making better lives, but to
manage and control, punish and inflict harm. They let you know
what they thought: You were being treated too well, each cruel punishment was deserved, and violence was the only way to communicate with the inmates, especially the colored girls. Miss Dawley,
the sociologist, interviewed them. She asked questions about whether
they liked school or preferred to work, who was their first lover, how
they felt about their mother and father, whether they enjoyed the
dance hall or the theater, whether they smoked or drank or had tried
drugs; she dutifully wrote down everything they said, but her recom-
mendation was always the same: Prison is the only place for her.

Mickey rebelled without knowing the awful things the staff said
about her in their meetings—she was simple-minded and a liar, she

thought too much of herself, "she had been with a good many men." The psychologist, Dr. Spaulding, noted she was trying to appear young and innocent, but clearly wasn't. "Was it possible that she was just fourteen years old?" Miss Cobb decided the matter: "Let's just assume she is eighteen." What was clear was that everyone believed prison was the best place for her, a young Negro on an errant path.

Staying out all night at a dance with her friends and stealing two dollars to buy a new dress so she could perform on stage were sufficient reasons to commit her. Mickey cursed and pummeled the wall with her fists and refused to stop no matter how tired she was. She didn't care if they threw her in the Disciplinary Building every single day—she would never stop fighting them, she would never submit.

Disciplinary Report: Very troublesome. She has been in Rebecca Hall and the Disciplinary Building. Punished continually. Friendship with the white girls.

She had been in the Disciplinary Building more times than her disciplinary sheet revealed. In Rebecca Hall, she schemed and plotted and incited the other girls to rioting and disorder. She was proud to have been the cause of considerable trouble during her entire time at Bedford. She raised so much hell there that even years later, after she had been released and a new superintendent was appointed, everyone remembered her name, and it was synonymous with troublemaker.

When confined in the prison buildings, she managed to send a few letters to her girlfriend. The love letter seized by the matron

Singer Too "Tight" For Reformatory

NEW YORK.—Loretta Jackson. a cabaret singer who was serving a term in the new Bedford Reformatory for Women for violating the Sullivan law, was transferred to the penitentiary to finish an indeterminate sentence of from six months to three years. The change was requested by the superintendent of the reformatory who complained that the prisoner was incorrigible.

Miss Jackson was arrested on 141st street recently when a detective learned that she was out gunning for a former lover. She pleaded guilty to the charge and was sent to Bedford, where it is charged that she immediately began stirring up strife among the inmates. Amos Baker, the superintendent, recalled that while serving a sentence in 1917 the young woman acted similarly. Miss Jackson is said to be well known in musical comedy circles.

was written in pencil on toilet paper because she was not allowed pen and paper in confinement. The missive to her girlfriend, Catherine, referred to the earlier riots of 1917 and 1918 and expressed the spirit of rage and resistance that fueled the December action in Lowell:

I get so utterly disgusted with these god d__ cops I could kill them. They may run Bedford and they may run some of the pussies in Bedford but they are never going to run Loretta Michie. . . . It doesn't pay to be a good fellow in a joint of this kind, but I don't regret anything I ever done I have been to prison [Rebecca Hall] three times and D.B. once and may go again soon and a few others and myself always got the Dirty End. Everytime prison would cut up in 1918 or 1917 when police came up whether we were cutting up or not we were [there]. . . . They would always string us up or put us in the Stairway sheets but we would cut up all the more. Those were the days when J.M. [Julia Minogue] was kept up all night and all day we would wait until she go to bed about 1 o'clock at night and then we would start and then we would quiet down about 4 o'clock and start again about 8 in the morning. . . . Then there was a good gang here then we could have those days back again if we only had the women but we haven't so why bother. . . . I have only one more day but when you've had as much punishment as I have you don't mind it. Well the Lights are being extinguished so Good Night and Sweet pleasant dreams. Loyally yours, Black Eyes or Mickey

Lowell Cottage roared with the sounds of revolt. The inmates smashed the cottage windows. Broken windows and shattered glass are the language of the riot. Furniture was destroyed. Walls defaced. Fires started. They screamed through the night. They sang. They yelled. These gestures would be repeated in the years to come as essential tactics of the riot. Like Esther Brown, Mickey didn't hesitate to smash things up. The cottage mates yelled and shouted and cursed for hours. Each voice blended with the others in a common tongue. Every utterance and shout made plain the truth: Riot was the only remedy within reach.

———

It was the dangerous music of open rebellion. En masse they announced what had been endured, what they wanted, what they intended to destroy. Bawling, screaming, cursing, and stomping made the cottage tremble and corralled them together into one large, pulsing formation, an ensemble reveling in the beauty of the strike. Young women hung out of the windows, crowded at the doors, and huddled on shared beds sounded a complete revolution, a break with the given, an undoing and remaking of values, which called property and law and social order into crisis. They sought *out of here, out of now, out of the cell, out of the hold*. The call and the appeal transformed them from prisoners into strikers, from faceless abstractions secured by a string of numbers affixed to a cotton jumper into a collective body, a riotous gathering, even if only for thirteen hours. In the discordant assembly, they found a hearing in one another.

The *black noise* emanating from Lowell Cottage expressed their rage and their longing. It made manifest the latent rebellion simmering beneath the surface of things. It provided the language in which "they lamented their lot and what they called the injustice of their keepers at the top of their voices." Sonic upheaval was a tactic, a creative resource of the riot, in December and January, and again in July, when a clash erupted in the laundry room between a group of mostly black girls, including their white friends and lovers, and a group of white girls who hated the nigger lovers as much as they hated the black girls. When the police and state troopers arrived, the battle shifted and the girls fought them. The state authorities and the journalists were eager to label the clash as a race riot, but even so, they described the sound of the struggle against the state in the terms of black music. To those outside the circle it was a din without melody or center. The *New York Times* had trouble deciding which among the sensational headlines it should use for the article, so it went with three: "Devil's Chorus Sung By Girl Rioters." "Bedford Hears Mingled Shrieks and Squeals, Suggesting Inferno Set to Jaz(z)." "Outbreak Purely Vocal." What exactly did Dante's Inferno sound like when transposed into a jazz suite? For the reporters, jazz was a synonym for primal sound, unrestrained impulse, savage modernism. It was raw energy and excitement, nonsense and jargon, empty talk, excess, carnal desire. It was slang for copulation and conjured social disorder and free love. Perhaps this was an oblique reference to the sexual dimension of the riot. Improvisation—the aesthetic possibilities that resided in the unforeseen, collaboration in the space of enclosure, the secondary rhythms of social life capable of creating an opening where there was none—exceeded the interpretive grid of the state authorities and the journalists.

You can take my tie
You can take my collar
But I'll jazz you
Till you holler

Sonic tumult and upheaval—it was resistance as music. It was a noise strike. In the most basic sense, the sounds emanating from Lowell were the free music of those in captivity, the abolition philosophy expressed within the circle, the shout and speech song of struggle. If freedom and mutual creation characterized the music, it too defined the strike and riot waged by the prisoners of Lowell. "The Reformatory Blues," a facile label coined by the daily papers to describe the collective refusal of prison conditions, was Dante filtered through Ma Rainey and Buddy Bolden. (The sonic upheaval of Lowell Cottage echoed and sampled the long history of black sound—whoops and hollers, shrieks and squawks, sorrow songs and blues.)

The chants and cries escaped the confines of the prison even if their bodies did not: "Almost every window [of the cottage] was crowded with negro women who were shouting, crying and laughing hysterically." Few outside the circle understood the deep sources of this hue and cry. The aesthetic inheritance of "jargon and nonsense" was nothing if not a philosophy of freedom that reached back to slave songs and circle dances—the sonic gifts of struggle and flight, death and refusal, became music or moanin' or joyful noise or discordant sound.

For those within this circle, every groan and cry, curse and shout insisted slavery time was over. They were tired of being abused and confined; they wanted to be free. Aaron had written almost those exact words in one of his letters: "I tell you Miss Cobb, it is no slave time with colored people now." So had Mattie's mother. All of them might well have shouted, *No slave time now. Abolition now.* In *the surreal, utopian nonsense of it all,* and at the heart of riot, was the anarchy of colored girls: treason *en masse,* tumult, gathering together, the mutual collaboration required to confront the prison authorities and the police, the willingness to lose oneself and become something greater—a chorus, swarm, ensemble, mutual aid society. In lieu of an explanation or an appeal, they shouted and screamed. How else were they to express the longing to be free? How else were they to make plain their refusal to be governed? It was the soundtrack to a history that hurt.

Outsiders described the din as a swan song, to signal that their defeat was certain and that they world return to their former state as prisoners without a voice in the world and to whom anything might be done. There was little that was mournful in the chants and curses, the hollers and squawks. This collective utterance was not a dirge. As they crowded in the windows of the cottage, some hanging out and others peeking from the corners, the dangerous music of black life was unleashed from within the space of captivity; it was a raucous polyphonic utterance that sounded beautiful and terrible. Before the riot was quashed, its force touched everyone on the grounds of the prison and as far away as the tenements, rented rooms, and ramshackle lodging houses of Harlem, Brooklyn, White Plains, and Staten Island.

The noise conveyed the defeat and aspiration, the beauty and wretchedness, which was otherwise inaudible to the ears of the world; it revealed a sensibility at odds with the institution's brutal realism. What accounts for the utopian impulse that enabled them to believe that anyone cared about what they had to say? What convinced them that the force of their collective utterance was capable of turning anything around? What urged them to create a reservoir of living within the prison's mandated death? What made them tireless? In January, the women confined in Rebecca Hall waged another noise strike. Loretta Michie and others who had testified against the prison authorities were among them. "Prisoners began to jangle their cell doors, throw furniture against the walls, scream, sing and use profanity." They yelled and wept. They "carried on" vocally. "The medley of sounds, 'the Reformatory Blues,'" one journalist quipped, "may yet make a hit on Broadway, even if the officials appear to disdain jazz." Those locked in the cells of the prison building carried on all night.

The chants and cries insisted: we want to be free. The strike begged the question: Why are we locked up here? Why have you stolen our lives? Why do you beat us like dogs? Starve us? Pull our hair from our heads? Gag us? Club us over the head? It isn't right. Most of us didn't do anything to deserve being locked up here. No one deserves to be treated like this.

All those listening on the outside could discern were "gales of cat-calls, hurricanes of screams, cyclones of rage, tornadoes of squeals." The sounds yielded to "one hair-raising, ear-testing Devil's chorus." Those inside the circle listened for the love and disappointment, the longing and the outrage that fueled this collective utterance. They channeled the fears and the hopes of the ones who loved them, the bad dreams and the nightmares about children stolen away by white men in the back of wagons or lost at sea. The refrains were redolent with all the lovely plans about what they would do once they were free. These sounds traveled through the night air.

The Socialist Delivers
a Lecture on Free Love

n his lecture, the Socialist questioned whether humans were
monogamist by nature or forced by social convention into such
arrangements, emphasizing "the difference between what we like
to say and what we like to do." In February 1917, Hubert Harrison
delivered a series of lectures that challenged middle-class propriety
and respectability by considering whether marriage was an institution esteemed primarily for the disposition of private property, suggesting that monogamy was unnatural, although imposed by state
law and social regulation, and ill-suited to our erotic longings. On
the topic "Is Birth Control Hurtful or Helpful?" he detailed what
every woman should know about protecting herself and advocated
for free love. Only a few blocks away from where the police seized
Harriet Powell on the dance floor and arrested Esther Brown and her
friend Rebecca for their willingness to make love with strangers, and
fifteen blocks away from where the police arrested Eleanor Fagan
and four other young women in a jump raid on a disorderly house,
the brilliant orator and stealth libertine gave political expression to
the manner in which they had chosen to live. Not that the young
women needed him to justify anything, but his words amplified the
radical breadth of their actions. They would have been surprised to

hear their lives described in these terms, but would have appreciated Harrison's willingness to defend the errant path they understood as freedom.

It is possible that he saw their faces in the far reaches of the crowd that gathered on the corner of 125th and Seventh Avenue or 135th and Lenox Avenue as he lectured on a soapbox or spotted Mabel and Ismay among the audience at the Temple of Truth on a Sunday

evening. Given his amorous nature, he would have noticed attractive *too fast* young women assembled on Harlem corners, especially those who made it a practice of strolling Seventh Avenue with their friends at all hours of the night.

No typescript or notes of his lectures on "Sex and Sex Problems" remain, so speculation is required to recover and sketch his ideas. Is it possible that Hubert Harrison's lectures extolled the erotic life

of the ungovernable? Would he have advocated for the serial relationships that defied monogamy, conjugal union, and the law? Or
defended the wild unapologetic manner in which Mamie Sharp and
Esther Brown lived? Would his sexual curiosity have found a mirror
in their polymorphous passions? Would he have been able to make
sense of the letters from Esther's husband as well as those sent by her
girlfriend Alice? Would his cheeks have warmed as he read Frances
Rabinowitz's letter to Lee Palmer, describing in graphic detail what
a blonde mama would do for her black daddy? Had his erotic wanderings made him the perfect listener, or would he have been greedy
for more details? Would his ideas about the struggle against capitalism and the color line have been expansive enough to describe the
sexual practices of the wayward without making claim to words like
inversion or *pathology* or *prostitution*? Would he have embraced their
sexual variance while remaining silent about his own? Or would
his lectures have captured only the broad contours of the lives of
these young women, but missed the truth of it, applying to them the
same double standard he utilized when chastising his daughters for
staying out late or stepping outside of the boundaries of the proper?
Would he have been as blind as other socialists and tried to save the
girls from the street by making them respectable women? Would he
have seen their gestures of refusal as "responding to the call of battle
against the white man's 'Color Line'"? Would he have been guilty
of mistaking an experiment in living for a chronicle of transgres-
sions, or capable of recognizing their yearning and passion? Might
he have understood that they also were embarked on a radical project? Harrison certainly would have objected to and denounced the
police harassment of young colored women and the targeting of Harlem's tenements by the vice squad and the police. Without question
he would have explained it as the assault of the color line, as part and
parcel of the law's effort to subject the race, control their aspirations
and longings, and restrict the lives of young people to a variation
of the plantation, impeding and obstructing every attempted depar-

ture. The protest and struggle enacted on Harlem streets might be thwarted, but impossible to stop or eradicate.

For him, there would have been personal reasons, too. As all of his friends knew, he could be all-embracing in sexual matters and cath-

olic in taste, often weighing the prerogative of freedom more heavily than the faculty of discernment. It made him something of a joke, and he barely escaped being named in Marcus Garvey's divorce suit because of his passionate affair with Amy Ashwood. It was one of at least ten affairs he had during the course of his marriage.

While the lives of Esther and Harriet and Rebecca were described as tragic, his sexual foibles and misdemeanors were made the stuff of farce. Neither view is adequate or able to grasp the raw need or the insurgent passions that longed to destroy the (white man's) world. Claude McKay, known less well for his indiscretions than for the ease and facility with which he cloaked them, derided Harrison, making a joke of his erotic appetites in print. McKay was affectionate but ruthless in his description of the satyr-socialist, describing him as "erotically very indiscriminate." A government intelligence report filed in 1921 described Harrison in similar terms, noting that one of the chief reasons for the failures of this very intelligent and highly educated man and scholar was his "abnormal sexualism," which was unabated despite the fact that he had a wife and had fathered several children. The government report hinted at something more than infidelity. Harrison never tried to cloak his love of drag balls, which he attended regularly. In his journals, he described the beauty of women he encountered there. Each woman was a different world, a discovery. A hand resting on a sequined hip might make a man bow down, the casual gesture outlining the contours of the body, the jeweled fabric soliciting the gaze of the onlooker, daring one to touch, to imagine what might be possible; *the feast on this* attitude an invitation which he found impossible to decline. Had he loved any of them? Had he been open to the ball's experiment? Or guided by curiosity and willing to explore intimacies not defined by the polarities of identity? Did he accept that practices were flexible and changing?

His extensive collection of erotic literature had filled his head with a range of lovely variations and offered diverse blueprints of the possible; this very adult library was second to none in New York. Finding it imperative to "translate his ideas about culture and the superiority of the black man into the Harlem idiom through which to harangue the man in the street from a soap box on any convenient corner," he sold his library of erotica. In all likelihood, the need of money also forced him to do so. For much of his life, he lived in deep poverty. This had been the case since 1911, when he was fired from his job at the post office after writing a letter to the *Sun* critical of Booker T. Washington and the Tuskegee machine and black leaders handpicked by white folks. (The letter, titled "Insistence upon Real Grievances the Only Course of the Race," condemned Washington for denying the realities of race hatred and the dispossession and social exclusion of Negroes, while apologizing for Jim Crow Democracy and insisting that black folks should be thankful.)

The young Henry Miller was enamored of Harrison and marveled at his skills as a street-corner orator. The consensus was that Harrison, the Black Socrates, was the most brilliant orator in New York. It is uncertain whether Miller was privy to the rumors about his personal life, but perhaps he suspected as much, perceiving the intensity of passion and the spirit of erotic adventure in the force of Harrison's political rhetoric. Miller took such lessons to heart in *Tropic of Cancer* and acknowledged the debt in *Plexus*, insisting that sexual freedom was as necessary as economic freedom and that the volcanic force of an orgasm might be compared justly to an uprising. It was not news. Emma Goldman said it; Ma Rainey and Bessie Smith and Lucille Bogan said it even better, but when the white boy said it, the world listened, and it became philosophy, not entertainment. Few would have suspected the lines of connection between *The Tropic of Cancer* and *The Negro and the Nation*, or discerned Miller's debt and the tribute to Harrison. The lines of affiliation and the shared entanglements are apparent in radical analysis and stream-of-consciousness prose, written in opposition to the police reports and the statutory laws, battling empire and the barbarism of civilization. The two men stand as icons of the radical spirit of the age. The others—the sweet boys who spent the savings from a year's wages trying to outdo the black Gloria Swanson at the Webster Hall or the Hamilton Lodge Ball, the fast types who eluded the eyes of private dicks and barricaded Harlem apartments against the police so that lady lovers could flirt and dance unafraid, the working girls and the madams who offered refuge to anarchists and bull daggers, the recalcitrant domestics and dreamy laundresses who kept company with celebrities and chorines, the wild children who made church in the dives and cabarets of Jungle Alley, who danced until spent in the Garden of Joy, who imagining themselves liberators filled their pockets with rocks on a March afternoon after the first brick had been thrown through the window of the Kress Five and Dime store—remain unknown. They were the faces in the crowd, yearning as avidly for another world as the fervent street-corner orator.

The Beauty of the Chorus

n the Red Summer of 1919, nothing appeared more improbable and untimely than colored girls, not yet broken by want and deprivation, dreaming of what might be possible. Despite the forty race riots that eradicated the last shreds of postwar optimism, and white folks on a killing rampage from Chicago to Texas, and black folks meeting them with violence, battling them for their lives and determined to prove, if only to one another, that freedom wasn't a mockery, and the death tables and the graphic pictures of lynched bodies published each month in *The Crisis: A Record of the Darker Races*, and the color line enclosing the city and solidifying the walls of the emerging black ghetto, and the inevitable servitude of domestic work and the intimate violence of hurtful things done behind closed doors, Mabel Hampton still imagined that she could live a beautiful life.

At seventeen, she was as weary of domestic work as she was of Jersey City. For the past two years, ever since she had graduated from school, she had been working as a domestic for the Parkers and taking care of their sons. The family was nice enough; she would have quit the job before she allowed herself to be abused. No matter, she hated the work. Servitude was servitude. It did not make a difference if it was called personal service or household service, or if you had been "trained" for it; Mabel, like most of her peers, ached for something better, for an arena other than the kitchen or bedroom for the display of her capacities and talents.

If she stayed in Jersey City, no better prospects than domestic work awaited her, and she wanted more than a servant's life. She was easy on the eyes and had a lovely voice. Everyone told her so. Her uncle had been the first to take advantage of her talent. When she was nine years old, she trudged behind him through the streets of lower Manhattan, singing on command in the alleys and court-yards of Greenwich Village. People looking out from their apartment windows, hanging wet sheets and undergarments on clotheslines, and relaxing on fire escapes marveled at the little wonder and tossed nickels and pennies at her feet. Her uncle George stuffed his pockets with the change and then dragged her on to the next block. He never told her she had a lovely voice, or offered her a dime, but even then she knew she could sing. With the hope that this gift might provide an escape route from cleaning house and caring for children, she took singing and dancing lessons, all the while imagining a life better than the one she had known, and a vocation other than the domestic service to which she had been sentenced. Like the thousands of oth-ers bound for Harlem, she wanted a larger part in the world than the one she had been assigned.

Her friend Mildred Mitchell had encouraged her to audition for the chorus of a musical revue at Coney Island, and to her delight she landed a part in the show. Mabel wasn't the best dancer; but she was enthusiastic, and her hair looked nice when freshly pressed, and she was slender enough to fit the velvet costume worn by the girl she replaced. Mabel bragged to her girlfriends Viola Bellfield and Maud Brown that she was moving to Harlem to pursue a life on the stage. This was true in the details, but inflated with wild hopes regard-ing where the chorus line might take her and the freedoms afforded by Harlem. The vision conjured by such a life was as seductive to Mabel as to her friends, who regularly boarded the train from Jersey City to Manhattan in search of romance and adventure. With the exception of Mildred, all the girls that Mabel knew labored in the kitchen or the factory or the brothel. She and Mildred were two of the lucky ones. Coney Island provided her exit from servitude, and the stage was the free territory. Dancing and singing fueled the radical hope of living otherwise, and in this way, choreography was just another kind of movement for freedom, another opportunity to escape service, another elaboration of the general strike. Joining the chorus encompassed much more than the sequence of steps or the arrangement of dances on the stage of a music hall or the floor of a cabaret. Like the flight from the plantation, the escape from slavery, the migration from the south, the rush into the city, or the stroll down Lenox Avenue, choreography was an art, a practice of moving even when there was nowhere else to go, no place left to run. It was an arrangement of the body to elude capture, an effort to make the uninhabitable livable, to escape the confinement of a four-cornered world, a tight, airless room. Tumult, upheaval, flight—it was the articulation of living free, or at the very least trying to, it was the way to insist *I am unavailable for servitude. I refuse it.*

Like other runaway domestics and young chorines, Mabel wanted to be free. She did not want to make her living scrubbing floors or washing clothes or mothering other people's children. She did not want to be bound in marriage. She did not want a man pushing inside her and making babies. She did not want to struggle to feed and raise children of her own. She did not want to bear the hurt and the shame of being unable to protect a child. So she moved to Harlem determined to escape all of that—the marriage plot: daddy, mommy, and child; life on her knees—intent on making an entirely new life and at seventeen she believed that this was possible. If it wasn't possible in Harlem, then it wasn't possible anywhere. This city-within-the-city provided necessary refuge for dreamers, artists, strikers, migrants, socialists, landless peasants, anarchists, idlers, faggots, communists, lady lovers, and all others determined to fashion a life not brutally constrained by the color line, not broken by servitude, not cowed by white violence, not dominated by a man.

Three small rooms of her own in the basement of a Harlem tenement were an incredible luxury. Mabel delighted in not having to take care of anyone but herself, not having to defend herself from uncles and stepfathers. She had cast off the starched white maid's uniform forever and entered a world where all the beautiful people were Negroes. Her apartment was on 122nd Street between Seventh and Lenox, and she paid ten dollars a week, which was a few dollars less than her weekly wages as a dancer. Black Broadway, which was what everyone called Seventh Avenue, was right outside her door. It was a street "teeming with life and blazing with color," and where the energy pulsing through the streets exemplified the vitality of the ordinary. The tenement blocks of Harlem were the most densely populated in the city and its population would triple by 1930. Five years later everything would explode.

Lenox Avenue was a grand thoroughfare in which every element could be seen—fast women, petty thieves, itinerant preachers, hawkers and elevator boys, cooks and domestics, painters, writers, socialists, and black nationalists; and the dicties: the black elite, the entrepreneurs and professionals. Every hue of black folk paraded down the avenue—from eight-rock (blackest black) to the barely discernible Negroes, or, as W. E. B. Du Bois described them, whites with Negro blood. Without question, the beautiful, throbbing heart of Harlem was the black multitude: the West Indian radicals perched on their soap boxes on Lenox Avenue lecturing about the violence of capitalist exploitation and the injustice of imperial war; the nationalists at Liberty Hall spouting dreams of a black man's country; the spiritualists luring the melancholy and the homesick to speak with their dear departed ones; the southern migrants selling baked yams and pickled pig feet at the corner of Fifth Avenue and 132nd Street; the domestics, exhausted and near dead, trudging home in the evening light with their uniforms balled up in brown paper bags, eager to be revived by a bath, face powder, and a new dress from Klein's department store purchased for the one evening a week they didn't have to work; the lady socialist declaring in the clear, crisp cadence, the formal idiom inculcated by the Negro college, the black church and the colonial schoolhouse that a new slave market had replaced the old and that black women were still being forced to sell their bodies and their labor to the highest bidder; the children playing ball in the street when the traffic permitted and until dusk yielded to night and they were called home; the sweet men dragged down in finery and cruising Fifth Avenue with a yaller gal on one arm and a high brown on the other. The low trade still slumbering in tenement apartments, because they rarely appeared before midnight or retired before five a.m. This was the multitude: the small players, anonymous members of the ensemble, common folk whose tears and laughter defined the vitality of the Black Belt, the heart and soul of the beauty and the disappointment that was Harlem. Walking down Seventh Avenue, Mabel delighted in getting lost in the crowd, in being carried away by the rush of black, brown, and tan bodies, in being one among the chorus.

————

In the small sideshow at Coney Island, the chorus consisted of eight girls, including Mildred and her. The famous Henderson's Music Hall dwarfed the small musical revue; but it was still the theater and that was what mattered. Mabel's career was just beginning and, no doubt, she would go on to better venues and proper shows—the Cherry Lane Theatre, Lafayette Theatre, Garden of Joy, the Alhambra, and Carnegie Hall. Every time she stepped on the stage, she felt like a bigger and greater version of herself, or not like Mabel at all, and both experiences made her feel wonderful. She could remember the first time she sat in the audience of a vaudeville theater watching the performers on stage: she was transfixed, as if some part of her that had been asleep for a very long time was awakened and that she might feel deeply yet not fear anything. She enjoyed tremendously the singers and the musical acts, but it was more than this. It was the ache of being alive in every part of her body and overtaken by this rush of sensation, by the awakening of perception. At that moment, she thought: I want to be up there. I can do that. It was a tangle of emotions hard to settle. Intuitively she knew that she was slipping into another arrangement of the possible, the costume of another existence, inhabiting a body different from the one violated in a coal bin. This other persona might enable her to be more deeply in the world, to inhabit it without being harmed, or at least to endure it. When the lights in the auditorium dimmed, she reveled in this other existence, which was not at all her, as if the stage possessed the capacity to transform her personal calculus, to augment the basic sense of who she was so that all the parts added up to someone so much greater than she had ever been. It wasn't just the lights and the velvet costumes and the pulsing rhythms of the latest rag, but the beauty of becoming with seven other girls, which unfolded in public under the pressure and encouragement of the gaze of strangers.

After the last performance of the evening, Mildred's mother would pick up the two girls, escorting them home on the long subway ride from Coney Island to Harlem. On the train, Mabel and Mildred talked about the glamorous life they anticipated and wondered if and when they would leave the chorus line for something better. After dancing for hours at Coney Island, they would go to a Harlem nightspot and dance a few hours more. Usually they went to one of the cabarets on 135th Street, Conner's or Parker's or Edmond's Cellar, any place that wasn't dicty, where they weren't too dark to get in. The night passed as they cut up on the dance floor and watched couples do the Slow Drag, a smooth bump and grind in which the pair, cemented at the hips, hardly moved from their spot on the dance floor, or, if asked, Mabel might follow a stranger onto the floor and dance the Turkey Trot, a fast, free-style marching one-step in which one dancer moved autonomously yet in the pull of the other's rhythms. No bumping and grinding for her.

Dancing in the cabaret was different from dancing on the stage. In the music hall, when the lights illuminated the stage, you became someone other than yourself, and this person guided how you moved, directed your gestures. The chorus was transformed from a line of separate dancers into a shared body finding a common rhythm. And this body moved as one, erasing the borders of the bounded self, feeling and moving in concert, and communicating with the audience through the cadence of voices, gestures, variations of movement, and the rhythm of clap and step. Legs kicked, turned, high-stepped and pivoted as if all were coordinated, finding and inhabiting a place in the music directed by the dictates of a common body. The dancers also moved independently, orbiting one another like small planets, one body pulling away from the others, yet still connected by force, gravity, and propulsion, then rejoining the line, engulfed once again in the collective composition and the collaborative movement. The chorus moved across the stage, delighting the onlookers, making them wish they were up there too.

In the cabaret, it was not as easy for Mabel to shed her individual skin. The cabaret was as different from the stage as it was from the private parties and buffet flats (an after-hours club in a private apartment, the kind of place where "gin was poured out of milk pitchers"). Each space had its own script and set of requirements, dictated the terms of possibility, decided the arrangement and comportment of the figure. The challenge was to improvise within the space of constraint, bending and breaking the rules without breaking the form. In the cabaret, Mabel and Mildred danced with men because couple or partner dancing had replaced the group or ensemble dancing of the jook joint and praise house. Mabel preferred dancing with women, but even in places like the Garden of Joy or the Clam House, which were filled with pansies and faggots and lady lovers and bull

WOMEN'S COURT

VAG :SUBD.4:LOIT.:SOL.PUB.PL.   N.H. D. N.   CASE No. 1549

SUBD. 4 887. C.C.P.   .:F.R.H.:T.C   DATE 7 - 6 - 24

SUBD. 150. T.H.L.   P.H: HOTEL   AGE   NATIVITY

WAYWARD MINOR

DEFENDANT   Mabel Hampton   21, U.S   B W

LOCATION OF OFFENSE 40 W 123 St. 3 fl.   APARTMENT

WITNESS Schlucker   S.S.   PRICE $ POLICE CTF.   SOL. J.R.

CUSTOMER'S ADDRESS

BAIL—BONDSMAN   COUNSEL   P.G. — P.N.   CONV. MAG. DISCH.   hours

ADJS. DATE 1 -7/7   SENTENCE Bedford   MAG. aw.

PRIOR CONV'S, PROST 0   INTOX, ETC   F. P. B. # ✓

HEALTH REPORT
INFECTIOUS   NON-INFECTIOUS   NO CTF.   MENTALLY SUB-NORMAL.   DRUG ADDICT

daggers, she didn't feel safe dancing with a woman in her arms. Off stage, she was extremely careful not to invite the scrutiny of men, and she dissuaded their pursuit. On more than one occasion when she deflected the advances of a would-be admirer, the man wondered aloud, "What's wrong with you?" or intoned in a voice that was part threat and part invitation, "I can see it in your eyes. I know what you want." The one time she feigned interest and played the part, it cost her dearly. She never told anyone the reason she didn't hear Fletcher Henderson and his Club Alabam' Orchestra that summer or why she disappeared. Why should everyone in the world know her business?

The private parties hosted by friends in Harlem flats were the only places she felt comfortable, safe. These gatherings had an entirely different set of arrangements. There were no white folks observing her like she was a rare specimen, or a strange kind of human. No men to intrude or force their way on a girl, unless an irate husband appeared. No downtown folks eager to gawk at faggots and Negroes, only the white wives and girlfriends of black bull daggers and lady lovers. Most of her friends were theater people, and half of them were women lovers and in the life. *Harlem was surely as queer as it was black.*

At the music hall, cabaret, and private party, Mabel tried to dance her way into feeling free, to compose a wild and beautiful life, to step onto an errant path that might guide her to the wonderful experiences afforded by Harlem. Every step executed on the dance floor was an effort to elude the prohibitions and punishments that increasingly hemmed in the ghetto and that awaited young women daring to live outside the boundaries of marriage and servitude or move through the city unescorted by a husband or brother. Mildred and Mabel risked the danger to enjoy the little freedom they could claim.

On the dance floor, they refused the world that refused them: to hell with the blocks where Negroes were not allowed to live, the restaurants that declined to serve them, the retail stores that shut their doors rather than hire them. Damn the dicty Negroes and the clubs and speakeasies that barred them at the threshold because they were too black and too poor.

The aspiration that fueled these bodies in motion and enabled assembly connected the chorus line to the bodies huddled on the floor of the cabaret, cruising down Seventh Avenue and grinding away in Harlem flats. All these sweaty bodies gathered on the floor sought escape from the dull routine of work and the new forms of capture waiting right outside the door and sometimes inside the club. Mabel moved with the rest, cramped and crushed on the dance floor. For a few hours after work or until the dawn broke, she was permitted a small reprieve from the fear and terror residing deep in the body, glistening and elated, she escaped loneliness.

At the small tables crammed into the space and surrounding the dance floor were the police informants and vice investigators trying to blend in with the crowd, to get lost in the swarm. They jotted notes about the layout of the club, the names of regulars, and guessed who was tricking, who was just out for a good time. The notes scrawled on the pages of a small lined pad described the suggestive moves of young women as low-class and obscene, and a too-bright smile or invitation to have a drink were all the proof needed to secure an

arrest the following night. The reports filed for the vice commission labeled young women like Mabel and her friends as prostitutes and described the cabaret as "a meeting place for cocaine fiends, street walkers, sissies and pimps. Colored and white frequent the place, although a sign at the door said, 'Colored Only.'"

In the broken circle of the dance floor, Mabel and her friends readied to get free. That little extra something, that improvisation of becoming together, that call to assembly, that two-step and slide announcing the struggle against an imposed life, that sensual embrace of a body unmarked by stigma and undisciplined by servitude.

It didn't matter whether it was a basement dive or a music hall. In its broadest sense, choreography—this practice of bodies in motion—was a call to freedom. The swivel and circle of hips, the nasty elegance of the Shimmy, the *changing-same* of collective movement, the repetition, the improvisation of escape and subsistence, bodied forth the shared dream of scrub maids, elevator boys, whores, sweet men, stevedores, chorus girls, and tenement dwellers—not to be fixed at the bottom, not to be walled in the ghetto. Each dance was a rehearsal for escape. The funky rhythms of a ragtime drag encouraged them to believe that they might evade the iron hand of social law and the prison of cold hard facts. The odds weren't in their favor, and in all probability they would remain exactly where they were: stuck in place, living on low wages, and with few signs of change on the horizon.

On the dance floor it was clear that existence was not only a struggle, but a beautiful experiment too. It was an inquiry about how to live when the future was foreclosed. How was it possible to thrive under assault? Could the joy afforded by the cabaret attenuate the assault of racism? Help dancers shake off the stranglehold of poverty for a few hours? Quiet any doubts about life in peril? Or was the experiment to remake the world that defined its mission against you and yours?

When Chandler Owen published his essay "The Cabaret as a Useful Social Institution" in the August 1922 issue of *The Messenger*, the most radical of black periodicals (and one described in a government memo by the architect of the Red Scare, Attorney General A. Mitchell Palmer, as "the most able and the most dangerous of all the Negro publications"), he identified the cabaret as the only democratic institution in the United States. It was the sole institution not defined by Jim Crow and that refused to embrace segregation. No doubt, Owen had in mind young women like Mabel and Mildred and their hunger for a new set of social arrangements. The young socialist charted clearly the connections between the sexual appetite and the movements of the dance floor—and the dance floor itself as a movement against racism and instrument in the reconstruction of American democracy. For him, the cabaret was an institution opposed to the confinement of the ghetto and segregation imposed by the color line. It had proven to be the single place capable of withstanding the violence and hatred of the race riot. Only in the cabaret, he wrote, can we find "hundreds of white men and colored men . . . white women and colored women, seated at tables, talking and drinking, enjoying the music, dancing when they cared to." This interracial sociality was policed and punished by the vice commission in an age that

Emma Goldman characterized as plagued by "an epidemic of vir-tue." Owen went so far as to describe the prohibition of interracial sociality and intimacy as a *race riot in the realm of pleasure*. Besides radicals and militants, artists and libertines, few others dared breach the color line.

Had he been privy to the parties Mabel and her friends were throwing in the private flats of Harlem, and observed the crowd assembled on the dance floor where the most handsome sheiks were sometimes named Jackie and Bobbie, or discerned the ways in which refusing the gender script was a frontal assault on the color line, then Owen might have been able to embrace what happened at private socials in Harlem tenements as another effort at the recon-struction of everything. The private parties and the buffet flats more ably eluded the scrutiny of the police and the state. The lady lovers who assembled in Harlem flats created freedom in sequestered zones beyond the reach of private investigators, voyeurs, and downtown folks slumming. Private homes and tenements provided a clandestine space, a loophole of retreat, within the highly policed and surveilled zone of the Harlem ghetto.

Spending an evening with Mabel and other young black women intent on defying the proscriptions of the ruling elites and the race leaders (who had entered a gentleman's agreement regarding segre-gation and abided the values of the patriarchal home) might have made Owen less uneasy about masculine women and enabled him to recognize that the fidelity to gender roles and punishment of sexual variance were other ways of maintaining and policing the color line.

————

A place like Edmond's Cellar was thick with lust and need, and this public intimacy was indifferent to privacy as well as the color line. The moan and cry of the Slow Drag's raw edge troubled the distinc-tion between shaking it and having sex, between dance and crime, as anyone listening to the conversations on the dance floor could attest:

"Oh baby, shake it!"

"I mean I can do it," she said.

"Yes you have such a little of it you ought to be able to do it."

"It may be little, but there is enough of it to snatch the [life] from you," she replied.

"Yeah. I believe it."

"Well. I'll show you."

"What's the matter, sweet papa? Don't you want some of this good stuff?"

"How much would it cost?"

"I charge white men five dollars, but colored men only three," she replied.

In the early hours of the morning, the two exhausted chorines returned to Mildred's house sweaty and aroused. In bed, they kissed and held each other as if they were husband and wife, as if Mabel were Mr. Hampton.

———

Mrs. Mitchell welcomed the motherless girl as her own. She especially liked Mabel because she was bright and charming, which was exactly the way Mabel desired to be seen, so she jumped at the attention, enjoying being treated like a second daughter. Since the age of ten, her life had depended on being able to charm her way into the families of strangers, as well as those of her friends. It was a skill honed by loss. Her mother died when she was just a month old, so her grandmother had raised her until she was eight, the last year she was a child. The thump of her grandmother's body hitting the kitchen floor was a sound that would stay with her for the rest of her life. When it was clear that her grandmother would not recover from the stroke, her aunt Nancy arrived from New York. Mabel could barely remember the funeral, only that her aunt packed up the entire house and sold off everything in two days. Aware that she would never again see the small clapboard house with its beautiful fence of rose bushes or the persimmon trees, or the Black Maples and the Shag-bark Hickory and the thickets of blackberries that populated the woods where she played with her friends, or smell the thick odor of overripe grapes decaying in the backyard arbor, Mabel sobbed the entire train ride from North Carolina to New York. Her aunt didn't try to comfort her. On the journey it was apparent that she didn't care at all for Mabel. In Winston-Salem she had made a great show of raising her dead sister's child, but really all she cared about was her grandmother's money. When they finally arrived at Pennsylvania Station, her aunt's husband was waiting to escort them home. Mabel, this is your uncle, Reverend George Mills. He was a tall man with chiseled features and pretty, wavy hair. But when she looked at him, she was afraid.

The granite cobblestones and red bricks that paved the path and the courtyard of her aunt's building were beautiful. When she looked out of the window, the sheets and clothes hanging on the line obstructed the sky and cast shadows in the yard. Greenwich Village looked nothing like Winston-Salem. They lived on the ground floor in a small apartment with a living room, a dining room and one bedroom. Mabel didn't have her own bed like she did in her grandmother's house. Her uncle forced her to sleep on the floor of the kitchen or in the coal bin, and her aunt said nothing to avoid a blow. On Sundays, the Reverend Mills's tiny congregation met in the living room. Mabel arranged the chairs so that the apartment resembled a church. She had attended a proper church with her grandmother, with a real minister who came to their house every Sunday for supper, so she didn't think that George Mills's living room looked like a church. During the week, she accompanied him throughout the city as he ministered to strangers and she sang spirituals and hymns. On their way back to Eighth Street, Mabel prayed that her aunt would be home, not because she was able to protect Mabel, but because at least she provided another object for his rage. The window in the bedroom opened onto the courtyard, and only the fear that the neighbors would hear sometimes made the reverend stop. He pinned Mabel's arms to the bed and muffled her screams with his hands. She kicked her legs and flinched with the weight of him. From the bed, she could see into the courtyard, and she tried to make her heart as hard as those stones. *He had already killed a white man, so he wouldn't think nothing of killing a nigger.* She knew not to tell anyone.

———

Ada Overton Walker or Ethel Waters? Ethel Williams or Inez Clough? Over plates heavy with fried chicken, potato salad, and collards, the girls argued about who was the best performer. They stuffed themselves, cussing and telling nasty stories because Mrs. Mitchell wasn't at home. Mabel and Mildred and the other girls from the chorus surrounded the table, but they sounded as if there were twenty of them, acting grown, talking over one another, the floor ceded to the loudest. They tried to shock and impress one another with how much they knew about men. Did it matter how long it was or just how thick? I know you didn't do French on that Negro. Girl, you are telling lies. It don't make a damn bit of difference if he just doing his business and not thinking at all about you. They compared their male lovers with their female lovers and agreed that women were sweeter lovers than men, although sometimes you needed the tool. Fingers could do just as well! Laughter erupted. Mabel stayed quiet. She was shy to admit that she had never had a lover. Only when they complained about life in the theater, damning the managers and producers who always found an excuse to put a hand where it was not wanted, or who tried to lure or harass a girl into a quick date under the boardwalk, did she feel free to speak with as much authority as the others. She was sick and tired of men trying to put their hands up her skirt and feel her pussy. All of them busted out laughing because they didn't expect sweet little Mabel to talk like a sailor. They worried about where they would work when the season ended. Mildred danced at a Harlem cabaret in addition to Coney

Island. There was sometimes work at the Lafayette Theatre, but unless you were an h.y., they wouldn't look at you. H.Y.? Welcome to the Negro theatre. They schooled Mabel about the color code: d.c. = dark cloud/black (there was never a place for a dark-skinned girl in the chorus); s.j. = smokey joe/brown-skinned; h.y. = high yellow. Virtually all of the female leads and dancers at the fancy Harlem clubs for downtown folks were light, bright, and damn near white. r.b. = red bone. There was a huge argument about whether a red bone was someone who was high brown with a reddish tone or a very fair-skinned person with light eyes or light hair. It didn't matter. The point was—your complexion decided where you could play, who looked up to you and who looked down on you. They argued about the best kind of face cream for lightening your skin and agreed that Madame Walker's face powder could make any brown skin look like a yellow girl, bleach you at least two or three shades. You didn't have to be light, just look it. Anyone could pass for a mulatto if the house lights were bright enough.

When Mrs. Mitchell entered the house with her friend Gladys, the tone of the conversation shifted. Mabel hardly said a word, but now

for different reasons. Gladys was about the same age as Mildred's mother, maybe even older, but she was handsome and dashing, a wild flash of a woman suggesting trouble. When Mabel looked at her, she started to feel funny, so she dropped her eyes, but when she looked up again, this beautiful woman, tall and brown skinned with gray hair, was looking at her, and a thrill shot through her like electricity. Gladys danced at Coney Island, but in a different act. Most of the girls in the chorus were not much older than Mabel, who at seventeen still looked like a child because she was so petite. She was unsettled by this woman and tried to sort out what made her feel so uncomfortable. Was it the ache in the pit of her stomach or the heat in her private parts? She felt powerless, and it frightened her; yet she couldn't stop looking at this woman. Mildred noticed it and so did Mrs. Mitchell. She certainly should have stopped staring after Mrs. Mitchell glanced back and forth between the two of them, but she wasn't able to stop looking, and every time Gladys was looking right back at her. Mabel believed you could tell everything by looking into someone's eyes, whether this person was good or evil, whether this person had the capacity to love, or would hurt you. The eyes of this woman were like a magnet drawing her close and preventing her from looking anywhere else. Mabel didn't say another word the rest of the night.

The next day after rehearsal, Gladys approached Mabel. The first thing she said was: "Now answer me truthfully. When I look at you, it thrills you don't it?"

"Yes, I think so," Mabel responded, nodding yes all the while because she was tongue-tied and unsure if any words had escaped from her mouth.

"I need to take that thrill away," Gladys whispered in Mabel's ear.

———

Perhaps, it was the sight of all those lovers seeking cover under the boardwalk or the incitement of the wall-to-wall bodies pressed

against one another on the beach, limbs sticky and entwined, proximate bodies barely within the legal limit of decency, that gave her
license. People poured into Coney Island from all over New York to
make love on the beach. No one bothered them unless they were the
wrong type of couple: a Negro or Chinese man with a white girl, or a

colored girl suspected of turning tricks, or a pansy and his boyfriend. All along the beach people had intercourse. It was as much a wonder as the ocean.

———

In a novel or play, a chorus girl romance had everything to do with ambition. Mabel's attraction to Gladys had little to do with the glamour of the stage or with the yearning to assume Gladys's much larger role in it. When Gladys said, "You'll have to find another baby now," Mabel was broken.

Mrs. Mitchell felt responsible for what happened because it all started in her house. "She is like a daughter to me," she told Gladys before the affair with Mabel began. "So don't ruin her. Don't mess up Mabel. If you don't plan to stay with her, leave her alone." Mrs. Mitchell knew Mabel had no one to hold onto, and how was Gladys going to change that? "Promise me you'll leave her alone." Gladys agreed, but a few days later, she broke her promise. Unable to resist the ardor of a first passion, she took Mabel; she took everything.

Mildred had tried to talk her out of the affair, before it began, before Mabel had used the word *lover* as if it belonged to her and she was practiced at saying it. My lover. It was new, but not unfamiliar like the other words Gladys taught her, which were offered in lieu of an explanation as to why they had no future; or imparted like an apology issued in advance of a crime that was about to be committed, or a bellwether of the bad things to come. Words like *ruin* tallied the want and the risk, *tribade* was thick with the promise of pleasure, while the word *lesbian*, which she had read in a book by Havelock Ellis, meant nothing to her and had little to do with those she wanted and how she wanted them. Mabel had never heard anyone utter the word *lesbian* until Gladys said it, and the way she said it was intended to push Mabel away. Too late she insisted, "No we can't." "I am married." "I don't want to ruin your life." Mabel thought, but didn't say, "You have already ruined it."

Was it unreasonable to hope that someone might actually love her? Her aunt and uncle had never loved her. Ellen White, her foster sister, had loved her. She was the only person who had ever tried to protect her. When Bessie, Ellen's older sister, found the ten-year-old Mabel abandoned in a Jersey City park, she brought her home. That first night, Ellen told Mabel not to be afraid and that no one would hurt her. Mabel was so hungry she devoured three eggs and a loaf of bread, but even with Mrs. White's coaxing, she refused to tell them anything other than her name and that her aunt had told her to wait and then left. No, she never returned. She didn't mention her uncle. No announcements looking for a lost girl who matched her description ever appeared in the paper. No detective or private dicks ever came looking for her and Mabel never uttered a word about her past. And she never told anyone, not even Ellen, what her uncle had done. It was too horrible for anyone to believe. Wouldn't they blame her?

After Ellen died in childbirth and the baby several weeks later, Mabel began dreaming about the mother she never knew. Years later she would say that a guardian angel had watched over her, always leading her out of trouble. She imagined her mother as this angel. She knew nothing about her mother and didn't even learn her name, Lulu Hampton or Simmons, until she was twenty years old. Her grandmother had refused to speak the name of her dead daughter or to display her picture anywhere in the house, as if even this small gesture might be mistaken for begrudging acceptance of the life Lulu had chosen. She had broken the law, and the baby girl, Mabel, was the proof of that. There was no father to speak of. Mabel tried not to think about what her life would have been like if her mother had not died when she was an infant. She loved her grandmother, but the woman was cold and dispensed her affection with a long-handled spoon. From reading books, Mabel learned what a mother was supposed to be, how her devotion and protection safeguarded the child, and that the bond between mother and child was unbreakable. Ellen was the person closest to being a mother in her life. The way Ellen held her and planted kisses on her face and lips made her feel loved. When the seventeen-year-old Ellen wrapped Mabel in her arms, she felt almost safe. Many a night she drifted off to sleep in those arms.

———

Gladys abandoned her as had every other person she had loved. To be so vulnerable and utterly without defense was unbearable. It terrified her. What Mabel had wanted most—the embrace of a woman's loving arms, the press of flesh against flesh, the heat and mass of a lover's body rising beneath her, the pound of Gladys's racing heart echoing in her chest, the sticky knot of coiled limbs—it wrecked her. Not because she was an outcast, but because love drained and emptied her, making it impossible for her to stand on her own two feet or live without her lover. Gladys taught Mabel everything, from how to dance to how to please a woman. At night, they would go out to different places, parties and cabarets, every adventure culminating in Gladys's bed. One night the girls played a joke on them and locked the front door, so they had to ring the bell and wake the landlady to gain entrance. The others had hoped to embarrass them, catch them red-handed, but they didn't care. In bed, it seemed like it was only the two of them in the world, in the vast stillness of the deep of night. In the few hours before dusk, there were no husbands to fear.

That Mabel was practiced in the exercise of losing the ones she loved did not lessen the pain of breaking up with Gladys. Her mother had died when she was an infant unable to differentiate between that body and her own, before the I emerged, marked, severed, fallen from this maternal plenitude, which in her case was abrupt and severe, premature like her mother's death. A dull throb that had accompanied her since her grandmother's death, and it warned: Watch out, when you least expect it, something terrible will happen. Her grandmother's glance from the deathbed, the blank glazed eyes looking through her; by the time her aunt had finished plaiting her hair, her grandmother was gone. Then Ellen. She would be alive if her parents hadn't forced her to marry a man she never loved. Mabel would be spared no one.

Sick. Depleted. Alone. She was ruined, not because she came to Harlem and got lost, not because she was hustling for some man on Fifth or Madison, not because of the terrible things she anticipated; she was ruined because love had broken her, and despite this, *she longed and longed and longed.* Gladys had warned Mabel about the price to be paid for loving her, but seduced Mabel anyway. That she had a husband didn't matter. That Mabel was seventeen didn't matter. That she had promised Mildred's mother not to mess with her didn't matter. Mabel tried hard not to think about all the things they had done, or about the weight of that beautiful brown resting against her, floating on top of her. Mabel tried not to think about what a husband might be able to do that she couldn't or to wonder if she would ever see Gladys again or if she was a fool to hope that Gladys might leave him, never return to Philadelphia but decide to live with a seventeen-year-old show girl in a three-room flat off Seventh Avenue.

When Gladys left, it didn't feel like the end of the affair, but the end of Mabel. What remained or who she might be was murky, uncertain. Could this bundle of feeling and impulse ever cohere into a person again? Ever manage to say "I" with any authority, or pretend to be the master of her sorry self? The ache of loving someone so unreservedly, so wholeheartedly, had nearly destroyed her. She had wanted everything from her lover—her lips against hers, her hands everywhere and then her mouth. The body's disregard of *should* and *ought* made her feel ashamed. Pleasure warred with common sense, even with self-preservation. The feelings unleashed by her first lover forced Mabel to retreat to her bed, to recoil from this sense of helplessness. She had spent so much of her life fearing what men might do to her that she never thought about what a woman might do. How a woman might hurt you? How was it that something so wonderful could break her apart?

Mildred pounded at the door until Mabel let her in. She tried to explain it, but she couldn't. All Mabel told her friend was, "I can't take it. It is too powerful. I don't want no part of it." It was not at all lovely to want someone so badly. Her heart was shattered. Everyone could go to hell. She had lost her mother, so who did she need? Nobody.

———

The city appeared far more glamorous and exciting from the passenger seat of the shiny Gray Touring Roadster. Her new lover, Ruth, was dashing and princely. Most of her friends were celebrities, entertainers, and those in the sporting life. In the 1920s New York was wild. Ruth's lover owned a brothel, so she knew everyone and guided Mabel through the best clubs, cabarets, and buffet flats in Harlem, Greenwich Village, and Brooklyn. Ruth never cared if people stared at them while they were dining at a restaurant, or if all of Mabel's neighbors turned their head and stared when Mabel plopped herself into the front seat of her car—all because they weren't accustomed to seeing such a pair, a handsome white woman with a Negro seated beside her who wasn't her servant. Most people, black and white, believed that they were bound for trouble and that there was something disreputable and suspicious about interracial intimacy. Few suspected they were lovers—their being friends was shocking enough.

The first time Ruth picked her up in Jersey City, you could have bought Mabel's landlady, Old Picklepuss, for a dime. Folks didn't know what to think as the chivalrous motorist opened the door for Mabel. The mouths of her neighbors were hanging open, and those ignorant Negroes didn't know what to say or how to greet a person and say hello. None said a word beside Picklepuss, who shouted upstairs for her after Ruth explained that she was looking for Miss Hampton. Her neighbor, Maude Brown, was grinning on the steps like a Cheshire cat. "Who's that white woman in the car?" she asked.

The next question was could she ride along with them? Ruth laughed and said she could come with them to Coney Island for an afternoon at the beach. The others were curious, but in the end their disapproval won out. No good would come of it. Picklepuss said, "Mabel, you best be careful. It just don't look right." Those busybodies would have passed out if Ruth had been wearing trousers too.

Mabel was no longer innocent. She had had a series of lovers—white women and black women, married women, bisexual women, and what she called true lesbians. Many of these were brief affairs; a few were with amorous friends like Mildred and Viola, performers working in the same shows, and dalliances with women moving in and out of the life. Mabel had learned to give and take pleasure. With Ruth, she traipsed through the city from the Village to Harlem, making love all afternoon, going to the theatre, frequenting parties, and hanging out in cabarets until the early hours of the morning changed her. She cultivated the pleasures to which Ruth had introduced her. Drinking champagne, smoking, indulging her appetites as she saw fit, learning to navigate the city so that she never had to be lonely. The people she now called friends were part of the glamorous world opened up by Ruth: Gladys Bentley, Jackie Mabley, and the two Ethels, Ethel Waters and her girlfriend Ethel Williams.

Bentley helped her to get a job dancing at the Garden of Joy, a Harlem nightspot that catered to a mixed crowd. Mamie Smith owned the place, and everyone knew Mamie because she recorded the first blues, "Crazy Blues," which sold 75,000 copies within a month of its release. The Garden of Joy was an open-air dance pavilion, and at some point during the night, Harlem's bohemians and notables stopped in, musicians and actors as well as the literary types. Bentley performed there; she had a huge following wherever she went, and white folks from downtown came to Harlem to see Bentley sing dirty songs in an elegant white tuxedo. Working in a cabaret frequented by lesbians, gay men, cross-dressers, and sissies gave Mabel some elbowroom; she could move without worrying about some man on

her ass. The Garden of Joy allowed her the space and time to flower
into a lover of women. For two years, she danced, waited on tables,
acted as hostess, and served drinks.

Now she was running with a "choosey crowd," composed of
mostly theatre people, dancers, singers, comedians, and almost all
of them were in the life. Ruth had introduced her to Bentley and
brought her to her first party at Jackie Mabley's house. Ruth knew
everyone who was anyone, entertainers, athletes, politicians, and the
wealthy. She was well connected because of her girlfriend. Everyone
in the sporting life passed through the brothel, to hear music, to
play piano or sing, whoring before they made a name, or cleaning
house if she was still green. Ruth was comfortable with colored folks
and introduced Mabel to many black women who also loved women.
Mabel was just a kid she was having fun with, just a lover for the
meantime, but Mabel was happy to go along for the ride.

"You want to go slumming?" Ruth asked. Sure, Mabel said. Slumming wasn't a word she and her colored friends used to describe
nightlife in Harlem. It was something white folks said to describe
their quest for pleasure uptown and their encounters with Negroes,
even if the black folks they met were rich or educated or accomplished. Mabel didn't give a damn either way, so long as it was fun.
As she waited in the foyer of A'lelia Walker's elegant apartment, it
was clear to Mabel that this was the opposite of slumming. Before
they entered, Ruth said, "Whatever you see, don't repeat."

A colored butler led them inside the stately apartment and asked
them to wait. A tall white man appeared, looked Mabel over and
asked Ruth if she was okay. Ruth said, yes I know her. She is my
friend; she's all right. The white man directed Mabel to follow. They
passed through the foyer, and then he escorted her to a private room
and instructed her to remove her clothes. She took off her white
fur coat and her belted gray jersey dress. She was nervous. Luckily,
she was wearing a very nice pair of undergarments. The white man
escorted her across the foyer and through the dining room, and then

opened a third door onto another room. For a moment, she was frozen; she stopped walking and gawked at the folks lounging in the room. She hoped no one had noticed. No one in the room had clothes on but her. A naked Ruth put her arm around Mabel's waist. How do you feel? Okay, she replied and looked around the room. Fourteen or more naked people were reclining on pillows spread across the floor. The guests—voyeurs, exhibitionists, the merely curious, queers, the polyamorous, and the catholic—lounged, drank, copulated. What first captured Mabel's attention was a man going down on a woman. She had never seen that before. As she stared at them, others gazed at the attractive newcomer, still wearing her stockings, slippers and a combination camisole. (She had been allowed to keep on her intimate apparel because this was her first time.)

A white fellow invited them to sit down. She and Ruth drank several bottles of champagne. They smoked reefer. They made love. The afternoon drifted into the evening and midnight into morning and morning into afternoon. No one seemed concerned about time. Folks talked, made love, ate, lounged, and listened to music. At first, it was hard for Mabel to do anything, or even to feel excited or aroused, she was so busy watching everyone else. Looking at others engaged in intimate acts seemed shocking and then funny, but as the hours passed it didn't seem unusual at all. People entered A'lelia's with a husband and exited with a wife. The collective lust washed over you; claimed you; dared you; transformed you. Mabel was as high as a Georgia pine and it all appeared lovely and free. Then she started to relax and was able to be comfortable with Ruth. They could do what they wanted and no one cared or bothered them. *They had a lovely time.*

When A'lelia Walker made an appearance, the room stirred in response. She conversed with her guests, wearing a little silk short set, but it might as well have been an ermine coat; she had the bearing of a queen, and wore the flimsy little outfit with a stately air. Even without her infamous riding crop, there remained something forbidding and dangerous about her. She smoked and drank with her guests, engaging in small talk. She was a tall, striking woman, who surrounded herself with beautiful women (Ethel Waters, Nora Holt, Edna Thomas) and gay men. She was lavish with her affection and her fortune. Her mother, Madame C. J. Walker, had invented the straightening combs and developed a line of beauty products; every girl in Harlem with straightened, slicked back, bobbed, and waved hair had her to thank. The dicties called A'lelia "the dekink queen" behind her back to belittle her, to make plain that she wasn't a rightful heir or deserving of a place among the aristocracy of the race. It goes without saying that they were jealous. The house she owned on 136th Street was said to be one of the most beautiful in Harlem. She also owned a villa on the Hudson, Villa Lewaro; she financed the Dark Tower, a literary salon in her palatial home of thirty rooms, although it was rumored that she never read books, only supported their authors. She drank excessively, played cards with her intimates, gorged on rich food. The apartment at 80 Edgecombe Avenue was grand, but it was a pleasure lair and not intended to be a show place, although the luxurious furniture, Persian rugs, the silk and satin pillows, the fur throws, the heavy velvet and brocade fabrics draped throughout the apartment were more fabulous than anything Mabel had ever seen. The luxury enveloped her and, like the bottles of champagne, made her feel exquisite. While she didn't especially like the taste of caviar, she loved the idea of eating it. A'lelia served champagne and caviar to her black guests, while whites fetied on pig feet, chitterlings, and bathtub gin, which was what they expected and wanted in Harlem, a delicious taste of the other.

Ruth brought Mabel to A'lelia's not to watch a show, but to enhance their pleasure. It was intended to be another lesson in the sensual education of Mabel Hampton. But it was more than this for Mabel. The shared intimacy of 80 Edgecombe Avenue was nothing like the crude display of sex acts offered at a buffet flat. The public sex and collective lovemaking, like the environment, were beautiful, worldly-wise, and testimony to a distinctly modern life. At A'lelia's place, the sharp edge of pleasure, the moans, whispers, and laughter blanketing the room, the choked breath of orgasm shattered the boundaries of the self, effaced the lines of social division, unmade men and women. The utter dissolution of the bounded, discrete self was the gift. The gay rebels and the gender queers savored the lush refuge; welcomed the opportunity to jettison propriety. Guests mingled across the divide of class and race, strangers became intimates, an English aristocrat fell in love with a Negro actress.

The opening and the possibility of the era seemed clear and palpable to Mabel in a lovely room filled with folks of all persuasions and proclivities lying about on velvet pillows. The transport of sex was welcome, even more, the experience of being liberated from all the details and encumbrances that organized her life, that fixed her in time and space. It permitted a deeper inhabitation, not of the self exactly, but of breath, touch, and taste, an acuity of the senses, a sharpening of the perceptual apparatus so that she could discern the varieties of blackness in a shadow and the world unfolding there, and take note of how the light refracting against a neighboring building inched its way along the windowsill until it spilled through the curtains, and it mattered little who received and who gave once clothes had been removed.

The lovely feel of the silk pillows brushing against her back or clutched between the palms of your hands. The soft amber lighting lulled her into a lazy peacefulness, and the lush carpets quieted the steps, cushioning the feet, so it felt like she was being carried or drifting away, or sinking deeper into the sandy undertow and being pulled into the ocean, buoyant, weightless, adrift. It was all so beautiful; it made her beautiful. The crystal champagne flutes and lovely décor of A'lelia Walker's generous fortune. Beautiful naked girls served the food and drink, chatting casually with guests. The music—piano rags yielded to sonatas, James P. Johnson to Rachmaninoff. Not one thing ugly or tawdry or off-key. This extended intimacy—the comfort and sumptuousness of shared passion, as if intimate acts were never intended to be private, to be owned like property. In the stunningly outfitted lair of an heiress even arousal was quiet and refined. The exchange of looks, the curious glance of a stranger, the shared rush of sensation, the shallow breath of release, enhanced the pleasure of everyone present, making eros into a communal luxury.

———

In 1924, the gorgeous fortune of the chorus seemed that it would be Mabel's forever. She landed a part in the famous bronze beauty chorus of *Come Along, Mandy*. It was the usual fare of the Negro theater—corked black faces, comedy skits, lovely songs, a clunky implausible plot, and young chorines. There were twenty girls, and when they performed, few of the critics failed to remark that virtually all of them were dark-skinned, they were labeled the bronze chorus, the nut-brown chorus, the sepia chorus, the not very beautiful chorus. In the *Messenger*, Theophilus Lewis exclaimed in a glowing review, *Finally a colored chorus*, by which he meant recognizably Negro, instead of the usual light, bright, and damn-near-white chorines who were the fixtures of the best houses and the biggest shows. When the lights dimmed in the house, Mabel and the other chorines crossed the stage in glittering costumes that shimmered in the darkness. The stage lights also were turned off to intensify the effect of the gorgeous luminescent outfits, which made the dancers appear like fireflies, floating and ethereal on the stage of the Lafayette Theatre. The hushed awe of the audience was palpable. One could almost hear them catch their breath. The chorus threatened to steal the show, despite the pale Gallic limbs of Jean Starr, the lead lady. The power and force of the voices and the collective frenzy of the Charleston won over the audience and critics alike.

The rows of black folks packed in the audience choked and laughed themselves to tears watching the comedians Whitney and Tutt, who some said rivaled Bert Williams and George Walker.

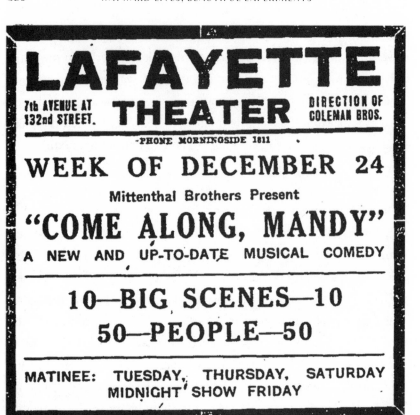

Negroes were not afraid to show their appreciation, and the audience stomped and clapped and whistled for the chorus. Even the reviews indifferent about the production, like the one published in the *Baltimore Afro-American*, noted how well the ensemble worked together, and singled out the chorus for praise. "The cast is a most meritorious one, and the chorus, while not especially beautiful, is a group of [dancing] youngsters who have pep that when the newness wears off will acquit themselves in a most creditable fashion." *Come Along, Mandy* was compared favorably to *Shuffle Along*, which had enjoyed an incredible run on Broadway. The costumes were hailed the most beautiful of the season. In the lavish costumes, Mabel and the other dancers appeared like fallen angels or gilded sepia dolls. The *Chicago Defender*: "The best beauty chorus in this city has been gotten together to entertain Harlem next week." The *Atlanta Constitution*: *Come Along, Mandy* "has taken by storm every southern city where it has been presented to a white audience." In the *New Journal and Guide*: "*Come Along, Mandy* is the latest of New York successes. A large and selected company, mostly girls, will present the comedy. Tuneful melodies, whirlwind dances and irresistible comedy will be the features, done in a costume and scenic setting of exceptional beauty." The *Chicago Defender*: "The famous bronze beauty chorus

was very capable. All song and dance numbers were well received and many were accorded unusual applause. Some of the costumes of the chorus were very elaborate and gaudy, typical of the Negro's love of highly colored raiment. One set of costumes worn by the chorus that showed up particularly well in one number was that used in 'On Parade.' The house and stage lights were turned off during the dance and the luminous trimmings of the costumes presented an attractive effect."

On the surface, Mabel's life resembled that of the average chorine, and if she was lucky singing and dancing might catapult her to something greater. The glamour of the stage might have lulled her into believing that the pleasure and liberties she enjoyed were enduring rather than provisional. This might have been the case had she been content with being a chorus girl or had she aspired to be a star. Neither was the case, because Mabel was still searching for a way to live in the world that allowed her to be comfortable in her own skin. She was no longer an ingénue or interested in passing for a pretty young thing. The glamorous outfits of the chorine now made her feel ridiculous. She preferred suits and low heels. Nobody knew who or what you were when you had a suit on.

———

She went to the theater all the time because she never felt lonely there. Watching Helen Mencken perform in *The Captive* (*La Prisonnière*) was an experience she would never forget. The show debuted at the Empire Theatre on September 29, 1926. There were 160 performances of the show before the police raided the theater, arrested the cast for obscenity, and permanently closed the doors. Mabel saw the play several times, and most of the audience were women in the life or were questioning or also felt like captives. Many wore violets pinned to their lapels and belts. Irène, who was played by Mencken, is a young woman, tortured by her love for Madame d'Arguines, but who pretends to love Jacques, the man to whom she is engaged. Resigning herself to this union, Irène utters the play's most oft-quoted line regarding marriage: "It's like a prison to which I must return captive, despite myself." It was the first time Mabel had seen the love between women represented anywhere, and Mencken played the part so true, surely she must love a woman. After meeting her backstage, Mabel was certain that Mencken was in the "girls' club," believing as she did that one-half the world was in the life. Irène probably reminded her of that first torrid affair with Gladys and the subsequent affair with Amanda Drummond, another gray-haired woman whom Mabel loved passionately and who was also

married. *The Captive, The Well of Loneliness,* Havelock Ellis's *Studies in the Psychology of Sex,* formed the textual web of Mabel's erotic and psychic life. This queer twist on the plot of the chorus girl was the open secret of the theater.

The Captive provided a language for desire and longing, an expression of what it meant to love women in a society in which heterosexuality was compulsory and marriage the prison that all women were expected to choose. To hear Irène espouse her love so convincingly not only was exhilarating, but also confirmed that so many others also loved as she did. For the first time, Mabel saw her desire, the desire for women, represented in a manner that was not tethered to the punitive language of "undesirable relation" or the psychopathology of the clinic or the deviance of blackness. Mabel had never imagined her life as a case study. Nor did she believe, as one psychiatrist suggested, that black women became lesbians because they were unattractive and so unable to achieve successfully their destiny as women, becoming "husbands" by default. An evolving understanding of how she loved and preferred to live made it more difficult for her to settle for the few options available to her: dancer, domestic, or whore. Her aesthetic and intellectual ambitions were so much greater than the possibilities afforded her by the corked antics and plantation spectacles of the Negro theatre. She regularly attended dramatic plays, operas, and concerts, and consumed novels and nonfiction voraciously, keeping lists of all the books she finished.

Myrtle Reed, *Later Love Letters of a Musician*
Marie Corelli, *The Secret Power*
Marie Corelli, *Ziska*
Marie Corelli, *Barabbas: A Dream of the World's Tragedy*
Gustavus Hindman Miller, *Ten Thousand Dreams Interpreted*
Cyril Falls, *Tales of Hoffman: Retold from Offenbach's Opera*
Sri Ramatherio, *Unto Thee I Grant,* Rosicrucian Library

Radclyffe Hall, *The Well of Loneliness*
Gustav Kobbe, *The Complete Opera Book*
Thomas Dixon, *The Clansman*
Booker T. Washington, *Working with the Hands*
Otto Weininger, *Sex and Character*
D. H. Lawrence, *Women in Love*
Eugene O'Neill, *Three Plays*

She read the New York dailies, as well as *The Crisis*, the *Amsterdam News*, the *Chicago Defender*, and the *Pittsburgh Courier*.

————

Her true passion was music, not the show tunes she sang in *Come Along, Mandy* and *Blackbirds of 1926*, or the rags and blues she listened and danced to at Harlem cabarets or house parties; none of this music touched her deeply or inspired her. She loved the opera, and there was no segregated seating at the opera houses. When she was sixteen or seventeen years old, a doctor's wife, whose house she cleaned, took her to see her first performance. The doctor and his wife were Jews from Europe. The Mrs. was always trying to educate her, pushing a book in her hand, ordering her to sit and listen to arias and sonatas, as if Mabel were her charge and not her servant. She read *The Encyclopedia of Opera* and learned the great stories of Puccini and Verdi and Bellini. When she decided to leave the chorus, forced out by her age as much as her blossoming masculinity, it was with the hopes that she would train as a classical singer and have a career in the concert hall.

Mabel adored Florence Mills and heard her sing the music of William Grant Still at Aeolian Hall. Mills's beautiful sharp clear voice filled the hall, and Mabel sat transfixed. She followed the rare stories about Negro musicians and singers working on the concert stages of Europe and would clip them from the papers and place them in her scrapbook, as if these bits of news might be capable of helping her navigate her way to the concert hall, as if their success against the odds meant that such dreams weren't foolish, not only because she was poor, black, and female, but also because she didn't have a soul in the world she could depend on. If it enraged her that no one expected greatness from her, it would have been reasonable. Some days she wanted to shout from the rooftop of her building for the whole world to step back and give her some breathing room. She listened to William Dawson and Stravinsky and Chopin just so she could breathe. She attended every performance by Negro opera societies performing in Harlem, and years later watched Marian Anderson and Paul Robeson on the stage at Carnegie Hall.

The tragic love, the recurring themes of loss, death, seduction and betrayal, no doubt struck a deep chord and provided an expressive language for Mabel's mother loss, a vehicle large enough to con-

Singer Gets $10,000 Award

PHILADELPHIA, March 17 (P).—Marian Anderson, colored singer, tonight was given the $10,000 Philadelphia award presented annually to the person who has "performed an act . . . calculated to advance the best interests of Philadelphia." A native of Philadelphia, Miss Anderson was honored before a distinguished audience at the Academy of Music. The award was established in 1921 by Ed-

tain all that abandonment. The discovery that her mother had been poisoned by a jealous rival for her father's love only confirmed the sense of her tragic life and deepened her appreciation of *Norma, Carmen,* and *Dido and Aeneas.* Music became Mabel's passion. It transformed every heartbreak, every terrible thing she had experienced into something magnificent and arresting. It took hold of her, it laid her low, it restored her, as if every lament was her mother speaking to her, every betrayed and abandoned lover a replay of her affairs, every dying and defeated heroine the girl child trapped in the coal bin. Music conveyed and echoed all the stories she never told anyone, the secrets she would never disclose, the cruel things she had endured, everyone she had lost. *Remember me.* All the queer endings. In the opera house, Mabel was not a domestic, not a prisoner, not a stud, not a woman, not colored, but a big, open heart. The music quieted the rush and rage booming inside her head. No need to scream, only to listen, permitting everything she felt to pour out—the aspiration, the love, the girl broken in two, the grief.

Her new girlfriend Ismay Andrews shared these passions. The two of them regularly attended concerts and performances and went to see French and German operas. Ismay eventually would write music for the National Negro Opera Company. Walking along Lenox Avenue and listening to the stepladder speakers was second only to her love of music. Ismay was a radical and identified with the young socialists and communists of Harlem. While her political views embraced the abolition of private property and welcomed the communal wealth that all would share when capitalism was overthrown, as a lover she was possessive and extremely jealous. If she suspected that Mabel was looking at someone else, she would turn nasty. When they went to parties, Ismay watched her like a hawk. They never fought publicly, but Mabel suspected that Ismay was capable of a good brawl. Perhaps, because she was a foreigner, which is how Mabel always thought of her, she didn't have a limited notion of what Mabel could aspire to or who she should be or what she should want. Ismay didn't think Mabel was trying to be superior or putting on airs because she loved the opera. To Mabel's ears, it con-

veyed the anguish of the blues and shared its chronicle of catastrophe; it simply spoke to her more deeply.

Ismay didn't think of herself as a foreigner. She was born in Lagos, Nigeria, but had been raised in the United States. In an article about her in the *Pittsburgh Courier*, she stressed that she had always felt at home in Harlem. Many of her friends were American. In the heyday of the young radicals, she lived in the streets and acquired her political education there. Ismay had listened raptly when Asa Randolph, Chandler Owen, Frank Crosswaith, and Hubert Harrison were holding forth on street corners from soap box stands; she was one of their warmest admirers.

All the things that the talented young Mabel longed to do, Ismay did, performing in operettas and in classical recitals. She started an African dance troupe, the Swahili Dancers, and shaped modern Negro concert dance. She composed music for the National Negro Opera Company. She performed with white theater companies and once was booed from the stage of a D.C. theatre for bossing two white actors in a farce. She would go on to act in film, share the stage with Paul Robeson, dance, and train other dancers and choreographers.

Had Mabel not lost her courage, had she not been poor, who knows what she might have achieved? Circumstances were different for Ismay. She had been raised comfortably in a doctor's house, and was educated and trained as a nurse, yet even with this, she died in utter destitution.

Every week the *Amsterdam News* and *Chicago Defender* documented the awful things done to Negroes and the great things Negroes were doing. Mabel tried to find her balance between these extremes, oscillating between hope and despair, as she read about girls and women abused, raped, and abducted, or who were so privileged they seemed like princesses in a fantasy world from which she was barred. When the world threatened to smother her, she opened her mouth, not to yell or shriek, but to find her way to song. Right outside her door was the menace that threatened to take her breath away. Some man might snatch you from a Harlem street; make you experience the worst things again, strip you and beat you. And she listened for all of that inside the music. There she could suffer it; she could weep openly.

Mabel dreamed of the concert stage at a time when black women were prevented from singing in the major concert halls of the United States and excluded from musical conservatories, with the exception of Oberlin and the New England Conservatory. What could one hope for under these circumstances? What could she reasonably expect to accomplish? She was poor, black, loved women, and preferred men's clothes. She needed music simply to survive and endure what it felt like to be in her skin.

Her last job in the chorus was at the Alhambra Theater. She was weary of the costumes and the silly songs; she was sick of being pawed and threatened and she worried about the rent because of uncertain work and unsteady wages. She no longer liked dancing, and if her option had been something other than the kitchen, she might have quit earlier. She tolerated what she had to, but refused to yield an inch more. Her friend, Ethel Waters, had once kicked a manager in the behind after he slapped her on the ass. The only reason she wasn't fired on the spot was that she was headlining the show. Mabel wouldn't allow anyone to touch her. Traveling with *Come Along, Mandy*, she barely escaped being raped by a producer by climbing out of a hotel window. The men in the theater forced chorus girls to sleep with them. It was the one way to get ahead, and she "didn't want no dicks ruining her and getting babies."

She had grown weary of being a Negro woman in all the ways expected of her. She wanted more than this. Looking out at the hundreds of folks filling the auditorium of the Alhambra, it was hard to believe that they didn't want more too.

Mabel envied the freedom of her friends Jackie Mabley and Gladys Bentley, who lived as they wanted. Bentley would "fight up a breeze" with anyone who crossed her. At the Clam House, Bentley became famous for a risqué act, dirty lyrics, and elegant tuxedos. Mabel admired her, but not for the same reasons as Langston Hughes, who described her as "a living piece of African sculpture." She respected Bentley for the same reasons she did Jackie Mabley—they wore trousers in the street, traipsed through Harlem with their women on their arms, and dared anyone to say a damn thing. Bentley would beat a man as easily as look at one. Bentley and Jackie wore slacks and jackets when few dared to, when you could be arrested for wearing men's clothes; they loved openly and flirted with women, they didn't apologize for who they were or try to pass for something they were not. Everyone in Harlem knew that Ethel Waters was a bull dagger, but it was different with her. Once she became famous it was like you weren't supposed to know; everything was suddenly hush-hush, but everyone knew what was what. A columnist in the *Afro-American* pointed a finger at her without calling names: "Female stars were chasing chorus girls. Some were so determined that the chorines were forced to lock their dressing room doors to deter the advances of leading ladies."

Bentley was in no way afraid to live however the hell she wanted. She never hid her love of women or soft-pedaled being a butch. In fact, she did just the opposite: she rubbed your face in it, so much so that it made folks embarrassed and hot around the collar, and they loved it and kept coming back to the Garden of Joy and the Clam House to hear Bentley sing her nasty songs decked out in an elegant white tuxedo. Mabel learned a lot from her about claiming space in a world that granted you none. Bentley also gave her a good piece of advice. She was the first to warn Mabel: Stay away from married women. They will get you killed.

The time spent with Bentley and Jackie made her question who she was and who she wanted to be. Did she have to be a woman? Did she have to be a man? Did she have to be anything at all, besides someone who loved women? What a woman could or should be was incredibly fraught, especially for a black woman. Even if she wore a dress or a skirt, she wasn't the same kind of woman as a white woman; and no matter how hard she worked or how many people she supported, she would never be considered the equal of a man, even when having the same load to bear.

Mabel called herself a stud because she didn't want to bother with men and she loved women. She had liked girls all her life. Her style became more masculine—low-heeled shoes, Panama hats, and skirt suits—but that had nothing to do with being a man, it was simply claiming the "he" who also defined her. When dressed in trousers, jacket, and tie, she was just being Mabel. Did she ever feel like a man? That was something she couldn't answer. She felt like herself. It was simple: she loved women and didn't bother about the rest. It didn't matter what other people called her, whether they called her a stud or a butch. Some of her friends called her Mr. Hampton. She called herself Mabel. The only thing that mattered was what she believed; the only script she had to abide was the one she created. That was the hope.

What was it that a colored woman was supposed to be? Whether they had bobbed hair or not, wore pants or dresses, had husbands or not, it didn't seem to matter; they all fell in between the categories or failed to conform to them. There was nothing the world wouldn't do to a colored woman. Everything they did to black men, they did to black women. Every time she read the papers she was reminded of this. Lynched them. Mutilated them. Beat them in the streets. Burned their homes. The ways you weren't a man were just an opportunity to commit another kind of violence. Rape you and then kill you. Make your children watch, so they knew no one in the

world could protect them. Hang you, and then slit your belly open like they did Mary Turner. When the baby dropped out, they killed the child. They lynched mothers with their sons. Raped little girls. Being black and female licensed every brutal act. In the face of all of this what could one do, but refuse the categories?

———

She was making her way to the Garden of Joy to meet friends when two men grabbed her on 133rd Street and Lenox. The man walking in front of her stopped abruptly and the one walking behind seized her. The men dragged her to a room on 135th Street, they made her strip, they beat her, they took her watch, and they inspected her body to determine her value. They tried to make her a piece of property, ass to be sold to the highest bidder. Strangers abducted her a few blocks from her apartment and tried to make her that girl with her arms pinned to the bed, as if she was something to be used then cast aside like garbage when he was through with her. They were moving her to another building when Mabel broke free from the man clutching her arm and she ran down into the subway. The train had just pulled into the station. She was lucky. A guardian angel protected and watched over her. She was alive. The men might have murdered her or made her wish she was dead. *They didn't give a damn what you were or who you were.* She was alive and for this she was thankful.

Coda: The Bronx Slave Market

The unlucky idled on a crate or bench waiting for the offer that never came, bargaining with themselves about the smallest amount they would be willing to accept for a day's work, hoping for but not counting on a stranger's decency. No matter how cold it was they lingered on the corner of Webster Ave or at the intersection of Simpson and Westchester from 8:00 a.m. until early afternoon. When it rained, they found shelter clustering in nearby doorways. The sullen and the resigned wore an expression "daring some one not to hire her." The whores gathered on one corner and the domestics on the other. The movement across the street was slow and regular. Most of those waiting on the corner to sell a hand job or cursory act of intercourse earlier had been in the paper bag brigade—the women with work clothes stuffed in the crumpled bags tucked under their arms. Now they worked on their backs as well as their knees, but at least it wasn't bone-breaking work. It paid more. In time, they would cross the street again. In the Bronx slave market, no one asked, "How can you do it?" It was "their own business," said one of the women waiting for housework. "If they can do it and get away with it, it is alright with the others." The domestics had no arguments with the other women working the street; the ones they wanted to run off the corner were the migrants and the new arrivals willing to work for almost nothing, who seemed to know no other words but: "I'll take what you will give me." "Yes ma'am. I do windows." Those were the girls who made it bad for the rest.

A Harlem Blues captured the exchanges of the market, the back and forth that concluded with meager wages or an empty hand:

Black Gal, Black Gal, Got some work for you
Tell me white folks what you want me to do
Got a big house to clean and scrub
Dishes to wash, floors to mop and scrub
White folks tell me, how much you going to pay
Well lemme see now, seeing it's a rainy day
Oh Thank you white folks, I done heard that before
Get away you white trash 'fore you get me real sore.

Sore or not, the general house worker shouldered the menial work that others avoided. Black women described this "free exchange" of their labor and capacity for paltry wages as the slave market. Ella Baker and Marvel Cooke characterized this new servitude as "the ruthless destruction of the Negro" by middle-class housewives and they offered a graphic picture of the new conditions of slavery:

> The Simpson Avenue block exudes the stench of the slave market at its worst. Not only is human labor bartered and sold for slave wage, but human love also is a marketable commodity. But whether it is labor or love that is sold, economic necessity compels the sale. With the invariable paper bundle, waiting expectantly for Bronx housewives to buy their strength and energy for an hour, two hours, or even for a day at the munificent rate of fifteen, twenty, twenty-five, or if luck be with them, thirty cents an hour. If not the wives themselves, maybe their husbands, their sons or their brothers, under the subterfuge of work, offer worldly-wise girls higher bids for their time.

Disguised as day laborers, Baker and Cooke waited to be hired, to be bought and sold—for as little as twenty-five cents an hour. The housewife "undresse[d] them with her eyes as she measure[d] their strength," judging how much work they could stand. The humiliation and the pitiable wages offered ample evidence that black women were the most oppressed sector of the working class. As they waited

to be hired, a man passed them by, uttering a sly "Hello Baby." He seemed familiar. They realized that he had been trailing them. Plainclothes notwithstanding, it was obvious that he was one of 'New York's finest' trying to entrap them for prostitution. The two of them waited all morning without finding work because their price was too high. Asked, "How much you charge?" they were unwilling to say, "I'll take what you give me."

———

Ten years after she appeared on the stage of the Alhambra Theater in *Blackbirds of 1926* with Florence Mills, Mabel Hampton entered the market for day laborers. She too might be found settled on a crate among the group of domestics as they waited for housewives from Yonkers and Westchester. For a short time after she left the theater, she labored in a shirt factory, but a strike forced her back into housework. After the crash of 1929, it was impossible to find a steady position with one family. That white uniform was the one dress she was still forced to wear.

The Chorus Opens the Way

Muses, drudges, washerwomen, whores, house workers, factory girls, waitresses, and aspiring but never-to-be stars make up this company, gather in the circle and fall into the line where all particularity and distinction fade away. One girl can stand in for any of them, can serve as the placeholder for the story, recount the history from the beginning, convey the knowledge of freedom disguised as jargon and nonsense. Few understand them, study them like they are worth something, realize their inherent value. If you listen closely, you can hear the whole world in a bent note, a throwaway lyric, a singular thread of the collective utterance. Everything from the first ship to the young woman found hanging in her cell. Marvel at their capacity to inhabit every woman's grief as their own. All the stories ever told rush from her opened mouth. A tome of philosophy in a moan. In the deepest darkest recess of an opaque song, it is clear that life is at stake.

She is an average chorine, just one of the girls, nobody special, part of the assembly, engulfed in the crowd, lost in the company of minor figures. The songs like her are an enigma, obscure and full of meaning, vital and *so old and raw*, like those voices echoing through the airshaft of the building or the stories of loss and betrayal bellowed from a second-story window, or the pleas whispered in a back alley: *Baby, let me come back home.* In unison, the voices give form to the tragedy:

Sometimes I feel like a motherless child,
A long way from home, a long way from home.

I saw my husband lying dead,
They took me over the sea

Love is like a faucet that turns off and on.
The very time you think you got it
It's turned off and gone.

Blues, please tell me do I have to die a slave?
Blues, please tell me do I have to die a slave?
Do you hear me pleading, you going to take me to my grave.

The song lines, the riotous refrains, the street-corner compositions are hard to explain or reduce to one thing, like a maternal song that makes you and marks you, yet is untranslatable. *Do bana cobe, gene, gene me!* The story exceeds the words, the verses. All the things secreted, harbored deep inside are felt and exclaimed. It is all so terrible and so beautiful. The weight of all that has happened is palpable, the immensity of hurt and betrayal, articulated in the rhythm of the line, conveyed in the length of breath. Living is not to be taken for granted. If you are able to bear the burden of what they have to bring, then there is a place for you inside the circle and what you have suffered is part of this inventory. The war, theft, rout, rape, and plunder are lodged in every line.

If you dare to listen and watch, or shout, "Speak—Tell it now," or clap your hands, you're in it and there's no escape. Now it is impossible to turn your back, to carry on like the world is the same. Don't waste a breath asking why she has to hold everything the rest can't bear, like you don't know, like you supposed things were some other way, like there was some gift other than what she offered in her outstretched hands; don't dare ask, you're in no position nor is anyone else except the ones with the crumpled paper bags stuffed with work clothes, or the kitchen conscripts, or the Middle Alley whores, or the fast girls acting like fools in the club and moving like angels on the stage, or girls trapped in an attic or raped in a coal bin, or women, bent over tubs, scrubbing and washing for the whole city, or sleeping in the room off the kitchen so they can raise the children and tend to the husbands and ensure the *future increase* of the world set against them. The chorus makes a plan, they draft a blueprint: move, escape, rush to the city, quit the job and run away from everything hell-bent on sucking all the life out of them. A moment of reprieve. Then trapped somewhere else, in a different city, a new place, a stranger's house, the boss's bedroom. No one else imagines anything better. So it is left to them to envision things otherwise; as exhausted as they are, they don't relent, they try to make a way out of no way, to not be defeated by defeat.

Who else would dare believe another world was possible, spend the good days readying for it, and the bad days shedding tears that it has not yet arrived? Who else would be reckless enough to dream a colored girl's or a black woman's future? Devote even an afternoon musing about the history of the universe seen from nowhere? Or be convinced that nothing could be said about the Negro problem, modernity, global capitalism, police brutality, state killings, and the Anthropocene if it did not take her into account? Did not reckon with the disavowed geography of the world: the barracoon, the hold, the plantation, the camp, the reservation, the garret, the colony, the attic studio, the bedroom, the urban archipelagoes, the ghetto, and the prison?

The chorus bears all of it for us. The Greek etymology of the word *chorus* refers to *dance within an enclosure*. What better articulates the long history of struggle, the ceaseless practice of black radicalism and refusal, the tumult and upheaval of open rebellion than the acts of collaboration and improvisation that unfold within the space of enclosure? The chorus is the vehicle for another kind of story, not of the great man or the tragic hero, but one in which all modalities play a part, where the headless group incites change, where mutual aid provides the resource for collective action, not leader and mass, where the untranslatable songs and seeming nonsense make good the promise of revolution. The chorus propels transformation. It is an incubator of possibility, an assembly sustaining dreams of the otherwise. *Somewhere down the line the numbers increase, the tribe increases.* The chorus increases. *So how do you keep on?* She can't help it. . . . *The struggle is eternal. Somebody else carries on.*

All of the details of the nothing special and the extraordinary brutality cohere to produce a picture of the world in all its beauty and death. In the whimsical girlish tones, in the loud laughter and the back-and-forth exchange of the hallway, in the girls dancing in the stairwell is a will to unsettle, destroy, and remake that is so forceful

it takes the breath away, so palpable it makes you reel with pain. To fall in step with the chorus is to do more than shake your ass and hum the melody, or repeat the few lines of the bit part handed over like a gift from the historian, as if to say, See, the girl can speak, or to be grateful that the sociologist has taken a second look and recognizes the working out of "revolutionary ideals" in an ordinary black woman's life. Guessing at the world and seizing at chance, she eludes the law and transforms the terms of the possible.

The bodies are in motion. The gestures disclose what is at stake—the matter of life returns as an open question. The collective movement points toward what awaits us, what has yet to come into view, what they anticipate—the time and place better than here; a glimpse of the earth not owned by anyone. So everything depends on them and not the hero occupying center stage, preening and sovereign. Inside the circle it is clear that every song is really the same song, but crooned in infinite variety, every story altered and unchanging: *How can I live? I want to be free. Hold on.*

ACKNOWLEDGMENTS

So much is owed to so many. This book would not have been possible without the work and words of so many brilliant, creative minds. To name a handful of them, the thinkers and artists and planners and rebels and teachers who come most immediately to mind, has as its unavoidable consequence the consignment of so many others to the background, an outcome which is at odds with my most fundamental intention. That said, I must thank the smaller and more immediate circle of those who enabled this work. The influence of Hazel Carby, Angela Davis, Judith Butler, Édouard Glissant, Jamaica Kincaid, Abbey Lincoln, Toni Morrison, Hortense Spillers, Gayatri Spivak, Michel-Rolph Trouillot, and Patricia Williams has been immeasurable.

The fellowship of friends and collaborators has nurtured this work. I have been inspired by conversation and engagement with Elizabeth Alexander, Jonathan Beller, Rizvana Bradley, Dionne Brand, Tina Campt, Anne Cheng, Huey Copeland, Ann Cvetkovitch, Denise Ferreira da Silva, Marisa Fuentes, Macarena Gómez Barris, Farah Griffin, Jack Halberstam, Sarah Haley, Tera Hunter, Arthur Jafa, Robin Kelley, Thomas Lax, Ralph Lemon, Fred Moten, Jennifer Morgan, Alondra Nelson, Tavia Nyong'o, Okwui Okpokwasili, Deborah Paredez, M. NourbeSe Philip, Anupama Rao, Evie Shockley, Neferti Tadiar, Krista Thompson, Ula Taylor, Alexander Weheliye, Mabel Wilson, and Jawole Willa Jo Zollar. The groups Black Modernities, Engendering Archives, Subaltern Urbanism, and Practicing Refusal have provided important spaces for the development of my thought. Tina Campt, Hazel Carby, Anne Cheng, and Christina Sharpe read an early draft of the manuscript and provided invaluable comments.

Many thanks to my agent Joe Spieler and my editor John Glusman for believing in and supporting this project. Their insights and guidance have made this a better book. Helen Thomaides provided abundant editorial support at Norton. Anna Jardine was a remarkable copyeditor. The design team produced the lovely book that I wanted. Tom Jenks encouraged me in an early stage of the project.

I would like to thank the Dorothy and Lewis B. Cullman Center for Scholars and Writers at the New York Public Library for providing me with a haven in which to think and write, and the Guggenheim Foundation for the support needed to complete this project.

Enormous thanks to the archivists at the Columbia Rare Book and Manuscript Library; the Lesbian Herstory Archives; the George Eastman House; Rochester University; the International Center of Photography; the Library of Congress; the Beinecke Library at Yale University; the New York City Municipal Archives; the New York Public Library, Rare Books and Manuscripts; the New York State Archives; the Rockefeller Archive Center; and the Urban Archives at Temple University. Joan Nestle at the Lesbian Herstory Archives extended her support and Tal Nader at the Rare Books and Manuscripts at the New York Public Library helped me to locate needed materials in the Committee of Fourteen records.

I would like to thank Donna Van Der Zee for helping me track down the photograph of Kid Chocolate and giving me permission to reproduce it.

Autumn Womack, Emily Hainze, Erica Edwards, and Eve Eure served as research assistants on this project. Their labor has been invaluable in collecting materials and tracking down elusive documents. The hours of conversation about photography, social surveys, experimental sociology, and, most importantly, the lives contained and condemned within these archival documents enriched the book. At the thirteenth hour, Sarah Haley gave me a great gift by volunteering to take charge of the endnotes. Eve Eure and Ellen Louis assisted her in this task. Abbe Schriber was relentless in tracking down images and acquiring permissions.

This book evolved in the intellectual laboratory that is the classroom. I would like to thank my students in Du Bois and His Circle; Du Bois at 150; Feminist Practice; Slavery, Coloniality, and the Human; Sexual Panic and Criminal Intimacy; and Race and Visuality. The weekly exchange and rigorous engagement honed my thinking. I have learned a tremendous amount by co-teaching with Tina Campt, Anne Cheng, Robert Gooding-Williams, and Neferti Tadiar.

I have benefited from the care and wise counsel of my dear friends Ula, Tina, Anne, and Neferti. These sisters have sustained me. My brother Peter stood by my side as our parents left the world.

This book could not have been written without the love and support of Samuel Miller. Thank you for reading on demand, for believing in me, for answering questions about abstruse matters of the law, and for nurturing me over the long course of the book's production. Thank you for the walks in the woods, for all the delicious meals, for taking care of me, for taking care of Kasia and my mother, for being the full-time parent on duty, for being my rock. My beautiful Kasia, thank you for all the love and the laughter, the zany adventures, the dance-a-thons, the time in the garden, and the thousand valiant attempts to pull me away from my desk, reminding me "it's only a book."

NOTES

A NOTE ON METHOD

xv   **the flapper was a pale imitation:** See Kevin Mumford, *Interzones* (New York: Columbia University, 1997) 108, 116–17. The flapper "symbolized the revolution in values." However, unlike young black women, her modes of sexual expression were not criminalized.

THE TERRIBLE BEAUTY OF THE SLUM

4   *dark ghetto*: Kenneth Clark, *The Dark Ghetto* (1967; repr. Middletown, CT: Wesleyan University Press, 1989).

6   **"terror to white neighbors and landlords alike":** Edwin Emerson, *Harper's Weekly*, January 9, 1897.

6   *broken up completely by the slave ship*: W. E. B. Du Bois, *The Philadelphia Negro: A Social Study* (1899; repr. Millwood, NY: Kraus-Thomson Organization, 1973), 67, 71, 178.

9   **a colored man, accused of stealing a loaf of bread:** Vincent Franklin, "The Philadelphia Riot of 1918," *Pennsylvania Magazine of History and Biography* 99, no. 3 (July 1975): 336.

9   **Then dragged a woman from the hallway:** The Citizens' Protective League, *Story of The Riot* (New York: Citizens' Protective League, September 1900).

9   **"What is to be done with them?":** Paul Laurence Dunbar, "The Negroes of the Tenderloin," in *The Sport of the Gods and Other Essential Writings*, eds.

Shelley Fisher Fishkin and David Bradley (New York: Random House, 2005) 264, 267.

9   **"vomit them back again to the South"**: Dunbar, "The Negroes of the Tenderloin," 267.

A MINOR FIGURE

15 **a different kind of likeness:** Deborah Willis and Carla Williams, *The Black Female Body: A Photographic History* (Philadelphia: Temple University Press, 2002) first introduced me to this image. See also Angela Davis, "Reflections on the Black Woman's Role in the Community of Slaves," *The Black Scholar* 2, November 1, 1981; Thavolia Glymph, *Out of the House of Bondage: The Transformation of the Plantation Household* (New York: Cambridge University Press, 2008); and Tera W. Hunter, *To 'Joy My Freedom: Southern Black Women's Lives and Labors after the Civil War* (Cambridge, MA: Harvard University Press, 1997). On the possibilities of a transformative annotation, see Christina Sharpe, *In the Wake: On Blackness and Being* (Durham, NC: Duke University Press, 2016), 116–24.

15 **anatomist . . . was found with a cache of nude pictures:** Herman Moens, a European "scientist" (he had neither scientific training or a medical degree) studying racial difference took a series of photos of black school-age children in Washington, D.C. The cache was found because the Dutch doctor was being investigated during WWI as a German spy.

19 **Despite their fugitive gestures of refusal:** see Tina Campt, *Listening to Images* (Durham, NC: Duke University Press, 2017), 32, 109, 113.

20 **the caption:** The caption, writes Roland Barthes, "appears to duplicate the image, that is, to be included in its denotation." *Image, Music, Text*, trans. Stephen Heath (New York: Hill and Wang, 1978), 26.

21 **surveillance . . . and the administered logic:** Simone Browne, *Dark Matters: On the Surveillance of Blackness* (Durham NC: Duke University Press, 2015); Nicole Fleetwood, *Troubling Vision: Performance, Visuality, and Blackness* (Chicago: University of Chicago Press, 2011); Kimberly Juanita Brown, *The Repeating Body: Slavery's Visual Resonance in the Contemporary* (Durham, NC: Duke University Press, 2015); Shawn Michelle Smith, *American Archives: Gender, Race, and Class in Visual Culture* (Princeton, NJ: Princeton University Press, 1999); Christina Sharpe, *Monstrous Intimacies: Making Post-Slavery Subjects* (Durham, NC: Duke University Press, 2010); Huey Copeland, *Bound to Appear: Art, Slavery and the Site of Blackness in*

Multicultural America (Chicago: University of Chicago Press, 2013); Nicholas Mirzoeff, *The Right to Look: A Counterhistory of Visuality* (Durham, NC: Duke University Press, 2011).

22 *you love in doorways*: Audre Lorde, "A Litany for Survival," in *The Black Unicorn* (New York: W. W. Norton, 1995), 255.

23 *beautiful flaws and terrible ornaments*: Gwendolyn Brooks, "Boy Breaking Glass," in *In the Mecca* (New York: Harper & Row, 1968).

23 Not until 1953: Roy de Carava, The Hallway, *Imageworks*, Art, Architecture and Engineering Library (Ann Arbor: University of Michigan Press, 1953).

24 compelled image: See Campt, *Listening to Images*, 49, 75.

25 Afterimages of slavery: "The residue of sexual exploitation on slave women's bodies is the afterimage of the black diaspora, the puncture of the past materializing in the present. . . . It presupposes a temporal aberration, an incessant invasion of the present moment by the past." The afterimage is a figure for the sexual legacy of slavery inscribed on black women's bodies. See Brown, *Repeating Body*, 18–19, 56. On annotation as practice of reckoning with violence and antiblackness, see Sharpe, *In the Wake*. Sharpe writes that "Black annotation [is a] way of imagining otherwise." It is a kind of wake work and part of a long history of imagining otherwise, "in excess of the containment of the long and brutal history." It is "a counter to abandonment, another effort to try to look, to try to really see." (126, 112, 115).

27 Art? Science? Pornography?: My reading of this photograph and the girl's experience in the studio is based on Susan Daly and Cheryl Leibold, "Eakins and the Photograph: An Introduction," in Susan Daly and Cheryl Leibold, *Eakins and the Photograph: Works by Thomas Eakins and His Circle in the Collection of the Pennsylvania Academy of the Fine Arts* (Philadelphia: Pennsylvania Academy of the Fine Arts, 1994); Anne McCauley, "'The Most Beautiful of Nature's Works': Thomas Eakins's Photographic Nudes in their French and American Contexts" in Susan Daly and Cheryl Leibold, *Eakins and the Photograph*; Jennifer Doyle, "Sex, Scandal, and Thomas Eakins's *The Gross Clinic*," *Representations*, vol. 68 (Fall 1999): 1–33; Elizabeth Johns, "An Avowal of Artistic Community: Nudity and Fantasy in Thomas Eakins's Photographs," in Susan Daly and Cheryl Leibold, *Eakins and the Photograph*; Mary Panzer, "Photography, Science, and the Traditional Art of Thomas Eakins" in Susan Daly and Cheryl Leibold, *Eakins and the Photograph*; Kathleen A. Foster and Cheryl Leibold, *Writing About Eakins: The Manuscripts in Charles Bregler's Thomas Eakins Collection* (Philadelphia: Pennsylvania Academy of the Fine Arts, 1989); Henry Adams, *Eakins Revealed: The Secret Life of an American*

Artist (New York: Oxford University Press, 2005); Fred Moten, "Taste Dissonance Flavor Escape: Preface for a solo by Miles Davis," *Women & Performance: a Journal of Feminist Theory* 17, no. 2 (July 2007): 217–46; Deborah Willis and Carla Williams, *The Black Female Body: A Photographic History* (Philadelphia: Temple University Press, 2002); Alan Braddock, *Thomas Eakins and the Cultures of Modernity* (Berkeley: University of California Press, 2009); William Innes Homer, *Thomas Eakins: His Life and Art* (New York: Abbeville Press, 1992); Thomas Eakins, *Thomas Eakins: His Photographic Works* (Philadelphia: Pennsylvania Academy of the Fine Arts, 1969); Sidney D. Kirkpatrick, *The Revenge of Thomas Eakins* (New Haven, CT: Yale University Press, 2006); and Thomas Eakins, "Notes on a Differential Action of Certain Muscles Passing More than One Joint," in Thomas Eakins, *A Drawing Manual* (Philadelphia: Philadelphia Museum of Art, 2005).

27   **"The body shows itself"**: This is the definition of pornography according to Roland Barthes, *Camera Lucida: Reflections on Photography*, trans. Richard Howard (1979; reprint New York: Hill & Wang, 2010), 59.

28   **a new era?**: Hazel Carby describes this period as the Woman's Era because of the political and literary activity of black women. See *Reconstructing Womanhood: The Emergence of the Afro-American Woman Novelist* (New York: Oxford University Press, 1989).

28   **statutory rape legislation**: Mary Odem, *Delinquent Daughters, Protecting and Policing Adolescent Female Sexuality in the U.S. 1885–1920* (Chapel Hill: University of North Carolina Press, 1995), 25–31, 33, 35; Carolyn E. Locca, *Jailbait: The Politics of Statutory Rape Laws* (Albany: State University of New York Press, 2004), 14–15; Michelle Oberman, "Regulating Consensual Sex with Minors: Defining a Role for Statutory Rape, *Buffalo Law Review* 48 (2000): 703–84; Jane E. Larson, "Even a Worm Will Turn at Last: Rape Reform in Late Nineteenth Century America, *Yale Journal of Law and the Humanities* 9, no. 1 (1997): 70–71; Ruth M. Alexander, *The "Girl Problem": Female Sexual Delinquency in New York, 1900–1930* (Ithaca, NY: Cornell University Press, 1995).

African American reformers were very wary of statutory rape laws. They were aware that they would fail to protect young black women while being deployed to criminalize black men. For an analysis of the intimacy of rape and racial violence, see Ida B. Wells, *Southern Horrors, Lynch Law in All Its Phases, A Red Record* and *Mob Violence in New Orleans* in *Southern Horrors*, ed. Jacqueline Royster (Boston: Bedford/St. Martin's Press, 1997).

29   **Black girls came before the law**: The law's negation of black personhood failed to recognize sexual injury. See *Scenes of Subjection* (New York: Oxford,

1997), 79–112; Danielle McGuire, *At the Dark End of the Street: Black Women, Rape, and Resistance—A New History of the Civil Rights Movement* (New York: Vintage, 2010).

29   **jeopardy:** Francis Beale, "Double Jeopardy: To Be Black and Female," in *The Black Woman: An Anthology*, ed. Toni Cade Bambara (New York: New American Library, 1970).

29   **had she no interest in it?:** See Ethel Waters, *His Eye Is on the Sparrow: An Autobiography* (Garden City, NY: Doubleday, 1951), 23.

29   *symphony of anger*: Audre Lorde, *Sister Outsider: Essays and Speeches* (1984; repr. Berkeley, CA: Crossing Press, 2007), 129.

29   *we were never meant to survive*: Audre Lorde, "A Litany for Survival," in *The Collected Poems of Audre Lorde* (New York: W. W. Norton, 2000), 255.

30   **potential history:** Ariella Azoulay, "Potential History: Thinking through Violence," *Critical Inquiry* 39, no. 3 (April 2013): 548.

31   **a new era, one defined by extremes:** For a discussion of the paradoxes and contradictions of this period, see Hazel Carby, "On the Threshold of the Women's Era," *Critical Inquiry* 2, no. 1 (October 1985): 262; and "Policing the Black Woman's Body in an Urban Context," *Critical Inquiry*, 18, no. 4 (July 1992): 738.

31   **Nazis' Nuremberg Laws:** James Q. Whitman, *Hitler's American Model: The United States and the Making of Nazi Race Law* (Princeton, NJ: Princeton University Press, 2017), 59–68, 113–24.

35   *eyes in advance of time and experience*: Marguerite Duras, *The Lover*, trans. Barbara Bray (New York: Harper Perennial, 1992).

AN UNLOVED WOMAN

38   **The conductor attempted:** Ida B. Wells, *The Memphis Diary of Ida B. Wells*, ed. Miriam DeCosta-Willis (Boston: Beacon Press, 1995), 77–79. This portrait is indebted to Paula Giddings's wonderful biography, *Ida: A Sword Among Lions—Ida B. Wells and the Campaign Against Lynching* (New York: Amistad, 2009).

38   **"the awful tragedies":** Mary Church Terrell, *A Colored Woman in a White World* (Washington, DC: Randall Inc., Printers and Publishers, 1940), 297, 296.

38   **"not a respectable person":** Brown v. Memphis & Co., 5 Fed. 499 (1880), U.S. App. 2696.

38   **"not-quite human":** In *Black Reconstruction, 1860–1880* (1935; repr. New York: Free Press, 1998), Du Bois writes that slavery damaged the Negro's reputa-

tion as human. Proponents of racial segregation would continue to doubt the Negro's status as human and to assert that crimes against his or her person were socially tolerable because "no human was involved." See Aime Cesaire, *Discourse on Colonialism* (New York: Monthly Review Press, 2000); Sylvia Wynter, "No Human Involved: An Open Letter to My Colleagues" (Stanford, CA: Institute N.H.I., 1994); and Alexander Weheliye, *Habeas Viscus: Racializing Assemblages, Biopolitics and Black Feminist Theories of the Human* (Durham, NC: Duke University Press, 2015).

39   *Ain't I a woman?*: See Nell Painter, *Sojourner Truth: A Life, a Symbol* (New York, W. W. Norton, 1997), 286–301.

39   "dirty-minded mulatress": Paula Giddings, *Ida: A Sword Among Lions*, 318.

39   hardheaded, and willful: These are the terms Wells used to describe herself. See *Crusade for Justice: The Autobiography of Ida B. Wells*, ed. Alfreda Duster (Chicago: University of Chicago Press, 1970), 18. For an examination of Wells's antilynching campaign, see Crystal Feimster, *Southern Horrors: Women and the Politics of Rape and Lynching*; Hannah Rosen, *Terror in the Heart of Freedom: Citizenship, Sexual Violence and the Meaning of Race in the Postemancipation South* (Chapel Hill: University of North Carolina Press, 2009); and Mia Bay, *To Tell the Truth Freely: The Life of Ida B. Wells* (New York: Hill and Wang, 2010). On feminism and willfulness, see Sara Ahmed, *Willful Subjects* (Durham, NC: Duke University Press, 2014).

40   fury of the mob: Ida B. Wells, *Southern Horrors: Lynch Law in All Its Phases* (*New York Age*, 1892; repr. Bedford/St. Martin's, 1997), 55.

40   *She was not in vogue*: Fannie Barrier Williams, "The Colored Girl," *Voice of the Negro* 2, no. 6 (1905), 400–403, reprinted in *The New Woman of Color: The Collected Writing of Fannie Barrier Williams*, ed. Mary Jo Deegan (DeKalb: Northern Illinois University Press, 2002), 63.

40   Then there were the stories: These incidents are described in Ida B. Wells, *Southern Horrors: Lynch Law in All Its Phases* (*New York Age*, 1892; repr. Bedford/St. Martin's, 1997), 58, 59, 71.

AN INTIMATE HISTORY OF SLAVERY AND FREEDOM

45   Mattie's chance: The story begins before the case file is assembled. It opens with her rushing to the city, packed on a steamer with hundreds of others in search of a better life. It opens in the midst of an experiment with freedom. It is a story that exceeds the archive.

46   **she was sure glad to be leaving:** This is a speculative account of Mattie's journey from Virginia to New York. The Old Dominion service was the primary mode of transportation from Norfolk and Richmond, and more generally along the Eastern Seaboard to New York City. There were smaller steamers that transported passengers from Hampton to Norfolk. See "Steamship Monroe, of the Old Dominion Line," *Marine Engineering* 8, no. 8 (August 1903): 396; and *The Official Railway* (New York: National Railway Publication Company, 1908), 1077. On Virginia migrants in New York City, see W. F. Osburg, "The Richmond Negro in New York" (master's thesis, Columbia University, 1909); Benjamin H. Locke, "The Community Life of a Harlem Group of Negroes" (master's thesis, Columbia University, 1913), 6; Robert Z. Johnstone, "The Negro in New York" (master's thesis, Columbia University, 1911), 8; and Paul Seymour, "A Group of Virginia Negroes in New York City" (master's thesis, Columbia University, 1912).

47   *field and the brothel:* Frederick Douglass described the plantation household as follows: "every kitchen was a brothel" in "Love of God, Love of Man, Love of Country: An Address Delivered in Syracuse, New York, on September 24, 1847," *Frederick Douglass Papers, Vol. 1: 1842–1852* (New Haven, CT: Yale University Press, 2009), 93. See also Sharpe, *Monstrous Intimacies.* This was no less true in the twentieth century. See Katherine McKittrick, "Plantation Futures," *Small Axe* 16, no. 3 (November 2013): 1–15. W. E. B. Du Bois also noted "the kitchen contains a whole social history" in *The Negro American Family: Report of a Social Study Made Principally by the College Classes of 1909 & 1910 of Atlanta University* (Atlanta, GA: Atlanta University Publications, 1908), 66.

47   *house of bondage:* The "house of bondage" is a figure for the afterlife of slavery, the domestic servitude of black women, and for prostitution. See Glymph, *Out of the House of Bondage*; Octavia V. Rogers Albert, *The House of Bondage or Charlotte Brooks and Other Slaves* (New York: Hunt and Eaton, 1891); and Reginald Wright Kauffman, *House of Bondage* (New York: Grosset & Dunlap, 1921).

47   **to steerage:** On segregation on the Old Dominion steamer, see Arthur Browne, *One Righteous Man: Samuel Battle and the Shattering of the Colored Line in New York* (New York: Beacon Press, 2016): "Nobody knows how it happened but on every Old Dominion Steamship that docked there (were) from two to three hundred Negroes landed in New York," p. 16; and Gilbert Osofsky, *Harlem: The Making of a Ghetto: Negro New York, 1890–1930* (Chicago: Ivan R. Dee, 1996), 30.

48   **"the one thing which seemed to offer hope":** John Berger, *A Seventh Man: A Book of Images and Words about the Experience of Migrant Workers in Europe* (Baltimore: Penguin, 1975; repr. New York: Verso, 2010), 33.

48   **what the future would hold:** In 1900, Mattie was just two years old and taking her first independent steps; that year, the state of Virginia had passed a law that mandated segregation in public transportation, curtailing the ways she could move in the world and fixing her place in it—she had been consigned to the bottom rung, always the eternal alien, the governed but never the citizen. In 1882, the *Chicago Tribune* began collecting lynching statistics. By the time Mattie arrived in New York City in the fall of 1914, nearly three thousand Negro men, women and children had been hanged, burned, castrated, and dismembered across the nation. While the majority of these acts occurred in the south, black folks were being murdered from New Jersey to Texas, from the heart of the Confederacy to Lincoln's birthplace. The tally of the lynched published in the *Tribune* and *The Crisis: A Record of the Darker Races* failed to account for the ordinary terror of life under Jim Crow; no one compiled statistics on the everyday and unspectacular acts of violence, kept count of the sexual assaults and insults, or recorded the daily humiliations of the color line.

48   **Matthews ... waiting for her at the pier:** On arrivals at the New York Dock, see the National League for the Protection of Colored Women, *1910 Annual Report* (New York, 1911), Schomburg Center for the Research in Black Culture, New York Public Library, New York, New York; Frances Kellor, "The Problem of the Young Negro Girl from the South," *New York Times* (March 19, 1905), 8; Frances Kellor, "Opportunities for Southern Negro Women in Northern Cities," *Voice of the Negro* (Atlanta, GA), July 1905; Victoria Earle Matthews, "Some of the Dangers Confronting Southern Girls in the North," *Hampton Negro Conference* 2, July 1898, and reprinted in Shirley Wilson Logan, *We Are Coming: The Persuasive Discourse of Nineteenth-Century Black Women* (Carbondale: Southern Illinois University Press, 1999), 215–20; "Migration of Colored Girls from Virginia," *Hampton Bulletin: Ninth Annual Report of the Hampton Negro Conference* (September 1905), 57–59; and Kelly Miller, "Surplus Negro Women," *Southern Workman* (October 1905): 522–28.

49   **they had escaped:** On views of black women's migration, see previous note and W. E. B. Du Bois, *Philadelphia Negro*, and New York Colored Mission, *Report of the New York Colored Mission* (New York: New York Colored Mission, 1871–1966).

49 *conditions of the Negro in the north*: Victoria Earle Matthews expressed her views on Dunbar's pessimism in a *New York Sun* editorial, September 14, 1897.

49 **"go home to God morally clean"**: Matthews, "Some of the Dangers Confronting Southern Girls in the North," 220.

49 **service was inculcated in every possible way**: *Everyday Life at Hampton Institute* (Hampton, VA: Hampton Institute, 1909).

51 **"monstrous intimacy"**: Sharpe, *Monstrous Intimacies*; Edouard Glissant, *Caribbean Discourse: Selected Essays*, trans. J. Michael Dash (Charlottesville: University Press of Virginia, 1989), 80.

51 **mistaken for white**: "It was her personality and natural endowment, physically, which gave her entree to places, and conditions in the South not accessible to many of our women." Elizabeth Lindsey Davis, *Lifting As They Climb* (New York: G. K. Hall, 1996), 22.

51 **death knell of Reconstruction**: The Spanish-American War was central to the making of a reunited white nation in the aftermath of the Civil War. The citizen-soldiers of north and south were reconciled on the stage of imperial war. In 1898, Mattie's parents were in Cuba. Twenty-five percent of the US soldiers were African Americans. Robin D. G. Kelley, "Mike Brown's Body: Meditations on War, Race and Democracy," Toni Morrison Lectures, April 13, 2015, Princeton University, Princeton, NJ; Amy Kaplan, "Black and Blue on San Juan Hill," in *Cultures of United States Imperialism*, eds. Amy Kaplan and Donald E. Pease (Durham, NC: Duke University Press), 219–36.

51 **the letter she received**: The letter was from Miss Hattie Morehouse, a white schoolteacher in Jacksonville, Florida, asking her to meet a girl soon to arrive by steamer. The young woman was found several days later, after a diligent search that involved police detectives, but by this time, she was a ruin of her former self. Victoria Earle Matthews, "Some of the Dangers Confronting Southern Girls in the North," *We Are Coming: The Persuasive Discourse of Nineteenth-Century Black Women*, ed. Shirley Wilson Logan (Carbondale, IL: Southern Illinois University Press, 1999), 215–220.

51 **"broken, disgraced young creature"**: Matthews, "Some of the Dangers Confronting Southern Girls in the North," 215.

52 **no past to which she could appeal**: Victoria Earle Matthews, "The Awakening of the Afro-American Woman" (1897), reprinted in *With Pen and Voice: A Critical Anthology of Nineteenth-Century African-American Women*, ed. Shirley Wilson Logan (Carbondale: Southern Illinois University Press, 1995), 151.

52   **"the depraved class commonly met with on the streets"**: Matthews, "Some
      of the Dangers Confronting Southern Girls," 219.

53   **something rotten, something spoiled**: See Erving Goffman, *Stigma: Notes
      on the Management of Spoiled Identity* (New York: Simon & Schuster, 1963),
      34, 42.

53   **Stigma isn't an attribute, it's a relationship**: Here I am paraphrasing Erving
      Goffman, who defines the impossible struggle to shake loose stigma as fol-
      lows: "the transformation of self from someone with a particular blemish into
      someone with a record of having corrected a particular blemish." *Stigma*, 9.

53   **respectable over and against**: Goffman, *Stigma*, 6.

53   **white people labeled a *Negress***: This is how she is described in the case file.
      See Bedford Hills Case File#2466. Bedford Hills Correctional Facility Col-
      lection, 14610–77B; inmate case files, ca. 1915–1930, 1955–1965, Records of
      the Department of Correctional Services, New York State Archives, Albany,
      New York. Hereafter referred to as Bedford Hills Case File.

54   **made Broadway into lyric**: Dunbar, *Sport of the Gods*.

55   **need of breathing room**: Philadelphia Housing Authority, "Negro Migrant
      Study," n.d., Philadelphia Housing Authority Papers, Urban Archives, Tem-
      ple University, Philadelphia; and The Chicago Commission on Race Rela-
      tions, "The Migration of Negroes from the South," *The Negro in Chicago: A
      Study of Race Relations and a Race Riot* (Chicago: University of Chicago Press,
      1922), 79–105.

55   **a feast of its meager opportunities**: All the usual sentimental reasons that
      are detailed in migrant studies and riot commission reports accounted for
      her presence in New York: freedom to move, the want of better opportu-
      nity, an escape from racist violence, an exit from slavery—reasons stated
      and replayed in songs, poems, letters, rumors and gossip. See The Chicago
      Commission on Race Relations, *The Negro in Chicago*.

55   **girls as dark as Mattie**: The biography of Mattie that follows is based
      upon her Bedford Hills Case File. The files are very detailed, particularly
      for 1917–1920, because the Laboratory of Social Hygiene conducted an
      extensive series of interviews with girls and women (between the ages of
      fourteen and thirty) on their arrival at the reformatory. The intake process
      included personal interviews; family histories; interviews with neighbors,
      employers, and teachers; psychological tests, physical examinations, and
      intelligence tests; and reports of social investigators and probation offi-
      cers. After a two-week evaluation of the compiled materials, physicians,
      psychologists, social workers, sociologists, and prison superintendents met

to discuss each individual case. The files also contain personal correspondence, discussions of sexuality, life experiences, and personal history, and photographs of the prisoners and their children; some files include poems and plays and love letters written by the young women; they also note the women's feelings and attitudes about their arrests. The case file was intended as a comprehensive account of the individual, which was critical to the state's practice of punishment and reform, management of the poor, and maintenance of the color line. The case file aimed to produce deep knowledge of the individual life, which was central to discourse of prison reform and the idea that incarceration, parole and probation need be contoured to the profile of the offender. This accounted for the shift to indeterminate sentencing as a "humane" and "scientific" approach to punishment. The modality of the case was grounded in a hermeneutics of suspicion and a horizon of reform. The case file was a product of the therapeutic state. See Michel Foucault, *Discipline and Punish: The Birth of the Prison*, trans. Alan Sheridan (New York: Vintage, 1995); David Rothman, *Conscience and Convenience: The Asylum and Its Alternatives in Progressive America*, chapter 2 (New York: Aldine Transactions, 2002); "On the Case," special issue, *Critical Inquiry* 33, no. 4 (Summer 2007); Karen W. Tice, *Tales of Wayward Girls and Immoral Women: Case Records and the Professionalization of Social Work* (Urbana: University of Illinois Press, 1998).

56   **queer arrangements of Chinatown:** See Nayan Shah, *Contagious Divides: Epidemics and Race in San Francisco's Chinatown* (Berkeley: University of California Press, 2001) and Mary Ting Yi, *The Chinatown Trunk Mystery: Murder, Miscegenation, and Other Dangerous Encounters in Turn-of-the-Century New York City* (Princeton: Princeton University Press, 2007).

59   *"I want that":* Tonya Foster, *A Swarm of Bees in High Court* (New York: Belladonna, 2015), 68.

60   **thought in deed:** Thought in deed is critical to anarchist practice. It is the foundation of a black feminist practice, which shares much with anarchism in its critique of state violence and struggle against enclosure on the plantation and in the city. The young women in this book are thinkers and radicals in this tradition. Also see Erin Manning and Brian Massumi, *Thought in the Act: Passages in the Ecology of Experience* (Minneapolis: University of Minnesota Press, 2014). On the relation between sexuality and the emergence of racism and coloniality, see Ann Stoler, *Carnal Knowledge and Imperial Power* (Berkeley: University of California Press, 2010); and Mumford, *Interzones*. Michel Foucault writes that sexuality is "a dense set of transfer points in

relations of power" in *History of Sexuality*, trans. Robert Hurley (New York: Pantheon Books, 1978), 96.

60 ***like any artist with no art form***: Toni Morrison, *Sula* (New York: Vintage, 1973), 121.

60 ***If she could feel deeply***: Audre Lorde, "Poetry is Not a Luxury," in *Sister Outsider*, 38.

61 **the third revolution of black intimate life**: See W. E. B. DuBois, "Of the Faith of the Fathers," in *The Souls of Black Folk* (1903; repr. New York: Penguin, 1989), 159–60; and *Negro American Family*.

61 **surpassed the status crimes**: See Carby, "Policing the Black Woman's Body," Sarah Haley, *No Mercy Here: Gender, Punishment, and the Making of Jim Crow Modernity* (Chapel Hill: University of North Carolina Press, 2016); Cheryl Hicks, *Talk With You Like a Woman: African American Women, Justice, and Reform in New York, 1890–1935* (Chapel Hill: University of North Carolina Press, 2010); Kali Gross, *Colored Amazons: Crime, Violence and Black Women in the City of Brotherly Love, 1880–1910* (Durham, NC: Duke University Press, 2006); Cynthia M. Blair, *I've Got to Make My Livin': Black Women's Sex-Work in Turn-of-the-Century Chicago* (Chicago: University of Chicago Press, 2010); and Emily Hainze, "Wayward Reading" (unpublished PhD diss., Columbia University, 2017).

62 ***verified history***: The Bedford case files label the state's gathering of rumor and fact as the "Verified History." The women's accounts are called "Statement of the Girl."

62 ***complete program of disorder***: Frantz Fanon, *The Wretched of the Earth*, trans. Richard Philcox (New York: Grove Press, 2005), 2.

63 **end of the world**: Black feminism is the desire for the end of the world as we know it. See Denise Ferreira da Silva, "Toward a Black Feminist Poetics: The Question of Blackness towards the End of the World," *Black Scholar* 44, no. 2 (Summer 2014), 81–97; Hortense Spillers, *Black, White & In Color: Essays on American Literature and Culture* (Chicago: University of Chicago, 2003); and Alexander Weheliye, *Habeas Viscus: Racializing Assemblages, Biopolitics and Black Feminist Theories of the Human* (Durham, NC: Duke University Press, 2014).

63 ***I liked doing it***: Mattie used each of these phrases to describe her relationship with Herman Hawkins.

63 **refusing shame**: On the willingness to inhabit and embrace deviance, see Cathy Cohen, "Deviance as Resistance," *Du Bois Review* 1, no. 1 (2004): 27–45.

65 *clutching at a way of life*: Fanon, "Grandeur and Weakness of Spontaneity," in *The Wretched of the Earth*, trans. Richard Philcox (1961; repr. New York: Grove Press, 2004).

68 **an exaggerated performance of what was expected or imposed**: Laurent Berlant, "Intimacy: A Special Issue," *Critical Inquiry* (Winter 1998), 285.

71 **more than an apology**: "The mother offered to make a restitution for them but the detective urged that a complaint be made." Bedford Hills Case File#2466.

71 **moral depravity**: "Her immoral life is the fact, the offense for which she is sentenced to the institution, the thing that is the crime in the eyes of the Law." Katherine Davis, "Preventive and Reformatory Work: The Fresh Air Treatment for Moral Disease," in *Informal and Condensed Report of the American Prison Congress* (Albany, NY, 1906), 24.

72 **Mattie screaming**: In December, the abuses at Bedford would be made public. Torture and abuse had been reported since 1913. See "Bedford Cruelty Charges Against Officials Upheld," *New York Tribune*, March 19, 1920.

73 **a guard was always present**: See Katherine Davis on "The Reformatory Plan," Proceedings of the National Conference of Charities and Corrections (Boston 1916). The supervised visits were discussed in the *Annual Reports of the State Commission on Prisons* (Albany, NY), 1915, 1920, and 1921.

75 **words travel even when we can't**: On the object of the prison letter, see Sora Han, "The Purloined Prisoner," *Theoretical Criminology* 16, no. 2 (May 2012): 157–74.

76 *if they destroyed much*: C. L. R. James, *The Black Jacobins: Toussaint L'Ouverture and the San Domingo Revolution* (London: Secker and Warburg, 1938; repr. New York: Vintage, 1989), 88.

AN ATLAS OF THE WAYWARD

This portrait of W. E. B. Du Bois is indebted to the work of many scholars. David Levering Lewis's magisterial two-volume biography, *W. E. B. Du Bois: Biography of a Race, 1868–1919* (New York: Henry Holt, 1993) and *W. E. B. Du Bois: The Fight for Equality and the American Century, 1919–1963* (New York: Henry Holt, 2000) have provided a treasure trove for my counter-narrative. As important is the critical secondary literature on Du Bois's scholarship: Nahum Dimitri Chandler, *X—The Problem of the Negro as a Problem of Thought* (New York: Fordham, 2014); Robert Gooding-Williams, *In the Shadow of Du Bois: Afro Modern Political Thought in America* (Cambridge, MA: Harvard University Press, 2009); Aldon

Morris, *The Scholar Denied: W. E. B. Du Bois and the Birth of Modern Sociology* (Oakland: University of California Press, 2015); Lawrie Balfour, *Democracy's Reconstruction: Thinking Politically with W. E. B. Du Bois* (New York: Oxford University Press, 2011); Hazel Carby, *Race Men* (Cambridge, MA: Harvard University Press, 1998); Farah Jasmine Griffin, "Black Feminists and Du Bois: Respectability, Protection, and Beyond," in "The Study of African American Problems: W. E. B. Du Bois's Agenda, Then and Now," special issue, *Annals of the American Academy of Political and Social Science* 568 (March 2000): 28–40; Lewis Gordon, "Du Bois's Humanistic Philosophy of the Human Sciences," in "The Study of African American Problems: W. E. B. Du Bois's Agenda, Then and Now," *Annals of the American Academy of Political and Social Science* 568 (March 2000): 265–80; Lucius Outlaw, "W. E. B. Du Bois on the Study of Social Problems," in "The Study of African American Problems: W. E. B. Du Bois's Agenda, Then and Now," *Annals of the American Academy of Political and Social Science* 568 (March 2000): 281–97; Cedric Robinson, *Black Marxism: The Making of the Black Radical Tradition*, (London: Zed Books, 1983); Kwame Anthony Appiah, "The Uncompleted Argument: Du Bois and the Illusion of Race," *Critical Inquiry* 12, no. 1 (1985): 21–37; Robert Stepto, *From Behind the Veil: A Study of Afro-American Narrative* (Urbana: University of Illinois, 2001); Kwame Anthony Appiah, "Illusions of Race," in *In My Father's House* (Oxford: Oxford University Press, 1992); Kwame Anthony Appiah, *W. E. B. Du Bois and the Emergence of Identity* (Cambridge, MA: Harvard University Press, 2014); Anthony Bogues, *Black Heretics, Black Prophets* (New York: Routledge, 2003); Joy James, *Transcending the Talented Tenth: Black Leaders and American Intellectuals* (New York: Routledge, 1996); Karen E. Fields and Barbara Fields, "Individuality and the Intellectuals: An Imaginary Conversation Between Emile Durkheim and W. E. B. Du Bois," in *Racecraft: The Soul of Inequality in American Life* (London: Verso, 2012), 225–60; Shatema Threadcraft, *Intimate Justice: The Black Female Body and the Body Politic* (New York: Oxford University Press, 2016); Cornel West, *The American Evasion of Philosophy* (Madison: University of Wisconsin Press, 1989); Shamoon Zamir, *Dark Voices, W. E. B. Du Bois and American Thought, 1888–1903* (Chicago: University of Chicago Press, 1995).

84   **threw a stone:** Patrick Chamoiseau, *Texaco*, trans. Rose-Myriam Réjouis and Val Vinokurov (New York: Pantheon, 1997).

85   **Bethel African Methodist Episcopal Church:** Bethel African Methodist Church was established after officials at St George's, the white Methodist church, denied unwelcome black parishioners even the right to pray.

88   **where they believed the cancer resided:** W. E. B. Du Bois, *The Autobiography of W. E. B. Du Bois: A Soliloquy on Viewing My Life from the Last Decade of its First Century* (New York: International Publishers, 1968), 194.

88   *race responsible for so much crime:* Du Bois, *The Philadelphia Negro: A Social Study* (1899; repr. Philadelphia: University of Pennsylvania Press, 1996), 241. The sponsors of the study hoped to quarantine and eradicate the threats posed by the ward. Civic leaders warned that the Negroes are a "hopeless element in the social wreckage" and they must be prevented from "accumulating too rapidly" or contaminating the respectable element "just outside the almshouse door." *Biography of a Race*, 188. Also see *Autobiography of W. E. B. Du Bois*, 194–204.

89   **residing in** *an atmosphere of dirt:* Du Bois, *Autobiography of W. E. B. Du Bois*, 195.

89   *labor blindly:* Du Bois was very critical of philanthropy. He described the "blind and aimless desire to do good," which characterized much charity and social reform work. "Aimless philanthropy" finds it easier to "labor blindly" than to "wait intelligently." W. E. B. Du Bois, "The Development of a People," *The Problem of the Color Line at the Turn of the Twentieth Century: The Essential Early Essays*, ed. Nahum Dimitri Chandler (New York: Fordham University Press, 2015), 244.

89   *where the refuse could be disposed:* Philadelphia Negro, 62.

89   *ghetto . . . an open-air prison:* W. E. B. Du Bois was the first to use the term *ghetto* to describe the racialized enclosure of black people. The column entitled The Ghetto was a regular feature of *The Crisis: A Record of the Darker Races* and it documented the expanding legal and social apparatus of racial segregation and the everyday violence of the color line. James Baldwin noted the impossibility of breathing in the ghetto along lines that anticipated Fanon's description of the native quarter in *Wretched of the Earth*. Baldwin writes that the ghetto is pervaded by a sense of congestion, "the insistent, maddening, claustrophobic pounding in the skull that comes from trying to breathe in a very small room with all the windows shut." Zygmunt Bauman echoes Baldwin and similarly observes that the "ghetto is a prison without walls . . . there is an ongoing exchange of a population between the prison and the ghetto and the urban space rendered as enclosure. See *Community: Seeking Safety in an Insecure World* (Cambridge: Polity Press, 2001), 120. Also see Loïc Wacquant, "From Slavery to Mass Incarceration: Rethinking the 'Race' Question in the US," *New Left Review* 1 (January 1, 2002).

90 **"Little Africa netted a courtroom"**: *Philadelphia Inquirer*, December 3, 1895 and June 17, 1895, quoted in Roger Lane, *Roots of Violence* (Cambridge, MA: Harvard University Press, 1986), 148; Du Bois, *Philadelphia Negro*, 313.

91 *as deep and dark a tragedy as any*: Kelly Miller, "Surplus Women," in *Race Adjustment: Essays on the Negro in America* (New York, Neale Publishing, 1908), 170–171; Charlotte Perkins Gilman, "The Duty of Surplus Women," *New York Independent* (January 1905).

93 *utter disregard of a black woman's virtue*: Du Bois, *Negro American Family*, 41.

93 **In a novel**: W. E. B. Du Bois, *The Quest of the Silver Fleece* (Chicago: A. C. McClurg, 1911).

93 **the role of chance**: W. E. B. Du Bois, "Sociology Hesitant," in *Problem of the Color Line: Negro American Family*, 42.

93 **the Negro slum**: Loic Wacquant, "What Is a Ghetto? Building a Socio-logical Concept," *Revista de Sociologia e Politica* (November 1, 2004): 155; Loic Wacquant, "From Slavery to Mass Incarceration: Rethinking the 'Race' Question in the US," *New Left Review* 1 (January 1, 2002); Erving Goffman, *Asylum: Essays on the Social Situation of Mental Patients and Other Inmates* (Chicago: Aldine, 1961); Kenneth Clark, *The Dark Ghetto* (New York: Harper & Row, 1965; Middletown: Wesleyan University Press, 1989); Mitchell Dunier, *The Ghetto: The Invention of A Place, the History of an Idea* (New York: Farrar, Straus & Giroux, 2016); Tommie Shelby, *Dark Ghettos: Injustice, Dissent, and Reform* (Cambridge, MA: Belknap/Harvard University Press, 2016); E. Franklin Frazier, *The Negro Family in Chicago* (Chicago: University of Chicago Press, 1932); St. Clair Drake and Horace R. Cayton, *Black Metropolis; A Study of Negro Life in a Northern City* (New York: Harcourt, Brace, 1945).

93 **weren't yet white**: On the process by which Europeans immigrants became white, see W. E. B. Du Bois, "The Souls of White Folk" in *Darkwater* (1920; repr. New York: Washington Square Press, 2004); Nell Irvin Painter, *The History of White People* (New York: Norton, 2011); David Roediger, *Wages of Whiteness: Race and the Making of the American Working Class* (New York: Verso, 1991); Noel Ignatiev, *How the Irish Became White* (New York: Routledge, 1995); Michael Rogin, *Blackface, White Noise: Jewish Immigrants in the Hollywood Melting Pot* (Berkeley: University of California Press, 1998); Eric Lott, *Love and Theft: Blackface Minstrelsy and the American Working Class* (New York: Oxford University Press, 1995); Matthew Frye Jacobsen, *Whiteness of a Different Color* (Cambridge, MA: Harvard University Press, 1999);

Thomas Lee Philpott, *The Slum and the Ghetto* (New York: Oxford University Press, 1978); Douglass Massey and Nancy Denton, *American Apartheid: Segregation and the Making of the Underclass* (Cambridge, MA: Harvard University Press, 1993); Toni Morrison, *Playing in the Dark: Whiteness and the Literary Imagination* (New York: Vintage, 1993).

94   **freedom was an open experiment:** Du Bois, *Souls of Black Folk*, 18, 25, 34.

94   **apparent harmony:** Du Bois, *Philadelphia Negro*, 81.

95   *All pimps look alike:* "All Pimps Look Alike to Me," was the tune Ernest Hogan appropriated and rewrote as the hit song "All Coons Look Alike to Me," which sold more than a million copies and was the bane of black existence in the 1890s. He earned nearly $30,000 in royalties for the song but on his deathbed expressed regret for having written it.

95   *All I ever wanted:* The line is from Me'Shell Ndegéocello, "Deuteronomy: Niggerman," *Peace beyond Passion*, Maverick Records, 1996. Format.

96   *loiterers on the ragged edge of industry:* Miller, "Surplus Women," in *Race Adjustment*, 171.

98   *crushing weight of slavery:* Du Bois, "Damnation of Women," in *Darkwater*, 115.

98   *count the bastards and the prostitutes:* W. E. B. Du Bois, "Of Our Spiritual Strivings," in *Souls of Black Folk*, 9.

98   **trembled:** In the introduction to *Philadelphia Negro*, Du Bois writes, "He must ever tremble lest some personal bias, some moral conviction or unconscious trend of thought . . . distort the picture in his view." The sexual immorality of the black community often made Du Bois "shudder" and "tremble." For a reading of his sexual politics, see Hazel Carby, "The Souls of Black Men," in *Race Men* (Cambridge, MA: Harvard University Press, 1998), 9–44; Melinda Chauteauvert, "Framing Sexual Citizenship: Reconsidering the Discourse on African American Families," *Journal of African American History* 93, no. 2 (Spring 2008): 198–222; Cathy Cohen, "Deviance as Resistance," *Du Bois Review* 1, no. 1 (2004): 27–45; Farah Jasmine Griffin, "Black Feminist and Du Bois: Respectability, Protection and Beyond," *Annals of the American Academy of Political and Social Science* 568 (March 2000): 28–40; Roderick Ferguson, *Aberrations in Black: Toward a Queer of Color Critique* (Minneapolis: University of Minnesota Press, 2003).

98   **the common hardship of poverty:** W. E. B. Du Bois, *The Souls of Black Folk*, 57; *W. E. B. Du Bois: Biography of a Race* (New York: Henry Holt, 1993). See Carby, "The Souls of Black Men," in *Race Men*, 9–44.

99   **835 hours:** Herbert Aptheker notes that if Du Bois spent twenty minutes with
      each household (2,500 households), the interviews for the survey would have
      added up to 835 hours, or about 104 days. See Introduction to W. E. B. Du Bois
      in *Philadelphia Negro*. In "My Evolving Program for Negro Freedom," in *What
      the Negro Wants*, ed. Rayford Logan (1944; Notre Dame: University of Notre
      Dame Press, 2001). Du Bois states that he interviewed 5,000 people. In his
      Autobiography of W. E. B. Du Bois, he claims to have interviewed 10,000.

100   **"dissected and by an unknown Negro":** In his *Autobiography of W. E. B. Du
      Bois*, he wrote: "The colored people of Philadelphia received me with no open
      arms. They had a natural dislike to being studied like a strange species."(198)
      See also Levering Lewis, *W. E. B. Du Bois: Biography of a Race* (New York:
      Henry Holt, 1993), 190.

100   **refused to tell him anything:** Du Bois, W. E. B. Du Bois, A Program for a
      Sociological Society 1897 Reel 80: 61, W. E. B. Du Bois Papers, University of
      Massachusetts, Amherst.

101   **He learned far more about the Negro problem from them:** Du Bois, "My
      Evolving Program for Negro Freedom," in *What the Negro Wants*; *Autobiog-
      raphy of W. E. B. Du Bois*.

101   **A third . . . were servants:** *The Philadelphia Negro*, 136.

101   **in the homes of white folks:** "Introduction: The Context of the Philadelphia
      Negro," *W. E. B. Du Bois, Race and the City*, eds. Michael Katz and Thomas
      Sugrue (Philadelphia: University of Pennsylvania Press, 1998), 10. See Isabel
      Eaton, "Special Report on Negro Domestic Service in the Seventh Ward,"
      Supplement to Du Bois, *Philadelphia Negro*, 454.

101   **white women's kitchens:** Du Bois, *Philadelphia Negro*, 133, 136; Tera Hunter,
      "The 'Brotherly Love' for which This City Is Proverbial Should Extend to All:
      The Everyday Lives of Working Class Women in Philadelphia and Atlanta in
      the 1890's," in *W. E. B. Du Bois, Race and the City*, 131, 132.

102   ***Degraded homes:*** Du Bois, "The Development of a People," in *Problem of the
      Color Line*, 254–55; "Family struggling to recover from debauchery of slav-
      ery," 257.

103   **Half . . . claimed to be widows:** Between 54.5 percent and 59.2 percent of
      black women between twenty and thirty-nine years old claimed to be wid-
      ows. Du Bois, *Philadelphia Negro*, 70; Lewis, *Biography of a Race*, 205.

104   **"I know I am not what I ought to be":** Du Bois, *Negro American Family*, 39.

105   **chosen vocations:** Du Bois, *Philadelphia Negro*, 60, 138.

105   **sheer physical existence:** Du Bois, "The Development of a People," in *Prob-
      lem of the Color Line*, 246, 355.

107 *open rebellion*: The Philadelphia Negro, 235.

107 *race that was responsible for so much crime*: Du Bois, *Philadelphia Negro*, 241. Crime in Philadelphia had increased steadily since 1880. For a critique of Du Bois's engagement with and reproduction of the discourse of black criminality, see Kevin Gaines, *Uplifting the Race: Black Leadership, Politics and Culture in the Twentieth Century* (Chapel Hill: University of North Carolina Press, 1996); Khalil Muhammed, *The Condemnation of Blackness: Race, Crime and the Making of Modern America* (Cambridge, MA: Harvard University Press, 2011); and Fred Moten, "Uplift and Criminality," in *Next to the Color Line: Gender, Sexuality and Du Bois* (Minneapolis: University of Minnesota, 2007), 317–49.

107 **seven times greater than their portion of the total population:** Monroe Work, "Crimes among Negroes of Chicago," *Journal of American Sociology* 6 (September 1900): 204–23; *The Nation*, July 1, 1897, 6–7.

108 **crime was the necessary outcome of racial policing:** Du Bois accepted the fact of black criminality, falling prey to the idea that Negroes committed more crime and that the reasons for black crime had to be explained. See Muhammed, *Condemnation of Blackness*; Gaines, *Uplifting the Race*; and Moten, "Uplift and Criminality."

108 **they *rushed to the city*:** The Philadelphia Negro, 254, 351.

108 **described the general strike:** W. E. B. Du Bois, *Black Reconstruction: An Essay toward a History of the Part which Black Folk Played in the Attempt to Reconstruct Democracy in America, 1860–1880* (1935; repr. New York: Free Press , 1999), 67.

108 ***The Negro was on strike***: T. J. Woofter Jr., "The Negro on Strike," *The Journal of Social Forces* 84 (1923–24): 84–88.

108 *a great human experiment*: Du Bois, *Black Reconstruction*, 383.

108 **"seeking political asylum within the borders of their own country"**: Isabel Wilkerson, *The Warmth of Other Suns: The Epic Story of America's Great Migration* (New York: Random House, 2010).

109 **knuckles put on *exhibition***: On the lynching of Sam Hose, see "Science and Empire," in *Dusk of Dawn* (New York: Oxford University Press, 2014). See Ida B. Wells's *Southern Horrors*, *A Red Record* and *Mob Violence in New Orleans*, collected in *Southern Horrors*, ed. Jacqueline Royster.

109 **refusal of the conditions of work:** Du Bois describes the general strike as a "great human experiment." See *Black Reconstruction*, 383. In *The Philadelphia Negro*, Du Bois produces a survey that will reform race relations by addressing white ignorance. The majestic *Black Reconstruction* attempts so

much more than this. It endeavors to radically transform our understanding of democracy by addressing the state of the enslaved and attending to the strike and flight of the enslaved as the remaking of American democracy. To do so requires Du Bois to foreground and to imagine the visions, aspirations, and practices that were never archived.

109 **"Life is elsewhere"**: Du Bois, "Of Beauty and Death," in *Darkwater*, 184.

110 *courage to greet them on the street*: Du Bois, *Philadelphia Negro*, 397–99.

110 **a story in motion**: Amiri Baraka, *In Our Terribleness* (New York: Bobbs, Merill, 1970). On Du Bois's use of visual graphics, see Alexander Weheliye, "Diagrammatics as Physiognomy," *CR: The New Centennial Review* 15, no. 2 (2015), 23–58.

111 **would one day be extinct**: Du Bois, *Philadelphia Negro*, 163, 319, 388.

111 **Hoffman's statistics**: See Frederick L. Hoffman, *Race Traits and Tendencies of the American Negro*, Publication of the American Economic Association 11, nos. 1–3 (1896), 1–329. Hoffman was an insurance actuary who argued that Negroes as a race were dying out and would be extinct. His prediction was based on a statistical analysis of death rates in the city.

113 *prostitutes of Middle Alley*: Du Bois, *Philadelphia Negro*, 193.

114 *Etta Jones . . . tragic stories*: Du Bois, *Philadelphia Negro*, 259–67.

114 *ripened too soon*: Jean Toomer, "Karintha," in *Cane* (1923; repr. New York: W. W. Norton, 2011), 1–2.

115 **Josie . . . was a thin homely girl**: "Of the Meaning of Progress," *The Souls of Black Folks* (1903; repr. New York: Penguin, 1989), 52.

115 *no touch of vulgarity or immorality*: When he describes ranks of Negroes, Du Bois characterizes the decent poor as being without a touch of immorality. He describes Mr. Dowell as being "calmly ignorant, with no touch of vulgarity." *Souls of Black Folk*, 53.

115 **She might have confided**: Du Bois, *Darkwater*, 102.

115 **sexual watershed**: The first time Du Bois wrote about Josie was in a personal essay, "A Negro Schoolmaster in the New South," in *The Atlantic Monthly* (January 1899, vol. 83, no. 495, 99–105). Josie would appear again in *The Souls of Black Folk*, *Dusk of Dawn*, and *Autobiography of W. E. B. Du Bois*. David Levering Lewis describes Du Bois's experience in the Dowell household as a "sexual watershed" in W. E. B. Du Bois's *Biography of a Race*, 71.

116 *I was literally raped*: *Autobiography of W. E. B. Du Bois*, 280.

116 *living example of the possibilities of the Negro race*: W. E. B. Du Bois, "The Talented Tenth" in *Problem of the Color Line*, 212. Du Bois's commitment

to the idea of race leadership by the elite persisted across the decades. As late as 1944, he writes of a "far-seeing leadership" and of the elites "those individuals and classes among Negroes whose social progress is at once the proof and measure of the capabilities of the race." See "My Evolving Program for Negro Freedom," (1944; repr. *Clinical Sociology Review* 8, no. 1, 1990), 51, 55.

116 **shudder:** *Autobiography of W. E. B. Du Bois*, 280. In "The Development of a People," Du Bois also uses the term "shudder" to describe the debauchery and nameless children in Negro homes: "Here is a problem of home and family. One shudders at it almost hopelessly." See Du Bois, *Problem of the Color Line*, 249.

117 *Crime and ornament:* See Adolf Loos, "Crime and Ornament," in *The Architecture of Adolf Loos: An Arts Council Exhibition* (London: London Arts Council, 1985), 101. "The reach of progress is thus equated with the suppression and erasure of erotic material excess, deemed to be the exclusive domain of sexual and savage primitives," such as "Negroes, Arabs, rural peasants." For a brilliant engagement of Loos, race and modernism, see Anne Cheng's *Second Skin: Josephine Baker and Modern Surface* New York: Oxford University Press, 2013), 24–25, 72–78.

117 *will to adorn:* Zora Neale Hurston, *The Sanctified Church* (Berkeley, CA: Turtle Island, 1981), 50.

117 **"Dandies" and "Clothes-bags":** Alexander Crummell, "Common Sense in Common Schooling," *Civilization and Black Progress* (Charlottesville: University of Virginia Press, 1995), 140.

117 **love of the baroque:** Zora Neale Hurston, "Characteristics of Negro Expression," in *The Sanctified Church* (Berkeley, CA: Turtle Island, 1981), 52.

117 **"gaudy and sensual":** Jane Addams, *The Spirit of Youth and City Streets* (New York: MacMillan, 1909), 8–9.

118 **"the fact of her existence":** Addams, *Spirit of Youth and City Streets*, 2.

118 **immoral habits and unhealthy bodies:** Du Bois, *Philadelphia Negro*, 162.

118 **reluctant lover:** Du Bois, *Autobiography of W. E. B. Du Bois*, 281.

119 **his *dear wife* unhappy:** *Autobiography of W. E. B. Du Bois*, 281.

119 *lusty young man:* *Autobiography of W. E. B. Du Bois*, 281.

A CHRONICLE OF NEED AND WANT

124 **Helen ordered Fanny Fisher:** See *Diary of Helen Parrish*, Octavia Hill Association (Philadelphia, PA) Records, SCRC 29, URB 46, Box 1, Spe-

cial Collections Research Center, Temple University Libraries, Philadelphia, Pennsylvania.

Helen Parrish wrote that Fanny Fisher cursed and used obscene language. Parrish didn't record the obscenities in her journal, however. The dialogue is recreated based upon Helen's detailed account of the exchange. She often paraphrased her conversations with tenants. When foul language was used, she noted that the tenant spoke to her in an offensive and disgusting manner or called her vile names or cursed. I have transcribed this indirect and reported speech into direct speech. My speculative and imaginative approach is based on archival research and a rigorous attention to sources.

124 **bringing her down to their level:** *Diary of Helen Parrish,* July 1 and July 8, 1888. Octavia Hill Collection.

124 **a debt that could never be paid:** On indebted personhood, see Saidiya Hartman, *Scenes of Subjection: Terror, Slavery, and Self-Making in Nineteenth Century America* (New York: Oxford University Press, 1997); and Denise Ferreira da Silva, "Accumulation, Dispossession, and Debt: The Racial Logic of Global Capitalism—An Introduction," *American Quarterly* 64, no. 3 (September 2012): 361.

125 **Saint Mary Street was in the ward:** John Sutherland, "Reform and Uplift among Philadelphia Negroes: The Diary of Helen Parrish, 1888," in *Pennsylvania Magazine of History and Biography* 94, no. 4 (October 1970): 499; Allen F. Davis and Mark Haller, *The Peoples of Philadelphia: A History of Ethnic Groups and Lower Class Life 1790–1940* (Philadelphia: University of Pennsylvania Press, 1998).

125 **Dark Hebrew women:** *Fourth Annual Report of the College Settlement Association,* from September 1, 1892 to September 1, 1893 (Philadelphia: College Settlement Association), 22–23.

126 **Hannah Fox purchased them:** Hannah Fox, Draft of an Address Talked, not Read before the Civic Federation, Washington, D.C. 1913, 2 (unpublished, Octavia Hill Association Collection, Urban History Archives, Temple University, Philadelphia).

126 **a very different tone:** The two women intended to transform the condition of the poor by improving their housing and physical environment and by providing a model of the moral conduct to which the less fortunate should strive. The poor were not immoral or criminal by nature, but made so by their condition. Fox and Parrish's plan, which was backed by family wealth, was based on the British housing reformer Octavia Hill's work with the Lon-

don poor. Hill espoused the mutuality of interests between the wealthy and the working classes and advocated a policy for slum reform that married the principles of philanthropy and capitalist investment. In short, the upper classes were to improve the housing conditions of the poor and inculcate the truly disadvantaged with the values of thrift, temperance, responsibility, and domesticity that they sorely lacked. For meeting their social duty, conscientious landlords were to be rewarded with a small profit of 5 percent on their initial investment. The experiment presumed that mutual interests and affection would bridge the divide between property owners and the propertyless, and alleviate class antagonism.

127 **their career as housing reformers:** Herbert Aptheker, Introduction, *Philadelphia Negro* (Philadelphia: University of Pennsylvania Press, 1973), 8, 10.

127 **Subjective need:** Jane Addams, "Subjective Need for Social Settlements" (1892), reprinted in *Twenty Years at Hull House* (New York: Macmillan, 1910), 94–100.

128 **en masse far from it:** The last four lines are verbatim from the *Diary of Helen Parrish* but have been recast in the third person.

130 **Poor Mary seemed content:** *Diary of Helen Parrish*, August 29.

131 **Negroes in the city lived in a state of poverty:** Du Bois, *Philadelphia Negro*, 171.

131 **Helen headed straight to the police precinct:** The entry in the *Diary of Helen Parrish* reads "While at no. 3 Katy Clayton came in, and quite unprovoked begin reviling me about writing her father lies. I quieted her and went about my rounds . . . . I went down to see Gallen. He said that on Saturday night, Katy, and the three Gallaghers, and others were on the steps. When he came again he met two Gallaghers leaving but not Jim. The steps was empty. He put his key in the door, heard a scuffle went through into the yard and Jim was there. He ordered him out and made him go. He slunk away. Two of the others were in the yard too. He says the officers are all alive about Katy, that if she can only be caught in the act she will be arrested. That he believed in her before but is convinced that things are wrong—I told him I would see the Lieutenant and spoke also about Mary Brown's."

133 *All are against me:* Helen wrote the majority of the entries, but another collector who served as a substitute in Helen's absence makes several. Perhaps not surprising is how little the perspective or voice changes across these entries.

137 **"floating on a sea of sense":** Dunbar, *Sport of the Gods*.

137 **lost in the silks and laces:** Stephen Crane, *Maggie and Other Tales of the Bowery* (New York: Modern Library, 2001).

139 **"encircled by disaster":** James Baldwin, *Sonny's Blues Going to Meet the Man* (1948; repr. New York: Vintage Books, 1995), 129.

151 **Shot in the Neck:** "Shot in the Neck: The Mysterious Affray That Startled Lisbon Street," *Philadelphia Inquirer*, October 4, 1888.

IN A MOMENT OF TENDERNESS THE FUTURE SEEMS POSSIBLE

155 **"What that niggah got to marry on?":** The mother, Sarah Jane, asks this of her daughter Isabelle and her fiancé, Sylvester. *Body and Soul* (1925) was directed by Oscar Micheaux.

This reading of *Body and Soul* is indebted to Charles Musser, who notes the open-ended and nonresolvable character of the film's layered plot. I take advantage of the film's disjunctive character in producing this counter-narrative. The "real" is abbreviated and hard to distinguish from the extended dream or nightmare sequence. "To Redream the Dreams of White Playwrights: Reappropriation and Resistance in Oscar Micheaux's Body and Soul," in *Oscar Micheaux & His Circle*, eds. Pearl Bowser, Jane Gaines, and Charles Musser (Bloomington: Indiana University Press, 2001); See also Hazel Carby, *Race Men: The Body and Soul of Race, Nation and Manhood* (Cambridge: Harvard University Press, 1998); Pearl Bowser, *Writing Himself into History: Oscar Micheaux, His Silent Films and His Audiences* (New Brunswick: Rutgers University Press, 2000); and Jane Gaines, *Fire and Desire: Mixed Blood Relations in Silent Cinema* (Chicago: University of Chicago Press, 2000).

157 **weather:** Christina Sharpe describes the weather as the all-encompassing atmosphere of antiblackness. Here, it is helpful to think about the precariousness of black life and imperiled love in the context of antiblackness, racist violence, and economic precarity. See "The Weather," in *In the Wake: On Blackness and Being* (Durham, NC: Duke University Press, 2016), 102–134.

1900. THE TENDERLOIN. 241 WEST 41ST STREET

162 **beached whale:** Hortense Spillers, "Interstices: A Small Drama of Words," in *Black, White and In Color: Essays on American Literature and Culture* (Chicago: University of Chicago Press, 2003), 153. Spillers writes: "Black women

are the beached whales of the sexual universe, unvoiced, misseen, not doing, awaiting their verb."

163 **New Negroes:** Henry Louis Gates, "The Trope of the New Negro and the Image of the Black," *Representations* 24 (Autumn 1988): 129–55; Henry Louis Gates and Gene Jarrett, *Readings on Race, Representation and African American Culture* (Princeton, NJ: Princeton University Press, 2007); *A New Negro for a New Century*, ed. Booker T. Washington (Chicago: American Publishing House, 1900). Alain Locke, ed. *The New Negro: Voice of the Harlem Renaissance* (1925; repr. New York: Touchstone, 1996).

164 **Colored folks hated him:** "Race Riot In New York City: Ten Thousand White People Spread Terror in the Tenderloin District," *New York Age*, August 23, 1900. This description of Thorpe is from his brother. See "Foresaw Brother's End," *New York World* (New York, evening edition), August 16, 1900.

165 **He was the one who told the police:** His friend George told May to get out of there, and she ran home. A white man smoking in the alley next to the theatre saw a light-skinned colored woman with a black eye rush up the street. He was the one who told the police where they could find May. This conflicts with Arthur Harris's version. See Trial Transcript. Case #32015, *People v. Arthur Harris*, County of New York, Box 608, District Attorney Indictment Papers, New York County, Court of General Sessions, New York City Municipal Archives.

165 **"lose control of your body":** Spillers, "Interstices: A Small Drama of Words," in *Black, White and In Color*. Also see "A Woman's Lot: Black Women Are Sex Objects for White Men," in *Black Women in White America: A Documentary History* (New York: Vintage, 1992).

165 **"negress," and "wench":** *New York Tribune*, August 17, 1900; *Sun* (New York), August 16, 1900.

166 *May Enoch's Rag:* Bryan Wagner contends that the blues emerge in the confrontation with police power. In support of this claim, he discusses an origin story recounted by the musician Jelly Roll Morton about rebel hero Robert Charles and a popular song about him that was never recorded. "The Black Tradition from Ida B. Wells to Robert Charles," in *Disturbing the Peace: Black Culture and Police Power after Slavery* (Cambridge, MA: Harvard University Press, 2009). On the public representation of May Enoch's character, see Judith Weisenfeld, *African American Women and Christian Activism* (Cambridge: Harvard University Press, 1998) and Hicks, *Talk with You Like a Woman*, 53–90.

166 **"He tried to lock up my woman":** Trial Transcript. Case #32015, People v.

Arthur Harris, County of New York, Box 608, District Attorney Indictment Papers, New York County, Court of General Sessions, New York City
Municipal Archives.

166   **"I fixed that son of a bitch"**: Trial Transcript. Case #32015, People v. Arthur
Harris, County of New York, Box 608, District Attorney Indictment Papers,
New York County, Court of General Sessions, New York City Municipal
Archives.

167   **"Lynch the niggers!"**: *New York Herald*, August 16, 1900; August 17, 1900.

168   **"the coolest monster on the corner"**: Lucius Shepherd, "Miles Davis," *The
Nation*, July 2, 2003.

169   **If courage made him an outlaw**: "So he lived and so he would have died had
not he raised his hand to resent unprovoked assault and unlawful arrest that
fateful Monday night. That made him an outlaw, and being a man of courage
he decided to die with his face to the foe." Lines from Ida B. Wells, *Mob Rule
in New Orleans* (1900), in *Southern Horrors and Other Writings*, ed. Jacqueline
Jones Royster (Boston: Bedford/St. Martin's, 1997), 202.

169   **covered with blood**: The Citizens' Protective League, *Story of the Riot*, 31.

170   **"jumped out of the window"**: Citizens' Protective League, *Story of the Riot*, 34.

171   **clubbing colored people**: Irene was a widow, doing general housework, ironing, washing and working hard. She was a thoroughly respectable woman.
Citizens' Protective League, *Story of the Riot*, 39.

171   **It didn't make a damn bit of difference if you were a woman or a man**:
Citizens' Protective League, *Story of the Riot*, 39.

171   **locked away in jail cells**: Citizens' Protective League, *Story of the Riot*, 41, 42.

171   **"treat niggers the same as down South"**: Citizens' Protective League, *Story
of the Riot*, 49.

171   **"We're going to make it hot for you niggers!"**: Citizens' Protective League,
Story of the Riot, 49.

171   **"Kill every damned one of the niggers!"**: Citizens' Protective League, *Story
of the Riot*, 53.

171   **"Set the House afire!"**: Citizens' Protective League, *Story of the Riot*, 53.

171   **"'Shut up, you're a whore'"**: Nettie Threewitts recounted "I was kept in
the station house without any clothes, except my nightgown, for about two
hours, when a woman who lives on 41st street gave me an underskirt, which
I put on." Citizens' Protective League, *Story of the Riot*, 60.

172   **"don't hit me!"**: Citizens' Protective League, *Story of the Riot*, 48.

172   ***Lord Help Me!***: Le'Andria Johnson, "Jesus," *The Awakening of Le'Andria
Johnson*, Music World Gospel, 2012.

172 **Women pleaded for their fathers and husbands:** Citizens' Protective League, *Story of the Riot*, 64–5.

173 **"[redress] now, when can we get it":** Reverend Cuyler, "Colored Pastor's Demand," *New York Times*, August 20, 1900.

173 **forty thousand Negroes:** By 1910, Black folks made up 1.9 percent of the city's population. See Osofsky, *Harlem*; and "Race Riot, 1900: A Study of Ethnic Violence," *Journal of Negro Education* 32, no. 1 (Winter 1963): 16–24. Also see Marcy Sacks, *Before Harlem: The Black Experience in New York City Before World War I* (Philadelphia: University of Pennsylvania Press, 2006), 72–106.

174 **stanch the flood of black folks:** See Kevin McGruder on the Property Owner's Protective Association of Harlem, "From Eviction to Containment," in *Race and Real Estate: Conflict and Cooperation in Harlem, 1890–1920* (New York: Columbia University Press, 2017), 62–97; David Levering Lewis, *When Harlem Was in Vogue* (New York: Penguin, 1997), 25; and Lewis Thorin Tritter, "The Growth and Decline of Harlem's Housing," *Afro-Americans in New York Life and History* 22, no. 1 (January 31, 1998); "$20,000 to Keep Negroes Out," *New York Times*, December 8, 1910.

174 **refusing to hire them:** As Matthew Frye Jacobsen writes: "It is not just that various white immigrant groups' success came at the expense of nonwhites, but that they owe their now stabilized and broadly recognized whiteness itself to the groups." *Whiteness of a Different Color*, 7–8. The 1924 Johnson Immigration Act further solidified this notion of whiteness.

174 **Negroes of the Tenderloin:** The Tenderloin was the vice district of the city. It extended between Twentieth and Fifty-Third Streets, west of Sixth Avenue and running to the waterfront. See Kenneth Jackson, ed. *The Encyclopedia of New York* (New Haven, CT: Yale University Press, 2010), 1289.

174 **invite the wrath of white folks:** *New York Times*, "Paul L. Dunbar Drugged," August 20, 1900.

175 *deep impassioned cry*: Paul Laurence Dunbar, "To the South on Its New Slavery," in *The Complete Poems of Paul Laurence Dunbar* (New York: Meade & Dunbar, 1913), 82.

1909. 601 WEST 61ST STREET. A NEW COLONY OF COLORED PEOPLE, OR MALINDY IN LITTLE AFRICA

177 **future of the race:** Mary White Ovington, *Half a Man: The Status of the Negro in New York* (New York: Longmans, Green, and Co., 1911). See also

Carolyn Wedlin, *Inheritors of the Spirit: Mary White Ovington and the Founding of the NAACP* (New York, John Wiley, 1998), 93.

179 **"fashionable coats, and well-creased trousers":** Ovington, *Half a Man*, 149.

179 **"never freer from insult":** "Vacation Days in San Juan Hill," *Southern Workman* 38 (November 1909): 628.

179 **"a fraternity of perverts":** "An Admonition," *New York Times*, April 29, 1908; Wedlin, *Inheritors of the Spirit*, 96–98.

179 **she was a race traitor:** "Dinner Minus Color Line: White Men of Club Dine with Negro Women and Decry Caste," *New York Times*, April 28, 1908; "An Admonition," *New York Times*, April 29, 1908; "Race Equality Feast," *Washington Post*, April 29, 1908; "Inter-Racial Dinners to be Given Monthly," *St. Louis Post-Dispatch*, April 29, 1908; The *Savannah News*, April 29, 1908, described Ovington as "the high priestess . . . whose father is rich and who affiliates five days in every week with Negro men and dines with them at her home in Brooklyn, Sundays. She could have had a hundred thousand Negroes at the Bacchanal feast had she waved the bread tray. But the horror of it is that she could take young girls into that den." Cited in Wedlin, *Inheritors of the Spirit*, 98.

180 **"Negro material":** Mary White Ovington, "Living on San Juan Hill," *Black and White Sat Down Together: The Reminiscences of an NAACP Founder*, ed. Ralph Luker (New York: Feminist Press, 1996).

180 **"a mass of humanity":** Ovington, *Half a Man*, 32.

180 **"human beehives":** "Vacation Days in San Juan Hill," 627.

181 **gave the hill its name:** Ovington, "Living on San Juan Hill," 26.

181 **entirely Negro blocks:** Ovington, *Half a Man*, 39.

181 **"likely to visit in the South":** Ovington, *Half a Man*, 39.

181 **"The buildings are *swarmed*":** *New York Times*, August 14, 1905.

181 **cordoned into exclusively black streets and neighborhoods:** Philpott, *Slum and the Ghetto*. John R. Logan, Weiwei Zhang and Miao Chunyu, "Emergent Ghettos: Black Neighborhoods in New York and Chicago, 1880–1940," *American Journal of Sociology* 120, no. 4 (January 2015): 1055–94. See Massey and Nancy Denton, *American Apartheid* (Cambridge, MA: Harvard University Press, 1993).

181 **Segregation leveled the distinctions:** Ellie Alma Wallis, "The Delinquent Negro Girl in New York, Her Need of Institutional Care" (master's thesis, Columbia University, 1912).

181 **opium-addled girls:** See Ryan Lane Bedford Hills File #2778. She grew up across the street from Ovington's model tenement.

182 **whore's *Internationale*:** Committee of Fourteen, Rockefeller survey of prostitution, White Slavery Grand Jury, Investigator's Report, Series V, Box 28, 1910 Committee of Fourteen Papers, Manuscript and Archives Division, New York Public Library.

182 **"Negro superiority":** Wedlin, *Inheritors of the Spirit*, 117; *Black and White Sat Down Together*, 61.

182 **the libertine colony:** See Doris Garroway, *The Libertine Colony* (Durham, NC: Duke University Press, 2005); Ann Stoler, *Carnal Knowledge and Imperial Power*; Achille Mbembe, *On the Postcolony* (Durham, NC: Duke University Press, 2001); and Jared Sexton, *Amalgamation Schemes: Antiblackness and the Critique of Multiracialism* (Minneapolis: University of Minnesota Press, 2008). All examine the sexual fantasy and libidinal economy of colonialism and the erotic investments that figure in the making of racial difference, colonial power, and antiblackness.

182 **distinctive geography:** Kevin Mumford describes the interzone as an area of cultural, sexual and social interchange. Interzones are inter-racial districts, stigmatized social spaces characterized by vice and prostitution. See Mumford, *Interzones*, 23. See Spiller, "Interstices," in *Black, White and In Color*, 156–57.

182 **"ceaseless sounds of humanity":** "Vacation Days in San Juan Hill," 628.

183 **"voices would come up the airshaft":** Ethel Waters, *His Eye Is On the Sparrow* (New York: Da Capo Press, 1992), 130; Nat Hentoff and Nat Shapiro, *Hear Me Talking to Ya* (New York: Dover Books, 1996), 224–25. Also see Shane Vogel, *The Scene of Harlem Cabaret* (Chicago: University of Chicago, 2009), 87–90.

183 **"threatening death to the degraded creature":** Ellie Wallis, "Delinquent Girls in New York" (master's thesis, Columbia University, 1920), 31.

183 **"*no acquiescence in slavery's status*":** "Vacation Days in San Juan Hill," 633.

183 **"the more he is sheltered and cared for":** "Vacation Days in San Juan Hill," 630.

184 **lexical gap between black female and woman:** Spillers, "Interstices," in *Black, White and In Color*, 156–57.

185 **"opportunity and larger freedom?":** Ovington, *Half a Man*, 164.

186 **As early as 1643, black women's labor:** See Tera Hunter, *Bound in Wedlock: Slave and Free Black Marriage in the Nineteenth Century* (Cambridge, MA: Harvard University Press, 2017), 9–10.

186 **"ungendering":** Hortense Spillers, "Mama's Baby, Papa's Maybe" and "Notes on Brooks and the Feminine" in *Black, White and in Color*, 149, 207–224.

186 **threshold between the dangerous and the unknown:** black women's refusal to work was even more threatening, according to Ovington, because it easily yielded to sexual promiscuity and prostitution. See "The Colored Women in Domestic Service," Bulletin of the Inter-Municipal Committee on Household Research 1, no. 7 (May 1905), 11.

187 *"Malindy of the hour":* Ovington, *Half a Man*, 148.

187 **extramarital affairs:** See Lewis, *W. E. B. Du Bois: Biography of a Race.*

188 **"purify his filthy imagination":** On the affair, see Wedlin, *Inheritors of the Spirit*, 68–70; and Linda Lumsden, *Inez: The Life and Times of Inez Milholland* (Bloomington: Indiana University Press, 2016), 25.

188 **maternal "weakness in the contour and color":** Ovington, *Half a Man*, 153.

188 **"vicious environment . . . strengthened her passions":** Ovington, *Half a Man*, 168.

188 **"she refuses to her colored neighbor":** Ovington, *Half a Man*, 162.

188 **"the ocean might rise up":** Ovington, *Half a Man*, 166.

188 **too heavy a load:** See Deborah Gray White, *Too Heavy a Load: Black Women in Defense of Themselves, 1894–1994* (New York: W. W. Norton, 1999).

189 **"sometimes she has not even tried":** Ovington, *Half a Man*, 168.

189 **"called to him a good-night":** "Vacation Days in San Juan Hill," 632.

189 **"I can dance now":** "Vacation Days in San Juan Hill," 632.

189 **fifteen or eighteen dollars a week:** Ovington, *Half a Man*, 157.

190 **Annabel glanced at the bare:** "Vacation Days in San Juan Hill," 632.

MISTAH BEAUTY, THE AUTOBIOGRAPHY OF AN
EX-COLORED WOMAN, SELECT SCENES FROM A
FILM NEVER CAST BY OSCAR MICHEAUX, HARLEM, 1920S

193 **If Gladys Bentley's life were an Oscar Micheaux film:** This sketch is based on Bentley's autobiographical essay, "I Am a Woman Again," *Ebony Magazine* (August 1952).

193 **he:** Throughout this section, I use the masculine pronoun to refer to Bentley to respect his masculine identification. He didn't feel like a woman or see himself as one during these decades. In his autobiographical essay "I Am a Woman Again," he describes the hormone therapy necessary to transform him into a woman. To my mind, this makes clear that he had abandoned the categories of *woman* and *female* decades earlier and justifies the use of "he."

194 **preening defiance and naked display of pleasure:** This list of queer traits is

culled from George Henry's *Sex Variants: A Study of Homosexual Patterns*, 2 vol. (New York: Hoeber, 1941).

196 **actuality of blackness:** Oscar Micheaux often used "actualities" or documentary footage in his films. The use of the actuality enabled him to archive forms of cultural practice and social assembly.

196 **in the clearing:** See Wilson Harris, "The Limbo Dance," in *Selected Essays of Wilson Harris*, ed. Andrew Bundy (New York: Routledge, 1999), 156–58; and Sterling Stuckey on the ring shout, "Introduction: Slavery and the Circle of Culture," in *Slave Culture* (New York: Oxford University Press, 1987).

197 **definitive of the cinema:** Rebecca Solnit, *River of Shadows* (New York: Penguin, 2004); Charles Musser, *The Emergence of Cinema: The American Screen to 1907* (Berkeley: University of California Press, 1994); Marta Braun, *Muybridge* (London: Reaktion Books, 2010).

197 **flow and frequency:** Tina Campt, unpublished paper, "Black Flow," delivered at Yale University, February 2018.

197 **reconstructed along radically different lines:** See Jacqueline Najuma Stewart, *Migrating to the Movies* (Berkeley: University of California Press, 2005), 94, on the ways that black cinema, including Micheaux's, enabled a "reconstructive spectatorship, a formulation which accounts for the ways in which Black viewers attempted to reconstitute and assert themselves in regard to cinema's racist and social operations." Leigh Raiford extends this line of argument in her reading of lynching photographs in *Imprisoned in a Luminous Glare: Photography and the African American Freedom Struggle* (Chapel Hill: University of North Carolina Press, 2013).

197 *celebrate with great solemnity*: "It hurts so much that we have to celebrate." Fred Moten, *Black and Blur* (Durham, NC: Duke University Press, 2017), xii; Amiri Baraka, *In Our Terribleness*.

197 **"the subject of much tongue wagging":** Wilbur Young, WPA, Negroes of New York, Sketches of Colorful Harlem Characters, "Gladys Bentley," September 29, 1938, Schomburg Collection, New York Public Library.

199 **"African sculpture animated by rhythm":** Langston Hughes, *The Big Sea* (New York: Hill and Wang, 1993); Anne Anlin Cheng, *Second Skin: Josephine Baker and Modern Surface* (New York: Oxford University Press, 2013); Jack Halberstam, *Trans*: A Quick and Quirky History of Gender Variance* (Berkeley: University of California Press, 2018); Lucas Crawford, "Breaking Ground on a Theory of Transgender Architecture," *Seattle Journal for Social Justice* 8, no. 2 (Spring/Summer 2010); Robert Farris Thompson, *African Art in Motion* (Berkeley: University of California Press, 1979).

199 **woman waited in the wings:** These are the story lines of various Micheaux films: *Within Our Gates*, *Scar of Shame*, *Ten Minutes to Live*, and *Swing*.

199 *to lay down their jive just like a natural man:* Lucille Bogan, "B. D. Blues":

> B. D. Women, they all done learnt their plan
> B. D. Women, they all done learnt their plan
> They can lay their jive just like a natural man

Quoted from *Shave 'Em Dry: The Best of Lucille Bogan*, Sony 2004. On the radical politics of women's blues, see also Angela Davis, *Blues Legacies of Black Feminism* (New York: Vintage, 1999); Hazel Carby, "It Just Be's that Way Some Time: The Sexual Politics of Women's Blues," *The Jazz Cadence of American Culture*, ed. Robert O'Meally (New York: Columbia University Press, 1996); Anne Ducille, "Blue Notes on Black Sexuality: Sex and the Texts of Jessie Fauset and Nella Larsen," *Journal of the History of Sexuality* 3, no. 3 (January 1993): 418–44; Farah Jasmine Griffin, *If You Can't Be Free, Be A Mystery: In Search of Billie Holiday* (New York: One World, 2002); Erin Chapman, *Prove It on Me: New Negroes, Sex and Popular Culture in the 1920's* (New York: Oxford University Press, 2012).

200 **intimate trespass afforded by the nighttime:** "Intimacy, as Harlem's history asserts, is a kind of trespass: the intimacy effects of the cabaret make conscious the boundaries between self and other as well as the conditions of their crossing." See Shane Vogel's *The Scene of Harlem Cabaret: Race, Sexuality, Performance* (Chicago: University of Chicago Press, 2009), 41–42.

200 **righteous propagation:** This term is borrowed from Michelle Mitchell to describe the conjugal arrangements deemed essential to the propagation of the race. See *Righteous Propagation: African Americans and Destiny after Reconstruction* (Chapel Hill: University of North Carolina Press, 2004). Also see Kevin Gaines, *Uplifting the Race* (Chapel Hill: University of North Carolina Press, 1996) and Evelyn Higginbotham, *Righteous Discontent: The Women's Movement in the Black Church* (Cambridge, MA: Harvard University Press, 1994).

200 **much discussed marriage to a white woman:** See Alfred Duckett, "The Third Sex," *Chicago Defender*, March 2, 1957. Duckett makes reference to Bentley's wives. The marriage in a New Jersey civil ceremony was common knowledge, yet I have not been able to find any verification of this in the press.

202 *I inhabited that half-shadow:* Gladys Bentley, "I Am a Woman Again,"

Ebony Magazine 7, no. 10 (August 1952): 92–98. See Eric Garber, "Gladys Bentley: The Bulldagger Who Sang the Blues," *Out/Look* 1, no. 1 (Spring 1988): 52–61. See also "Spectacle in Color: The Lesbian and Gay Subculture of Jazz Age Harlem," in *Hidden from History: Reclaiming the Gay and Lesbian Past*, ed. Martin Duberman et al. (New York: Meridien, 1990); David Serlin, "Gladys Bentley and the Cadillac of Hormones," in *Replaceable You: Engineering the Body in Postwar America* (Chicago: University of Chicago Press, 2004), 111–58; Carmen Mitchell, "Creations of Fantasies/Constructions of Identities: The Oppositional Lives of Gladys Bentley," *The Greatest Taboo: Homosexuality in Black Communities*, ed. Delroy Constantine-Simms (Los Angeles: Alyson Books, 2000), 211–225; and James F. Wilson, *Bulldaggers, Pansies and Chocolate Babies* (Ann Arbor: University of Michigan Press, 2011). On female masculinity, see Jack Halberstam, *Female Masculinity* (Durham, NC: Duke University Press, 1998). On black transgender analytics and identity, see C. Riley Snorton, *Black on Both Sides* (Minneapolis: University of Minnesota Press, 2017); Kai Green, "Troubling the Waters: Mobilizing a Trans* Analytic," in *No Tea, No Shade: New Writings in Black Queer Studies*, ed. E Patrick Johnson (Durham, NC: Duke University Press, 2016); Matt Richardson, *The Queer Limit of Black Memory* (Columbus: Ohio State University, 2016).

202 *walk just like a natural man:* Lucille Bogan, "B. D. Blues."

FAMILY ALBUMS, ABORTED FUTURES: A DISILLUSIONED WIFE BECOMES AN ARTIST, 1890 SEVENTH AVENUE

This portrait of Edna Thomas is based on newspaper clippings and a confidential interview conducted by Dr. George W. Henry in his extensive case study of homosexuals, *Sex Variants: A Study of Homosexual Patterns* (New York: Hoeber, 1941). The project was sponsored by the Committee for the Study of Sex Variants and the interviews were conducted in the 1930s. Jan Gay collected more than three hundred case histories of lesbian women in the hopes of countering the discrimination and criminalization of queer sexuality. The Committee for the Study of Sex Variants wanted to decriminalize homosexuality, although defining it as an abnormal sexuality and the result of failed and broken families and/or the gender nonconformity of parents. In the context of her collaboration with the committee, Jan Gay's role as the initiator of the project and as a primary researcher was greatly minimized, if not erased, and her work incorporated without due recognition. Gay was responsible for the great numbers of artists and leftist activists included in the study. (She was the daughter of Ben Reitman, who abandoned his family to become Emma Goldman's lover.) John Katz first identified Edna Thomas as Pearl M in *Gay/Lesbian Almanac: A New Documentary* (New York: Harper & Row, 1983): 526–28. Edna Thomas had appeared earlier as Mary Jones in "Psychogenic Factors in Overt Homosexuality," *American Journal of Psychiatry* 93, no. 4 (January 1937): 889–908. For an extensive discussion of this study and an insightful reading of the interviews, see Henry Minton, *Departing from Deviance: A History of Homosexual Rights and Emancipatory Science in America* (Chicago: University of Chicago Press, 2001) and Jennifer Terry, *An American Obsession: Science, Medicine and Homosexuality in Modern Society* (Chicago: University of Chicago Press, 2014). See also George Hutchinson, *In Search of Nella Larsen: A Biography of the Color Line* (Cambridge, MA: Harvard University Press, 2006); Verene D. Mitchell and Cynthia Davis, *Literary Sisters: Dorothy West and Her Circle* (New Brunswick: Rutgers University Press, 2012); Verene Mitchell and Cynthia Davis, *Dorothy West: Where the Wild Grape Grows* (Amherst: University of Massachusetts Press, 2005); *The Harlem Renaissance: A Historical Dictionary*, ed. Bruce Kellner (New York: Metheun, 1984); Darlene Clark Hine, *Black Women in White America* (Brooklyn: Carlson Press, 1993); A'lelia Bundles, *On Her Own Ground: The Life and Times of Madame C. J. Walker* (New York: Washington Square Press, 2001); *Encyclopedia of the Harlem Renaissance*, vol. 2, eds. Cary Wintz and Paul Finkelman (New York: Routledge, 2004).

205 *concubines of their servant girls*: Du Bois, "The Servant in the House," in *Darkwater*, 92.

205 *monstrous intimacy*: Sharpe uses this term to account for the "extraordinary sites of domination and intimacy, slavery and the Middle Passage [that] were ruptures with and a suspension of the known world that initiated enormous and ongoing psychic, temporal and bodily breaches." It encompasses the "series of repetitions of master narratives of violence and forced submission that are read and reinscribed as consent and seduction: intimacies that involve shame and trauma and their transgenerational transmission." Sharpe, *Monstrous Intimacies*, 4.

205 *daughters labor even now under the outcome*: Spillers, "Interstices," in *Black, White and In Color*, 155.

206 kitchen contained a "whole social history": See Du Bois, "The Servant in the House," in *Darkwater*, 92; and *The Negro American Family*, 66.

206 "all who could scramble or run": Du Bois, "The Servant in the House," in *Darkwater*, 92.

206 **Dissemblance was the way:** Darlene Clark Hines, "Rape and the Inner Lives of Black Women in the Middle West," *Signs* 14, no. 4 (Summer 1989): 912–20.

206 **slavery and its afterlife:** On perverse lines of descent, see Eduoard Glissant, *Caribbean Discourse: Selected Essays* (Charlottesville: University of Virginia Press, 1999). On the "afterlife of slavery," see Saidiya Hartman, *Lose Your Mother* (New York: Farrar, Straus & Giroux, 2007), 45, 73, 107.

206 *snakes in her belly:* See "Case of Pearl M" in Henry, *Sex Variants*, 563–70.

207 **a very nice colored neighborhood:** While Pearl says that her family moved to Philadelphia, the actor Edna Thomas reported growing up in Boston.

211 **lost to the world:** "One's queerness will always render one lost to a world of heterosexual imperatives, codes and laws . . . . To be lost is not to hide in the closet or perform a simple (ontological) disappearing act; it is to veer away from heterosexuality's path. Freedmen escaping slavery got lost too." Jose Munoz, *Cruising Utopia: The Then and There of Queer Futurity* (Durham, NC: Duke University Press, 2009), 66, 73.

212 *It made her know:* See "Case of Pearl M" in Henry, *Sex Variants*, 563–70.

212 **Edna was among the circle:** See Lewis, *When Harlem Was in Vogue*; George Hutchinson, *In Search of Nella Larsen: A Biography of the Color Line* (Cambridge: Harvard, 2006) 159, 204, 256; and A'lelia Bundles, *On Her Own Ground: The Life and Time of Madame C.J. Walker* (New York: Scribner, 2002), 238. Harlem was a center of queer culture and social life. Among her best friends were Caska Bonds, Wallace Thurman, and Jimmy Daniels. On queer Harlem, See George Chauncey, *Gay New York: Gender, Urban Culture and the Making of the Gay Male World* (New York: Basic Books, 1995); Michael Henry Adams, "Queers in the Mirror: Old Fashioned Gay Marriage in New York, Part II," *Huffington Post* blog, July 7, 2009, https://www.huffingtonpost.com/michael-henry-adams/queers-in-the-mirror-a-br_b_227473.html.

212 **distant cousin of Oscar Wilde:** *Encyclopedia of the Harlem Renaissance*, eds. Cary D. Wintz and Paul Finkelman (New York: Routledge, 2004), 1176.

214 **"tidal waves of chance":** W. E. B. Du Bois, "Criteria of Negro Art," *The Crisis: A Record of the Darker Races* (1926).

214 **The world kept Edna guessing:** " 'The World Has Us Guessing,' Says Clever Lulu Belle Star," *Pittsburgh Courier*, March 10, 1928. This guessing fundamentally attends the question "Ain't I a woman?" and the doubt and negation that attend such a question, which, as Spillers writes, is almost too much to bear. "Interstices," in *Black, White and In Color*, 157.

REVOLUTION IN A MINOR KEY

217   "rebellious flame": See Wallace Thurman, "Cordelia the Crude, a Harlem Sketch," *Fire!!* 1, no. 1 (1926): 5–6.

217   what the war . . . would bring: Sentiment about World War I was divided. Most Negroes were reluctant to fight in a white man's war in a segregated army, especially when Negroes were being lynched and assaulted in their uniform. Dates of official U.S. involvement in WWI: 6 April 1917 to 11 November 1918.

218   The spirit of Bolshevism: Michelle Stephens, *Black Empire: The Masculine Global Imaginary of Caribbean Intellectuals in the United States, 1914–1962* (Durham, NC: Duke University Press, 2005); Barbara Foley, *Spectres of 1919: Class and Nation in the Making of the New Negro* (Urbana: University of Illinois Press, 2008); Brent Hayes Edwards, *The Practice of Diaspora: Literature, Translation, and the Rise of Black Internationalism* (Cambridge: Harvard University Press, 2003).

218   "conscious sway of invitation": Thurman, "Cordelia the Crude," 5–6.

218   *Why shouldn't I go out*: Bedford Hills Case File#2682.

219   a few blocks from the Palace Casino: This is the same address as Josephine Schuyler's place. All of the girls were associates and friends of Josephine Schuyler and spent time at her place, which was a gambling den, buffet flat and collective. The cartography of black life and spaces of experiment include the alley, the rooftop, the hallway, the disorderly house, the cabaret, the black-and-tan dive, etc. The prison cottage is the extension and continuation of the ghetto as a zone of racial enclosure. Arrest and confinement defined the effort to eradicate this unruly and promiscuous sociality. The straight world thought of these places as the shadow world or the underworld. The cabarets, dives, and dance halls were subterranean and fugitive spaces to the degree that they evaded the police.

220   their *training* in slavery: Slavery was the source of black women's immorality, observed Frances Kellor, noting that "Negro women [were] expected to be immoral and [had] few inducements to be otherwise." See Frances Kellor, "Southern Colored Girls in the North," *Bulletin of the Inter-Municipal Committee on Household Research* 1, no. 7 (May 1905). Jane Addams wrote, "Black women yielded more easily to the temptations of the city than any other girls." Negroes were "several generations behind the Anglo-Saxon race in civiling agencies and processes." See "Social Control," *The Crisis: A Record of the Darker Races* (January 1911): 22.

220   **civilizing agencies and processes:** "Social Control," *The Crisis: A Record of the Darker Races* (January 1911): 22.

220   **"his [or her] sexual mores":** Du Bois, *Negro American Family.*

221   **no cash exchanging hands:** Girls between fourteen and twenty-one, but sometimes as young as twelve, were sentenced to reformatories for being in a house with a bad reputation or suspected of prostitution, or having friends or neighbor who were thieves or prostitutes, or associating with lowlifes and criminals, or being promiscuous. Hicks, *Talk with You Like a Woman,* 184.

221   **practices of intimacy and affiliation:** See Carby, "Policing the Black Woman's Body," *Critical Inquiry* 18, no. 4 (Summer 1992); Sarah Haley, *No Mercy Here: Gender, Punishment, and the Making of Jim Crow Modernity* (Chapel Hill: University of North Carolina Press, 2016); Hicks, *Talk with You Like a Woman*; Blair, *I've Got to Make My Livin'*; and LaShawn Harris, *Sex Workers, Psychics, and Number Runners: Black Women in New York City's Underground Economy* (Bloomington: University of Illinois Press, 2016).

222   *Only* **young women were adjudged wayward:** See Title VIIA of the Code of Criminal Procedure Section 913a. Also see Raphael Murphy, "Proceedings in a Magistrate's Court Under the Laws of New York," *Fordham Law Review* 24, no. 1 (1955). In 1925, the Wayward Minors Act was expanded to include males. See Chapter 389, Laws 1925, which extended the provisions. Clinton McCord, "One Hundred Female Offenders: A Study of the Mentality of Prostitutes and 'Wayward' Girls," *Journal of the American Institute of Law and Criminality* 6, no. 3 (September 1915): 385–407.

222   **"the minor upon a career of prostitution":** Willoughby Cyrus Waterman, *Prostitution and Its Repression in New York City, 1900–1931* (New York: Columbia University Press, 1932), 40–41; Timothy Gilfoyle, *City of Eros: New York, Prostitution and the Commercialization of Sex, 1790–1920* (New York: W. W. Norton, 1994).

223   **provisions of the Wayward Minors Act:** Waterman, *Prostitution and Its Repression in New York City,* 39.

223   **Billie Holiday appeared before the Women's Court:** Julia Blackburn, *With Billie* (New York: Pantheon, 2005), 61–62, and Donald Clarke, *Wishing on the Moon: The Life and Times of Billie Holiday* (New York: Viking, 1994), 38. See also *Lady Sings the Blues,* which offers a complex account of hustling, as well as being framed and targeted. Billie Holiday, *Lady Sings the Blues* (1956; repr. New York: Three Rivers Press, 2006), 28–29.

224   **different ways of conducting the self:** See Michel Foucault, *Security, Territory, Population: Lectures at the Collège De France, 1977–78* (New York: Pic-

ador, 2009), 198; Michel Foucault, *History of Sexuality, Volume 2: The Use of Pleasure* (New York: Vintage Books, 1988).

WAYWARD: A SHORT ENTRY ON THE POSSIBLE

This entry on the wayward is in dialogue with notions of the respectable, the queer, and the willful. See Evelyn Brooks Higginbotham, *Righteous Discontent: The Women's Movement in the Black Baptist Church* (Cambridge, MA: Harvard University Press, 1994); E. Patrick Johnson, *No Tea, No Shade: New Writings in Black Queer Theory* (Durham, NC: Duke University Press, 2016); Eve Sedgwick, *Tendencies* (Durham, NC: Duke University Press, 1993); Jack Halberstam, *The Queer Art of Failure* (Durham, NC: Duke University Press, 2011); and Sarah Ahmed, *Willful Subjects* (Durham, NC: Duke University Press, 2014).

228   **queer resource of black survival:** See C. Riley Snorton, *Nobody Is Supposed to Know: Black Sexuality on the Down Low* (Minneapolis: University of Minnesota Press, 2014).

THE ANARCHY OF COLORED GIRLS
ASSEMBLED IN A RIOTOUS MANNER

229   *somebody's angel child:* Bessie Smith, vocalist, "Reckless Blues" by Fred Longshaw and Jack Gee, recorded 1925, Columbia 14056D, 10-inch LP.

229   **speak of potentialities:** Emma Goldman, "Anarchism: What It Really Stands For," in *Anarchism and Other Essays,* 2nd revised ed. (New York: Mother Earth Publishing Association, 1910).

229   **Harrison encountered her in the lobby of the Renaissance Casino:** On the life and work of the Harlem radical, see Jeffrey Perry, *Hubert Harrison: The Voice of Harlem Radicalism, 1883–1918* (New York: Columbia University Press, 2010); and Shelley Streeby, *Radical Sensations: World Movements, Violence, and Visual Culture* (Durham, NC: Duke University Press, 2013).

230   **ex-slave's refusal to work:** "The *Quashees* (the free blacks of Jamaica) content themselves with producing only what is strictly necessary for their own consumption, and, alongside this 'use value,' regard loafing (indulgence and idleness) as the real luxury good; how they do not care a damn for the sugar and the fixed capital invested in the plantations, but rather observe the planters' impending bankruptcy with an ironic grin of malicious pleasure ..." Karl Marx, *Grundrisse: Foundations of the Critique of Political Economy* (1939; repr. London: Penguin, 2005), 325–27.

230 *real luxury good*: Marx, *Grundrisse*, 325–27.

230 *thousand new forms*: Rosa Luxemburg, "The Russian Revolution," in *Reform or Revolution and Other Writings* (New York: Dover Books, 2006), 215.

231 **cooperation and mutuality found among ants, monkeys, and ruminants**: Pyotr Kropotkin. *Mutual Aid* (1902; repr. Boston: Extending Horizons Books, 1955); Darlene Clark Hine, "Mutual Aid and Beneficial Association," in *Black Women in America*, 3 vols. (New York: Oxford University Press, 2005); Jacqui Malone, "African American Mutual Aid Societies," *Stepping on the Blues: The Visible Rhythms of African American Dance* (Urbana: University of Illinois, 1996), 167–86; Ron Sakolsky, "Mutual Acquiescence or Mutual Aid?" *The Anarchist Library* (November 2012), https://theanarchistlibrary .org/library/ron-sakolsky-mutual-acquiescence-or-mutual-aid; Avery Gordon, *The Hawthorne Archive* (New York: Fordham University Press, 2017).

232 **"Neglect of the Problems of the Negro Woman"**: Ella Baker, *The Crisis: A Record of the Darker Races* (November 1935); Claudia Jones, "An End to the Neglect of the Problems of the Negro Woman!," *Political Affairs* 28 (June 1949): 51–67; Carole Boyce Davies, *Left of Karl Marx: The Political Life of Black Communist Claudia Jones* (Durham, NC: Duke University Press, 2007).

232 **revolt against . . . "unjust labor conditions"**: Du Bois, "The Servant in the House," in *Darkwater*, 90.

232 **jazz chorus**: "Girls on 'Noise' Strike," *New York Times*, January 25, 1920; "Vocal Hostilities of Bedford Girls Finally Halted," *New York Times*, January 27, 1920.

232 **the very idea of work**: Narrative drawn from "Information concerning the Patient," August 12, 1917; and "Information concerning the Patient," September 15, 1917; Bedford Hills Correctional Facility, Inmate case files, Series 14610–77B, Records of the Department of Correctional Services, New York State Archives, Albany, Bedford Hills Case Files #2507 and #2505. Also see Elizabeth Ross Haynes, "Negroes in Domestic Service," *Journal of Negro History* 8, no. 4 (October 1923), 396.

233 **then propose to marry her**: "See Harlem Elopers are Thrust in Cell," *Afro-American*, June 30, 1928.

233 **bound by need and want**: "Statement of the Girl, Work History," August 12, 1917, Bedford Hills Case File #2507.

233 **Service carried the stigma of slavery**: See Sophonisba Breckinridge, "The Legal Relation of Mistress and Maid, with Some Comment Thereon," *Bulletin of Household Research* 1, no. 2 (1904): 7–8. Breckinridge understood the continuities between domestic work and slavery and detailed the fea-

tures of involuntary servitude produced by the contract between mistress and maid. "There is as yet no legislation defining hours, and providing for humane treatment and sanitary conditions" of household workers. "There is no law forbidding children to work in the kitchen; and in some jurisdictions, delinquent children are habitually placed in household work by probation officers. Legislation looking toward betterment of conditions in domestic service is confined at present, to compelling payment of wage when earned." See also Margaret Livingston Chanler, "Domestic Service," *Bulletin of the Inter-Municipal Committee on Household Research* 1, no. 6 (April 1905): 7.

233   **captive maternal:** Joy James, "Captive Maternal Love: Octavia Butler and Sci-Fi Family Values," in *Literature and the Development of Feminist Theory*, ed. Robin Truth Goodman (Cambridge: Cambridge University Press, 2015), 185–99. On black female surplus, see Rizvana Bradley, "Reinventing Capacity: Black Femininity's Lyrical Surplus and the Cinematic Limits of *12 Years A Slave*," *Black Camera* 7, no. 1 (Fall 2015): 162–78.

234   **colored woman's piano day:** A general houseworker loved her washing so much that she called Mondays her "piano day." See Mary White Ovington, "The Colored Woman in Domestic Service in New York City," *Bulletin* 1, no. 7 (May 1905), 10.

234   **sacrificial devotion:** R. R. Wright, "Negro Household Workers," *Bulletin of the Inter-Municipal Committee on Household Research* 1, no. 7 (May 1905); Miller, "Surplus Negro Women."

234   **"care for their precious darlings":** Hutchins Hapgood, *An Anarchist Woman* (New York: Duffield, 1909), 40.

234   **like a swarm or swell of an ocean:** Du Bois described the collective action of the general strike as a swarm or swell. See *Black Reconstruction*. In the chapter "The General Strike," he uses the term *swarm* repeatedly to describe the movement of the enslaved and the fugitive.

234   **long poem of black hunger and striving:** This line is a riff on de Certeau's long poem of walking. See Michel de Certeau, *The Practice of Everyday Life* (Berkeley: University of California Press, 1984), 101.

234   *the wild rush from house service*: Du Bois, "The Servant in the House," in *Darkwater*, 92.

234   *All the modalities sing a part*: Certeau, *Practice of Everyday Life*, 99.

234   **The map of what might be:** Saidiya Hartman, "Venus in Two Acts," *Small Axe* 12, no. 2 (June 2008): 1–14; Ula Taylor, "Street Strollers: Grounding the Theory of Black Women Intellectuals," *Afro-Americans in New York Life and History* 30, no. 2 (July 2006): 153–71; Sarah Cervenak, *Wandering: Philo-*

sophical *Performances of Racial and Sexual Freedom* (Durham, NC: Duke University Press, 2015), 2; and Giuliana Bruno, *Streetwalking on A Ruined Map: Cultural Theory and the City Films of Elvira Notari* (Princeton, NJ: Princeton University Press, 1993).

234 *l'overture*: *L'overture* is another way to think about tumult, upheaval, and the radical practice of everyday life. It is also a reference to the revolutionary practice of the enslaved.

235 **to fight back, to strike out:** On discrimination against black girls and segregation at the Hudson Training School, see "Inquiry Board Hits Negro Segregation," *New York Times*, November 20, 1936, 9; and "Hits Race Discrimination," *New York Times*, August 7, 1936. See also Weekly Comment, *Chicago Defender*, June 28, 1919; and "Demand Unabated in Child Welfare," *New York Times*, September 14, 1933. A former superintendent recalled that when she took over charge of the Hudson Training School, "she made a bonfire of the manacles, restraining sheets and straitjackets which had been in use in the institution."

235 *to smash things up*: "Notes of the Staff Meeting," September 29, 1917, Bedford Hills Case File #2507: "She is the sort of girl who would not hesitate to smash out"; "the unruly who smash windows and furniture": State Commission of Prisons, "Investigation and Inquiry into Allegations of Cruelty to Prisoners in the New York State Reformatory for Women, Bedford Hills," in *Twenty-Sixth Annual Report of the State Commission of Prisons for the Year 1920*, March 12, 1921, 93; young women "smashing and yelling," State Commission of Prisons, "Investigation and Inquiry into Allegations of Cruelty," 94. Also see M. Fleming, "Ungovernability: The Unjustifiable Jurisdiction," *Yale Law Journal* 83, no. 7 (June 1974): 1383–1409.

235 *That was the offering*: Gwendolyn Brooks, *Maud Martha: A Novel* (New York: Harper and Row, 1953; repr. Chicago: Third World Press, 1993), 22.

236 *tried to kill her and failed*: Lucille Clifton, "Won't you celebrate with me," *Collected Poems of Lucille Clifton 1965–2010* (New York: BOA Editions, 2012).

236 **"to bring things into relation"**: Elaine Scarry, *On Beauty and Being Just* (Princeton, NJ: Princeton University Press, 1999), 30.

236 **Subsistence:** Karl Marx on forms and modes of life, see *German Ideology* (New York: International Publishers, 1970) and *Economic and Philosophic Manuscripts of 1844* (New York: International Publishers, 1964).

237 **survival was an achievement:** Saidiya Hartman, "Belly of the World," *Souls: A Critical Journal of Black Politics, Culture, and Society* 18, no. 1 (January/March 2016): 166–173.

237 **"reproduction of physical existence"**: Roderick Ferguson, "The Erotic
     Life of Diaspora: Black Queer Formations in the History of Neoliberalism,"
     unpublished talk, Institute for Research on Women, Gender, and Sexuality,
     Columbia University, New York, 2013.

237 **subject to frequent police raids**: Stephen Robertson, "Disorderly Houses:
     Residences, Privacy, and the Surveillance of Sexuality in 1920's Harlem,"
     Journal of the History of Sexuality 21, no. 3 (September 2012): 457. See Carby,
     "Policing the Black Body in an Urban Context," *Critical Inquiry* 18, no. 4
     (Summer 1992): 738–55.

238 **"charity girl"**: Kathy Peiss, *Cheap Amusements* (Philadelphia: Temple Uni-
     versity Press, 1986), 110–12.

238 **no clear line between desire and necessity**: On the survival strategies of
     young black women, see Aimee Cox, *Shapeshifters* (Durham, NC: Duke Uni-
     versity Press, 2015), 171.

238 **then he'd marry her**: This account is based upon "Statement of the Girl,"
     August 10, 1917, Bedford File#2505.

238 *Oh my man I love him so*: Billie Holiday, "My Man," *The Billie Holiday Song-
     book* (New York: Verse, 1986).

240 **she had violated those codes**: See Ruth Reed, *Negro Illegitimacy in New York*
     (New York: Columbia University Press, 1926), 48, 68.

240 **require the commitment of a criminal act**: George E. Worthington and
     Ruth Topping, *Specialized Courts Dealing with Sex Delinquency: A Study of
     the Procedure in Chicago, Boston, Philadelphia, and New York* (New York:
     Frederick Hitchcock Publisher, 1925); Christopher Tiedeman, *A Treatise on
     the Limitations of Police Power in the United States* (St. Louis: F. H. Thomas
     Law Book Company, 1886); Saidiya Hartman, *Scenes of Subjection*, 63, 69,
     186–206; Bryan Wagner, *Disturbing the Peace* (Cambridge, MA: Harvard
     University Press, 2009).

241 **running the streets**: In the case of status offenses, it is *status and not conduct
     that determines whether an act is a transgression of the law.* See Cynthia Godsoe,
     "Contempt, Status, and the Criminalization of Non-Conforming Girls," *Car-
     dozo Law Review* 35, no. 3 (February 2014): 1091–116; "Ungovernability: The
     Unjustifiable Jurisdiction," *Yale Law Journal* 83, no. 7 (June 1974): 1383–409.

241 **"a struggle to transform one's existence"**: Willfulness is a struggle to exist
     or to transform an existence. See Ahmed, "Willfulness as a Style of Politics,"
     in *Willful Subjects*, 133.

241 **"The history of disobedience"**: Ahmed, *Willful Subjects*, 137.

241 **"Leading the life of a prostitute"**: See George J. Kneeland, *Commercial-*

ized Prostitution in New York City (New York: Century Co., 1913). Of the 647 cases examined in the study of the Bedford Hills Reformatory, Katherine Bement Davis writes: "not all of them were convicted for prostitution but all were leading the lives of prostitutes" in "A Study of Prostitutes Committed from New York City to the State Reformatory at Bedford Hills," appendix to Kneeland, *Commercialized Prostitution in New York City*, 190.

241 *the manner of walking*: Civil Rights Division, United States Department of Civil Rights Division and Theodore M. Shaw, *The Ferguson Report, Department of Justice Investigation of the Ferguson Police Department* (New York: New Press, June 2015).

242 **target young women for prostitution**: By 1917, vagrancy statutes and Tenement House Laws were the primary vehicles for arresting and indicting young women as prostitutes.

242 **rate of conviction**: Worthington and Topping, *Specialized Courts Dealing with Sex Delinquency*, 217–18, 245, 274, 276, 287, 397–403, 418–19; Frederick Whitin, "The Women's Night Court in New York City," *Annals of the American Academy of Political and Social Science* 52 (March 1914): 183.

242 **predict the future**: The anticipation of future criminality was at the heart of anti-vagrancy statutes and the overwriting of blackness as criminality.

242 **refused to work**: Girls between fourteen and twenty-one, but sometimes as young as twelve, were sentenced to reformatories for being in a house with a bad reputation or suspected of prostitution, or having friends or neighbors who were thieves or prostitutes, or associating with lowlifes and criminals, or being promiscuous. See Hicks, *Talk to You Like A Woman*, 184.

243 **"without visible means of support"**: William J Chambliss, "A Sociological Analysis of the Law of Vagrancy," *Social Problems* 12, no. 1 (Summer 1964): 66–77.

243 **"no man knows from where they came"**: Tiedeman, *Treatise on the Limitations of Police Power*, 118.

243 **from idler to convict and felon**: Tiedeman, *Treatise on the Limitations of Police Power*, 117.

244 **"Silks and Lights:** "Silks and Lights Blamed for Harlem Girls' Delinquency," *Baltimore Afro-American*, May 19, 1928; "Lure for Finery Lands Girl in Jail," *New York Amsterdam News*, August 14, 1926.

245 *the wild world of fun and pleasure*: See letter from husband to Esther Brown, Bedford Hills Case File #2507.

246 **paid directly by the police**: "Frame-up and Blackmail," *New York Age*, January 7, 1928; "Be Careful Girls," *Amsterdam News*, May 14, 1920.

246   **"That's no straight road"**: Mrs. Scott, an elderly woman who took care of
       Esther's son, blamed what happened to Esther on her mother and told the
       caseworker that Rose Saunders "consorted with one of the men who lodged
       in her apartment."

247   *old love wishing you well*: Letter in Bedford Hills Case File #2507.

247   *assembled in a riotous manner*: The governor of New York, Lord Cornford
       (who was Queen Anne's cousin), issued a scathing proclamation to "take
       all methods for the seizing and apprehending of all such Negroes found to
       be assembled and if any of them refuse to submit then fire upon them, kill
       or destroy them, if they otherwise cannot be taken . . . . Several Negroes in
       Kings County have *assembled themselves in a riotous manner*, which if not
       prevented may prove of ill consequence." As a precaution against conspir-
       acy, the assembly of slaves was severely restricted. When not engaged in
       their master's service, no more than three slaves could meet together on a
       penalty of being whipped not more than forty lashes. No more than twelve
       slaves, in addition to the coffin bearers and gravediggers, could assemble at
       any funeral on pain of public whipping. Another prohibited the gathering of
       slaves after nightfall. See Roi Ottley and William J. Weatherby (eds.), *The
       Negro in New York: An Informal Social History, 1626–1940* (New York: New
       York Public Library, 1967), 22. Slave codes in colonial New York targeted
       black assembly. See Edwin Olson. "The Slave Code in Colonial New York,"
       Journal of Negro History, 29, no. 2 (April. 1944): 147–65; Ira Berlin and Les-
       lie Harris, *Slavery in New York* (New York: New York Historical Society,
       2005). See Simone Browne, *Dark Matters* (Durham, NC: Duke University
       Press, 2015).

248   **whipped not more than 40 lashes**: See Colonial Laws of New York, i, 520,
       cited in Olson, "The Slave Code in Colonial New York." See also Berlin and
       Harris, *Slavery in New York*.

248   **Board of Charities**: On the role of philanthropy and charity in produc-
       ing a racialized order see Alice O'Connor, *Poverty Knowledge: Social Sci-
       ence, Social Policy, and the Poor in Twentieth-Century U.S. History* (Princeton,
       NJ: Princeton University Press, 2001); Paul Boyer, *Urban Masses and the
       Moral Order in America, 1820–1920* (Cambridge, MA: Harvard University
       Press, 1992); Ralph Luker, *Social Gospel in Black and White: American Racial
       Reform, 1885–1912* (Chapel Hill: University of North Carolina Press, 1991);
       David Rothman, *Conscience and Convenience: the Asylum and its Alternatives
       in Progressive America* (Boston: Little Brown, 1980); Michael McGerr, *A
       Fierce Discontent: The Rise and Fall of the Progressive Movement in America*

(New York: Free Press, 2003); Richard Hofstadter, *Age of Reform* (New York: Vintage Books, 1955). Robert Allen, *Reluctant Reformers: Racism and Social Reform Movements* (Washington, DC: Howard University Press, 1974).

249 *"Disorderly is worse than discrimination"*: Frederick Whittin to Du Bois, 10 October 1912, box 11 (Du Bois 1911–1912) folder, W. E. B. Du Bois Correspondence. Frederick Whittin to Du Bois, 10 October 1912, box 2 (General Correspondence) folder, W. E. B. Du Bois Correspondence 1912 October 11–20. For a study of the committee's work in New York City, see Jennifer Fronc, *New York Undercover: Private Surveillance in the Progressive Era* (Chicago: University of Chicago Press, 2009).

249 **vagrants and prostitutes:** See William Fryer, *Tenement House Law of the City of New York* (New York: The Record and Guide, 1901); Robert de Forest and Lawrence Veiller (eds.), *The Tenement House Problem* (London: Macmillan, 1903); and The Tenement House Law of the State of New York and Chapter XIXa of the Greater New York Charter (New York: Tenement House Department, 1912).

250 **incubator of crime:** The law also established guidelines for the improvement of extant houses and the building of new tenements; however, reinforcement of the law proved difficult. Many social reformers believed that social problems were determined by poor environmental conditions, so that improving housing conditions would improve the morality and life chances of the poor by transforming the ecology of the slum. "The Tenement Law of the City of New York" Section 141, "Vagrancy"; William John Fryer, ed., *The Tenement House Law of the City of New York* (New York: Clinton W. Sweet, 1901).

250 **overcrowding that was the prolific source of sexual immorality:** Committee of Fifteen, *The Social Evil: With Special Reference to Conditions Existing in the City of New York* (New York: G. P. Putnam, 1902), 173–174.

250 **consolidate the meaning of prostitution:** See Mumford, *Interzones*; Fronc, *New York Undercover*; Timothy Gilfoyle, *City of Eros: New York City, Prostitution, and the Commercialization of Sex 1790–1920* (New York: W. W. Norton, 1992); and Jessica R. Pliley, *Policing Sex Districts: The Mann Act and the Making of the FBI* (Cambridge, MA: Harvard University Press, 2014); Waterman, *Prostitution and Its Repression in New York City*, 39.

250 **"the vagrant as the chrysalis of every criminal":** Tiedeman, *Treatise on the Limitations of Police Power*, 117.

251 **"vagrancy clause of the Tenement House Law":** 1,099 persons were

arrested for this violation. Committee of Fourteen, *Committee of Fourteen Annual Report 1914* (New York, 1914).

251 **Thirty-six percent of these convictions were of black women:** Committee of Fourteen, *Committee of Fourteen Annual Report 1914*, 32–33; Val Marie Johnson, "Defining Social Evil: Moral Citizenship and Governance in New York City, 1890–1920" (PhD diss., The New School for Social Research, New York, New York, 2002), 396–397, fn. 121. The Tenement House Committee and the Committee of Fourteen targeted landlords whose primary tenants were African Americans. In 1910, black women comprised 1.9 percent of the city population, 8 percent of those charged with prostitution, and 7.6 percent of those charged with disorderly conduct. In 1914, the vast majority of women charged with prostitution was through the vagrancy clause of the Tenement House Law. Although African American women comprised little more than 2 percent of the population of the city, they were 36 percent of those arrested for violation of the Tenement House Law. Foreign-born women were 24 percent of those arrested, although they were 40.8 percent of the city. Because of the segregated labor market, black women were frequently employed in sex venues, but in non-sex-work as housekeeepers, maids and washerwomen. By 1928, there were four times more Negro women than white women in court. By 1930, there was a dramatic increase in rates of arrest. Three Negro women were arrested for every two white women, even where there was one Negro woman to eight white women living in New York City. The "policing relation" had everything to do with this disparity. See Sophia Robison, *An Inquiry into the Present Functioning of the Women's Court in Relation to the Problem of Prostitution in New York City* (Welfare Council of New York, Research Bureau, May 1935).

251 **arrest of black women and tenement residents:** "There has been an increase, as compared with 1913–1914, of cases from tenements on the East Side and in Harlem, while decreases were noticed in the central part of the city, which includes the . . . Tenderloin. This latter decrease, as well as the increase in the Harlem district, is probably explained by the movement of the negroes from one section to the other." Kneeland, *Commercialized Prostitution in New York City*, 165; also see Committee of Fourteen, *New York City Annual Report*, 1915–1916, pp. 32, 42, 55, 58.

251 *willingness* **to have sex or engage in "lewdness":** Criminal Code, Section 887, defined the vagrant as follows: "Any person (a) who offers to commit prostitution; or (b) who offers or offers to secure a female person for the purpose of prostitution, or for any other lewd or indecent act; or (c) who

loiters in or near any thoroughfare or public or private place for the purpose
of inducing, enticing, or procuring another to commit lewdness, fornication,
unlawful sexual intercourse or any other indecent act; or (d) who in any
manner induces, entices or procures a person who is in any thoroughfare
or public or private place to commit any such acts is a vagrant." In 1921, the
definition was again expanded in *People v. Breitung*, although the first item
was unchanged since the fourteenth century: "A person who not having visible means to maintain herself, lives without employment."

N.Y. PEN. LAW § 240.20: NY Code-Section 240.20: Disorderly conduct: A person is guilty of disorderly conduct when, with intent to cause
public inconvenience, annoyance or alarm, or recklessly creating a risk
thereof: 1. (S)He engages in fighting or in violent, tumultuous or threatening behavior; or 2. (S)He makes unreasonable noise; or 3. In a public
place, (s)he uses abusive or obscene language, or makes an obscene gesture; or 4. Without lawful authority, (s)he disturbs any lawful assembly or
meeting of persons; or 5. (S)He obstructs vehicular or pedestrian traffic;
or 6. (S)He congregates with other persons in a public place and refuses
to comply with a lawful order of the police to disperse; or 7. (S)He creates
a hazardous or physically offensive condition by any act which serves no
legitimate purpose.

Disorderly House, Penal Law, Section 1146: A person or person who
keeps a house of ill-fame or assignation of any description, or a house or
place for persons to visit for unlawful sexual intercourse, or for any lewd,
obscene or indecent purpose, or disorderly house, or a house commonly
known as a stale beer dive, or any place of public resort by which the
peace, comfort, or decency of a neighborhood is habitually disturbed, or
who requests, advises or procures any female to become an inmate of any
such house or place, or who as agent or owner, lets a building or any portion, knowing that it is intended to be used for any person specified in this
section, or who permits a building or portion of a building to be so used,
is guilty of a misdemeanor. This section shall be construed to apply to any
part or parts of a house used for the purposes herein specified.

Disorderly Person. Code of Criminal Procedure, Sections 899, 911.

4. Keeps of bawdy houses or houses for the resort of prostitution,
drunkards, tipplers, gamesters, habitual criminals, or other disorderly
persons. (Disorderly persons overlap with the meaning of the vagrant.)

Section 911 Court may also commit [her] to prison; nature and duration of imprisonment. The court may also in its discretion, order a person convicted as a disorderly person, to be kept in the county jail, or in the City of New York, in the city prison or penitentiary of that city, for a term not exceeding six months of hard labor.

Public Nuisance, Penal Law, Sections 1530 and 1532:

Section 1530: A public nuisance is a crime against the order and economy of the State and consists in unlawfully doing an act, or omitting to perform a duty, which act or omission:

1) Annoys, injures or endangers the comfort, repose, health or safety of any considerable number of persons; or,
2) Offends public decency; or
3) (Actually Point 4) In any way renders a considerable number of persons insecure in life, or the use of property.

Section 1532. Maintaining a nuisance. A person who commits or maintains a public nuisance, the punishment for which is not specially prescribed, or who willfully omits or refuses to perform any legal duty relating to the removal of such a public nuisance, is guilty of misdemeanor.

252 **by force and without warrants:** See Grace Campbell, "Tragedy of Colored Girl in Court," *New York Age*, April 25, 1925; "Women Offenders and the Day Court," *New York Age*, April 18, 1925. See Campbell quoted in "Harlem Love Girls Get 25 cents, Whites $5," *Afro-American*, January 29, 1938.

252 **police raid without a warrant:** Committee of Fourteen, *Annual Report of the Committee of Fourteen 1915–1916*.

254 **being in the wrong place at the wrong time:** Pat James and many other women were arrested for prostitution in taxicabs. She left a club at 1:30 a.m. Two men entered the cab after she did. She started screaming and fighting with them, fearing that they would rob her, but instead she was arrested for prostitution. Bedford Hills Case File#3489. Nancy Lacewell was arrested in a hallway. The officers first charged her with robbery and then changed the charge to prostitution. Bedford Hills Case File#3501. Henrietta Dawson was arrested for prostitution after agreeing to a date with a man she had met at a Harlem club. Her mixed-race child convinced the court that she had been living the life of a prostitute. Bedford Hills Case File#3499.

254 **"it was the word of some dirty grafting cop against theirs":** Billie Holiday, *Lady Sings the Blues* (1956; repr. New York: Three Rivers Press, 2006), 27.

254 **rockin' me, with one steady roll:** Trixie Smith, 1922, "My Man Rocks Me (With One Steady Roll)," Black Swan Records, 14127-B.

256 **"respectable members of the community":** "Race Actresses Said Framed by Cop." *Baltimore Afro-American.* December 26, 1925, 5.

256 *to live in its clauses and parentheses:* Anne Winters, "MacDougal Street, Old Law Tenement," *The Displaced of Capital* (Chicago: University of Chicago Press, 2004).

256 **the problem of crime was the threat posed:** See Christopher Muller, "Northern Migration and the Rise of Racial Disparity in American Incarceration," *American Journal of Sociology* 118, no. 2 (September 2012), 281–326; Muhammed, *Condemnation of Blackness*; Bryan Wagner, *Disturbing the Peace*; and Michelle Alexander, *The New Jim Crow* (New York: The New Press, 2012).

THE ARRESTED LIFE OF EVA PERKINS

257 **Eva Perkins:** This account of Eva Perkins is based on Bedford Hills File#2504.

259 **he was every man who wanted more and had failed:** See James Weldon Johnson, *Autobiography of An Ex-Colored Man* (1912; repr. New York: W. W. Norton, 2015) and Sutton Griggs, *Imperium in Imperio,* (1899; repr. New York: Random House, 2007).

259 **the dramaturgy of struggle:** Sylvia Wynter, "Beyond Miranda's Meanings: Un/silencing the Demonic Ground of Caliban's Woman," *Out of the Kumbla: Caribbean Women and Literature* (Trenton, NJ: Africa World Press, 1990), 363.

259 **an absent presence:** Evelynn Hammonds, "Black (W)holes and the Geometry of Female Sexuality," *differences: A Journal of Feminist Cultural Studies* 6, no. 2–3 (1994), 127–45. Katherine McKittrick, *Demonic Grounds: Black Women and the Cartographies of Struggle* (Minneapolis: University of Minnesota, 2006), 37–64.

260 **"reduced to having no will or desire:** Wynter, "Beyond Miranda's Meanings," 363.

261 **dissemblance:** Darlene Clark Hine, "Rape and the Inner Lives of Black Women," *Signs: Journal of Women in Culture and Society* 14, no. 4 (Summer 1989): 912–20.

261 **agree 'em to death and destruction:** Ralph Ellison, *Invisible Man* (1952; repr. New York: Vintage, 1995), 16.

RIOT AND REFRAIN

263 **names that appeared in the newspaper:** "Girl Chained, Bed to Crash If She Moved," *New York Tribune*, December 13, 1919. Also see "Screaming Girl Manacled to Cell," *Washington Post*, December 7, 1919; "Girl 'Strung Up' Before Prison Inquiry Board," *New York Tribune*, December 7, 1919; " 'Stringing Up' Bedford Girls Called Useless," *New York Tribune*, December 21, 1919; "Expert Condemns Stringing Up Girls," *New York Times*, December 14, 1919; "Handcuff Girls at Reformatory," *Los Angeles Times*, January 4, 1920; and "Harsh Penalty Meted to Girls," *Louisville Courier Journal*, January 4, 1920.

263 **cells in the Disciplinary Building:** "Doctor Assails Stringing Up of Bedford Girls," *New York Tribune*, December 14, 1919, 14; New York Department of Efficiency and Economy, *Annual Report Concerning Investigations of Accounting, Administration and Construction of State Hospitals for the Insane, State Prisons and State Reformatory and Correctional Institutions* (Albany, NY: J.B. Lyon Company, 1915), 932–933; State Commission of Prisons, "Investigation and Inquiry into Allegations of Cruelty," 74.

263 **two hundred and sixty-five inmates:** State Commission of Prisons, "Investigation and Inquiry into Allegations of Cruelty to Prisoners in the New York State Reformatory for Women, Bedford Hills," in *Twenty-Sixth Annual Report of the State Commission of Prisons for the Year 1920* (March 21, 1920), 146.

263 **crowded tenements on the Lower East Side:** Katherine Davis, "Preventive and Reformatory Work" and "Salient Facts about the New York State Reformatory for Women, Bedford Hills, New York," pamphlet, Women Prison's Association of New York, Rare Books and Manuscripts, New York Public Library, 4–5.

264 **the cells of Rebecca Hall:** State Commission of Prisons, "Investigation and Inquiry into Allegations of Cruelty," 78.

264 **cruel and unusual punishment:** State Commission of Prisons, "Investigation and Inquiry into Allegations of Cruelty," 68.

264 **mortification of the self:** Erving Goffman, *Asylums: Essays on the Social Situation of Mental Patients and Other Inmates* (New York: Anchor Books, 1961); Colin Dayan, "Civil Death," *The Law is A White Dog* (Princeton, NJ: Princeton University Press, 2013); Frank Wilderson, "The Prison Slave as Hegemony's (Silent) Scandal," *Social Justice* 30, no. 2 (2003).

265 **"If you don't quell them:** State Commission of Prisons, "Investigation and Inquiry into Allegations of Cruelty," 78.

265 **"treatment, not punishment":** State Commission of Prisons, "Investigation and Inquiry into Allegations of Cruelty," 72.

265 **too friendly with the white girls:** In Case #2503, "friendships with white girls" was listed as a disciplinary infraction. Interracial intimacy and undesirable sexual relations had been a concern for state authorities and the public since 1914. In 1916, two segregated cottages were built for black women because the state feared "undesirable sex relations grow out of this mingling of the two races." See "Annual Report of the State Board of Charities for the Year 1915" (Albany 1916), 32, 854–67. For a critical examination of these issues, see Regina Kunzel, *Criminal Intimacy: Prison and the Uneven History of Modern American Sexuality* (Chicago: University of Chicago, 2010); Sarah Potter, "Undesirable Relations: Same-Sex Relationships and the Meaning of Sexual Desire at a Women's Reformatory," *Feminist Studies* 30, no. 2 (Summer 2004), 394–415; Estelle B. Freedman, "The Prison Lesbian: Race, Class, and the Construction of the Aggressive Female Homosexual," *Feminist Studies* 22, no. 2 (Summer 1996), 397–423; and Cheryl Hicks, *Talk With You Like a Woman: African American Women, Justice, and Reform, 1890–1935* (Chapel Hill: University of North Carolina Press, 2010), 204–33.

265 **a moment of privacy:** Mattie Jackson was punished for complaining about the food: "Disciplinary Report," Bedford Hills Case File #2466; women were punished for "insignificant offenses": State Commission of Prisons, "Investigation and Inquiry into Allegations of Cruelty," 91; on education, see State Commission of Prisons, "Investigation and Inquiry into Allegations of Cruelty," 81; on discrimination against colored girls and denials of education, see "Doctor Assails Stringing Up."

265 **a colored girl was expected to work:** State Commission of Prisons, "Investigation and Inquiry into Allegations of Cruelty," 80, 148.

265 **"feeble-minded":** The failure of the reformatory was blamed on the mental deficiency of the prisoners. Almost all accounts of Bedford characterize colored girls at Bedford as feeble-minded: see "State Board of Charities Annual Report." Prison officials constantly established a relationship between riotous behavior and feeble-mindedness. See Edith R. Spaulding, "The Problem of the Psychopathic Hospital Connected with a Reformatory Institution," *Medical Record: A Weekly Journal of Medicine and Surgery* 99, no. 20 (May 14, 1921): 819. Girls escaped from Bedford after others were confined to the psychopathic unit. Most often young black women were classified as "intellectually inferior" and having the mental ability of ten-to-twelve-year-olds. See

"Brief Case Histories of Twenty One Women Recommended for Custodial Care," Committee of Fourteen Records, Manuscripts and Archives Division, New York Public Library; In the *Twenty-Sixth Annual Report*, prison officials established a relationship between riotous behavior and feeble-mindedness.

266 **rest of their natural lives:** Most black women paroled from Bedford were made to perform "general housework": *Twenty-First Annual Report of the New York State Reformatory for Women*, Legislative Report of the State of New York (Albany, NY: J.B. Lyon, 1922), 25. Most of the black women paroled to domestic labor complained about the arduousness of the labor; some voluntarily returned to Bedford rather than do general housework.

266 **All a "Bedford girl" was good for:** Davis, "Preventive and Reformatory Work," in *Informal and Condensed Report of the American Prison Congress* (New York, October 21–26, 1906), 25. Davis conceded that young women were at greater social risk after being sentenced to Bedford: "Girls who have been here are considered fair game by almost all the 'white slavers' in the state, with the result that they are confronted with twice the temptations that face girls who have never been here." "Woman Defines Virtue," *New York Tribune*, April 27, 1913.

266 **confined in segregated housing:** In 1917, segregated housing was introduced at Bedford to prevent "harmful intimacy" or interracial sexual relationships and friendships.

267 **Eva had been paroled:** Bedford Hills File#2504.

267 **half of the folks in Harlem lived this way:** See Ira De A. Reid, *Twenty-Four Hundred Negro Families in Harlem: An Interpretation of the Living Conditions of Small Wage Earners* (New York: National Urban League, May 1927).

267 **"spend more money in a week than you can earn in a month":** Davis, "Preventive and Reformatory Work" (Albany, NY: *National Prison Association*), 205–206.

267 **sole pair of shoes and walked away:** When released from Bedford Hills, young women were provided with these items. See *Twenty-Sixth Annual Report of the State Commission of Prisons* (March 12, 1921), 105.

268 **The cottage system:** See Eugenia C. Lekkerkerker, *Reformatories for Women in the United States* (The Hague: J. B. Wolters, 1931), 101–11; and Davis, "Salient Facts about the New York State Reformatory for Women."

268 **ten isolation cells:** *Annual Report of the New York State Department of Efficiency and Economy Concerning Investigations of Accounting, Administration and Construction of State Hospitals for the Insane, State Prisons and*

State Reformatory and Correctional Institutes February 1, 1915 (Albany, NY, 1915), 932.

270 *own the earth forever and ever:* W. E. B. Du Bois, "The Souls of White Folks," in *Darkwater.*

270 **disenchanted with the idea of property:** Patricia Williams, "On Being the Object of Property," *Alchemy of Race and Rights* (Cambridge, MA: Harvard University Press, 1992).

274 **it is my duty as a man:** Bedford Hills File #2504. On nonbinary blackness, see Toni Cade Bambara, "On the Issues of Roles," *The Black Woman: An Anthology*, ed. Toni Cade Bambara (1970; repr. New York: Washington Square Press, 2005), 123–35.

274 *the Negress* **occupied a different rung of existence:** On the Negress, see Hilton Als, *The Women* (New York: Farrar, Straus & Giroux, 1996); Huey Copeland, "In the Wake of the Negress," in *Modern Women: Women Artists at the Museum of Modern Art* (New York: Museum of Modern Art, 2010), 480–97. On the Negress, Copeland writes: "A figure, a tactic, a subject, a structural position and a means of mark-making, the Negress stands at the boundary of hegemonic and resistive discourses. . . . To grasp the Negress, to conjure her into being, is to collapse a limit, to bring the world unbearably close, to perform an alchemy that transmutes subjects into objects and back again. Such transformations are made possible by the flows of bodies that have turned black women into fungible property."(484) Janell Hobson, *Venus in the Dark: Blackness and Beauty in Popular Culture* (New York: Routledge, 2005); T. Denean Sharpley-Whiting, *Black Venus: Sexualized Savages, Primal Fears, and Primitive Narratives in French* (Durham, NC: Duke University Press, 1999), 56.

275 **I would not have all this trouble:** Letter of July 7th, 1919, Bedford Hills File #2504.

275 **His letters were honest and passionate:** This description of Aaron's letters are based on the 60+ letters he sent the prison authorities. His longing for a different life and his defiant and unapologetic tone is evidenced throughout the letters.

276 **Kiss for you indeed my baby:** "Letter from Eva to Aaron," Bedford Hills File #2504.

276 *Sociological note:* Bedford Hills File #2504.

277 **"handcuffed to the bars of her cell:** "Doctor Assails Stringing Up."

277 **toes touching the ground:** State Commission of Prisons, "Investigation and Inquiry into Allegations of Cruelty," 91.

277   **washed out with soap and water:** "Doctor Assails Stringing Up"; State
      Commission of Prisons, "Investigation and Inquiry into Allegations of Cru-
      elty," 74.

277   **string up girls about one hundred times:** State Commission of Prisons,
      "Investigation and Inquiry into Allegations of Cruelty," 88.

277   **"feet were wholly on the floor":** State Commission of Prisons, "Investiga-
      tion and Inquiry into Allegations of Cruelty," 87–88.

277   **lift them a little higher:** State Commission of Prisons, "Investigation and
      Inquiry into Allegations of Cruelty," 88.

278   **Lowell Cottage made their voices heard:** According to reporters, the cot-
      tage "was heard before it was seen." See "Girl Chained, Bed to Crash If She
      Moved," *New York Tribune*, December 13, 1919, 22. The next year Flower
      Cottage rebelled. See "Bedford in Tumult under Rule of Man," *New York
      Times*, July 24, 1921.

279   **"din of an infernal chorus":** "Girls on 'Noise' Strike," *New York Times*, Jan-
      uary 25, 1920. "Vocal Hostilities of Bedford Girl Finally Halted," *New York
      Tribune*, January 27, 1920.

279   **"innocent girl in the jailhouse":** Letter from Aaron Perkins, Bedford Hills
      Case File #2504.

279   **as if they were not human:** "Girl Chained, Bed to Crash If She Moved,"
      New York Tribune, December 13, 1919, 22. "Girl Prisoners Mutiny," *New York
      Times*, January 3, 1920.

279   **The uproarious din:** "Girl Chained, Bed to Crash If She Moved," *New York
      Tribune*, December 13, 1919, 22.

279   **The chorus spoke with one voice:** Eva was not at Bedford in December,
      but she was there for the previous upheavals. In Rebecca Hall, Michie had
      incited the other girls to riot. Eva returned to Bedford and was there for sub-
      sequent riots. I have condensed the time to place these stories alongside one
      another.

279   **Mattie Jackson joined the chorus:** Bedford Hills Case File, #2466; State
      Commission of Prisons, "Investigation and Inquiry into Allegations of Cru-
      elty," 74; "Girl Chained, Bed to Crash if She Moved," *New York Tribune*,
      December 13, 1919.

280   **bellowed, cursed, and screamed:** Bedford Hills Case File #2503. In 1926,
      Loretta Michie was arrested on a Harlem street for carrying a revolver in her
      purse. She was not allowed to return to Bedford because of her involvement
      with the riots. See Bedford Case File #4092, superintendent's letter.

280 **"sweetheart in my dreams I'm calling you"**: "Letter from Loretta Michie to 'Devoted Pal,'" Bedford Hills Case File#2503.

280 **Miss Dawley, the sociologist, interviewed them**: Almena Dawley was the sociologist at the Laboratory of Social Hygiene; the summary of her interviews appear in Bedford Hills Case files.

280 **"she had been with a good many men"**: "Staff Meeting," Bedford Hills Case File#2503.

281 *Friendship with the white girls*: Bedford Hills Case File,#2503.

282 **I get so utterly disgusted**: Missive to her girlfriend, Bedford Hills Case File,#2503.

282 **essential tactics of the riot**: On window breaking in the past, see "Annual Report of the New York Department of Efficiency and Economy" (Albany, NY: Lyon Company Printers 1915), 932; "Window-Breaking Girls Handcuffed," *Washington Post*, January 4, 1920.

283 *out of here, out of now*: Fred Moten, "Erotics of Fugitivity," *Stolen Life* (Durham, NC: Duke University Press, 2018), 266.

283 **eager to label the clash as a race riot**: "Bedford Rioters Keep Up Din in Cells," *New York Tribune*, July 26, 1920. The ready solution proposed by the prison commissioner was "to classify and segregate different classes of prisoners." Other officials proposed a return to the severe methods of restraint and punishment that earlier had been condemned.

284 **Improvisation**: Secondary rhythms and improvisation: On chance and secondary rhythms, see W. E. B. Du Bois, "Sociology Hesitant"; and George Lewis, *Oxford Handbook of Critical Improvisation Studies* (New York: Oxford University Press, 2017).

284 **You can take my tie**: Charles A. Ford, "Homosexual Practices of Institutionalized Female," *Journal of Abnormal Psychology* 23, no. 4 (1929), 444.

285 **"jargon and nonsense"**: Frederick Douglass, *Narrative of the Life of Frederick Douglass, an American Slave, Written by Himself* (1845; repr. New York: New American Library, 1968.)

285 **"it is no slave time with colored people now"**: Letter of May 4, 1919. Also see May 12, 1919.

285 *surreal, utopian nonsense*: Moten, "Uplift and Criminality."

285 **to whom anything might be done**: "Devil's Chorus Sung by Girl Rioters," *New York Times*, July 26, 1920.

286 **"appear to disdain jazz"**: "Girls on Noise Strike," *New York Times*, January 25, 1920, 19. See also "Girl Prisoners Mutiny."

286   **"Devil's chorus"**: "Devil's Chorus Sung by Girl Rioters," *New York Times,*
        July 26, 1920. "Girl Inmates Attack Troops in New Riots," *San Francisco
        Chronicle,* July 26, 1920, and "How the State Failed in Its Care of the Way-
        ward Women at Bedford," *Brooklyn Daily Eagle,* August 1, 1920.

286   **lost at sea:** Eva's mother describes her nightmare in a letter to Prison Super-
        intendent, Bedford Hills File#2504. Successive generations were lost at sea:
        Mattie Jackson, Bedford Hills Case File #2466.

THE SOCIALIST DELIVERS A LECTURE ON FREE LOVE

287   **"what we like to do"**: This sketch of Hubert Harrison is indebted to Jeffrey
        Perry, *Hubert Harrison: The Voice of Harlem Radicalism* (New York: Colum-
        bia University Press, 2010), 276; Winston James, *Holding Aloft the Banner
        of Ethiopia: Caribbean Radicalism in early Twentieth-Century America* (New
        York: Verso, 1998), 129, 320. See also Shelley Streeby, *Radical Sensations:
        World Movements, Violence and Visual Culture* (Durham, NC: Duke Univer-
        sity Press, 2013); Joyce Turner, *Caribbean Crusaders and the Harlem Renais-
        sance* (Urbana: University of Illinois Press, 2005), 53.

288   **possible that he saw their faces:** This sketch about Harrison's encounters
        and erotic life are based on the reminiscences by his friends Bruce Nugent,
        Gay Rebel of the Harlem Renaissance: Selections from the Work of Bruce Nungent
        (Durham, NC: Duke University Press, 2002); Claude McKay, "Harlem,"
        in *A Long Way from Home* (1937; repr. New Brunswick: Rutgers University
        Press, 2007); and Gary Holcomb, *Code Name Sasha: Queer Black Marxism
        and the Harlem Renaissance* (Gainesville: University Press of Florida, 2009).

289   **lectures on "Sex and Sex Problems"**: His series on Sex and Sex Problems
        included such topics as "The Mechanics of Sex," "Analysis of Sex," "Analysis
        of the Sex Impulse" and "Sex and Race." See Perry, *Hubert Harrison,* 276;
        and Streeby, *Radical Sensations,* 199.

292   **Marcus Garvey's divorce suit:** See Ula Taylor, *The Veiled Garvey: The Life
        and Times of Amy Jacques Garvey* (Chapel Hill: University of North Carolina
        Press, 2002); James, *Holding Aloft the Banner of Ethiopia,* 129, 320.

292   **"abnormal sexualism"**: See James, *Holding Aloft the Banner of Ethiopia,*
        129, 320. See also Shelley Streeby, *Radical Sensations: World Movements,
        Violence and Visual Culture* (Durham, NC: Duke University Press, 2013).
        See Jeffrey Perry, *Hubert Harrison* (New York: Columbia University Press,
        2009), 107–8, 276, 352–54. Harrison barely escaped being mentioned in the
        divorce proceedings of Amy Ashwood and Marcus Garvey. On the divorce,

see Taylor, *Veiled Garvey*, 30, 34, 37–38. On Claude McKay, see Gary Edward Holcomb, *Claude McKay, Code Name Sasha: Queer Black Marxism and the Harlem Renaissance* (Gainesville: University Press of Florida, 2009); Brent Hayes Edwards, "The Taste of the Archive," *Calalloo* 35, no. 4 (Fall 2012); and "Vagabond Internationalism: Claude McKay's Banjo" in *The Practice of Diaspora: Literature, Translation and the Rise of Black Internationalism* (Cambridge, MA: Harvard University Press, 2003).

292 **extensive collection of erotic literature:** See Bruce Nugent, *Gay Rebel of the Harlem Renaissance: Selections from the Work of Richard Bruce Nugent*, ed. Thomas Wirth (Durham, NC: Duke University Press, 2002), 149.

293 **to "translate his ideas about culture:** As quoted in Nugent, *Gay Rebel of the Harlem Renaissance*, 149.

THE BEAUTY OF THE CHORUS

297 **Red Summer of 1919:** "In several of the over forty urban race riots that occurred in the summer of 1919—most notably in Washington and Chicago—residents of black neighborhoods took up arms." Barbara Foley, *Spectres of 1919*, 13. This was also the case for the New York City Race Riot of 1900.

297 **Mabel Hampton:** The portrait of Mabel that follows is based upon approximately thirty-three audiotapes that comprise her oral history (spanning approximately twenty-four hours of interviews). Mabel Hampton Oral History Collection, Special Collection #7929, Lesbian Herstory Archives, Brooklyn, NY). The interviews address a wide range of ideas and experiences from attitudes about sexuality, lesbian experiences across the decades, her life in the theatre, childhood, and work history. Mabel was an archivist and collected playbills, scrapbooks, photo albums, black postcards, and musical theatre programs. See also Joan Nestle, " 'I Lift My Eyes to the Hill': The Life of Mabel Hampton as Told by a White Woman," *Queer Ideas: The Kessler Lectures in Lesbian and Gay Studies* (New York: Feminist Press at the City University of New York, 2003), 23–48; Joan Nestle, "Excerpt from the Oral History of Mabel Hampton," *Signs: Journal of Women in Culture and Society* (Summer 1993), 925–35; Joan Nestle, "The Bodies I Have Lived With," *Journal of Lesbian Studies* 17, nos. 3–4 (2013), 215–39; and Nestle's blog, joannestle2.blogspot.com/2011/10/i-lift-my-eyes-to-the-hill-the-life-of -mabel-hampton. Nestle observed that Hampton's life "revolved around two major themes—her material struggle to survive and her cultural struggle for

beauty." This effort to make a beautiful life in the context of material deprivation and racial and sexual violence has shaped my portrait of Mabel. As well, I have tried to illuminate her aspirations as an artist and her life experience as a gender-fluid and nonbinary black person. Mabel met her life partner Lillian Foster in 1932. They remained together until 1978.

300 **the most densely populated in the city:** Osofsky, *Harlem*; Marcy S. Sacks, *Before Harlem: The Black Experience in New York City before World War I* (Philadelphia: University of Pennsylvania Press, 2006); Lewis, *When Harlem Was in Vogue*; Cheryl Lynn Greenberg, *Or Does It Explode: Black Harlem in the Great Depression* (New York: Oxford University Press, 1997); Jervis Anderson, *This Was Harlem: A Cultural Portrait* (New York: Farrar, Straus & Giroux, 1983); Harris, *Sex Workers, Psychics and Number Runners*.

302 **a smooth bump and grind:** Slow drag was "a couple's dance in which a man and a woman pressed their bodies tightly together in a smooth bump and grind as they kept to the rhythm of the music." John O. Perpener III, *African American Concert Dance: The Harlem Renaissance and Beyond* (Urbana: University of Illinois Press, 2001), 37. The Slow Drag was too sexual and too much defined by pelvic movement and naked sexuality to cross over and become a mainstream white dance. It was too black, with the sensual, deeply felt rhythms of the Negro.

The Turkey Trot was "a fast marching one-step, arms pumping out at the side, with occasional arms flapping emulating a crazed turkey." Marshall Stearns, *Jazz Dance: the Story of American Vernacular Dance* (New York: Macmillan, 1968), 95–96. The reviews of William Jourdan Rupp and Wallace Thurman's *Harlem* were obsessed with the Slow Drag represented in the play. As the reviewer in the *New York Sun* (1928) wrote: The play is "a motion picture thrown upon the background of negro dancing. The dancers lustily, swaying shamelessly and reveal the simplicity and deep earthiness of their race's hold on life. . . . Men and women who dance like that have the strength for violence." As quoted in Perpener, *African American Concert Dance*.

303 **"gin was poured out of milk pitchers":** Eric Garber, "A Spectacle in Color: The Lesbian and Gay Subculture of Jazz Age Harlem," in *Hidden from History: Reclaiming the Gay and Lesbian Past*, ed. Martin Duberan, Martha Vicinus, and George Chauncey (New York: Penguin, 1990).

303 **jook joint:** Katherine Hazzard Gordon, *Jookin': The Rise of Social Dance Formations in African American Culture* (Philadelphia: Temple University Press,

1992). On black social dance, see Thomas DeFrantz, *Dancing Many Drums: Excavations in African American Dance* (Madison: University of Wisconsin Press, 2001) and Lynne Fauley Emery, *Black Dance: From 1619 to Today* (Princeton, NJ: Princeton Book Co., 1989). On chorus line dancers, see Jayna Brown, *Babylon Girls: Black Women Performers and the Shaping of the Modern* (Durham, NC: Duke University Press, 2008), 189–237; Daphne Brooks, *Bodies in Dissent* (Durham, NC: Duke University Press, 2006), 207–78.

304 **Why should everyone in the world know her business:** Mabel Hampton, Tape 3, July 1986. She also liked to say "break it in half" and "figure it out."

304 **an irate husband:** "Rent Parties Are Menace," *New York Amsterdam News*, October 28, 1925, 1.

304 **half of them were women lovers:** Mabel described her sexual practices and community by using the terms "women lovers," "lady lovers," "bull daggers," "true lesbians," and "faggots."

304 *Harlem was surely as queer:* Henry Louis Gates, "The Black Man's Burden," *Fear of a Queer Planet* (Minneapolis: University of Minnesota Press, 1993), 23.

306 **"a meeting place for cocaine fiends":** Investigators' Report, Committee of Fourteen Papers, Box 38. MssCol 609, Rare Book and Manuscripts, New York Public Library. If movement provided the language for articulating freedom, rehearsing it, then the Committee of Fourteen hoped to quash it and to strengthen and extend the color line despite New York City's antidiscrimination laws and lack of a legal apparatus to enforce segregation.

306 **the *changing-same* of collective movement:** On the "changing-same," see Leroi Jones, *Blues People: Negro Music in White America* (1963; repr. New York: Harper Perennial, 1999); James Snead, "Repetition as a Figure of Black Culture," *Black Literature and Literary Theory*, ed. Henry Louis Gates (New York: Routledge, 1984).

307 **"dancing when they cared to":** Chandler Owen was writing about Chicago cabarets, but he also had New York City in mind. He explicitly criticized the Negro members of the Committee of Fourteen, which included Fred Moore of the *New York Age* and Booker T. Washington's successor. Owen condemned Negro leaders for entering a gentlemen's agreement to secure the adoption of segregation in cabarets. It hurt such gentlemen to see white and colored people drink and dance together. "The cabaret is an institution. It is doing in many cities what church, school, and family have failed to

do. It is destroying the hydra-headed monster of race prejudice." See "The Cabaret—A Useful Social Institution," *Messenger* 4 (August 1922), 461. Contrary to those like Hannah Arendt and others who feared that the spectacle of raw need threatened to undermine the Republic and its ideals, the black socialist envisioned this "struggle for joy," the hunger for sex and pleasure, as capable of toppling the color line and creating an interracial sociality that would undercut the force of law and custom. Owen championed the Black-and-Tan Cabaret in a second essay published in February 1925. "The Black and Tan Cabaret—America's Most Democratic Institution," *Messenger* 7 (February 1925), 97–99. However, he had less to say about the radical experiments conducted in all black spaces. Intraracial spaces of intimacy challenged the conscription of second-class citizenship and servitude by nurturing all our kin—that is other arrangements of intimacy, sociality, love, and affiliation. What Owen strived to articulate in print was enacted in the cabaret—the social experiments enacted in the space of the cabaret, as well as house parties and halls.

308   **"an epidemic of virtue":** Emma Goldman, "The Traffic in Women," *Anarchism and Other Essays* (New York: Mother Earth Publishing, 1917), 198.

308   **might have made Owen less uneasy:** Observing Mabel and Mildred and other young bobbed-haired girls would have also made him nervous and uneasy. He feared "masculine women" and didn't imagine that transgressing gender distinctions served any social usefulness and dismissed it as rebellion for the sake of it.

309   **"I charge white men five dollars":** "Investigative Report," Committee of Fourteen Records, Manuscripts and Archives Division, New York Public Library, Box 38.

312   **You didn't have to be light, just look it:** Jayna Brown, *Babylon Girls Black Women Performers and the Shaping of the Modern* (Durham, NC: Duke University Press, 2008); Daphne Brooks, *Bodies in Dissent: Spectacular Performances of Race and Freedom* (Durham, NC: Duke University Press, 2006).

315   **along the beach people had intercourse:** Hampton Collection, Tape XV, Lesbian Herstory Archives.

315   **"You'll have to find another baby now":** Dunbar, *Sport of the Gods*, 162.

315   *lesbian*: Havelock Ellis and John Addington Symond, *Sexual Inversion* (London: Wilson and McMillan, 1897).

318   *she longed and longed and longed*: Theodore Dreiser, *Sister Carrie* (1900; repr. New York: Penguin Classics, 1994), 83.

319 **"I can't take it. It is too powerful":** Mabel describing the act of oral sex. Hampton Collection, Tape X, Lesbian Herstory Archives.

321 **a very nice pair of undergarments:** Mabel vividly remembered the party because she was required to take her clothes off. "I can't forget that because I had to take it all off. So naturally I wouldn't forget it." She was wearing a gray dress and a white fur coat. Tape XXI, January 13, 1983.

325 *Finally a colored chorus:* Lewis Theophilus, "Theater," *Messenger* 6, no. 2 (February 1924).

328 **"the costumes presented an attractive effect":** *Chicago Defender*, December 22, 1923; *Atlanta Constitution*, December 4, 1924; *New Journal and Guide*, March 1, 1924; *Chicago Defender*, March 29, 1924.

328 **Nobody knew who or what you were when you had a suit on:** December 18, 1988 (Tape 1), Lesbian Herstory Archives.

330 **becoming "husbands" by default:** On racism and the construction of homosexuality: Estelle Freedman, "The Prison Lesbian," *Feminist Studies* 22, no. 2 (Summer, 1996): 397–423; Regina Kunzel, *Criminal Intimacy: Prison and the Uneven History of Modern American Sexuality* (Chicago: University of Chicago Press, 2010); Siobhan Somerville, *Queering the Color Line: Race and the Invention of Homosexuality in American Culture* (Durham, NC: Duke University Press, 2000); Roderick Ferguson, *Aberrations in Black: Toward a Queer of Color Critique* (Minneapolis: University of Minnesota Press, 2003).

330 **all the books she finished:** Special Collections Record, Lesbian Herstory Archives, Partial List of Mabel Hampton's Books, Box 4 and 5.

331 **Florence Mills:** Mabel and Florence worked together briefly at the Lafayette Theatre and, according to Mabel, enjoyed a casual intimacy. Tape 1, April 8, 1989, Lesbian Herstory Archives.

333 **all the queer endings:** Wayne Koestenbaum, *The Queen's Throat: Opera, Homosexuality and the Mystery of Desire* (New York: Da Capo, 2001).

335 **Ismay had listened raptly:** Ismay was born in Lagos, Nigeria. She was married to a photographer from Barbados, Raymond Percival Talma, around 1921. The marriage probably didn't last long since there is little mention of her husband. (Ismay was one of several married women with whom Mabel was involved.) See the *Pittsburgh Courier*, "Native African Woman Has Won Success in Two American Careers," April 11, 1931.

337 **"a living piece of African sculpture":** Langston Hughes described Bentley in these terms. See Hughes, *Big Sea*. Carl Van Vechten adored her. She made

an appearance in *Parties* (1930; reprint Avon Books 1977), 34–35. Bentley also features in Blair Niles, *Strange Brother* (1931; repr. New York: Heretic Books, 1991).

337 **"to deter the advances of leading ladies"**: "Where Are the Chorus Girls of Yester-Year?" *Baltimore Afro-American*, July 6, 1935.

338 **she loved women and didn't bother about the rest**: Mabel Hampton, Tape 1, June 18, 1982.

339 **refuse the categories**: In *Black on Both Sides*, C. Riley Snorton argues that captive flesh "figures a critical genealogy of modern transness" and considers the ways in which the fungible life of the captive unsettles gender and makes possible its rearrangement. He also writes, extending Spillers, that "gender is itself a racial arrangement that expresses the transubstantiation of things." (57, 83) Kara Keeling, "Looking for M: Queer Temporality, Black Possibility and Poetry from the Future," *GLQ* 15, no. 4 (2009), 556–82. Zakiyyah Iman Jackson, "'Theorizing in a Void': Sublimity, Matter, and Physics in Black Feminist Poetics," *South Atlantic Quarterly* 117, no. 3 (July 2018), 617–48.

340 **The movement across the street**: Ella Baker and Marvel Cooke describe sex workers and domestics waiting on opposite corners of the street for work. See "The Bronx Slave Market," *The Crisis*, November 1935. Before they entered sex work, the profession of the majority of prostitutes had been domestic service. See Kneeland, *Commercialized Prostitution in New York City*. Especially see Katherine Davis's report on women at Bedford Hills, "Salient Facts about the New York State Reformatory for Women, Bedford Hills, New York."

340 **cross the street again**: Most of those arrested for prostitution had worked as domestics and after serving time were often paroled to domestic work or had no other choice but to return to it. See Kneeland, *Commercialized Prostitution in New York City* and Blair, *I've Got to Make My Livin'*.

341 **Black Gal, Black Gal**: Harlem Blues: WPA, Negroes in New York, collected by Lawrence Gellert in "Blues Songs," Schomburg Library, New York Public Library.

341 **"bids for their time"**: Ella Baker and Marvel Cooke, "The Bronx Slave Market," *The Crisis*, November 1935.

341 **The housewife "undresse[d] them with her eyes"**: Ella Baker and Marvel Cooke, "The Bronx Slave Market," *Crisis*, November 1935; Marvel Cooke, "The Bronx Slave Market," *New York Sunday Compass Magazine* (Parts I and II), January 8, 1950; Louise Mitchell, "Slave Markets Typify Exploitation of Domestics," *The Daily Worker*, May 5, 1940 (reprinted in Gerder Lerner's

Black Women in White America, 231); Vivian Morris, "Bronx Slave Market," WPA Harlem Interviews, Schomburg Center for Research on Black Culture; Dayo Gore, *Radicalism at the Crossroads: African American Women Activists and the Cold War* (New York: New York University Press, 2012); and Harris, *Sex Workers, Psychics, and Number Runners*; and "Running with the Reds: African American Women and the Communist Party during the Depression," *Journal of African American History* 94, no. 1 (Winter 2009): 21–43.

THE CHORUS OPENS THE WAY

346 **maternal song that makes you:** See Du Bois, "The Sorrow Songs," in *The Souls of Black Folk* and *Dusk of Dawn*.

347 *future increase*: See Jennifer Morgan, *Laboring Women: Reproduction and Gender in New World Slavery* (Philadelphia: University of Pennsylvania Press, 2004); Daina Berry, *Their Pound of Flesh* (Boston: Beacon Press, 2017); and Dorothy Roberts, *Killing the Black Body* (New York: Vintage, 1998).

347 *dance within an enclosure*: See John Gould, "Tragedy and Collective Experience," in *Tragedy and the Tragic*, ed. M. S. Silk (New York: Oxford University Press, 1996), 217–36; Page du Bois, "Toppling the Hero: Polyphony in the Tragic City" and David Scott, "Tragedy's Time: Post-Emancipation Futures," in *Rethinking Tragedy*, ed. Rita Felsi (Baltimore, MD: Johns Hopkins University Press, 2008); David Scott, *Conscripts of Modernity: The Tragedy of Colonial Enlightenment* (Durham, NC: Duke University Press, 2004); Jeremy Glick, "Bringing in the Chorus: The Haitian Revolution Plays of C. L. R. James and Edouard Glissant," in *The Black Radical Tragic: Performance, Aesthetics, and the Unfinished Haitian Revolution* (New York: New York University Press, 2016).

348 **ceaseless practice of black radicalism:** On the radical experiments conducted by the chorus and the motley crew, see Laura Harris, "What Happened to the Motley Crew? C.L.R. James, Hélio Oiticica, and the Aesthetic Sociality of Blackness," *Social Text* 30, no. 3 (2012): 49–71; and Fred Moten, "Entanglement & Virtuosity," and "Not in Between," *Black & Blur* (Durham, NC: Duke University Press, 2017).

348 *Somebody else carries on*: Interview with Ella Baker. See Ellen Cantarow, *Moving the Mountain: Women Work for Social Change* (New York: Feminist Press, 1980), 93; Barbara Ransby, *Ella Baker and the Black Freedom Movement* (Chapel Hill: University of North Carolina Press, 2005). For a critique of the

model of political leadership, see Erica Edwards, *Charisma and the Fictions of Black Political Leadership* (Minneapolis: University of Minnesota, 2012); Cedric Robinson, *Terms of Order: Political Science and the Myth of Leadership* (Chapel Hill: University of North Carolina Press, 2016); Cathy Cohen, *The Boundaries of Blackness: AIDS and the Breakdown of Black Politics* (Chicago: University of Chicago Press, 1999).

LIST OF ILLUSTRATIONS

INDEX

Entries that reference page 355 and subsequent pages refer to endnotes.